THIS
GREAT STRUGGLE

THIS
GREAT STRUGGLE

AMERICA'S CIVIL WAR

STEVEN E. WOODWORTH

ROWMAN & LITTLEFIELD PUBLISHERS, INC.

Lanham • Boulder • New York • Toronto • Plymouth, UK

Published by Rowman & Littlefield Publishers, Inc.
A wholly owned subsidiary of The Rowman & Littlefield Publishing Group, Inc.
4501 Forbes Boulevard, Suite 200, Lanham, Maryland 20706
http://www.rowmanlittlefield.com

Estover Road, Plymouth PL6 7PY, United Kingdom

Distributed by National Book Network

British Library Cataloguing in Publication Information Available

Library of Congress Cataloging-in-Publication Data
Woodworth, Steven E.
   This great struggle : America's Civil War / Steven E. Woodworth.
     p.   cm.
   Includes bibliographical references and index.
   ISBN 978-0-7425-5184-8 (cloth : alk. paper)—ISBN 978-1-4422-1087-5 (electronic)
     1. United States—History—Civil War, 1861–1865.   2. United
States—History—Civil War, 1861–1865—Social aspects.   3. United
States—History—Civil War, 1861–1865—Political aspects.   4. United
States—Politics and government—1861–1865.   I. Title.
E468.W88 2011
973.7—dc22

                                                                           2010050535

∞ ™ The paper used in this publication meets the minimum requirements of American National Standard for Information Sciences—Permanence of Paper for Printed Library Materials, ANSI/NISO Z39.48-1992.

Printed in the United States of America

For Ralph L. Woodworth, 1933–2010
and
Erma J. Woodworth, 1935–2010

"The lines are fallen unto me in pleasant places;
yea, I have a goodly heritage."
Psalm 16:6

To God Alone be the Glory.

CONTENTS

PROLOGUE

The afternoon sun beat down, and the high humidity that was typical of the District of Columbia in August made the atmosphere stifling. In their blue woolen uniforms, the near one thousand men of the 164th Ohio Regiment sweated patiently and for the most part happily. It was not usually this hot in their homes in Seneca and Summit counties in northern Ohio, but they had had all summer to get used to it. Since May they had manned the defenses of forts Corcoran, Woodbury, Bennett, Strong, Hagerty, and C. F. Smith, on the Virginia side of the Potomac, part of the chain of forts that ringed the capital city.

There the men of the 164th had done their three months of soldiering. The eighteen deaths within the regiment had come not from enemy bullets or shells but from camp diseases. They were just as dead nonetheless. The men of the 164th may not have seen a single Rebel all summer long, even when a small Rebel army had approached the capital defenses on the Maryland side back in July, but their stint of duty had not been without its dangers. The deceased ranged in age from forty-one-year-old Private Daniel Frederick, who died at Fort Strong in July, all the way down to nineteen-year-old Private William Wilson, who had died at the same fort the month before.

The spring of 1864 had opened amid high hopes that the next few months of campaigning would bring Union victory and an end to the war that was then entering its fourth year and had already shed blood on a scale out of proportion to anything the young republic had seen in its almost four score and eight years of independence. In anticipation of the spring and summer's big push for victory, Governor John Brough of Ohio had offered President Abraham Lincoln additional help from his state. Ohio had already raised scores of regiments that now formed a significant part of the strength of the nation's armies, but the state had recently reorganized its militia, changing the organization's name at the same time to the National Guard to emphasize its new, more serious purpose. Brough visited Lincoln in Washington that spring and asked if the summer's big push could be strengthened by the addition of several dozen regiments of National Guard troops to cover the rear areas and supply lines and free more of the veteran troops for duty on the front lines.

Lincoln had gratefully accepted and suggested that Brough call on the governors of the other midwestern states to join in the effort. He did, and the result was eighty-five thousand troops enlisted for a hundred-day tour of duty that summer, thirty thousand of them from the Buckeye State. Among them was the 164th Ohio Regiment, which on this eighteenth day of August was standing in the tidewater heat, happy because they had finished their tour of duty and were about to ship out for home and also happy because they were stopping by the White House on their way to the train station to pay their parting respects to President Lincoln. Several of them had seen Lincoln once or twice before during their time around Washington, and a few had gotten to shake hands with the him, but seeing the president was always an exciting prospect, and the presumption was that he would have a few words to say to the regiment.

Lincoln had much less reason to be in high spirits than did the soldiers of the 164th Ohio. The high hopes of spring had withered in the heat of summer. Despite the maximum effort—enhanced by the help of the Ohio National Guardsmen—Grant had not taken Richmond, and Sherman had not taken Atlanta. The casualties on the fighting fronts had been horrendous, and the public was both appalled with the losses and disappointed in the lack of tangible progress. The nation's most prominent newspaper publisher, Horace Greeley, had been writing defeatist editorials and had written to Lincoln urging a negotiated peace that would have abandoned the goals for which the nation was fighting the war. "Our bleeding, bankrupt, almost dying country . . . longs for peace," Greeley had written.

Worse, this was a presidential election year, and though Lincoln had his party's nomination for another term, dissidents within the party had already nominated a rival candidate on a third-party ticket. A congressman and senator from his own party had sponsored a bill that had repudiated Lincoln's program for trying to restore loyal governments in the Rebel states, and when Lincoln had vetoed it, its sponsors had written a manifesto condemning him and, just two weeks prior, published it in Greeley's paper. With fellow party members like that, Lincoln hardly needed Democrats, but Democrats there were, vociferously denouncing Lincoln and the war for all the opposite reasons from those of his Republican foes save that both complained that war progress was too slow. The Democratic convention was scheduled to open in Chicago eleven days after this parting visit at the White House by the 164th Ohio, and although it was not clear yet who would garner the nomination, it would plainly be someone who at least tacitly hewed to the Democratic Party's line that the war was a failure and should be abandoned. Slavery, the Democrats believed, should continue.

Politicians in those days had no tracking polls to tell them how their ideas were playing with the public or what their chances were of winning the next election. They had to try to gauge such things from the tone of newspaper editorials and from the assessments of friends and associates. Lincoln was one of the most astute politicians of his era and had an excellent sense of which way the political wind was blowing. By mid-August 1864, all his instincts were telling him that he was in serious electoral trouble. Five days after this brief speech to the troops he would write, "This morning, as for some days past, it seems exceedingly probable that this Administration will not be re-elected. Then it will be my duty to so co-operate with the President elect, as to save the Union between the election and the inauguration; as he will have secured his election on such ground that he cannot possibly save it afterward." He put the paper in an envelope and had his cabinet members sign the flap without knowing the contents. Lincoln wanted the Democrat who defeated him in the November election to know he had seen it coming since August.

A soldier of the 164th who had seen Lincoln at a public event in late May shortly after the regiment arrived in Washington had noted, "The countenance of the President when sitting alone was inexpressibly sad." It could not have been any better on August 18 as he sat in the White House before going out to meet the troops to acknowledge their salute, thank them for their service, and send them on their way back to their homes in northern Ohio towns like Tiffin, Tallmadge, and Akron. Observers had noticed on many occasions that once Lincoln began to address an audience, his face always became more animated and cheerful, and so it would have been as he spoke to the 164th.[1]

"You are about to return to your homes and your friends," Lincoln began, "after having, as I learn, performed in camp a comparatively short term of duty in this great contest. I am greatly obliged to you, and to all who have come forward at the call of their country."

Four days later Lincoln would tell another of the departing Ohio National Guard regiments, "I almost always feel inclined, when I happen to say anything to soldiers, to impress upon them in a few brief remarks the importance of success in this contest." That was true, and his brief talk to the men of the 164th was no exception.

"I wish it might be more generally and universally understood," Lincoln continued, "what the country is now engaged in. We have, as all will agree, a free Government, where every man has a right to be equal with every other man. In this great struggle, this form of Government and every form of human right is endangered if our enemies succeed. There is more involved in this contest than is realized by every one. There is involved in this struggle the question whether your children and my children shall enjoy the privileges we have enjoyed."

Of course, as Lincoln well knew, the reason the nation was now involved in this civil war was the fact that all did not agree that "every man has a right to be equal with every other man." Almost all white southerners and, as Lincoln was painfully aware, all too many northern voters emphatically rejected that proposition if the term "every man" included a black man. Yet Lincoln was right in saying they all agreed that they had "a free Government," and he seemed to imply that since that was the case they ought also to recognize that in such a government "every man has a right to be equal with every other man." If it were not so, if freedom was only for those whom society or the government chose to favor, then it was not a free government at all, and no one's freedom was safe. If one man's freedom necessarily meant his right to deprive another man of freedom or if one region's freedom meant the right to break up the nation and create anarchy, then the American people might as well admit that "a free Government" was impossible. That was why Lincoln went on to emphasize that there was "more involved in this contest than is realized by every one." If they did realize it, the president might well have thought to himself, they would not presently be flirting with the prospect of voting for a Democratic candidate who would be pledged to give up emancipation and practically obligated to give up the Union as well. Lincoln could not speak face-to-face with the more than four million northern voters, but he could speak to these soldiers. He wanted them to understand that it was *their* freedom and their children's that was at stake in the war.

Lincoln went on to admit, "There may be mistakes made sometimes," but he urged his listeners not to let that divert them from their devotion to the cause for which the nation was striving. "I beg of you, as citizens of this great Republic," Lincoln said, "not to let your minds be carried off from the great work we have before us. This struggle is too large for you to be diverted from it by any small matter."

Then Lincoln gave them a parting commission: "When you return to your homes rise up to the height of a generation of men worthy of a free Government, and we will carry out the great work we have commenced."[2]

As Lincoln strove to make clear to those citizen-soldiers, the Civil War was worth fighting. One hundred and fifty years later, it is still eminently worth studying—worth studying because of what was at stake in the war, because of how the war changed America, and because of what "this great struggle" showed of the height to which that generation of Americans rose and its challenge to future generations to be worthy of a free government.

THIS
GREAT STRUGGLE

1

AMERICA'S LONG ROAD
TO CIVIL WAR

SLAVERY IN AMERICA DURING
THE COLONIAL ERA AND THE
AMERICAN REVOLUTION

Long before the April night when a Confederate artillerist in Charleston, South Carolina, jerked the lanyard of a heavy cannon and fired the opening shot of the Civil War, the seeds of the dispute that would send millions of Americans into battle against each other in what still stands as the republic's deadliest war had already taken deep root in American culture. That dispute was about slavery. Slavery's beginnings in America lay far back in colonial times long before the four score and some odd years the United States had been in existence on that April night in 1861 when the shooting finally started in earnest.

When the first Englishmen had come to the New World almost three centuries before, they had prided themselves that their laws, unlike those of already established colonial power Spain, knew no such thing as a slave. Over the next century, however, that was to change. Englishmen in their country's first permanent settlement in what was to become the United States, Jamestown, found their economic fortune in the cultivation of the tobacco plant. Tobacco was a labor-intensive crop. With land abundant in colonial Virginia, the only practical limit on how much a man could grow and, therefore, how much money he could earn, was how much labor he could command. Hired labor was out of the question. Any potential hired man could readily obtain his own land and enjoy all the fruits of his own labor rather than only part of them as an employee. So the only way a large landowner could work his acres was with nonfree labor.

At first the solution Englishmen chose was that of indentured servitude. An indentured servant was a poor Englishman who could not afford passage to America but still wanted to take his shot at making his fortune in the New World. In order to do so, he would sign a contract, called an indenture, binding him to service for a certain specified period of years, usually seven, in exchange for the cost of his transportation to the colony. Indentured servants were the most common form of nonfree labor in Virginia during the colony's first half century. They could be male or, relatively rarely, female; could be bought and sold; and were sometimes mistreated, and their terms of service could be legally extended for various infractions, such as, in the case of a female servant, giving birth to a child. However, the child in that case was free, not the property of the master, who, under English law, owned the indentured servant's labor but not his or her person. As long as mortality remained extremely high in early colonial Virginia, reliance on indentured servants, rather than actual slaves, was not only familiar but also economically sensible since both the indentured servant and the more expensive lifetime slave were statistically likely to be dead before seven years were up.

The shift from indentured servitude to race-based slavery was gradual. Life spans slowly increased, making lifetime slaves a better investment. The Spanish in the Caribbean, Central America, and South America were already using slavery on a vast scale and had been doing so for over a century. A well-developed transatlantic slave trade, carried in Spanish, Portuguese, Dutch, and English ships, served the constant demand of Latin American colonial economies for ever more bondsmen. It was easy enough for Englishmen in the North American colonies of Virginia and its junior partner on the Chesapeake Bay, Maryland, to begin importing slaves when the stream of indentured servants failed to meet demand or when a longer-term investment seemed appealing. It remains unclear what, if any, additional factors drove the shift toward slavery, and historians have long argued as to whether racism caused slavery or was caused by it. In any case, by the 1660s, the economies of both Virginia and Maryland had shifted overwhelmingly to the use of slaves rather than indentured servants, though a few of the latter continued to be present in the colonies for several decades more. By that time, the law codes of these two colonies fully recognized and protected the institution of slavery.

During that same decade, other Englishmen established the Carolinas as colonies just south of Virginia. South Carolina in particular quickly adopted a slave culture and economy, not, like those of its neighbors to the north, by developing it internally but rather by importing a complete and operating slave economy and culture from the British-owned sugarcane plantation island of Barbados, where indentured servitude had given way to slavery even more quickly than it had in the Chesapeake colonies amid the brutal, killing labor and conditions of sugar cultivation. Barbados planters seeking to expand or younger sons of such planters seeking establishments of their own migrated to the new colony of South Carolina and brought their slaves and the associated culture and laws with them. Though South Carolina planters came to grow rice and indigo rather than tobacco or sugar, their economy, like that of the Chesapeake colonies and Barbados, rested on the foundation of staple-crop agriculture, well suited for cultivation by large gangs of fairly unskilled and unmotivated workers. By about 1715 South Carolina had become the only one of the colonies in which slaves made up a majority of the population. North Carolina, though with a somewhat more diverse economy, followed the cultures of its neighbors to the north and south. Georgia's founders, James Oglethorpe and his philanthropic fellow proprietors, never intended their experiment in enlightened reform to include slavery, but the colonists eventually managed to introduce the institution there as well.

While slavery thrived and became the mainstay of the economies of the southern colonies, the northern colonies developed along different lines. Slavery existed there as well but in far smaller numbers. Some of the colonies, such as Massachusetts and Pennsylvania, had originally been born out of religious motivations that were more or less hostile to slavery and at least initially hindered its growth. All the northern colonies developed economies that lent themselves less well to the use of slave labor than did the southern colonies' virtually uniform dependence on staple-crop agriculture. Mixed small manufacturing, small farming, shipping, and fishing in New England; grain cultivation in Pennsylvania; and commerce in port cities such as Philadelphia, New York, and Boston all presented less temptation for the wholesale exploitation of slaves. Thus, conscience and economics combined to limit the total number of bondsmen in the northern colonies to a tiny fraction of those in the South.

The American Revolution turned the colonists' attention to issues of liberty and the rights of man. If indeed "all men are created equal and are endowed by their Creator with certain unalienable rights," then it would be impossible to justify slavery, as the Revolutionaries, including the slaveholders among them, were painfully aware. Patrick Henry, who rhetorically asked if even life itself was worth the price of "chains and slavery" and answered his own question in the negative with his famous demand for liberty or death, was nevertheless a slaveholder. "Would any one believe that I am Master of Slaves of my own purchase!" he asked in another, less well known, rhetorical question. Yet though he called slavery "this Abominable Practice," he could only express the hope that some time, somehow, the opportunity would arrive to abolish it. He was not alone in his conflicted state of mind. The prevailing view in the South was that immediate emancipation would turn loose on society an unrestrained racial underclass and spark the onset of a race war. "We have the wolf by the ears," Henry's fellow Virginia slaveholder Thomas Jefferson would later remark, "and feel the danger of either holding or letting him loose."[1]

In the northern states during the Revolutionary era, the situation was different. Minute slave populations there aroused little worry about the dangers of emancipation. Many northern slaveholders voluntarily freed their slaves, as did some in Virginia, and each of the northern legislatures adopted laws either abolishing or gradually phasing out slavery within the boundaries of its own state. The southern legislatures did not. In short, the Revolutionary era turned American minds to liberty and thereby etched the line between liberty and slavery deeper into the landscape of American culture. On the map that line now became the border where the southernmost original free state, Pennsylvania, met the northernmost original slave state, Maryland, a boundary that took its name from colonial surveyors Charles Mason and Jeremiah Dixon. Thus, the intellectual dichotomy over slavery birthed a tangible geographical division. The Mason-Dixon Line would be the demarcation between bondage and freedom.

The ambivalence of the founding generation toward the institution of slavery left its mark on the new republic's early policies. When in 1787 Jefferson wrote and Congress passed the Northwest Ordinance, that act banned slavery in all of what was to become the states of Ohio, Indiana, Illinois, Michigan, and Wisconsin. The Ohio River thus became the boundary between slave and free states west of the Appalachians as the Mason-Dixon Line was east of them.

That same year the Philadelphia Convention wrote the new Constitution. The framers carefully avoided using the painful word "slave" in the document, referring instead to "persons bound to servitude." In concessions to the concerns of the slave states, especially South Carolina, the Constitution provided that when such persons escaped from a slave state to a free state, they were to be returned. Congress would have no power to abolish the slave trade until 1808. When slave state delegates proposed that slaves be counted as part of population for the apportionment of representatives in Congress but not for the purposes of direct taxation, northern members of the convention balked. The two sides finally settled on a compromise stipulating that for both purposes each slave should count as three-fifths of a free inhabitant. This was a clear gain for the South since Congress never levied a direct tax, and the three-fifths clause therefore served only to secure the overrepresentation of southern whites in Congress and the Electoral College. Although the founders recognized the contradiction between republican liberty and slavery, they incorrectly concluded that slavery would eventually wither and die. Unfortunately, slavery was not capable of self-correction. This clouded their policymaking and thrust the slave issue onto future generations.

SLAVERY IN THE EARLY REPUBLIC

What from a modern perspective may seem the founders' inexplicable complacence about slavery's existence as a blatant contradiction of their ideals within their system of ordered liberty rested partially on the belief that the institution was in fact in the process of dying out. That belief in turn stemmed in part from wishful thinking and in part from certain economic and agricultural developments of the mid-eighteenth century. As soil in Virginia lost its fertility for further profitable cultivation of tobacco, farmers and planters had shifted increasingly to wheat, a much less labor-intensive crop. A plantation that converted from tobacco to wheat would at once find itself with a large surplus of labor, and slaveholders could readily imagine strong economic motivations for eventual manumission (voluntary freeing) of their slaves, provided that the problem of free blacks within white society could be solved.

All of this changed when in 1793 Connecticut Yankee Eli Whitney, while serving as a tutor on a Georgia plantation, invented a practical cotton gin—a device that would separate the seeds of the cotton plant from its white fibers. The cotton gin revolutionized the southern economy, making possible the profitable cultivation of cotton throughout the Deep South. The favorable treaties made with southern Indian tribes at the close of the War of 1812 opened vast expanses of land that was ideal for cotton farming. Textile mills in Britain, built to process wool, provided a ready market for American cotton, which soon became one of the country's most valuable exports. Cotton was a labor-intensive crop, requiring many pickers during the harvest season. The plantations and farms of Georgia, Alabama, Mississippi, and Louisiana became a market for the surplus slaves of Virginia and other Upper South states. The spread of cotton as a cash crop during the generation after the writing of the Constitution meant that whereas economic forces had previously pressured slaveholders to free their bondsmen, those same forces now encouraged the profit-minded planter to hang on to his slaves or sell them to the Deep South for substantial sums. Thus, cotton engrained slavery even more deeply into southern culture and economics.

The new economic conditions slowly, almost imperceptibly at first, fostered new attitudes in the South regarding slavery. With cordial southern support, Congress banned the slave trade in 1808 as soon as constitutionally permitted, but the support of southerners came in part from representatives and senators from the Upper South, a region whose chief crop for export to the other states, surplus slaves, would become much more valuable if the flow of imported slaves were cut off. Indeed, slave prices rose steadily decade after decade. Slaves became one of the favorite and most lucrative investments in the South.

Then in 1819 the Missouri Territory petitioned for admission to the Union as a slave state. This alarmed some northern congressmen. Louisiana, the first state to be formed from the territory acquired by the Louisiana Purchase, had entered the Union as a slave state in 1812, but geography had assuaged northern concerns about the spread of slavery. Louisiana lay farther south than any other American state at that time, and slavery had existed there under French and Spanish rule before America acquired the territory. It appeared only natural that the Pelican State would bring slavery along with statehood. Missouri was different. It lay directly west of Illinois, where Jefferson's own Northwest Ordinance had banned slavery. If admitted, it would become the northernmost slave state. Worse, the land that made up the would-be state of Missouri had known no slavery under French or Spanish rule. The implication of admitting Missouri as a slave state was that slavery was the natural and normal arrangement in all future American territories— slavery followed the flag.

This was exactly the reverse of how some northern congressmen wished to view their flag and country, and so one of them, New York Representative James Tallmadge Jr., introduced an amendment to the Missouri statehood act, stipulating that slavery was to be phased out in the state over the next generation. Southern representatives and senators reacted with startling ferocity. Despite their vociferous opposition, the amendment passed in the

House, where northern representatives outnumbered southern, but the Senate, where slave and free states were evenly balanced, rejected it.

Into this heated impasse stepped Henry Clay, with the first of several compromises he would sponsor during his long congressional career. Under the terms of his proposal, which Congress finally adopted after lengthy wrangling, Missouri would enter the Union as a slave state, and Maine, hitherto part of Massachusetts, would enter as a free state, thus preserving the balance in the Senate. The line that formed most of the southern boundary of Missouri, latitude thirty-six degrees, thirty minutes, would be extended all the way across the remainder of the land acquired in the Louisiana Purchase. All lands south of the line would be reserved for future slave states, while all lands north of it, with the exception of Missouri itself, would be forever closed to slavery. At the time, southerners thought it no bad bargain, for although the lands north of thirty-six thirty were far more extensive than those south of it, the prevailing belief at the time was that persons of African descent—and therefore the institution of slavery—could not thrive in those northerly regions.

Southern reaction to Tallmadge's relatively mild proposal provided a stark revelation of the change in attitudes over the preceding generation. Even Jefferson, who had once favored the limitation of slavery's spread and written that limitation into the Northwest Ordinance, now saw in any attempt to place a boundary on slavery the potential doom of the Union. "This momentous question," he wrote,

> like a fire bell in the night, awakened and filled me with terror. I considered it at once as the knell of the Union. It is hushed indeed for the moment, but this is a reprieve only, not a final sentence. A geographical line, coinciding with a marked principle, moral and political, once conceived and held up to the angry passions of men, will never be obliterated; and every new irritation will mark it deeper and deeper.[2]

The Missouri Compromise quieted the clamor over slavery in the national political arena, and it soon came to be viewed with a feeling akin to reverence by the American people. Yet the fundamental contradiction that slavery posed in the midst of a society dedicated to freedom remained a continued source of periodic irritation, much as Jefferson had predicted.

Throughout the 1820s and 1830s those irritations remained small but occurred with disturbing regularity. In 1822 South Carolina slaveholders purported to have uncovered an elaborate conspiracy of slaves bent on revolt and subsequent mayhem. They blamed the ferment on the widely publicized Missouri Compromise debates, which, they said, had introduced evil ideas of freedom into the minds of their otherwise contented slaves. Some modern scholars suspect the slaveholders may have fabricated the entire story in order to justify a more strident defense of slavery.

ABOLITIONISM, NULLIFICATION, AND TERRITORIAL EXPANSION

An 1831 Virginia slave revolt was real enough. In August of that year a slave preacher and mystic named Nat Turner led fellow slaves in a bloody uprising, killing almost every white man, woman, and child who came across their path, fifty-five in all, before finally being suppressed by the aroused Virginia militia in less than forty-eight hours. Captured several weeks later, Turner and fifty-five of his fellow slaves were executed. Other blacks may have died at the hands of mobs during the reaction to the uprising. It was the bloodiest slave revolt in U.S. history.

Some southerners saw the outbreak as the result of more evil Yankee ideas, this time emanating from a group known as abolitionists who presented the country with a new kind of opposition to slavery. Prior to this time, moral witness against slavery in America had mostly been expressed in genteel manner by members of an organization called the American Colonization Society. The society advocated persuading America's free blacks to migrate to Africa as a first step toward persuading planters that it would be safe to manumit their slaves since the freedmen would no doubt quickly follow the other members of their race to their ancestral continent. As a means of bringing about the end of slavery in the United States, the American Colonization Society had been notable chiefly for its complete ineffectiveness, which won it the good opinion even of some slaveholders, including Henry Clay. The abolitionists were something else entirely. They called for the immediate, uncompensated emancipation of all slaves. Most of them were evangelical Christians, and they made it plain that they considered the ownership of slaves to be a sin.

The abolitionists' loudest and most strident spokesman was in some ways not representative of the movement. William Lloyd Garrison was unorthodox in his religious views and more radical even than most other abolitionists, but he became one of the most recognized public voices and faces of the movement thanks to the weekly abolitionist newspaper he founded in 1831 in Boston. Garrison's rhetoric was inflammatory. "I am in earnest," he wrote in his first issue, "I will not equivocate—I will not excuse—I will not retreat a single inch—AND I WILL BE HEARD." He certainly was. Though the paper, named *The Liberator*, had fewer than four hundred subscribers that first year and its circulation grew only very slowly, Garrison's shocking statements made him and his message well known throughout the country. The state of Georgia offered a five-thousand-dollar reward for his arrest, and death threats were numerous.

Much as abolitionists like Garrison might fill the hearts of southern whites with fear and loathing, they posed almost as little practical threat to slavery as did the prim and stuffy gentlemen of the American Colonization Society. The abolitionists were earnest enough, but their numbers were few. Nowhere in the country were they in the majority, and even in the Northeast they could easily become the objects of popular outrage and mob violence. Abolitionist preachers were sometimes arrested out of their pulpits by the local sheriff as disturbers of the peace. Garrison once narrowly escaped a lynch mob in Boston. Outside of the Northeast and some strongly antislavery parts of the upper Midwest, abolitionism was an extremely dangerous creed to embrace. When Presbyterian minister Elijah P. Lovejoy began publishing an abolition newspaper in Alton, Illinois, near St. Louis, a proslavery mob destroyed his printing press. Supporters helped him purchase a replacement press, and the mob destroyed it too. His third press met a similar fate, and when in November 1837 Lovejoy attempted to prevent the destruction of a fourth press, the mob killed him.

Southern whites and their northern sympathizers reacted aggressively toward abolitionism in legal ways as well. One southern countereffort took the form of South Carolina "nullifying" the federal tariff. In November 1832 a special South Carolina state convention declared the tariff unconstitutional and therefore null and void within the state. The tariff was a foolish economic policy, highly unpopular in the South. Getting free of it would have been a welcome development, but establishing a state's right to nullify federal laws would have been a much larger accomplishment. Southern states could then have nullified any federal act they might feel impinged on the rights of slaveholders without the tiresome and, to southern minds, dangerous debates that had surrounded the Missouri Compromise. President Andrew Jackson handled the situation with both firmness and finesse, putting the South Carolinians in a position in which they would have to become the aggressors in order to stop collection of the tariff. Knowing that Jackson would throw the whole armed might of the Union against them if they attacked and disappointed that no other southern states had joined them in their stand, the South Carolinians sullenly backed down.

Slavery advocates invented additional means to preserve the peculiar institution. Later during the 1830s southern congressmen persuaded the U.S. Post Office to ban the transmission of abolitionist literature through the mail. Throughout the decade abolitionists had sent petitions to Congress requesting the banning of slavery within the District of Columbia or at least of the slave trade there. So in 1836 proslavery members of Congress led the way in imposing, with the help of sympathetic northerners, the so-called Gag Rule stipulating that Congress would not receive any petition against slavery and implying that the petitioners had committed an offense, at least against good manners, by sending it. Slavery supporters did not intend to let perceived abolitionist radicalism infect the U.S. government.

Party politics helped suppress abolitionist agitation. By the mid-1830s the United States had an established two-party system, pitting Democrats against Whigs. Democrats favored strict adherence to the Constitution and very limited government. Whigs played fast and loose with the Constitution and advocated government intervention in the economy in hopes of boosting prosperity, at least for some people. Both parties were alike, however, in appealing to a nationwide constituency, and therefore both were committed to avoiding any national debate over slavery. Party leaders cracked the whip vigorously to keep their members of Congress in line on such issues as the banning of abolitionist literature from the mail or the maintenance of the odious congressional Gag Rule. Within the South, both parties billed themselves as the surest defenders of slavery, while in the North the Whigs, always more loosely organized, sometimes presented themselves as principled foes of slavery, and the Democrats maintained that the issue was none of any northerner's business. So effective was the two-party system in muzzling all criticism of slavery at the national level that frustrated abolitionists in 1840 formed a party of their own, but in that year's presidential election the ideologically pure Liberty Party garnered fewer than ten thousand votes and had no impact on the outcome of the election.

The momentous events of the 1840s fundamentally changed this situation and made it drastically more difficult for politicians to dodge the issue of slavery. Early in the decade President John Tyler made the friendly annexation of the Republic of Texas a goal of his administration. Beginning in the 1820s, Americans had settled in Tejas, Mexico's northeastern province, first with the blessing of the government in far-off Mexico City, then with its suspicion and finally outright hostility. Mexican misrule had led in late 1835 to an uprising in Texas. The rebellious Texians, as they called themselves, won their independence the following April at the Battle of San Jacinto and established the Republic of Texas. Mexico sullenly maintained its claim to the province it could no longer rule. Tyler's move to annex Texas, though warmly welcomed by the Texians, drew the ire of abolitionists and of more moderate antislavery Americans since the Texians, being mostly migrants from the American South, had legalized slavery in their new republic. Adding Texas to the United States would increase the number of slave states in the Union.

The potent crosscurrent of slavery, which some Americans opposed regardless of the consequences for national growth, and of territorial expansion, which many Americans favored regardless of their views on slavery, now generated a political maelstrom that grew in size and strength. As the election of 1844 approached, the Democrats dumped their antiannexation frontrunner in favor of dark-horse annexationist James K. Polk of Tennessee on a platform calling for annexation not only of Texas but also of the entire Oregon Territory, hitherto jointly occupied by the United States and Great Britain. The Whigs nominated their own antiannexation candidate, Mr. Whig himself, Henry Clay, but as election day approached, Clay, fearing his anti-Texas stand might cost him at the polls, began hedging. His efforts to straddle the issue served only to prompt slavery opponents to bolt his party in favor of the Liberty Party. Enough of them did so in key states to throw the election to the expansionist Polk. Reading Polk's victory as a mandate for annexation, the lame-duck Tyler renewed his efforts and finally added Texas to the Union in March 1845, days before Polk's accession to office.

On entering the presidency, Polk found that Britain would negotiate its differences with the United States, but Mexico would not. The result was an amicable division of the Oregon Territory but war with Mexico when the latter declined to remove its troops from territory claimed by Texas. To the astonishment of European military pundits, including the renowned Duke of Wellington, who had defeated Napoleon at Waterloo, the United States triumphed over Mexico. General Winfield Scott, a veteran of the War of 1812, captured Mexico City with a small but excellent American army whose junior officers included Captain Robert E. Lee and lieutenants Ulysses S. Grant, Pierre G. T. Beauregard, Thomas J. Jackson, and George B. McClellan, among others who were destined to become far better known a decade and a half later.

The 1848 Treaty of Guadalupe-Hidalgo, which ended the war, granted the United States, in exchange for a fifteen-million-dollar payment to Mexico, the vast tract of territory that now comprises all or most of New Mexico,

Colorado, Utah, Arizona, Nevada, and California. The value of this tract, known as the Mexican Cession, increased drastically when a few months later news reached the East that American settlers in California had discovered gold there. The California Gold Rush was on, and multitudes flocked to the Pacific slope of the Sierra Nevada, not only from the rest of the United States but also from nearly every other country of the globe.

The acquisition of the Mexican Cession, combined with the rush of gold seekers to California, changed the political situation in America so that the two-party system was no longer able to keep the issue of slavery out of national politics. The new territories would have to be organized sooner or later, and when they were organized they would have to be either open to slavery or closed to it. Congress would have to decide. It had not faced that type of decision since the 1820 Missouri controversy, Jefferson's "fire bell in the night." Now Congress would once again face the slavery issue, which had in the meantime become far more polarized and intense than it had been a generation before. The rush of settlers to California meant that the problem of organizing at least that particular portion of the Mexican Cession could not be postponed. In a state of virtual anarchy, California must have a government at once. The question of slavery there could not be delayed.

THE WILMOT PROVISO AND THE COMPROMISE OF 1850

Some Americans did not wish to delay settlement of the slavery issue. Among them were northern Democrats who felt betrayed that Polk had passed up the kind of massive territorial acquisition in the Northwest that he had achieved in the Southwest, notwithstanding the 1844 Democratic platform's promises of both. This laid northern Democratic officeholders open to the northern Whigs' charge that their party was merely a front for the slaveholders' quest to increase the extent and power of the slave system. One such disgruntled northern Democrat was freshman Congressman David Wilmot of Pennsylvania. In order to demonstrate that his and other northern Democrats' support of the war and expansion did not equal support of slavery, Wilmot introduced a proviso, or limitation, to one of the first major spending authorizations for the war.

The Wilmot Proviso specified that slavery would not exist in any lands acquired as a result of the Mexican War. Southerners of both parties were enraged, partially because they did indeed hope the war's southwestern expansion would increase the power of the slave system and partially because they were insulted by the very suggestion that slavery was a morally questionable practice that needed limitation. The proviso passed the House, where northern numbers predominated, but failed in the Senate, where the South still possessed an equal number of states and at least a few northern senators could always be trusted to vote for the interests of slavery, whether to guard the interests of northern cotton mills that used the fiber grown largely by slaves or simply to keep southerners happy. Subsequently, northern representatives reintroduced the Wilmot Proviso on one spending bill after another. The result each time was the same, and southern rage grew.

Meanwhile, the leadership of each of the two parties did its best to dodge the issue of slavery completely. In the presidential election of 1848, the Democrats nominated Lewis Cass of Michigan on a platform featuring Cass's own concept of popular sovereignty—the idea of allowing the settlers in any given territory to decide the status of slavery there. The Whigs countered by nominating successful Mexican War general Zachary Taylor, who was also the absentee owner of a plantation and many slaves in Louisiana. In the best Whig fashion, the party declined to adopt any platform at all. Taylor's slave ownership, as well as his prominent role in a war that had been popular in the South, won him added support in that region, but some strongly antislavery northern Whigs were displeased enough to bolt the party, joining with some equally discontent antislavery Democrats as well as the old Liberty Party supporters to form the new Free Soil Party, a politically somewhat disparate group united in opposition to any further spread of slavery in the territories. The Free Soilers polled considerably more votes than had the old Liberty Party but this time not in such a way as to influence the outcome of the election. Instead, the Whigs, with their war hero and lack of any specifically defined policies to defend, took the White House.

Slaveholders felt complacent, abolitionists disgusted; both were stunned when, only a few months into his tenure, Taylor proposed admitting California directly to statehood, without passing through territorial status. This was de facto popular sovereignty, the policy of his defeated opponent, since California residents would draw up a state constitution either with or without legalized slavery, and since few slaveholders had chosen to bring their valuable human investments into turbulent and nearly lawless California, the vote of its residents was almost certain to make it a free state. That, as angry white southerners pointed out, amounted to de facto imposition of the Wilmot Proviso. To the compounded horror of slavery supporters, this would bring the total of free states to sixteen as against fifteen slave states, giving the free states a majority in the Senate as they had had in the House for many years, with little prospect of ever adding enough additional slave states to catch up again.

At the urging of aged proslavery extremist John C. Calhoun of South Carolina, delegates from several southern states met in October 1849 in Mississippi to denounce the Wilmot Proviso. There the delegates also called for a convention to represent all of the slave states the following June. The implication was clear that if slavery were not permitted to expand into the Mexican Cession, the Nashville Convention would become an opportunity for the slave states to declare themselves out of the Union.

With this tacit threat hanging over the country, Henry Clay in January 1850 presented a comprehensive compromise plan to Congress. Clay's eight-part package aimed at settling all of the issues then threatening to divide the country, each of which had at its core the dispute over slavery. The public closely followed the extensive debates in Congress over the course of the next eight months. Passions ran high. Proslavery extremists opposed the compromise because they considered it too hostile to slavery, especially because it admitted California as a free state. Abolitionists and more moderate opponents of slavery were equally opposed to the compromise but for opposite reasons, chiefly because it provided for the imposition, nationwide, of a draconian new Fugitive Slave Law, much tougher than the one previously on the books.

A coterie of senators and congressmen, led by Clay and Massachusetts Senator Daniel Webster, championed the cause of compromise. Those two, as well as Calhoun, who opposed the compromise, had dominated congressional politics for nearly half a century and were now obviously near the end of their careers. Calhoun actually died of tuberculosis in March 1850. All three men were considered to have given their most dramatic and moving speeches during the compromise debates. Yet despite Webster's legendary eloquence and Clay's unparalleled legislative skills, the compromise proposal stalled.

The Nashville Convention met in early June, but southern moderates prevailed and prevented any call for the slave states to leave the Union. The convention did, however, call for the extension of the Missouri Compromise boundary between slavery and freedom in the Louisiana Purchase, thirty-six degrees, thirty minutes latitude, all the way through the Mexican Cession to the Pacific, including the southern half of California. Such a step would provide land for several more slave states. The implication was that if the demand was not met, secession-minded southerners could schedule another convention.

The outlook for compromise began to change in midsummer. Anticompromise President Zachary Taylor took ill on the Fourth of July and died five days later. Vice President Millard Fillmore, a proponent of compromise, succeeded to the office. The influence of the presidency was now pulling the other way. Clay had left Washington to escape the sweltering summer heat, but thirty-six-year-old Democratic Senator Stephen A. Douglas of Illinois took up the compromise and began again the effort to put it through Congress. At five feet two inches tall, Douglas was four or five inches shorter than the average man and decidedly pudgy, but his reputation for legislative prowess, first in his adopted state of Illinois (he was a Vermont native) and then in the national capital, was already winning him the nickname "Little Giant."

Douglas skillfully divided the compromise's eight points into several separate packages. Then he used shifting coalitions to hustle them through Congress. Many—though by no means all—northern members resolutely opposed the Fugitive Slave Act whenever it came up, and nearly every southern member bitterly opposed acceptance of California as a free state each time that proposal reached the floor, but Douglas threaded his way through the legislative opposition, adding the votes of his relatively small band of dedicated compromisers to the votes in favor of each point of the compromise until all had passed and President Fillmore had signed each of them into law between September 9 and September 20, 1850, leaving large majorities in both houses of Congress in stunned dismay at the passage of a compromise they had bitterly opposed.

With that, the crisis was past, for the moment, and the problem of slavery contention in Washington seemed to have been permanently solved. The American public breathed a collective sigh of relief that secession and possible civil war had been averted. Yet the Compromise of 1850 was more illusion than reality. The majority of the members of Congress had opposed it, though for quite opposite reasons. Neither side in the dispute had been ready to accept any portion of the other side's demands. The compromise had simply been forced on an unwilling Congress by a small segment of compromisers using skillful legislative maneuvering.

For once, the politicians, who interacted regularly with persons from the other section of the country, may have understood the problem better than their constituents, few of whom were acquainted with persons outside their section. Few white southerners could bring themselves to believe that "Yankees" really cared so much for the slaves. They must be after some mere political and mercantile advantage and would back down when they saw there was no profit to be made from their hypocritical cant about freedom. Most northerners could not imagine that white southerners were so committed not only to the survival but even to the extension of slavery that they would destroy the country and risk war in order to secure it. As was to be the case steadily until almost 1865, each side underestimated the other's earnestness and determination. For now, large numbers on each side of the sectional divide imagined that the other side had backed down, at least to some degree, and they considered the compromise a godsend.

FUGITIVE SLAVES, *UNCLE TOM'S CABIN,* AND THE KANSAS-NEBRASKA ACT

The Compromise of 1850 had not removed the underlying fundamental difference of values regarding slavery, and over the next several years, while sectional peace reigned in Washington, slavery conflict flared up in various places around the country. The largest cause of that strife was the new Fugitive Slave Act that had been part of the Compromise of 1850. The act was so draconian that it made it relatively easy for any white southerner to come north and kidnap any black person, whether a former slave of his or a freeborn citizen of a northern state, and carry him or her off into slavery. Further, it mandated, under threat of severe criminal penalty in case of refusal, the use of northern state and local facilities, such as jails, and the active cooperation of northern state officials, sheriffs, and even common citizens. The latter might be drafted into a posse to hunt down alleged runaways. Thus, northerners, some of whom were opposed to slavery, were compelled not only to acquiesce but actively to participate in the enforcement of a law they held to be positively immoral. No amount of abolitionist speeches, sermons, or pamphlets could have created as many converts to abolitionism as did the Fugitive Slave Act.

The Fugitive Slave Act was a slap in the face of state rights. Nothing else the federal government had ever done or proposed doing throughout all of the nation's history up to that time had so thoroughly trampled on the rights and sovereignty of the individual states. This was especially ironic in view of the fact that less than twenty years later some white southerners would already be claiming that their cause had been that of state rights. The history of the 1850s does not bear that out. Southern political leaders during that decade, as during the preceding decades, championed either the cause of state rights or that of federal authority according to whichever seemed most likely to protect the institution of slavery. Since southerners had generally controlled the federal government during that era, they had more often than not been the active enemies of state rights.

The Fugitive Slave Act soon sparked resistance. Some abolitionists already maintained a network of secret routes and safe houses known as the Underground Railroad, aimed at aiding runaway slaves in making their way through the northern states to ultimate freedom in Canada. Perhaps one hundred thousand slaves had already taken the route to freedom, most of them to Canada, and the Underground Railroad came to carry its peak traffic in the 1850s, as the Fugitive Slave Act drove more northerners to take the step of outright civil disobedience by aiding the slaves in their escape.

Animosity toward the Fugitive Slave Act and its high-handed enforcement in the North led in 1851 to violence in the town of Christiana, Pennsylvania. On September 11 of that year, a group of escaped slaves shot and killed a slaveholder who was leading a posse with the intent of apprehending one of them. A celebrated trial followed in which Pennsylvania authorities, compelled by law to cooperate in a process they hated, allowed two of the accused to escape and otherwise did their best to assure a just, if not a legal, outcome. Southerners took notice and angrily determined to see the Fugitive Slave Act enforced in the North.

They got their chance for a high-profile case two years later. In 1853 Virginia slave Anthony Burns escaped and managed to board a ship at Richmond and sail to Boston. His master got wind of his whereabouts and invoked the Fugitive Slave Act to secure his return. Boston contained more abolitionists than any other major city in America, though even there they were a minority. Some of them determined to free Burns and launched a mob assault on the jail where he was being held, killing a deputy U.S. marshal but failing in their purpose. President Franklin Pierce, who had been elected in 1852 as a "northern man of southern principles," determined to make an example of this case and teach northerners a lesson about the supremacy of law and the return of fugitive slaves. Pierce sent in large numbers of federal troops to line the streets leading down to the docks. More soldiers formed a moving square around Burns as they marched him through Boston in chains and put him aboard a ship bound for Virginia. Bostonians watched in impotent rage, and thousands who had previously been apathetic turned overnight into what one of them called "stark, raving abolitionists." The return of Burns had cost the federal government forty thousand dollars, or perhaps fifty times the price he would have brought at the slave market.

Meanwhile a growing war of words was raging over the subject of slavery. In June 1851 the magazine *National Era* began running a serialized fictional story by a Lane Seminary professor's wife named Harriet Beecher Stowe, who had been inspired to write by her outrage at the Fugitive Slave Act. The story she wrote continued in installments through forty weeks and gained a large following. Published the next year as a book titled *Uncle Tom's Cabin*, it became a runaway best-seller. Based on careful research, *Uncle Tom's Cabin* was meant to show the evil not of southern whites but of the system of slavery. Some of its slaveholding characters were kindly, and its chief villain was Connecticut-born Simon Legree, who had moved to Louisiana and bought a plantation. Such refinements were lost on proslavery readers, however, who reacted with howls of rage and a flurry of books of their own purporting to show that slavery was a benevolent institution and that slaves were far better off than white northern factory workers. It remained unclear why no one sought the allegedly privileged status of slave. On the other hand, so many slaves were willing to attempt escape that southerners had felt the need of a ferocious new Fugitive Slave Act.

Despite the rival publications and the controversies stemming from the Fugitive Slave Act, the country could at least take comfort in the fact that slavery had not been an issue of dispute in Washington since the passage of the Compromise of 1850. That changed abruptly in 1854, and ironically the man who sparked the change was the chief architect of the final passage of the Compromise of 1850 and perhaps the politician who had the most to lose from a revival of the national political controversy over slavery. Illinois Senator Stephen A. Douglas had not intended to reignite the slavery debate in Washington in 1854. He had wanted to get a transcontinental railroad built across the plains and mountains to connect California with the rest of the country.

In the strange logic of politics, railroad building connected directly to slavery. Douglas shared the mistaken but widespread belief that building such a large railroad required federal subsidies. That in itself made the railroad's construction a political prize to be fought over by the various sections of the country, each wanting the route to originate in its region. During the 1850s the only sort of federal subsidy that was considered feasible was some sort of land grant, along the right-of-way. The government could not grant land until it was properly surveyed, and the land could not be properly surveyed until it was within an organized territory. Thus, in order to build a transcontinental railroad where he wanted it, stretching westward from Iowa, Douglas had to organize a territorial government in the remaining unorganized lands of the Louisiana Purchase, lands that had been forever closed to slavery by the 1820 Missouri Compromise. Southern congressmen and senators would therefore be hostile to Douglas's bill for two reasons. First, they would wish to see the transcontinental railroad built on a southern route rather than across the central plains. Second, and more significant, organizing those lands into territories would be the first step toward turning them into states that, under the terms of the Missouri Compromise, must be free states.

To line up the southern votes he needed in order to get his bill through Congress, Douglas had to include language repealing the Missouri Compromise and opening the new territories to slavery under popular sovereignty. His Kansas-Nebraska Act set up a large Nebraska Territory on the northern plains and a smaller Kansas Territory, directly west of slaveholding Missouri. The status of slavery in these territories was now to be determined by popular sovereignty, the vote of their inhabitants at some unspecified time in the future. The separation of the smaller Kansas Territory directly west of Missouri was clearly meant to invite proslavery settlers to claim the territory as a future slave state.

Douglas grimly predicted that the bill would create a political storm in the North but introduced it anyway. He was right about the storm. Indeed, he had no idea. The outrage in the North gave birth to the Republican Party. The country was ripe for a new party. The Whig Party, always a loose coalition of interest groups, had finally all but disintegrated in the first few years of the decade, largely as a result of the tensions placed on political unity by southern Whigs claiming to be the staunchest defenders of slavery while northern Whigs presented themselves to voters as the principled opponents of the South's "Peculiar Institution." With the Whig Party's demise, almost half the American electorate was in search of a new political home.

The new Republican Party also incorporated diverse political elements. That portion of northern Whig voters who did indeed oppose slavery flocked to the new party, as did free-soil, or "Anti-Nebraska," Democrats, as well as members of the old Free Soil Party. They were a disparate lot. Some favored high tariffs, others low. Some backed a national bank, others hard money. Some were abolitionists who believed in racial equality, others were racists who wanted to limit the spread of slavery only so that the territories would be exclusively a white man's country. Yet there was an adhesive that bound the seemingly conflicting elements of the party: they all came together on a platform that called for no further spread of slavery. They could not prevent the passage of Douglas's bill, but they now provided a major free-soil party that was strong enough to carry the North in elections and might, in a few years, be able to put together enough northern electoral votes to choose a president.

BLEEDING KANSAS AND THE LINCOLN–DOUGLAS DEBATES

Implementation of Douglas's Kansas-Nebraska Act proved even more problematic than its passage. Proslavery Missourians determined to see Kansas become another slave state by fair means or foul. Thousands of them, heavily armed and threatening, flocked across the Kansas line on the territory's first election day, casting fraudulent ballots and intimidating antislavery and free-soil voters with threats of beatings, whippings, or worse. So effective were these Missouri "Border Ruffians" that the proslavery side won in a landslide that numbered several times more votes than there were eligible voters in the territory. The Pierce administration nevertheless certified the obviously fraudulent results and officially recognized the new proslavery government of Kansas, with its capital at Lecompton. Free-state settlers, along with the large majority of new Kansans who cared nothing for slavery one way or the other but disliked election fraud, held an unauthorized revote and elected a rival, antislavery government with a large majority of the territory's legal voters. Pierce denounced the free-state government as illegitimate and threatened its adherents with dire punishment. It appeared as though slavery would triumph in Kansas.

In May 1856 proslavery militia destroyed the free-state Kansas capital at Lawrence. Several days later, a small band of antislavery militia, led by hardcore abolitionist John Brown, retaliated with a stealthy nocturnal raid on the proslavery settlement of Pottawatomie Creek, where they killed several men in cold blood who had previously been threatening death to free-staters (i.e., settlers like Brown and his large family who favored turning the Kansas Territory into a free state). The details of the killings were disputed, but Americans were shocked by the news. Slavery advocates had previously murdered several abolitionists, both in Kansas and elsewhere in the country, but they were outraged that an abolitionist had finally reciprocated.

Almost simultaneously in Washington, D.C., Massachusetts Republican Senator Charles Sumner delivered a speech titled "The Crime against Kansas," tacitly likening the attempt to make Kansas a slave state to the crime of rape. Sumner named names, especially that of aged, proslavery South Carolina Senator Pierce Butler, who was absent that day because of illness. Two days later Butler's nephew, Congressman Preston Brookes of South Carolina, entered the Senate chamber and attacked Sumner with a loaded cane, leaving the Massachusetts senator lying unconscious in a pool of blood. Sumner barely survived and was unable to return to his Senate seat for several years, during which time his constituents reelected him, leaving his empty chair in the Senate as a silent witness against the brutality of the slave power.

Meanwhile the election campaign of 1856 was in full swing. The Democrats passed over their most prominent figure, Douglas, because of his notoriety in both sections of the country on the issue of slavery. Instead, they chose aged political cipher James Buchanan, a man whose nickname, "Old Public Functionary," neatly summarized his career. His chief qualification for office, aside from the fact that having been out of the country the past four years as an ambassador in Europe he had had little chance to make controversial statements on slavery, was that he was, like Pierce, another "northern man of southern principles." The Republicans chose Mexican War veteran John C. Frémont, political heir of the powerful Missouri Benton family. His qualifications to govern, in terms either of experience or of temperament, were highly questionable, but he was famous and had announced a free-soil position.

Some southern political leaders threatened to have their states secede from the Union on the election of Frémont or any "black Republican," as they contemptuously called all members of the party. Their threats were not put to the test that year, as Buchanan edged out Frémont, but Republicans noted with hope and their opponents with apprehension that if Frémont could have carried Pennsylvania—a probable Republican state had not its native son been the Democratic candidate—and either Illinois or Indiana—both thoroughly winnable states for the Republicans—Frémont would have won the election after all. The outcome might be different in another four years.

Meanwhile, back in Kansas, violence escalated between pro- and antislavery settlers, with the Missouri Border Ruffians mixing in. Skirmishes took place between rival militias as the press began to refer to the territory as "Bleeding Kansas." John Brown won recognition among antislavery circles for leading his free-state militia in several of the skirmishes. Slave-state guerrillas killed one of Brown's sons. A number of additional deaths occurred before the federal government finally restored a reasonable degree of order in the territory.

James Buchanan came into office in March 1857 devoutly wishing that all abolitionists would go away and stop making trouble. He saw what he thought was a chance to make that happen in a case then before the Supreme Court. Slave Dred Scott had sued for his freedom on the basis that his owner, an army doctor, had brought him to the free state of Illinois and the free territory of Wisconsin. Rabidly proslavery chief justice Roger B. Taney had lined up a majority of justices to support a narrow decision dismissing Scott's case on the grounds that, as a black man, he was not a citizen and therefore had no standing to sue. Buchanan secretly convinced Taney to broaden his decision into the nation's first great piece of judicial legislation, a sweeping decree meant to establish once and for all the legality of slavery throughout the territories. Taney obliged, striking down as unconstitutional all restrictions on slavery, including the venerable Missouri Compromise. No one, Taney announced, had the right to prevent slaveholders from taking their slaves into any of the territories of the United States. Contrary to Buchanan's hopes, however, the court's decree did not end all debate of the issue of slavery.

The unabated virulence of the issue of slavery became immediately obvious when Buchanan tried to secure admittance of Kansas as a slave state on the basis of a constitution drawn up by the blatantly fraudulent proslavery territorial government headquartered in Lecompton. Douglas, though he cared nothing about slavery, denounced this action as a travesty on popular sovereignty and majority rule. A bitter division sprang up within the Democratic Party between the followers of Douglas and those of Buchanan.

Increasingly it seemed that almost no action in national politics could escape the slavery controversy. The House of Representatives went through a long deadlock unable to elect a speaker as the result of a book written by an obscure North Carolinian. Hinton Rowan Helper was no friend of African Americans, but he was a foe of slavery because he saw how it degraded non-slaveholding southern whites. In his 1857 book *The Impending Crisis at the South*, Helper attacked the system of slavery and exhorted his fellow non-slaveholding southern whites to vote it out of existence. Slaveholding southerners were furious—and seriously frightened. Nonslaveholders were the majority in the South, and if they ever gave up their commitment to maintaining slavery as the best way of maintaining white supremacy, the institution would be in serious trouble. Slaveholders' rage multiplied when they learned that the Republican Party, eager to win a hearing among the common folk of the South, had printed and distributed a condensed version of Helper's book and that a number of Republican politicians had signed a statement endorsing it. Among them was Ohio Republican John Sherman, the party's candidate for Speaker of the House. Proslavery House members kept that body in turmoil for months and finally succeeded in blocking Sherman's election. The House chose a compromise candidate instead.

In 1858, as for the past half dozen years since the deaths of Henry Clay and Daniel Webster, Stephen A. Douglas was the most prominent political figure in the United States. In political terms, "the Little Giant" towered over even the president of the United States, with whom he was now in the bitterest of political feuds because of his opposition to Buchanan's cherished Lecompton constitution in Kansas. Douglas was up for reelection to the U.S. Senate that year, and Republican newspapers on the East Coast, notably Horace Greeley's influential *New York Tribune*, began to call for the Illinois Republicans to give Douglas their nomination. Prairie State Republicans were appalled and none more so than Abraham Lincoln. A successful Springfield lawyer, Lincoln had come out of political retirement in 1854. No longer simply a Whig Party hack intent on bringing home the bacon for his district, Lincoln, though still ambitious, now had a cause to which to devote his political efforts, and that cause was fighting slavery. In eloquent speeches he made clear that Douglas's policy of not caring whether the people voted slavery up or voted it down was not good enough for the Republican Party and not good enough for the United States.

Lincoln won the Illinois Republican nomination for the Senate. His acceptance speech, given in Springfield on June 16, 1858, set the tone for the campaign. "'A house divided against itself cannot stand,'" Lincoln said, quoting the twelfth chapter of the Gospel According to Matthew:

> I believe this government cannot endure, permanently, half slave and half free. I do not expect the Union to be dissolved—I do not expect the house to fall— but I do expect it will cease to be divided. It will become all one thing or all the other. Either the opponents of slavery will arrest the further spread of it, and place it where the public mind shall rest in the belief that it is in the course of ultimate extinction; or its advocates will push it forward, till it shall become alike lawful in all the States, old as well as new—North as well as South.[3]

Lincoln's contest with Douglas was a David-and-Goliath battle that pitted the five-foot-four-inch Little Giant against the gangly six-foot-four-inch but politically relatively unknown Lincoln. Reluctantly Douglas agreed to a series of seven debates, to be held in venues throughout the state. The debates brought out more clearly than ever the issues that divided the country. Douglas race-baited Lincoln relentlessly, accusing him, in the coarsest of terms, of a belief in racial equality that would have been very unpopular in much of that state. He put Lincoln so badly on the defensive in one down-state venue that the lanky Republican actually did deny a belief in the social equality of the races but came back to assert that an African American had as much right to freedom as any man present, including himself or Douglas. Lincoln took the offensive reminding voters again and again that Douglas's belief in democracy was not a sufficient moral absolute and that the same moral law that gave any men the right to govern themselves also gave black men and women the right to own themselves.

Despite a strong performance in the debates, Lincoln lost the election, largely because the state of Illinois had not been redistricted lately, leading to the underrepresentation of Republicans in the legislature. In those days before the Seventeenth Amendment, state legislatures still elected U.S. senators, thus guarding the sovereignty of the states. Since Republicans were underrepresented in the Illinois legislature, they were unable to elect Lincoln despite the slightly higher number of Republican ballots that Illinois voters had cast. Still, the lanky Springfield Republican had made a name and a national reputation for himself.

2

AND THE WAR CAME

JOHN BROWN'S HARPERS FERRY
RAID AND THE ELECTION OF 1860

Throughout the decade of the 1850s, the momentum seemed to shift constantly back and forth between politics and practical action, between the men in frock coats and other men who would not hesitate at all to dirty their hands in any number of ways. John Brown was one such man. He had perpetrated the Pottawatomie killings in Kansas back in 1856. He had also led antislavery militia in battle there against their proslavery opponents. After Kansas had grown quiet, Brown had led armed raids into Missouri, liberating a handful of slaves and appropriating their owners' horses as well as punishment for the crime of slaveholding and further support for the cause of freedom. Thereafter he had taken his family to live in a racially mixed upstate New York community, an extreme rarity at that time, specifically for the purpose of showing his solidarity with African Americans.

All the while Brown was planning what he confidently believed would be his greatest stroke against the slave power. He would lead a band of abolitionist fighters into slave territory somewhere in the southern Appalachians. There escaping slaves would flock to join him, and he would organize them into a freed-slave republic that would, he hoped, grow until it overthrew the slave-tolerant U.S. government and replaced the imperfect U.S. Constitution with its own charter, over which Brown had labored many an hour by candlelight in Kansas and New York. When Brown presented the plan to his friend, black abolitionist Frederick Douglass, the latter was appalled. The plan seemed like suicide and would discredit the abolitionist movement. Nevertheless Brown and his small band of adherents, both white and black, forged ahead.

In October 1859 he led them to the U.S. arsenal at Harpers Ferry, Virginia (now West Virginia), seizing the undefended facility and taking hostages. Brown hesitated before leading his raiders away from Harpers Ferry, however, and soon found himself surrounded by Virginia militia. No slaves came to join him. That particular section of Virginia contained relatively few slaves. Instead of help from those he had hoped to free, Brown soon found that federal authority had arrived in the person of U.S. Army Lieutenant Colonel Robert E. Lee, supported by a company of U.S. Marines, hastily shipped up from the Washington navy yard. When Brown refused Lee's summons to surrender, Lee sent in the marines, who successfully stormed Brown's remaining enclave within the arsenal.

Though badly wounded, Brown survived, and Virginia authorities lost no time in arraigning and trying him for treason against the state of Virginia and other crimes. The trial's outcome was never in doubt. Guaranteed a place on the gallows before year's end, Brown conducted himself with impressive dignity, winning the grudging respect of his captors and the admiration of many across the North who had initially recoiled from the violent and lawless nature of his raid. Southerners took note of and exaggerated the degree of northern sympathy for Brown. The most radical of slavery advocates, known as Fire-Eaters, warned that he was a harbinger of the bloody intentions of the abolitionists toward all white southerners.

One Fire-Eater, Virginia agricultural writer Edmund Ruffin, acquired some of the pikes, or spears, Brown had brought with him in hopes of arming the slave allies who never came. Ruffin sent one pike to each southern state capitol as a graphic reminder to his fellow white southerners of what the North supposedly wanted to do to them and their families. When Virginia authorities hanged Brown that December, surrounded by almost the whole of the state's militia, the septuagenarian Ruffin, complete with flowing white hair, had himself temporarily inducted into the corps of cadets of the Virginia Military Institute so that he could be on hand to have the pleasure of seeing the famous abolitionist fighter twist in the wind. Commanding the contingent of cadets was one of their professors, stern Presbyterian and Mexican War veteran Thomas J. Jackson. Jackson admired the courage and calmness with which Brown faced death but disapproved of his cause.

Brown's raid and the subsequent publicity surrounding his trial and execution, including displays of public mourning in some northern cities, culminated in an entire decade of political and sometimes violent and bloody sectional strife over the issue of slavery. Each clash, whether in the national capital or in places like Lawrence, Kansas, or Harpers Ferry, Virginia, had intensified the bitter feelings between North and South. Thus polarized, the nation faced the election of 1860.

The Democratic convention took place in Charleston, South Carolina, the most extreme proslavery city in the most extreme proslavery region of the most extreme proslavery state in the Union. Local crowds packing the visitors' gallery roared their approval for every proslavery speech and jeered any mention of the candidacy of Stephen Douglas, whom they hated for having denied the inherent right of slavery to go into all of the territories regardless even of the majority vote of white inhabitants.

Through more than one hundred ballots, the convention could not achieve the two-thirds vote needed to make a nomination. Southerners had more than one-third of the delegates committed to stopping Douglas or any candidate not completely dedicated to slavery expansion. Douglas had a solid majority of delegates behind him, and this time his supporters, many of them from the Midwest, were tired of backing down to the demands of the slave power every four years—and then paying the price for it at the polls in the North. Unable to nominate a candidate, the convention turned instead to selecting a platform, but when the majority refused a southern demand that the federal government actively protect slavery in every territory, southern delegates walked out. An attempt to restore party unity at a special convention in Baltimore several weeks later also broke up over the issue of slavery, and the severed wings of the Democratic Party nominated rival presidential tickets—Vice President John C. Breckinridge for the southern Democrats, Douglas for what was left of the national Democratic Party.

During the period between the first Democratic convention in Charleston and that party's attempt to reconstitute itself in Baltimore, the Republican Party met in Chicago, Illinois, and, passing over front-runner William H. Seward as being perhaps too controversial a figure, instead nominated Lincoln. The Illinois lawyer had seemed like the ideal candidate, dedicated to the party's cause of halting the spread of slavery yet without the harsh edge that public perception attributed to Seward. In a speech in New York City the preceding February, Lincoln had showed an ability to articulate Republican principles in surprisingly clear and eloquent language, arguing persuasively that what the Republicans wanted was a return to the thought and policies of the founders of the republic, who had wished to contain slavery so that it would be "in the course of ultimate extinction." Lincoln also had common-man appeal and a set of very savvy political managers.

The 1860 campaign was not to be a three-way race. As if the field of candidates were not already crowded enough, a group of former southern Whigs, dissatisfied with both the Democrats and the Republicans, held a convention and formed itself into the Constitutional Union Party. The new party nominated John Bell of Tennessee as its presidential candidate—the fourth major-party candidate in that year's race—and, in the best of old-time Whig tradition, declined to adopt any platform other than "the Constitution and the enforcement of the laws"—a creed to which every party claimed to subscribe. Voters understood that what the Constitutional Unionists stood for was a moderate proslavery position without the Fire-Eaters' constant demands for slavery expansion and strident threats of secession if their demands were not met or their candidate was not elected.

The election turned into two separate two-way races: Bell versus Breckinridge in the South and Lincoln versus Douglas in the North. Breckinridge carried the Deep South and Bell the Upper South. Douglas garnered more votes than either but carried only Missouri and half of New Jersey. Lincoln was the top vote getter, edging out Douglas in all the rest of the free states and locking up an electoral majority with scarcely more than 39 percent of

Former U.S. Vice President and Confederate General and Secretary of War John C. Breckinridge

Secretary of State William H. Seward

the popular vote. Curiously, this was not because his opposition was split three ways. Even if all the votes cast for all three of Lincoln's opponents had been cast for one man, Lincoln would still have won since he carried nearly all of the northern states by moderate to narrow margins but garnered virtually no votes at all in the South.

THE SECESSION OF THE DEEP SOUTH STATES

Throughout the campaign, southerners, particularly the Fire-Eaters, had loudly and frequently repeated that they would take their states out of the Union if any "Black Republican" was elected. At news of Lincoln's triumph, secessionists in all of the slave states went to work to make good on their threat. By a campaign of manipulation and voter intimidation, they strove to bring about secession. South Carolina led the way on December 20, 1860, and thereby undercut the attempts of southern unionists to stop the momentum for secession by persuading southern voters to wait until all of the slave states could go out together. Though a two-week delay followed, South Carolina's action was like the bursting of a levee, as one after another of the slave states seceded. During January 1861, five more Deep South states declared themselves out of the Union, and Texas, on February 1, became the seventh state to do so.

Later that month representatives of the seceded states met in Montgomery, Alabama, and constituted themselves the Confederate States of America, electing as their president Mississippi Senator Jefferson Davis. Davis, a West Point graduate and Mexican War veteran, originally coveted a military appointment in the newly forming Confederate army, but he accepted the presidency and prepared to lead the new slaveholders' republic. The Confederacy, seeking further legitimacy, adopted a constitution modeled on the U.S. Constitution but altered to recognize slavery specifically. They knew what their revolution was intended to protect, even if some of them would later deny it and claim they were fighting for state rights. Another difference from the U.S. Constitution was that the Confederate constitution limited its president to one six-year term without eligibility for reelection. Davis was to serve as provisional president until a regular president could be elected in the fall of 1861 and inaugurated the following February. As it turned out, no candidate opposed him, and the Mississippian was elected to succeed himself and become the Confederacy's first—and only—regular president.

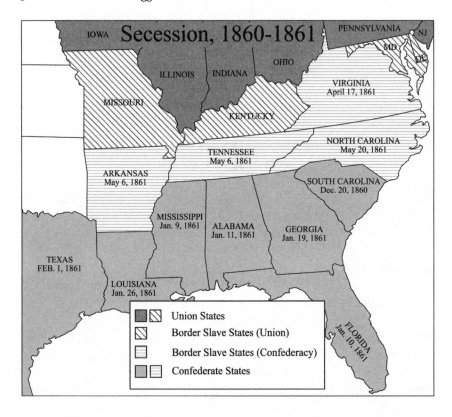

While the Deep South states seceded and formed a rival government, lame-duck President Buchanan did nothing. In the face of his idleness, rebellious state militia throughout the Deep South seized every federal installation in those states except for two: irrelevant Fort Pickens outside the harbor of Pensacola, Florida, and all-too-relevant Fort Sumter inside the harbor of Charleston, South Carolina. Much to Buchanan's dismay, the commander of the seventy-six-man U.S. Army garrison at Charleston had moved his troops on Christmas night 1860 from the indefensible old Fort Moultrie to the new and modern (as well as incomplete) Fort Sumter, where it would be much more difficult for rebellious militia to bring him to grips. Southern leaders cried foul and demanded that Sumter be evacuated as part of an overall U.S. government acceptance of the secession of the southern states. Such acceptance did not seem unlikely in view of the fact that Buchanan, in his last State of the Union Address, had proclaimed that states had no right to secede and that the federal government had no right to stop them if they did.

Jefferson Davis as he appeared during the Civil War.

Public opinion in the North was divided. Some northern Democrats, naturally hostile to Lincoln and his platform of limiting slavery expansion, were inclined to sympathize with the seceding states. Horace Greeley, influential editor of the *New York Tribune* and one of the most prominent Republican journalists in the country, urged, "Let erring sisters go in peace," and some other Republicans took up his refrain. This was not so much because they desired to see the Union broken up as because they were afraid that the Buchanan administration would knuckle under to the southern threat of secession and agree to some sort of compromise that might negate all that antislavery Americans had achieved in the recent campaign.

The Cotton South seemed unified and determined, the North confused and uncertain. The Upper South—Virginia, Maryland, North Carolina, Kentucky, Arkansas, and Missouri—seemed to teeter on the brink of secession, as the Fire-Eaters in those states had fallen just short of their goal of rushing secession past a skeptical electorate. Secessionists in the Upper South tended to believe that what their cause needed was some aggressive action on the part of the Confederacy to demonstrate that it truly was independent and was not going to put up with any trifling from the Lincoln administration.

As Virginia Fire-Eater Roger Pryor told a crowd in Charleston, South Carolina, the way to bring Virginia out of the Union and into the Confederacy was to "strike a blow."

In a demoralized Washington, D.C., guarded by large numbers of U.S. Army troops deployed by aged General in Chief Winfield Scott to prevent any attempt at disrupting the inauguration, Lincoln took office March 4, committed to preserving the Union intact. Standing in front of the capitol with its unfinished dome, Lincoln read an inaugural address couched in conciliatory terms. He was duty bound to preserve the Union, Lincoln explained, but he would not be the aggressor. He would not attack the southern states or their institution of slavery unless they attacked first. He would enforce all of the laws, even the Fugitive Slave Act, but otherwise he would respect the rights of the states within the Union. He would maintain current garrisons like Fort Sumter, but they would attempt neither to collect the tariff nor to take any other action against the secessionists. In conclusion, Lincoln showed some of the eloquence that has led scholars to consider him the most adept user of the English language of any American statesman:

> In *your* hands, my dissatisfied fellow-countrymen, and not in *mine*, is the momentous issue of civil war. The Government will not assail *you*. You can have no conflict without being yourselves the aggressors. *You* have no oath registered in heaven to destroy the Government, while I shall have the most solemn one to "preserve, protect, and defend it."
>
> I am loath to close. We are not enemies, but friends. We must not be enemies. Though passion may have strained it must not break our bonds of affection. The mystic chords of memory, stretching from every battlefield and patriot grave to every living heart and hearthstone all over this broad land, will yet swell the chorus of the Union, when again touched, as surely they will be, by the better angels of our nature.[1]

White southerners were for the most part as unmoved by Lincoln's eloquence as they were by his restraint. His statement that secession was not a constitutional right, guaranteed to the states and to be accepted without question by the federal government, they characterized as a virtual declaration of war.

FORT SUMTER

On taking over the presidency, Lincoln found the nation's situation even worse than he had imagined. The army was small and scattered, most of it defending the western frontier against Indians. The navy was also small and scattered, most of it patrolling against the Atlantic slave trade. The aged commanding general had little encouragement to offer. Winfield Scott had been one of the greatest military minds of his time but his time was most emphatically passed by 1861. Once a majestic sight in full dress uniform, the six-foot-four-inch Scott had grown so old, fat, and gouty that he could not mount a horse but had to be hoisted onto its back by something like a small crane. Scott told Lincoln that getting an expedition through to Fort Sumter would require more men than the army had and counseled giving up the fort. Most of the president's cabinet agreed, including the forceful and cunning Secretary of State Seward, who thought that he should have been president instead of Lincoln. Worst of all, reports from Fort Sumter indicated that the garrison was running out of food. If not resupplied within a few weeks, Anderson and his men would have no choice but surrender or starvation, and surrender of the fort would be read in the South and in the rest of the world as the government's acceptance of southern secession.

A desperate Lincoln seized on a plan presented by Assistant Secretary of the Navy Gustavus V. Fox. What army leadership thought impossible, the navy proposed to do: get a relief expedition through to Fort Sumter. Though most of the fleet was unavailable, one reasonably powerful unit was on hand in the side-wheel steamer USS *Powhatan*, mounting sixteen guns, eleven of them heavy. It would form the nucleus of a task force whose mission would be resupplying Sumter. If the Rebels offered no resistance, *Powhatan* and the other warships would wait outside the harbor while a supply ship carried in the needed rations. If the Rebels opened fire, then *Powhatan* and the smaller warships, such as ten-gun steam sloop of war USS *Pawnee*, would, in theory at least, shoot their way into the harbor and see to the insertion not only of rations but of additional troops as well. A Union agent would alert Anderson of the expedition's approach so that the fort's garrison could cooperate with its own heavy guns. At the same time, a letter from Lincoln went to South Carolina Governor Francis W. Pickens (pointedly not to Jefferson Davis, whose office as president of the self-styled Confederate States Lincoln did not recognize), blandly informing him that an expedition would be resupplying Fort Sumter and that no shot would be fired or any troops, guns, or ammunition inserted unless the attempt was resisted.

Meanwhile, Seward was playing a deep game of his own. Convinced that the southern states could somehow be convinced to give up the idea of secession if only they were placated about Fort Sumter, he had entered into an indirect, unofficial, and completely unauthorized negotiation with several

Confederate commissioners whom Davis had sent to Washington for that purpose. Seward hinted broadly to the Confederate agents that Fort Sumter would be abandoned, a decision he had no authority to make. When he learned of Lincoln's authorization of Fox's plan to resupply the fort, Seward drew up an order that he cunningly got Lincoln to sign without knowing what it was, diverting *Powhatan* to other duty. When Lincoln discovered the move and ordered Seward to revoke the order, Seward did so over his own signature. The ship's commander obeyed the order signed by the president rather than that signed by the secretary of state, and before Lincoln could discover this second subterfuge, *Powhatan* was beyond recall and unavailable for the expedition.

Lincoln could see little choice but to go ahead with the expedition anyway. It lacked the firepower now to shoot its way into the harbor, but the attempt to insert the unarmed supply ship was the last chance for preserving peace and Union by maintaining the status quo in Charleston harbor. Lincoln knew that, given the aggressiveness of the southern leadership, the chance for peace was slim, but he had to try. There was little else for him to do other than accept the dismemberment of the United States, and that he would not do.

On receiving Lincoln's notification of the planned relief expedition, Governor Pickens had immediately forwarded it to Jefferson Davis in Montgomery, the Confederate capital. Davis was determined to have Fort Sumter as a symbol of Confederate sovereignty. He hoped to get it peaceably but was quite willing to do so by force if necessary. On learning that the relief expedition was on the way, he ordered the commander of the Confederate forces ringing Charleston harbor, Louisianan Pierre G. T. Beauregard, to demand the fort's immediate surrender and, if that were refused, to blast it into submission.

Beauregard was a veteran of the prewar U.S. Army who, like many southern officers, had resigned his commission when his state seceded and taken a commission in the new Confederate army. An 1838 graduate of West Point, where Robert Anderson had been his artillery instructor, Beauregard was a skillful military engineer who had supervised the arrangement of dozens of batteries of Confederate guns trained on Fort Sumter.

In response to Davis's order, Beauregard, on the afternoon of April 11, 1861, sent a trio of staff officers in a small boat with a flag of truce to demand Anderson's surrender. The leader of the Confederate delegation was Colonel James Chesnut, until a few months earlier a U.S. senator from South Carolina. To Chesnut's summons to surrender, Anderson replied that his orders would not allow him to give up the fort at that time but that if the Confederates waited long enough, lack of provisions would force him to do so. Chesnut and his cohorts piled back into their boat and took this message back to Beauregard, who in turn telegraphed it to Montgomery.

Davis had his secretary of war reply that if Anderson would specify a time when he would evacuate the fort, Beauregard could hold off on the attack. Back into the boat went Chesnut and the other two staff officers for the long pull across the harbor. By the time they reached the fort, it was well after midnight on the morning of April 12. When Anderson met with them and heard their demand for a date to evacuate the fort, he gave April 15, if resupply did not reach him first. Everyone knew that the Union relief expedition was scheduled to arrive before then, so Chesnut took the responsibility, though very much in keeping with the wishes of Beauregard and Davis, of refusing Anderson's terms and informing him that Confederate guns would open fire on the fort in one hour.

Once again plying their boat across the harbor, the three Confederate officers proceeded to the nearest Confederate battery, located on James Island, and gave the order to fire. Among the Confederate soldiers there was Virginia Fire-Eater Edmund Ruffin, still sporting his long, white hair. Having had himself temporarily inducted into the Virginia Military Institute so that he could have the pleasure of watching John Brown hang seventeen months before, Ruffin had now temporarily joined a South Carolina unit and was thus on hand for the first shot of the war. Indeed, according to some stories he actually fired the first shot, though this is generally discounted. It was 4:30 a.m., on Friday, April 12, when the guns on James Island roared into action, and the rest of the Confederate guns around the harbor quickly joined them in opening fire.

Low on ammunition, Anderson held his fire for the first several hours, then had his men reply sparingly. Outside the harbor, Fox and his relief expedition stood by helplessly, unable to force their way to the fort. By the afternoon of April 13, with ammunition almost gone and flames out of control inside the fort, threatening its powder magazine, Anderson surrendered. He and his seventy-six men had done all that could have been expected of them and by putting up a stout fight had demonstrated that the United States was not willingly acquiescing in the surrender of its fort. Amazingly, the thirty-four-hour-long bombardment had killed no one. Beauregard, always an admirer of the chivalrous niceties of war as it had been practiced in an earlier age, allowed Anderson to fire a fifty-gun salute to his flag in a formal surrender ceremony the following day before leaving the fort to board Fox's ship and head north. Ironically, a gunner firing the salute accidentally ignited a pile of cartridges, and two U.S. soldiers died in the blast.

LINCOLN CALLS FOR TROOPS AND THE UPPER SOUTH AND BORDER STATES REACT

News of Fort Sumter shocked the nation, and both North and South reacted strongly. As Lincoln would later explain the situation, "Both parties deprecated war, but one of them would *make* war rather than let the nation survive, and the other would *accept* war rather than let it perish, and the war came."[2]

On April 15, the day following the surrender ceremony in Charleston, Lincoln, following the Constitution as well as Washington's example in the Whiskey Rebellion, issued a proclamation: "Whereas the laws of the United States have been and are opposed in several States by combinations too powerful to be suppressed in the ordinary way," the president requested the states to provide seventy-five thousand militia for federal service. Proslavery governors in Upper South states like Virginia, North Carolina, and Kentucky indignantly refused, but the response across the North was more than enthusiastic. The flag had been fired on, and the North rose up in a surprisingly unified reaction. Stephen Douglas pledged his support to Lincoln in suppressing treason. Patriotic rallies took place in scores of towns, and men flocked to enlist. Recruiting quotas were exceeded almost overnight, and several state governors begged Lincoln to accept additional regiments and in some cases kept those regiments on hand as state troops until the federal government, in due time, was more than happy to receive them. The first seventy-five thousand militia were limited by constitutional restraints to a maximum term of ninety days' service.

Reaction in the slave states that had not previously declared themselves out of the Union was quite different and proved the truth of Pryor's advice that the South Carolinians "strike a blow." Once it became clear that they would have to fight either for a slave republic or for a republic in which slavery might be limited, Upper South residents, especially those who held political power, had no doubts as to which side they would take. On April 17 the Virginia state convention voted for secession. Theoretically the vote was subject to ratification in a state referendum to be held the following month, but by that time Virginia's secessionist governor had already all but incorporated the state into the Confederacy. Within a few weeks, North Carolina, Tennessee, and Arkansas had followed suit.

The part of the Upper South known as the border states—Maryland, Kentucky, and Missouri—was divided internally. Kentucky and Missouri had secessionist governors with moderately Unionist legislatures. In Maryland, those relationships were reversed. Baltimore and the eastern counties of Maryland, with the highest slave population, were the hotbed of secessionism in that state. When on April 19 the Sixth Massachusetts Regiment, the first of the northern regiments responding to Lincoln's call, passed through Baltimore on its way to Washington, trouble broke out. Rail connections through Baltimore were discontinuous, and troops traveling to Washington from the North had to detrain at one station and march through the streets of Baltimore to another station where they could entrain for the national capital. As the Massachusetts men did so, an angry secessionist mob attacked them, throwing stones and firing pistols. The soldiers shot back, and when the fray had ended, four soldiers and twelve civilians were dead.

The mayor of Baltimore and the governor of Maryland demanded that Lincoln allow no further Union troops to pass through the city and inflame the citizens and, when Lincoln refused, had the railroad bridge burned so that none could. Secessionist Marylanders cut the telegraph wires leading north from Washington. This made for some very tense days in the capital, cut off as it was from communication with the North or from the arrival of any additional troops. Benjamin F. Butler, general of the Massachusetts militia (and peacetime lawyer and politician), found a way around Baltimore, commandeering a steamer and using it to carry his troops down Chesapeake Bay to Annapolis, Maryland, whence a railroad led to Washington. Maryland secessionists had damaged both engines and tracks, but Butler's troops, among whom were men who had worked in the shop that made the locomotive, repaired both and got the line running. Other Union troops followed in a steady stream along the same route until, on May 13, Butler and his troops took control of Baltimore.

Semirebellious Maryland continued to be a problem. Near the end of the month, Union troops there arrested a man named John Merryman for recruiting for the Confederacy. Merryman's lawyer filed for a writ of habeas corpus in federal circuit court. In those days U.S. Supreme Court justices doubled as circuit court judges, and this circuit belonged to Chief Justice Roger B. Taney of Maryland, who had already shown his proslavery colors in the 1857 case of *Dred Scott v. Sandford*, in which he had said that "no black man had any rights that a white man need respect."[3]

True to form, Taney on May 27 ordered Merryman released, claiming that only Congress, not the president, could suspend the writ of habeas corpus as Lincoln had recently done in areas crucial to communication between Washington, D.C., and the loyal states. In fact, the Constitution is silent on the issue of who may suspend the writ, noting only that it may indeed be suspended in times of rebellion or invasion. The officer in charge of Merryman refused Taney's order, and Lincoln backed him up, following the example of Andrew Jackson by defying the chief justice's decision. Lincoln explained his action to Congress some weeks later. Assuming for the sake of argument that his suspension of the writ had been a technical infraction of the law, Lincoln asked rhetorically, "Are all the laws, but one, to go unexecuted, and the government itself go to pieces, lest that one be violated?" Lincoln believed the answer was no, and Congress agreed. It later ratified his suspension of the writ of habeas corpus in selected areas as needed throughout the rest of the war. That sometimes included Maryland, where the Lincoln administration took a firm hand in suppressing secessionism by occasionally locking up some of its most vocal adherents for a month or two.

Simultaneous with Maryland's flirtation with rebellion, the state of Missouri faced a similar crisis. Recently elected Governor Claiborne Jackson was dedicated to the cause of slavery and had led Border Ruffians into Kansas during that territory's troubles in the 1850s. He directed secessionist state militia in capturing the federal arsenal at Liberty, Missouri, on April 20, the day after the Baltimore riot. With his newly enhanced firepower, Claiborne made plans to take the much larger U.S. arsenal at St. Louis. To improve his chances still further, he requested cannon from Jefferson Davis, who obligingly dispatched several that Louisiana Rebels had plundered from the U.S. arsenal at Baton Rouge, shipped in crates labeled "Marble."

Defending the arsenal was a fiery, diminutive captain of the regular army named Nathaniel Lyon. Alerted to the danger by Unionist Missouri politician Frank Blair, Lyon reconnoitered a camp of some of the secessionist militia outside St. Louis disguised as Blair's mother-in-law, complete with a dress and a veil to hide his brushy, red beard. Satisfied of the secessionists' hostile intent, Lyon preempted them, and on May 10 surrounded their camp with Union-loyal, antislavery German American militia regiments from the St. Louis area as well as a few U.S. Army regulars. The secessionists, about seven hundred in number, surrendered without a fight, but as the Union troops marched their prisoners away, a secessionist mob attacked, hurling bricks and firing pistols. In the ensuing riot, four soldiers and about twenty-four civilians were killed. More died in further clashes the following day.

Many Missourians had previously been at best tepid Unionists, and the news that German troops in Federal uniforms had shot down civilians in the streets of St. Louis, even if those civilians had been in the act of rioting, outraged public opinion and brought new recruits to Jackson's secessionist militia. The state legislature also threw its support to the governor. On June 11 Jackson and the commander of his secessionist militia, General Sterling Price, who had commanded a regiment of Missouri volunteers during the Mexican War, met with Lyon and Blair at the Planters' House Hotel in St. Louis to discuss restoring peace to the state. By this time, Lincoln had promoted Lyon to brigadier general and given him command of all U.S. troops in Missouri. Jackson and Price demanded that Lyon withdraw all Federal troops from the state, leaving it to the secessionists, who said it would then be neutral. The suggestion outraged Lyon, who said he would see every Missourian dead before he would accept any such agreement. "This means war," growled the fiery Lyon before stalking out of the room. Jackson and Price returned to Jefferson City, where the governor issued a call for fifty thousand volunteers to oppose Lyon. He did not get nearly that many, and he and the secessionist legislature soon found themselves fleeing toward the southwestern corner of the state as Lyon advanced with his troops from St. Louis.

Kentucky presented a different case entirely. Like Maryland and Missouri, it was a slave state with strong economic ties to the North and a deeply divided population. Also like the other border states, it wished to remain neutral. Unlike them, Kentucky got the chance to do so, at least for a time. Both presidents, Lincoln and Davis, had been born in Kentucky, scarcely one hundred miles apart, but they need not have been Kentucky natives to have understood the political importance of the state. As Lincoln explained the situation that fall, "I think to lose Kentucky is nearly the same as to lose the whole game. Kentucky gone, we can not hold Missouri, nor, as I think, Maryland. These all against us, and the job on our hands is too large for us. We would as well consent to separation at once, including the surrender of this capitol"—meaning Washington, D.C.[4]

Neither side could afford to offend Kentuckians by flouting their state's announced neutrality. Both scrupulously kept their troops out of Kentucky, though they quietly slipped weapons across the border to equip sympathetic militia within the state and maintained training camps just outside its borders, Union to the north and Confederate to the south, for organizing Kentuckians willing to leave their state and enlist on one side or the other. As some observers pointed out at the time, neutrality amounted to secession. The situation was bizarre and could hardly be expected to last, but for the time being it was a tremendous boon to the Confederacy. At the same time that a inviolably neutral Kentucky provided an impenetrable shield for the heartland of the Confederacy against Union invasion, it also provided a conduit for a very valuable trade with the North, bringing even weapons and ammunition into the industrially weak Confederacy. Still, Lincoln was willing to tolerate it for the time being rather than run the risk of alienating Kentuckians.

VIRGINIA AND ITS PLACE
WITHIN THE WAR

Despite the bloodshed in various places and the gathering of newly recruited troops at a number of points on either side of what had become a long, hostile boundary between the Union and the Confederacy, much of America looked for the decisive action to occur in Virginia. Throughout the war, a large segment of the population, the press, and, to a certain extent, both governments showed a fixation with Virginia out of proportion to its importance to the outcome of the conflict. With Maryland secessionists held in check both by the firm hand of the federal government and by its own sizable Unionist population, especially in its western counties, Virginia was the frontline state of the Confederacy. In the older, better-known, and more populous eastern part of the nation, Virginia held the boundary between the Union and the Confederacy. It was the part of the war closest to the major population centers and the major media markets.

The Virginia theater of the war also came to include, by the end of May, the capitals of the two rival governments within a hundred miles of each other. Impressed with both the importance and the prestige of Virginia, the Confederate congress voted on May 20 to accept Virginia's invitation and move its capital from Montgomery to Richmond. Virginia was the state of Madison, Jefferson, and, most of all, Washington, whom the Confederates assumed would have favored their cause and whose image, mounted on horseback and gesturing, presumably to his troops, they placed on their national seal. Locating the capital in Richmond was a bid to identify with all of Virginia's past greatness. It was also an assurance to the Virginians that the Confederacy would make every effort to defend their state.

And there were very genuine reasons for the Confederacy to defend Virginia. It was now one of the Confederacy's most populous states, and it contained the largest share of the South's industry. The Tredegar Iron Works in

Richmond was the only mill in the Confederacy that could make a railroad locomotive and one of a very few that could make a heavy cannon. Virginia's accession greatly strengthened the Confederacy, and the state's loss would be a severe blow. Moving the national capital to Richmond would both reassure Virginians and place the South's foremost military hero, President Jefferson Davis, immediately adjacent to the presumed scene of the most important fighting.

Yet not all Virginians were enthusiastic about the new Confederacy. Every southern state contained Unionists, but Virginia held an unusually large number, and they were concentrated in the state's northwestern counties, not far from Pennsylvania and Ohio. These areas had economic ties to the northern states and, more important, contained few slaves. Slaves made up about one-tenth the percentage of the population (4 percent) in northwestern Virginia that they did in the South as a whole (about 40 percent). Many citizens of the northwestern counties, west of the Allegheny Mountains, felt that their region had always been treated as the redheaded stepchild by the state government in Richmond, paying more than its fair share of taxes and receiving less than its fair share of state spending. When it came to being dragged into a rebellion to make the continent permanently safe for slavery, the northwesterners were ready to draw the line.

With the northwestern counties of Virginia filled with a mostly Union-loyal population ready to throw off the yoke of the tidewater and piedmont slaveholding aristocracy, the region was ripe for the arrival of Federal troops looking to restore loyal government in the region. Washington had no troops to send, but Ohio did. Like several other governors, Ohio's William Dennison had found himself with more recruits than the state's quota under Lincoln's call for seventy-five thousand men. He wisely enlisted them anyway and so had them on hand to deal with the opportunity developing just beyond his state's southeastern boundary.

To command them he snagged a highly reputed professional officer. Born in Philadelphia in 1826, George B. McClellan had received special dispensation to enroll in the U.S. Military Academy at West Point prior to his sixteenth birthday. Graduating second in the class of 1846, McClellan had served as an engineer officer in the Mexican War and then in the peacetime army before resigning in 1857 to take up a career as a railroad executive. He had been considered one of the brightest of the rising young officers within the army, and by 1861 he was president of the Ohio and Mississippi Railroad.

On the issue of slavery, McClellan more or less agreed with the Confederates, but he rejected secession and was disturbed when the Confederates had fired on Fort Sumter. Deciding to reenter the military, McClellan set out for Pennsylvania to offer his services to its governor. Dennison was one of several governors seeking his services and got him to stop by Columbus and give some advice on the organizing of Ohio's troops. By April 23, he was commanding general of the state's militia, and on May 3, Lincoln promoted him to major general, making him one of the most senior generals in the army, and assigned him to command the Department of the Ohio, comprising the states of Ohio, Indiana, and Illinois.

McClellan's first assignment was to liberate the Unionist citizens of northwestern Virginia and protect the vital Baltimore & Ohio Railroad, a strategic link between Washington and the Midwest, as it ran through that region. Leading an army of Ohioans and Indianans, McClellan advanced in early June through Grafton toward a Rebel force at Philippi. The Confederates retreated so rapidly in the face of McClellan's advance that northern newspapers derisively christened the event "the Philippi Races."

On July 11 McClellan's troops met the Confederates in battle at Rich Mountain. In what was meant to be a pincers movement, McClellan sent Brigadier General William S. Rosecrans with a large brigade to strike the Rebels in the rear, on which McClellan would attack with the rest of his force in front. When the moment came, however, McClellan convinced himself that the Confederates badly outnumbered him when, in fact, the reverse was the case. Hesitating, he left Rosecrans to fight the battle alone. Rosecrans won anyway, capturing numerous Confederates and sending the others off in headlong retreat. Union forces followed up, and on July 13 in a small rearguard action at Corrick's Ford, Confederate Brigadier General Robert S. Garnett fell, the first general on either side to die in the war.

Meanwhile, delegates from the twenty-five northwestern counties of Virginia had met in convention at Wheeling in May. Later that month in the formal secession referendum called by the Virginia secession convention, the northwestern counties voted almost two to one against secession. Early in June a second convention met in Wheeling, denounced secession, and declared the offices of all secessionist state officials to be vacant. In their place, the second Wheeling convention set up a Union-loyal government for the state of Virginia, headed by Francis H. Pierpont as governor. Though the new government claimed rightful sovereignty over all of Virginia, its action, coupled with McClellan's successful campaign, represented the first steps in the eventual separation of trans-Allegheny Virginia into a new state of West Virginia, a process that would not be formally complete until 1863.

While the North might take satisfaction from its success in trans-Allegheny Virginia, all eyes were turned anxiously on the eastern part of the state, where Washington and Richmond confronted each other across scarcely one hundred miles of piedmont and tidewater Virginia. A first, tentative and halting Union effort in eastern Virginia occurred in early June. When Virginia had seceded, Union forces had retained control of Fort Monroe at the tip of the peninsula formed by the broad estuaries of the York and James rivers where they emptied into Chesapeake Bay. From that base, a small Union column of about 3,500 men under the command of Benjamin Butler advanced northwestward, up the peninsula, in the direction of Richmond. On June 10, the day before the second Wheeling convention gathered four hundred miles to the northwest, Butler's men encountered the Rebels, dug in behind Brick Kiln Creek near Big Bethel Church about fourteen miles from Fort Monroe and seventy from Richmond. The Federals immediately attacked. The Fifth New York Regiment, colorfully dressed in the uniforms of Algerian Zouaves (colonial units of the French army), complete with baggy red pants, moved toward the Rebel flank. The Seventh New York, filled with the scions of Gotham's social elite, advanced in the center, then became confused, turned about, and fired into the ranks of the Third New York, coming up in support. Both regiments wore the gray uniforms then common among militia throughout the country. The Seventh, despite its own appearance, had become convinced that the Third was in fact a Confederate regiment that had gotten behind it.

The gaudy and nonstandard uniforms and the rampant confusion set the tone for the day's action. The Confederates were as inexperienced as the Yankees, but all they had to do was hunker down behind their entrenchments, then known as breastworks, and shoot the Federals as they advanced. It proved all too easy. Only the First Vermont got across Brick Kiln Creek and then only briefly before retreating. One Confederate was killed, and seven were wounded, as against eighteen Union dead, including an officer descended from both Massachusetts's first governor, John Winthrop, and its greatest divine, Jonathan Edwards. Another sixty Yankees suffered wounds. Butler's force retreated disconsolately back to Fort Monroe, and the Rebels celebrated what soon came to be dignified with the title of the Battle of Big Bethel, citing it, despite recent setbacks in the western part of Virginia, as further proof, if any was needed, that one Rebel could lick ten Yankees with a cornstalk.

In reality Butler's forlorn foray had demonstrated two important facts. The first of these was that it would prove difficult and costly in this war to overcome troops defending entrenchments, even when the attacker enjoyed, as Butler did, an almost three-to-one superiority in numbers. The second lesson of Big Bethel was that Benjamin Butler, like most men of his type, was a much better lawyer than general. Good political skills did not necessarily bring with them the ability to lead troops in battle. Leaders of both sides would require much time and repetition before absorbing either lesson.

THE FIRST BATTLE OF BULL RUN

Butler's probe up the York–James peninsula had not been anything like a serious Union effort to penetrate to Richmond and put the Confederate government there out of business. For such a grand offensive, northern newspaper editors began to clamor with increasing insistence, led as usual by press doyen Horace Greeley, who placed on the masthead of his influential *New York Tribune* that summer the slogan "On to Richmond." The Rebel congress was scheduled to convene in that city in late July, and northern editors demanded that the Union army should get there first. Greeley's strategically naive slogan operated on the false premise that capturing the enemy's capital would deliver a swift victory—a popular misconception that helped shape military movements in the East during much of the war.

Commanding the main Union field army in northern Virginia was Brigadier General Irvin McDowell. A big, bluff regular army officer; classmate of Beauregard in West Point back in 1838; and veteran of staff duty in the Mexican War, McDowell had not been Lincoln or Scott's first choice. That had been Virginian Robert E. Lee, recently promoted to colonel of the army's Second Cavalry Regiment, both because of Lee's sterling reputation as an engineer officer in the Mexican War and because of the political benefit to be found in giving the command to a Virginian. Lee had turned them down and gone with his state, so Lincoln and Scott had turned to McDowell, by all accounts a loyal and capable officer, though he had never before commanded troops in battle.

McDowell was painfully aware of his army's lack of experience and training and badly wanted more time for drill. America's militia system had lapsed into disarray in the decades before the war, existing in most states only in name and imparting no training at all. The most active part of the prewar militia had been the so-called volunteer companies, local drill teams that doubled as social clubs and turned out on ceremonial occasions in fancy uniforms but had almost as little real military training as their fellow citizens who never even showed up for the perfunctory annual militia muster. The lack of mili-

Campaigns of 1861-1862

tary order in McDowell's army was visually evident in its polyglot array of uniforms—several species of Zouaves, French chaussers, Prussian jaegers, regular army blue (sometimes worn by the volunteers as well), militia gray, and, in the case of the First Minnesota Regiment, simple red flannel shirts—but the army possessed none of the military skills suggested by any of its garbs, foreign or domestic, except perhaps the Minnesotans, who were, as their uniforms suggested, a collection of lumberjacks and farmers.

Lincoln disagreed with McDowell. Taking the same line as the newspaper editors, he insisted that McDowell launch an early advance against Richmond. This was not merely the product of overheated bravado like Greeley's but stemmed at least as much from Lincoln's appreciation of the massive political and economic cost to the country with each week that the war continued. To McDowell's protest that his men were green, Lincoln allowed that this was true. "But so are the Confederates," he countered. "You are all green together." This sort of horse sense would often give Lincoln better insight than his generals during the course of the war. In this case, however, it overlooked the fact that the green Union troops would have to perform the more difficult task of taking the offensive. All the Confederates had to do was get in their way and stay there.

McDowell devised an intelligent plan for defeating the Confederates in front of his army, then encamped near Washington, D.C., and opening the way to Richmond. A smaller Union army of about eighteen thousand men under aged Pennsylvania militia general and War of 1812 veteran Robert Patterson would continue to operate near Harpers Ferry, holding in check a Confederate army of twelve thousand men operating in the lower Shenandoah Valley (because the Shenandoah River flows roughly south to north, the lower Shenandoah Valley always refers to the northeastern end of the valley and the upper valley to its southwestern end). While Patterson kept Johnston's attention, McDowell himself with thirty-five thousand men would advance from Washington about twenty-five miles due west to Centreville, Virginia. Just beyond Centreville, on the other side of a sluggish stream called Bull Run, waited the twenty-thousand-man Confederate army of Brigadier General Pierre G. T. Beauregard, hero of Fort Sumter, guarding the important rail nexus called Manassas Junction. McDowell would outnumber him, outflank him, and drive him back in retreat. At least that was the plan.

McDowell's army marched away from Washington on July 16, and things began going wrong immediately. Staff officers were insufficient in numbers and woefully unprepared by training or experience for moving the largest army yet seen on the North American continent. The troops fell out to pick blackberries, and company officers, who had been elected by these same men and were their neighbors back home, lacked the moral authority to get them back on the march. Commanders of regiments, brigades, and divisions proceeded cautiously, frequently halting to scout ahead lest they lead their columns into an ambush, against which McDowell's march orders had strictly warned. A march that was supposed to have taken one day—and regulars could have done it in that time—instead took five before all the army's units were in place near Centreville. The neophyte army's inexperience was painfully obvious as the Union troops trudged slowly south. Meanwhile, in case Confederates had failed to give timely notice to their commanders of the impending Union attack, one of McDowell's subordinates on July 18 probed forward contrary to orders toward Blackburn's Ford on Bull Run and suffered a sharp repulse, alerting the Confederates and giving further proof of the martial superiority of the southern soldier.

In fact, Beauregard was already well aware of McDowell's approach, having been warned on the Union army's first taking the road by Confederate female spy and prominent member of Washington society, Rose O'Neal Greenhow. Beauregard, who was in a state of pronounced nervous excitement, not to say panic, notified Davis at once and lamented that his impending defeat was the president's fault for not reinforcing him sooner. Now, he wrote, it was too late.

But it was not too late for the Confederates. Davis ordered Johnston to slip away from Patterson and hurry to Beauregard's aid. Since Patterson was doing nothing even remotely interesting to his enemies, Johnston, who was to prove one of the war's most adept retreaters, had no trouble getting away and leaving the Pennsylvania septuagenarian guarding a valley devoid of almost all Confederate troops. Patterson remained for some time none the wiser. On the way to Manassas Junction, Johnston discovered, somewhat to his surprise, that he could move his troops by railroad, thus speeding their approach.

By the morning of July 21, 1861, as McDowell launched his carefully planned attack, Johnston and almost all of his troops had joined Beauregard, and with additional reinforcements Davis had dispatched from other parts of Virginia, the Confederate army behind Bull Run numbered about the same strength as McDowell's. Johnston, who outranked Beauregard, exercised nominal command but allowed Beauregard the actual direction of the fight.

McDowell's men set out well before dawn, and by first light a third of them had crossed Bull Run west of Beauregard's position and were bearing down on his flank while the other two-thirds of McDowell's army confronted the Confederates in front, across the creek. Beauregard, who had been planning an attack of his own that would have been something of a mirror image of the assault McDowell had launched, abandoned his offensive plans and rushed reinforcements to his crumbling left flank. At first, it seemed no use, as the Federals drove forward relentlessly, rolling up the Confederate line. The key terrain feature turned out to be a hill topped by the farmhouse of eighty-five-year-old widow Judith Henry. Stubbornly refusing to leave her house even as the fighting approached, Mrs. Henry suffered a fatal wound.

Meanwhile, she was not the only one who stubbornly refused to leave Henry House Hill. Brigadier General Thomas J. Jackson was there with his brigade of five Virginia regiments drawn up in line awaiting the next Union push. Informed that the Federals were coming, the 1846 West Point graduate, noted Mexican War artillery officer, and recent Virginia Military Institute professor replied, "Then, Sir, we will give them the bayonet." Amid the wreckage of several brigades fleeing from the Confederate left, Brigadier

N

Patterson
(18,000)

Harper's
Ferry

Northern Virginia, 1861
First Bull Run
July 18, 1861

MARYLAND

Winchester

Potomac River

J.E. Johnston
(12,000)

McDowell
(35,000)

Washington,
D.C.

Manassas Gap R.R.

Beauregard
(20,000)

Alexandria

Shenandoah River

Orange & Alexandria R.R.

☐ Union Forces

▨ Confederate Forces

← Confederate Movements

VIRGINIA

General Barnard Bee tried to rally his troops. "There is Jackson standing like a stone wall," he shouted to his men. "Let us determine to die here and we will conquer." Several other versions of the famous statement exist, and Bee, who was killed moments later, could never clarify his exact words or even his intent, but Jackson, who now had his famous nickname, worked together with additional reinforcements from the Confederate right to hold Henry House Hill. The other Confederate troops rallied around them, and the tactical situation began to stabilize.

Things began to go wrong again for McDowell. He and his inexperienced officers could not orchestrate a mass assault—no easy task on a battlefield with tired and untrained troops—and his attack devolved into a series of regimental charges. The assault stalled. A Confederate regiment attacked one of McDowell's key artillery batteries, and because the Rebels wore blue uniforms, the Federals mistook them for friendly troops until it was too late to stop them or to save the battery. As the Union troops began to fall back, the already extreme confusion produced by battle, even a hitherto victorious battle, was compounded. The army began to disintegrate.

As organization broke down, panic seized the weary, fought-out soldiers. With no training to steady them, they broke and ran. The Confederates whooped with delight and set off in pursuit, giving a high-pitched cry that would soon be known as the "Rebel Yell." Caught in the tangle of the hasty retreat were Union civilians, including some members of Congress, who had come out from Washington in buggies with picnic baskets to enjoy the show from a safe distance. They now added their carriages to the confusion on the roads and their panic to the emotional distress of the retreating Union soldiers.

The Confederate pursuit did not last long, as Beauregard and Johnston halted their own exhausted and disorganized troops within sight of the battlefield that their side would soon be calling Manassas and the Federals would call Bull Run. McDowell had unbroken reserves at Centreville and was able to cover an orderly retreat, but for the great mass of his army, the retreat was anything but orderly, as the troops, many of them having thrown away their weapons and ammunition, kept on running or at least walking until they were back in Washington, having covered the return trip in about one-fifth the time they had taken going out.

3

ALL QUIET ALONG
THE POTOMAC

SETTLING DOWN FOR A REAL WAR

The dramatic Confederate victory at Bull Run shocked the nation. Southern whites felt more certain than ever of the superiority of their martial prowess, and for once northerners were almost tempted to believe they were right. "We are utterly and disgracefully routed, beaten, whipped by secessionists," wrote New York businessman George Templeton Strong in his diary. The casualties of the battle were about 1,800 Confederates killed and wounded and about 1,600 Federals, plus another 1,300 or so Federals captured in the final disastrous rout. Each side had suffered almost twice as many killed and wounded as United States forces had sustained in the bloodiest battles of the Mexican War and the War of 1812. Far greater than the loss of life and limb, however, was the impact on the spirits of the warring sections of the country. Confederate morale had never been higher, while Unionists were almost in despair.

Recent wars in Europe had tended to be short, decided by a single great battle. Many Americans assumed that their own conflict would be much the same. Especially Confederates reveled in the thought that their independence had been won on the field of Manassas. Some northerners were inclined to agree with that. The never quite stable Horace Greeley, who had so vociferously urged an early advance against Richmond, now wrote Lincoln an anguished letter imploring him not to shrink from the difficult necessity of abandoning the war, accepting defeat, and granting Confederate independence. Fortunately for posterity, Lincoln was not yet ready to give up. Neither, as it turned out, were the people of the North. With the approval of Congress, Lincoln had already expanded the regular army and called for another forty-two thousand volunteers, not for the obviously inadequate ninety-day term but for three years. Now in the wake of Bull Run he issued a call for three hundred thousand three-year volunteers, and the country responded enthusiastically as recruits flocked to the colors once again in more than adequate numbers. Most of the ninety-day regiments promptly reenlisted for the three-year term, determined to see the rebellion suppressed and the Union saved.

The North's determined response to the defeat and obvious willingness to make much greater efforts was a sobering development for Confederates. Within weeks of Bull Run, the luster began to wear off of their great victory as it became apparent that the battle had not come close to winning the war at a single stroke. With that, recriminations began within the Confederate public and high command as to whose fault it was that the victory had turned out to be barren. Confident that such a feat could have been easily done, newspaper editors wanted to know why Confederate forces had failed to pursue the beaten Yankees into Washington. Beauregard wrote and published, contrary to regulations, a report of the battle implying that he had had an excellent plan that, if implemented by Davis before the battle, would have won the war by now. In fact, Beauregard's plan had been all moonshine and nonsense, completely impractical, and Davis had been right to turn it down. In the face of Beauregard's postbattle grandstanding, the president did his best to keep his well-known temper and wrote his general a mild rebuke.

Curiously, though the war had grown out of a dispute over the future of the institution of slavery, the two sides in the conflict were not equally eager to admit the fact that they were fighting over slavery and the status of African Americans. Confederate leaders made no secret of the fact that they were fighting for slavery and white supremacy. In a March 21, 1861, speech in Savannah, Georgia, Confederate Vice President Alexander H. Stephens proclaimed, "Our new government is founded upon exactly the opposite idea [to that of the equality of the races]; its foundations are laid, its cornerstone rests, upon the great truth that the negro is not equal to the white man; that slavery, subordination to the superior race, is his natural and normal condition. This, our new government, is the first, in the history of the world, based upon this great physical, philosophical, and moral truth."[1]

By contrast, Union leaders during the first half of the war were not nearly so forthright about what kind of war this was and why they were fighting it. This was never more true than in the immediate aftermath of Bull Run, when a traumatized U.S. Congress feared that support for the war might collapse in the wake of the humiliating defeat. In a July 22, 1861, proclamation, authored by Kentucky Representative John J. Crittenden, Congress announced "that this war is not waged upon our part in any spirit of oppression, nor for any purpose of conquest or subjugation, nor purpose of overthrowing or interfering with the rights or established institutions of those States, but to defend and maintain the supremacy of the Constitution and to preserve the Union."[2]

In a very narrowly technical sense, this was correct. Although the southern states had seceded because they did not accept the incoming administration's position on slavery, the U.S. government was presently waging war simply to suppress the rebellion and restore obedience to the law without regard to the cause for which the rebellion had been launched and the law defied. It was not fighting directly for the cause of freeing the slaves—yet. Nevertheless, even at this early stage of the conflict, the most cursory observer of American politics could easily predict the likely results of Union victory. Lincoln had previously expressed his and his party's goal as placing slavery "in the course of ultimate extinction." A rebellion that tried and failed to break up the Union for the sake of slavery would only tend to bring that extinction closer than it would otherwise have been. Notwithstanding Congress's bland denials, even in these early days it was clear to all concerned, especially to the slaves themselves, that a Union victory would shorten the days of slavery.

Northern leaders had political reasons for their desire to emphasize the cause of saving the Union and enforcing the law and to play down the issues of slavery and race. White southerners were virtually unanimous in their support for slavery and white supremacy, but a significant minority of them opposed secession, especially in places like western Virginia, East Tennessee, and other parts of the upland and Appalachian South. On the other hand, although support for the war to preserve the Union was far from unanimous in the North, it did command a fairly sizable majority of support across the region. By contrast, the cause of abolishing slavery would scarcely command a majority, even in the North, much less in border slave states like Crittenden's own Kentucky. Emphasizing that they were waging a war solely for the restoration of the Union and not for the abolition of slavery was a way that northern leaders could unite their own section of the country and divide the South, at least to some degree.

MCCLELLAN RISES IN THE EAST;
FIGHTING BEGINS IN THE WEST

In the immediate aftermath of Bull Run, however, Lincoln and those around him in Washington had little leisure to think about the meaning of the war, how it should be presented to the public, or even of the great mobilization about to begin across the North. The president's immediate concern was keeping the Rebels out of Washington. Lincoln could not know, on the day after the battle, that the Confederate army was too disorganized to follow up its victory, but he could not ignore the disorganized and demoralized state of the main Union army in Virginia, with thousands of its soldiers scattered throughout the capital city, many of them in bars drinking themselves into oblivion while appalling their fellow patrons with exaggerated tales of disaster. The public had lost confidence in McDowell. More important, the army had lost confidence in McDowell and in itself. Lincoln needed a general who could restore the army's confidence in itself and win its confidence for himself, a general who had won victories and who was not too far away from Washington since Lincoln needed him right away. The obvious choice was George McClellan, fresh from his victories in western Virginia. On July 22 a telegram from the secretary of war summoned the thirty-four-year-old major general to Washington without delay.

McClellan the conquering hero officially assumed command of the troops around Washington on July 27 and immediately went to work to restore order and discipline. Provost guards swept the stragglers out of the Washington bars and off the streets. Back in their camps, the men, including regiment after regiment of new troops arriving in the Washington area in response to the president's latest call, learned what it was to be soldiers, observing military discipline, maintaining military bearing, and drilling for hours on end. Uniforms and equipment became somewhat more standardized, though the army would continue to contain a number of Zouave regiments.

Shortages of U.S. manufactured weapons testified to the Union's early unreadiness for waging war and forced the federal government to procure arms from European manufacturers. This meant that different regiments carried a variety of weapons, from the standard U.S. Harpers Ferry or Springfield rifle-muskets to the highly similar British Enfield. Meanwhile, badly inferior Belgian or Austrian rifles or obsolete but still lethal U.S. Model 1820 smooth-bore muskets also found their way into the Union ranks. Although muskets and rifles of varying calibers posed a logistical nightmare, the Union made do with its odd assortment of weaponry until gradual standardization of military armaments occurred as the conflict progressed. To his credit, McClellan transformed the collection of troops around Washington, some of them demoralized and all of them green, into something that looked and felt like an army. He called it the Army of the Potomac, and its men soon came to feel an exuberant faith in themselves and their commander.

So far, McClellan had been all that Lincoln, the cabinet, or Congress could have hoped, and the youthful warlord's reputation seemed to be expanding more rapidly than a bursting shell. Newspapers christened him "the young Napoleon." Lincoln was deferential. Cabinet members and congressional leaders fawned on the new commander of the Army of the Potomac, suggesting that he was the only man who could save the country. Washington was safe, and the army was growing in size and proficiency. Its commander was dapper in his tailored uniform and so deep chested that he looked short at his slightly above average five feet, seven inches, cutting a splendid figure on horseback and looking the very image of the Currier & Ives war that people imagined they were about to fight. Civilians visiting the army's camps gazed admiringly on the general, and his adoring troops cheered him to the echo.

While McClellan continued to make his preparations in the East, serious fighting broke out in the West, which during the Civil War referred to the part of the country west of the Appalachian Mountains. Because both sides were still respecting Kentucky's bizarre claim to neutrality, the four-hundred-mile stretch from the mountains to the Mississippi was, for the present, out of bounds. That left Missouri, where Nathaniel Lyon had occupied Jefferson City on June 15 and then pursued Sterling Price and his army of secessionist Missourians toward the southwestern corner of the state, winning skirmishes at Booneville on June 17 and Carthage on July 5. By July 13 he had reached Springfield.

Meanwhile, about seventy-five miles to the southwest, in the extreme corner of Missouri, Price had been joined by Brigadier General Ben McCulloch along with a force of Confederate troops who had moved up from Arkansas. Price and McCulloch found it difficult to work together. Both were proud veterans of the Mexican War. Price maintained that as a major general of Missouri forces, he should command. McCulloch contended that his Confederate brigadier general's commission took precedence. With Lyon closing in, they agreed to set aside their differences for the moment. Together their combined forces turned, advanced toward Lyon, and encamped August 6 near Wilson's Creek, ten miles from the town.

Outnumbered more than two to one, the always aggressive Lyon decided to attack. On the night of August 9 he led his army of about 5,400 Kansans, Iowans, and German American Missourians, as well as a few U.S. Army regulars, out of Springfield. Lyon's second in command was Colonel Franz Sigel. A graduate of the Karlsruhe Military Academy and sometime lieutenant in the army of the German state of Baden, Sigel had led revolutionary forces in the German uprisings of 1848. When they failed, he, like many another German, had come to America. He was a great favorite of his fellow German émigrés. Sigel pressed on Lyon a plan to allow him, Sigel, to take an independent column of 1,200 men and try to surprise the Rebels with a flank attack.

Lyon's column struck the Rebels first at 5:00 a.m., August 10, surprising Price's Missourians and driving them back. Later in the morning Sigel attacked and also scored initial success, but McCulloch counterattacked and routed Sigel's column, driving it from the battlefield. The Rebels were then free to turn their united strength against Lyon's woefully outnumbered troops. The Federals held on doggedly along a ridge that became known as Bloody Hill. Lyon suffered two wounds but continued to encourage his men until a third bullet killed him instantly. Major Samuel D. Sturgis (West Point, 1846) took over command of the Union army and shortly thereafter ordered it to retreat. The Confederates and their Missouri allies were in no shape to pursue. Losses from the battle were about equal—1,317 Union to 1,230 among Price's and McCulloch's men.

In the aftermath of the Battle of Wilson's Creek, McCulloch and Price fell out again. The former took his Confederates back to Arkansas, while the latter led his Missourians on a foray 150 miles north to the valley of the Missouri River, where on September 20 he defeated a small Federal force at the Battle of Lexington. Governor Jackson and the pro-Confederate legislature that had fled with him to Arkansas declared Missouri a Confederate state and incorporated Price's force into the Confederate army. Nevertheless, most Missourians stood by the Union and supported a Union-loyal state government set up by the state convention that had rejected secession that spring. As more Federal troops entered the state, Price found himself compelled to fall back and join McCulloch. By the end of October, his army and Jackson's secessionist Missouri government were back in Arkansas.

THE WAR COMES TO KENTUCKY

By that time, Kentucky was no longer neutral. Lyon's superior in Missouri was Major General John C. Frémont, commander of the Department of the West. Frémont was a prime example of what historians sometimes call a political general. Every Civil War general was in some sense political since the president who appointed him hoped that his victories would achieve the political goals of the nation and perhaps of the president's own party as well. Many generals, including professionally trained officers, benefited from having good political connections. A political general, however, was one whom a president appointed to the rank of general directly from civilian life, not because of any victories he was expected to win, though the president certainly hoped he would win victories, but rather because simply having him in uniform, with a general's insignia on his collar, would increase public support for the war, often in some particular segment of the population. Many Americans believed that military leadership was a natural gift, not something that could be taught at an academy or learned by experience, and they wanted their favorite political heroes to lead them into battle.

Leading small army exploring expeditions in the Far West during the 1840s, Frémont had won popularity as the Pathfinder, though the paths he found were those his guide Kit Carson showed him. He had gained political influence by marrying the daughter of powerful Missouri Senator Thomas Hart Benton and notoriety by helping to win California during the Mexican War and then being court-martialed for insubordination to a superior officer. Great wealth had come to him when someone had discovered gold on land Frémont owned near Mariposa, California, and the adoration of antislavery Americans when he had declared for free soil and accepted the 1856 Republican presidential nomination. His public reputation made him exactly the sort of great man who many northerners believed would be a natural military leader. As a former Republican presidential candidate, he had political stature Lincoln could not afford to ignore.

Like most political generals, Frémont proved a far better politician than general, and in the end he was not a very good politician. He failed to support Lyon adequately, remaining ensconced in his St. Louis headquarters surrounded by a lavish staff that included foreign officers seeking adventure in the American war. Missourians and midwesterners found them off-putting. Allegations of financial corruption arose, and the War Department began to investigate. Meanwhile, in the aftermath of Wilson's Creek, Frémont continued to accomplish nothing as a general.

Aware that Lincoln could well be considering removing him, Frémont played to the gallery by issuing a proclamation announcing the imposition of martial law in Missouri and the emancipation of the state's slaves, a move he had absolutely no authority to make. Abolitionists reacted with delight, but Lincoln realized the proclamation could have disastrous results for the allegiance of wavering Kentuckians in the still-neutral Bluegrass State and wrote Frémont suggesting that he quietly withdraw the proclamation. Instead of doing so, Frémont dispatched his formidable and politically savvy wife to Washington to make his case to Lincoln directly. Jessie Benton Frémont was nothing if not forceful, making implied threats of her husband's future political opposition—or worse. Lincoln was unmoved, and since Frémont refused to withdraw the proclamation himself, the president issued an order of his own revoking it.

As the Frémonts had intended, abolitionists fumed with rage that their Republican president apparently cared nothing for the freeing of slaves, but they were wrong. Lincoln was eager to do what he could to bring about an end to slavery, but he knew that he would have to do so in a way that would stand up to legal scrutiny (very likely by Roger B. Taney) and that would, he hoped, be acceptable to border-state Unionists. He would bide his time. For the next few months, Lincoln sought by means of suggesting programs of gradual, compensated emancipation, along with the deportation of the freed slaves to Africa or Central America, to persuade border-state Unionists to give up slavery voluntarily, starting a process he hoped would spread to the rebellious states as well.

For the present, Lincoln had prevented Frémont from making a move that would have damaged the Union cause seriously in Kentucky and the other border states. It was a Confederate general who prevented Frémont's next political blunder by beating him to it. The importance of the Mississippi River was obvious to practically everyone on both sides. The "Father of Waters" was both the great east–west divider of the continent and the great north–south conduit of commerce. The Confederates had on July 28 occupied the town of New Madrid, Missouri, in a bend of the river opposite the Tennessee–Kentucky line, and had begun fortifying it. Frémont noticed another key position, the only place north of Memphis where high bluffs overlooked the Mississippi, fifty miles upstream from New Madrid at Columbus, Kentucky. Frémont ordered a subordinate to occupy it.

Fortunately for the Union cause, Confederate troops under the command of Major General Leonidas Polk got there first. Polk was Frémont's Confederate equivalent in a number of ways. He was a political general despite having graduated from West Point in 1827, where he was the idol of underclassman Jefferson Davis. He had resigned from the army immediately on graduation to pursue a career as an Episcopal priest, in which he had been a great success and risen to the rank of bishop of Louisiana. Though Polk had never actually held a command in the army and had not so much as picked up a book on military affairs for thirty-four years, Davis commissioned him to the rank of major general directly from civilian life, partially because he hoped that the well-known bishop would boost popular support for the war in the lower Mississippi Valley and partially out of a youthful hero worship toward Polk that Davis never outgrew. Aside from being completely unqualified for his position, Polk's chief drawback as a general was that he never really saw the need of taking orders from anyone below the rank of God, with Whom he tended to confuse himself. At the beginning of September 1861, he showed his regard for Davis's announced policy of respecting Kentucky neutrality by marching his troops into the state and occupying those alluring bluffs at Columbus.

The result was outrage among previously nonaligned Kentuckians and consternation among those Kentuckians and Tennesseans who had been working to bring the Bluegrass State into the Confederacy and now saw the ruin of all their efforts. One of them was Tennessee Governor Isham G. Harris, who now frantically telegraphed Richmond to have Polk recalled. Confederate Secretary of War Leroy Pope Walker initially issued a recall order, but Polk ignored it, and presently Davis revoked it, accepting Polk's claim that it had been a matter of military necessity. With that, the political damage was done. Kentucky might have gone for the Union eventually anyway. Now it did so emphatically, the state legislature demanding that the Confederates withdraw and calling on Union forces to enter the state and help expel the invaders. A few Kentuckians left the state to side with the Confederacy, including Governor Beriah Magoffin and Senator (former U.S. vice president) John C. Breckinridge, but three times as many Kentuckians fought for the Union.

Meanwhile, having incurred the full political cost of being the first to invade Kentucky so as to gain the bluffs overlooking the Mississippi at Columbus, Polk failed to secure the military dividend of his move. Sixty miles east of Columbus the Tennessee River flows through Kentucky on a north–south course. Ten miles farther east, the Cumberland River does the same. Whereas the Mississippi flows from north to south, the Tennessee and Cumberland, here in their lower reaches, flow from south to north. That made no difference to steamboats, including several iron-plated gunboats the Federals were known to be building near St. Louis. Polk was soon fortifying his bluff tops at Columbus with a view to stopping those gunboats, but the vessels could just as easily come up the Tennessee or the Cumberland and open the way for ground forces that could turn (get behind) Polk's stronghold, forcing the Confederates to retreat to avoid being trapped. Polk recognized the importance of taking control of the other two rivers by seizing the towns at their mouths, Paducah and Smithland, but he waited, and the Union commander beat him to it.

That Union commander was a subordinate of Frémont's named Ulysses S. Grant. An 1842 West Point graduate, Grant had served creditably in the Mexican War and then been stationed to California. Lacking the independent wealth necessary to bring his wife and family out to the West Coast on a captain's salary, Grant had grown bored and lonely and had sought solace in drink. Easily intoxicated, Grant in 1854 faced the choice of resigning or being court-martialed and chose the former. For the next seven years, he strove for success in various occupations but found none.

When the war broke out, Grant offered his services to the government and eventually received a commission as colonel in command of a regiment of unruly volunteers. He handled them well, but his advance in rank would have been much slower had his military career not become the particular project of his congressman, Elihu B. Washburne. Political backing could help good generals as well as bad ones. As a subordinate of Frémont's, Grant commanded Union troops in southern Illinois with his headquarters in Cairo, at the confluence of the Mississippi and the Ohio, the southernmost town in the free states. He had just taken over his new assignment in Cairo when he learned of Polk's incursion into Kentucky at Columbus. He saw both the threat and the opportunity and immediately occupied Paducah and Smithland. Applauded as a liberator by the Kentucky legislature, Grant left Polk with all the political cost of having broken Kentucky neutrality and none of the military benefits.

Years later, Grant would sum up his philosophy of war: "Get at the enemy as quick as you can; hit him as hard as you can, and keep moving on." He lost no time putting that philosophy into practice in his new command. A small Confederate cavalry foray into southwestern Missouri gave Grant the excuse he needed to make an attempt on Columbus, presenting it to Frémont as a diversion to keep the Confederates away from Union forces in Missouri. As a first step he took his small force of about three thousand men down the

Mississippi from Cairo in riverboats, supported by two of the navy's gunboats (earlier models protected with heavy oaken planks rather than iron plates), and attacked the Confederate encampment at Belmont, Missouri, just across the river from Columbus.

After overrunning the Rebel position at Belmont, Grant's inexperienced volunteers broke ranks to celebrate their victory. Their equally inexperienced officers, including Illinois Democratic politician John A. McClernand, encouraged them, making Fourth-of-July-style speeches. While this went on, more Rebels crossed the river from Columbus and got between Grant's force and its steamboats. Cut off and badly outnumbered, some of Grant's officers suggested they ought to surrender, but Grant calmly replied that as they had cut their way in, so they would cut their way out again. And so they did, amid fierce fighting, regaining the steamboats and returning to Cairo. Grant's first attempt to take Columbus had failed, but his men had learned something— both about warfare and about their commander.

BALL'S BLUFF AND THE JOINT COMMITTEE ON THE CONDUCT OF THE WAR

Meanwhile back in the East, McClellan continued to drill his splendid Army of the Potomac, but he did not undertake any offensive movement toward the Confederates whose flags could be seen from the U.S. capital at their forward outposts at Mason's and Munson's hills, just a few miles south of the Potomac. Confederate batteries on the Virginia shore downstream from Washington made navigation of the Potomac too dangerous for unarmed vessels without heavy naval escort, effectively cutting off the capital's contact with the sea. Yet despite the beautiful fall campaigning weather with crisp temperatures and cloudless skies that kept Virginia's dirt roads dry and firm, McClellan left his magnificent army in its camps. Admiration for the young general's stirring martial appearance and obvious love for all the pomp and circumstance of war began to wear thin for some of the more aggressive-minded Republican politicians in Washington.

"All quiet along the Potomac," read the general's regular communiqués to the War Department. In the weeks immediately following Bull Run, those missives had been reassuring, both to the administration and to the public, which had read them in the next day's newspapers. By late summer, some people were reading that line with distinctly sardonic overtones. Ethel Lynn Beers of New York saw the phrase in a newspaper one morning in September and noticed just below it a small item about a picket (soldier on outpost duty beyond the front line) being killed. The ironic juxtaposition moved her to compose a poem titled "All Quiet along the Potomac Tonight," lamenting the picket's death on a night when the high command deemed that nothing significant had happened in the war. It was a poignant reminder that while the largest armies on each side sat idly regarding each other's advanced positions through field glasses and peace and victory came no nearer, the nation was still at war, ordinary men were still dying, and families suffered the absence and possible loss of loved ones. *Harper's Weekly* magazine published the poem November 30, 1861. Later it was set to music.

By the time Beers's poem appeared in *Harper's*, the situation expressed in its title had become a very bitter one to many in Washington and elsewhere, and a good deal more than the "stray picket" had become casualties. Along the Potomac, upstream from Washington, scattered outposts of troops kept watch on America's new internal frontier: Confederates on or within a few miles of the south bank and Federals on the north. On October 19 McClellan ordered Brigadier General George McCall to take his division and reconnoiter across the Potomac to the town of Dranesville, Virginia, about twenty miles northwest of Washington. McClellan also suggested to Brigadier General Charles Stone, commanding a division farther up the Potomac, diverting attention from McCall by making "perhaps some slight demonstration," or diversion, against the Rebel forces near Leesburg, Virginia, fifteen miles to the northwest of Dranesville.

The next day Stone sent a small probe across the river, and when all went well, on October 21, he dispatched a three-hundred-man battalion to the south bank at a place called Ball's Bluff, where the Virginia shore rose steeply from the Potomac. A few hundred yards beyond the top of the bluff the battalion encountered a small Confederate force with which it skirmished inconclusively. Stone dispatched Colonel Edward D. Baker to the bluff to determine whether to withdraw the reconnaissance force or to reinforce it.

The fifty-year-old Baker was a very special sort of colonel. Born in England, Baker had come to Illinois as a teenager, studied law, and entered politics. A veteran of the Black Hawk and Mexican wars, Baker also served in the Illinois legislature and U.S. House of Representatives, first as a Whig and then as a Republican, becoming a close friend of Abraham Lincoln, who named his second son Edward Baker Lincoln. Baker moved to Oregon in

1860 and immediately won election to a U.S. Senate term that began October 2 of that year. In May 1861, like many other politicians on both sides who considered themselves great natural leaders of men both in war and peace, Baker had obtained authorization from the War Department to raise a regiment of troops and become its colonel. By the fall of 1861, he commanded a brigade within Stone's division while retaining his seat in the Senate, where he would occasionally appear and make speeches in uniform. "I want sudden, bold, forward, determined war," he had once intoned on the Senate floor.

Finding the troops at Ball's Bluff engaged in light skirmishing with the Confederates, Baker at once decided the time had come for "sudden, bold, forward, determined war" and ordered as many troops as possible across from the north bank to reinforce the Federals on the bluff. It was a slow business getting the men across the river since only three small boats were available for ferrying, but Baker was in his glory, quoting Thomas Babington Macaulay's poem about Henri IV, King of France, going into battle 271 years before: "Press where ye see my white plume shine/Amidst the ranks of war." He did not have the military acumen to realize that he was bringing his troops into a trap, with their backs to a steep bluff and a river for which they lacked adequate boats to make a quick crossing.

By 3:00 p.m. Baker had about 1,700 troops on the bluff. The Confederates, under the command of thirty-seven-year-old Colonel Nathan G. "Shanks" Evans (West Point, 1848), a prewar regular army officer and veteran of Bull Run, were present in about equal numbers and began to press hard against Baker's ill-chosen position. The poorly led Federals fell back fighting until they were pressed against the bluff top. Baker took four bullets almost simultaneously and fell dead around 4:30, the first and, thus far, only U.S. Senator to die in battle. The fighting continued until nightfall, as the Confederates drove the routed Union soldiers pell-mell down the bluff and into the river. When it was over, more than two hundred Federals were dead, as many more were wounded, and more than five hundred had become prisoners of war. Confederate casualties totaled 155.

In the larger accounting of the war as a whole, the nearly one thousand Federal casualties would prove to be very small change indeed. Nor had the Battle of Ball's Bluff done anything to change the course of the war in military terms. It was, however, going to change the course of politics in the Union and therefore also of the war as well. The North had suffered another humiliating defeat and a traumatic one. Baker's body, recovered under flag of truce, lay in state in Washington, deeply mourned by members of the Senate as well as the president and his family. Eleven-year-old Willie Lincoln wrote a poem for the occasion: "There was no patriot like Baker, / So noble and so true; / He fell as a soldier on the field / His face to the sky of blue. . . ." The bodies of Baker's men who had drowned or been shot attempting to swim the river could be seen floating past the city in the Potomac.

Someone was bound to be held responsible for such a disaster. Baker, who had been its author, was, as a martyred hero, unavailable for blame. That left Stone, and he made an uncommonly good target. In the midst of a civil war in which (from a Union point of view) several million Americans had betrayed their country, including several hundred who as army officers had previously taken oaths of loyalty to the country, it was easy to wonder who else might be disloyal. Stone, like McClellan and many other army officers, was a Democrat and had no sympathy with Republicans or abolitionists, whom most Democrats held to be only slightly less responsible for the war than the southern Fire-Eaters.

Such Democratic officers' disdain for Republicans was returned with interest, especially by the more radical members of that party in Congress. To make matters worse, Stone had ordered his men to return to owners any fugitive slaves who entered the camps of his division. This was in keeping with the orders of his superiors and the official policy of the government at that point in the war since the Lincoln administration was pursuing a policy of attempting to conciliate rebellious southerners. When a Massachusetts regiment of his division carried out Stone's orders, the incident earned Stone the wrath of Massachusetts Republican Governor John A. Andrew and of one of the state's Republican senators, Charles Sumner, both powerful men in Washington. Stone replied to their criticisms with an intemperate letter.

Now in the wake of Ball's Bluff, Radical Republicans who wondered why the Union had suffered two embarrassing defeats in Virginia within three months took action by establishing the Joint Committee on the Conduct of the War, the brainchild of Michigan Senator Zachariah Chandler and chaired by Ohio Senator Benjamin Wade. Among the committee's first items for business was General Charles P. Stone, and since he was under orders from McClellan not to discuss any of McClellan's orders or arrangements and since he was, in any case, not particularly sympathetic to the committee, the members found his testimony highly unsatisfactory. In February 1862 Secretary of War Edwin M. Stanton, himself closely allied with the congressional radicals, had Stone arrested and imprisoned for six months without charges. Eventually he was released but held only minor positions throughout the remainder of the war.

Stone seems to have been loyal, an officer guilty only of tactlessness and bad luck. His fate, however, was an indication that the Radical Republicans in Congress were determined to have "sudden, bold, forward, determined war," to wage it without regard for niceties, and to strike against slavery as the root of the southern rebellion and the source of much of its strength. Every Union general, especially in the eastern theater of the war, henceforth would have to wage war under the baleful gaze of these grim and uncompromising veterans of the long political war against slavery. Nor was Lincoln immune to their criticism when they thought he was being too lenient or too slow in moving against slavery or removing generals whose hearts did not appear to be in the war. Sometimes the committee made Lincoln's job easier, more often harder, but it would be a fact of political life in Washington for the remainder of the war.

McClellan would eventually come in for some of the committee's closest scrutiny, but for the moment he continued riding high. When Winfield Scott retired, old and fatigued both by the war and by McClellan's uncooperativeness, Lincoln added the duties of general in chief to the position McClellan already held as commander of the Army of the Potomac. When Lincoln questioned whether McClellan would be up to filling both positions, the general assured him, "I can do it all."

Secretary of War Edwin M. Stanton

THE BLOCKADE AND DIPLOMACY

Back in April, shortly after calling out the seventy-five thousand militia in the wake of the attack on Fort Sumter—indeed, on the same day that the Baltimore mob attacked the Sixth Massachusetts—Lincoln had issued a proclamation declaring a blockade of the southern states. Under international maritime law, a nation blockading another nation could stop and seize any ships attempting to enter or leave the blockaded nation's ports, including those of neutral nations. In order to do so, the blockading nation was required to maintain at all times a naval presence off those ports sufficient to pose a credible threat to ships entering and leaving. Apart from a properly maintained blockade, the seizing of neutral ships would, with certain exceptions, be an act of war against the countries whose flags those ships flew, in this case, most significantly, France and, especially, Great Britain.

Britain was the greatest naval power in the world at that time and had been for the better part of three centuries. The British had used blockades in nearly every one of their wars during that time and were accustomed to pushing the practice of blockading to and sometimes beyond the uttermost boundary of what international law contemplated. Indeed, British abuses of blockading had helped provoke the Americans to war in 1812. Now the shoe was on the other foot. The United States, with its massive naval preponderance over the Confederacy, was eager to interpret blockade law in the broadest possible terms, often at the expense of British merchants who would have liked very much to have traded with the Confederacy. The British government, though by no means well disposed toward the United States, nevertheless accepted the new broad American interpretations of what it meant to blockade, filing them away to be trotted out when next Britannia had occasion to demonstrate that it really did rule the wave by blockading a future enemy.

One British response to the blockade, however, infuriated many Americans. No sooner had Lincoln announced the blockade than the British government formally declared its neutrality. As innocuous as this might sound, it alarmed northerners because it implied that the Civil War was a conflict between two independent, sovereign nations. That of course was exactly what the Confederates claimed, and it seemed perilously close to implying that British recognition of the Confederacy would follow in short order. Confederates had been counting on that, and they confidently expected that it would be followed by British military intervention to secure their independence. Lincoln was annoyed but had to admit, when American experts on international law pointed it out to him, that Britain had been technically legally correct in its reaction to the blockade, which, as a clear act of war against the Confederacy, did at least recognize the slaveholders' republic as a warring party and thus justified a declaration of neutrality.

Years later, after the war was over, some merchants even went to court claiming that since the United States maintained that the Confederacy had never been legally independent, the blockade had never been legal and that their seized ships and cargoes should be returned. The Supreme Court held, with surprising common sense, that a civil war was, after all, still a war and that the methods of war were appropriate in waging it.

In fact, though Britain had been precisely legally correct in its declaration of neutrality, its government was not particularly favorable to the United States. It is an oversimplification but still generally true in very broad terms that the middle and lower classes in Britain favored the Union cause because they opposed slavery on religious or philosophical grounds and correctly identified the Union as fighting against the spread and perpetuation of that institution. The upper class, on the other hand, tended to sympathize with the Confederacy, perhaps because the gentry did not mind slavery as much as their social inferiors, but chiefly because they resented and envied America's growing wealth and power. Britain was still what twenty-first-century people would call the world's superpower, but perceptive Britons could already see that the United States would someday surpass its mother country—unless something somehow happened to weaken or destroy it. The Civil War seemed just the thing for that purpose. Since the upper classes tended to have a disproportionate influence in government, their outlook was largely reflected in the British government's approach to the Civil War.

Confederates promised themselves much from this. A large proportion of the factories of Britain and France were textile mills that fed on the raw material of American-grown cotton. In theory, if the flow of that cotton were cut off, Britain and France would suffer economic upheaval, as hundreds of thousands of workers became unemployed. Unwilling to suffer such a fate, the governments of those countries would use military and naval force if necessary to see to it that nothing—for example, a Union invasion or blockade—interfered with the steady growing and shipping of large amounts of the white fiber. At least, that was what Confederates theorized, and it was the idea of the commercial supremacy of the South's chief staple crop, even before secession, that led South Carolina Senator James Henry Hammond to proclaim in an 1858 speech to the Senate, "You dare not make war on cotton. No power on earth dares to make war upon it. Cotton is king."[3]

That remained to be seen, but one thing was certain. However much the British government might enjoy seeing Americans killing each other and the United States being weakened, it did not wish to secure that result at the expense of British blood or the even greater commercial dislocation that would result from plunging into the American war. Nor could the British government afford to have its constituents see it as committing the country to a war to preserve slavery. For the time being, at least, her majesty's government would smile unofficially on the Confederacy but endeavor to stay out of the war. As the government and its supporters, particularly in the press, had in past condemned the United States as the great slaveholding power, so now they sneered at the Union cause as not being that of freedom but rather only of preserving the United States with slavery intact.

During the early months of the war, the Union blockade was notably porous. The navy lacked adequate numbers of ships, and many of those it did have were laid up "in ordinary," moored in harbors in various states of disrepair and in need of much work to be made ready for deployment. Many of those that were ready for sea were deep-draft vessels unsuitable for use in the shallow waters close inshore near the entrances to southern ports. Secretary of the Navy Gideon G. Welles and his staff wrought mightily to acquire the needed vessels to make the blockade effective, purchasing ferry boats and other shallow-draft civilian steamers, fitting them out with a few guns, and manning them with crews of bluejackets from the navy's rapidly expanding manpower pool. Purpose-built gunboats rapidly began to take shape in shipyards along the northern coast, especially a class of small warship specially designed for blockade duty and nicknamed "Ninety-day Gunboats" from the speed at which they could be constructed.

The blockade eventually became severely damaging to the Confederacy, choking the supply of foreign-made arms and ammunition and other vital war supplies and contributing to the eventual Union victory. Nevertheless, throughout the course of the war, a steady trickle of cargo vessels successfully ran the blockade, especially the sleek, fast steamers designed for blockade-running (at the expense of much reduced carrying capacity) and built in Britain. During the early days of the war, no such purpose-built blockade-runners were available, and none were needed, as ordinary merchant vessels came and went from southern harbors with only a moderate risk of apprehension by the thin cordon of blockaders. Thus, southern planters could have exported virtually the entire cotton crop of 1860—and probably much of that of 1861 as well—with only moderate losses that would have been more than compensated by rising cotton prices in Europe.

They could have—but they did not. Thinking that an abrupt and complete stoppage in the flow of cotton to European textile mills would be the most effective way of shocking the British and French into recognition of the Confederacy and then military intervention on its behalf, vast numbers of southern planters and cotton factors (merchants) held on to their cotton, declining to send it to market and creating what amounted to a Confederacy-wide cotton embargo. Although it was never official Confederate government policy and it was never absolutely effective in preventing all cotton exportation, it did drastically diminish the amount of cotton that left American shores during 1861, and in that it was far more effective than the as-yet-feeble efforts of the U.S. Navy to impose a blockade. In triggering European intervention, however, the Confederacy's spontaneous citizen-imposed cotton embargo was an utter failure. European warehouses bulged with the accumulated cotton surpluses of the previous few years, including the year in which Senator Hammond had announced that cotton was king. European textile mills were yet to feel the pinch of cotton deprivation, and their governments were content to watch the Americans destroy their own country without European help or expense.

THE PORT ROYAL EXPEDITION AND THE *TRENT* AFFAIR

One of the problems that made blockading difficult for the U.S. Navy on the southern coast was the need of warships to take on coal at frequent intervals. Only a steam-driven warship could be an effective blockader against steam-driven blockade-runners, and to have any chance of catching them, the warship would have to keep its boiler fires going at all times. That entailed frequent trips back to a Union naval base to refill its bunkers with coal, leaving minimal time to cruise or station off a southern port. The problem could be minimized if the Union possessed naval bases near the ports it was blockading. A U.S. Navy commission studied the southern coastline and decided that Port Royal, South Carolina, should be the first target since it could support blockading squadrons off both Charleston, South Carolina, and Savannah, Georgia.

The navy put together a large expedition under Flag Officer Samuel Du Pont, consisting of warships as well as transports carrying thirteen thousand army troops, and dispatched it to the southern coast in late October. After suffering delay and some damage from an autumnal gale off the South Carolina coast, the ships of the fleet arrived off Port Royal one by one during the first few days of November, and on November 7, the same day Grant made his foray against Belmont, Missouri, half a continent away, Du Pont led them into the sound to attack the two Confederate forts defending the harbor. It was an all-navy operation, as the transport carrying the army's ammunition had been blown far off course and still had not arrived. After several hours of bombardment, the Confederates fled, leaving the harbor and its environs to the Federals. Within a few days the army troops had landed and secured a coastal enclave that included the town of Beaufort, South Carolina, and eventually extended up the coast more than fifty miles almost to Charleston. The victory at Port Royal Sound greatly facilitated blockading southern ports on the Atlantic coast and showed the way for other similar operations around the whole coastline of the Confederacy, a threat the Confederate high command would never really be able to meet effectively.

The acquisition of the Port Royal enclave also brought Union forces suddenly and rather unexpectedly into possession of an enormous slave population. The coastal reaches of South Carolina had some of the highest slave concentrations in the nation, and the question now was what the Union forces would do with them. Following a pattern set by the always cunning lawyer Benjamin Butler during the early days of the war, they classified the African Americans as contraband of war, technically enemy property that has been used in the enemy's war effort. As such, the slaves were now the property of the U.S. government, which more or less granted them freedom. During the course of the rest of the war, some of the first halting steps toward black freedom would be made at Port Royal, including the enlistment of blacks into the Union army and experiments with settling the former slaves to farm for their own profit on the lands they once had worked as slaves.

Du Pont and his U.S. Navy fleet had won one of the first major Union victories of the war at Port Royal and brought Union victory appreciably closer. The very next day, however, another commander with another unit of the navy brought on what may well have been the Union's most dangerous crisis of the war. Captain Charles Wilkes commanded the U.S. steam frigate *San Jacinto*, which had been since 1859 cruising off the coast of Africa to help suppress the illegal international slave trade. It was on its way back to the United States to join in the Port Royal expedition, but Wilkes had delayed along the way to search for a reported Confederate commerce-raiding vessel. When *San Jacinto* put in at the port of Cienfuegos, Cuba, for coal, Wilkes learned that Confederate emissaries James M. Mason and John Slidell, bound for Britain and France, respectively, had successfully run the blockade at

Charleston in a speedy, coastal vessel on October 12 and were at that very moment in Havana waiting to take passage in the British mail packet *Trent*, bound for St. Thomas in the Bahamas, where they planned to take a British liner for the final leg of their trip to Europe.

The crusty, sixty-three-year-old seadog Wilkes, considered his options. After consulting several books on the law of the sea, he decided that Mason and Slidell were a form of living diplomatic dispatches. Diplomatic dispatches were contraband, articles whose warlike purpose allowed the vessel of a warring power to seize the neutral vessel carrying them. This would not be an exercise of the blockade since the ships involved would be far from any American harbor. It would depend for its justification solely on the claim that the *Trent* was carrying contraband. Wilkes was a fiery, impetuous officer, and he immediately got under way and placed the *San Jacinto* in the Old Bahama Channel, through which the *Trent* was bound to pass on its voyage to St. Thomas.

On November 8, the day after the capture of Port Royal Sound, the royal mail packet appeared, right on time. It took two shots across the bow to convince *Trent*'s captain to heave to. When he did, a cutter from the *San Jacinto* brought on board U.S. Navy Lieutenant Donald M. Fairfax, leading a boarding party. The British captain haughtily refused to produce his ship's registration and passenger list or to allow a search of the vessel for contraband, as a cruising warship was entitled to require of a neutral vessel, and Fairfax seemed hesitant to press the point. He did nonetheless find Mason, Slidell, and their secretaries and, in compliance with his orders from Wilkes, conveyed the four men and their baggage to the *San Jacinto*. Perhaps somewhat taken aback by the British captain's display of outraged arrogance, Fairfax did not carry out the portion of Wilkes's orders that required him to seize the *Trent* as a prize of war, as *San Jacinto* was entitled to do with any ship carrying Confederate contraband.

When *San Jacinto* arrived in the United States with the captured Confederate emissaries, the North erupted in jubilation, celebrating the frustration both of the Rebels' plans and of Britain's underhanded efforts to aid them. The British reaction was national outrage. Wilkes's action was, at worst, a milder version of exactly the sort of thing British captains had been doing to foreign ships for decades, including to U.S. vessels in the run-up to the War of 1812, but this was different as far as the British government and populace were concerned. Those incidents had been done by Britain to others, including Americans. By contrast, this had been done by Americans to a British ship. It was not to be tolerated. Prime Minister Palmerston, always hostile to the United States, told his cabinet with an oath that he would not stand for such a provocation from the Americans. To Queen Victoria he wrote that the time was right to teach "a lesson to the United States which will not soon be forgotten."[4] It certainly would not have been, but fortunately for both countries, the crisis did not go that far. Nevertheless, British troops stationed in Canada were put on alert, and further reinforcements were dispatched from the Isles. The *Trent* Affair was the closest the United States and Great Britain came to armed conflict during the Civil War.

Lincoln and his cabinet were at a loss to know what to do with the diplomatic "white elephants," as Lincoln called them, that Wilkes had brought them. The Confederate emissaries, now cooling their heels at Fort Warren in Boston Harbor, were doing more to bring about armed foreign intervention in the American Civil War than they could conceivably have done had they been running loose in the courts of Europe. Lincoln commented that the nation would do best to limit itself to "one war at a time." Yet northern public opinion made it hard to release Mason and Slidell since this would appear to be (and indeed really would be) backing down to British bullying. The problem would have become insoluble and another Anglo-American war almost inevitable had the British cabinet sent to the United States the harshly worded ultimatum it initially composed, an insulting demand for groveling with which no American president could ever have complied. Queen Victoria, invited by the cabinet to send her comments on the message, referred the matter to her husband, Prince Albert, even then dying of typhoid. The prince suggested modifying the language of the message so as to give the Americans the option of claiming, as was indeed the case, that Wilkes had acted without instructions from his government.

Backing down was still a difficult dose for Lincoln and his cabinet to swallow, but Seward wrote the British a lengthy letter explaining that Wilkes had indeed acted without authorization and that although his halting and search of the *Trent* had been legal, he had erred in not bringing the entire ship to an American port to be adjudicated in a prize court and possibly condemned for carrying contraband. Since Wilkes (actually Fairfax) had erred by simply removing the emissaries and letting the ship go, Seward was happy to apologize and to recognize with satisfaction that the British had now come around to the American position about the rights of the sea and admitted that they had done wrong for the past sixty years. With that, the United States released Mason and Slidell to go on their ways, and the Rebel diplomats reached their respective destinations in January 1862. Palmerston grumbled that there was much in Seward's message with which he did not agree, including the assertion that Mason and Slidell had constituted "diplomatic dispatches." In fact, as Mason's daughter later revealed, the Confederates had had with them on the *Trent* a pouch of actual diplomatic dispatches that remained undiscovered because Fairfax did not search the ship. A British officer carried the pouch to waiting Confederate agents in England in flagrant violation of neutrality law.

As 1861 came to an end the Confederacy seemed to be riding high. It had won the great battle of the war, Bull Run, and most of the smaller ones—Big Bethel, Wilson's Creek, and Ball's Bluff. Its chief losses were in western Virginia and along the southern coast at Port Royal. More significantly though less visibly, it had suffered a major blow to its security in the evaporation of Kentucky neutrality. For now, though, the Confederacy's situation seemed secure. Britain had not yet intervened, though it had come perilously close, and southerners continued to expect that event—all the more so now since Mason was in London to explain to British officials why it was their duty to recognize the Confederacy.

The outlook appeared correspondingly gloomy for the Union—military defeats, near war with Britain, and a finance crisis within the government all combined to create a dismal picture. When in late December McClellan contracted a severe case of typhoid, Lincoln thought matters could hardly get worse. "The people are impatient," he lamented to Quartermaster General Montgomery C. Meigs. "Chase [Secretary of the Treasury Salmon P. Chase] has no money and he tells me he can raise no more; the General of the Army has typhoid fever. The bottom is out of the tub. What shall I do?"[5]

4

THE EMERGENCE OF
GRANT

TWO PRESIDENTS
AND THEIR PROBLEMS

Lincoln was painfully aware of what the war was costing the country each day not only in terms of money, of which Secretary of the Treasury Salmon P. Chase did somehow manage to raise a continuing supply, but also of the people's will to see the cause through to victory. He wished his generals might somehow have the same perspective, realizing that they did not necessarily have the luxury of unlimited delay to prepare to meet the Rebels in battle. With one exception, none of his generals saw that angle. McClellan was the worst, and by the beginning of 1862, Lincoln was beginning to lose patience with his dashing young general in chief who not only did nothing but also refused to reveal to Lincoln any of his plans for future operations. McClellan was also insulting. In letters to his wife, McClellan referred to the president as "nothing more than a well-meaning baboon" and "the original gorilla."

He may not have used quite that language in talking with others, but the attitude came through. To one general he called Lincoln "a rare bird." In November Lincoln and Seward, accompanied by Lincoln's secretary John Hay, stopped by McClellan's house in Washington one evening to discuss strategy. Told that McClellan was out, they said they would wait and were shown into the parlor. About an hour later McClellan came home, was told that the president and secretary of state were waiting for him, and went

George B. McClellan with his wife,
Ellen Marcy McClellan.

upstairs. Half an hour later the visitors asked the porter to take the message upstairs to McClellan that they were still waiting. The servant returned a few moments later with word that McClellan had gone to bed for the night. As they walked back to the White House, Hay expressed outrage, but Lincoln said, "It was better at this time not to be making points of etiquette and personal dignity." To another Lincoln commented, "I would hold General McClellan's horse" if the general would only win a victory.

With Scott far off in New York in retirement, with the nation's new top military man unwilling to cooperate with him, and with some in Washington even suggesting that there might be a sinister reason why McClellan, the Democrat, would not cooperate, Lincoln desperately turned to studying books on military science to try to educate himself in matters of strategy. Then shortly before Christmas, McClellan came down with typhoid and was out of commission for nearly three weeks.

Reports from the West were equally discouraging. Frémont was gone now, sacked by Lincoln for corruption and failure to accomplish anything useful. In his place the president appointed Henry W. Halleck (West Point, 1839), the army's leading intellectual and author of the main textbook Lincoln was studying on the art of war. To command in Kentucky, now that that state was open as an avenue of Union advance, Lincoln had assigned Don Carlos Buell (West Point, 1841), a McClellan protégé with a reputation as a professional's professional. Yet despite all of Lincoln's urging, neither general was willing to undertake any action at all.

Lincoln was especially frustrated that Buell would not advance to relieve the Unionist population of East Tennessee, which had risen up against secessionist rule and was currently being schooled by several thousand Confederate troops in just how much the Rebels truly believed in self-determination. East Tennessee was not an easy place to reach, especially from the north and especially in winter, but Buell was ready to provide plenty of reasons why his command could not reach anyplace at all within Rebel control. Halleck was no better, and the two steadfastly declined to cooperate with each other. On one dispatch from Halleck, Lincoln sadly endorsed, "It is exceedingly discouraging. Here as everywhere else nothing can be done."

In Virginia at least, Lincoln could try to force the pace of the action in person. To Lincoln's lament that the bottom was out of the tub, Montgomery Meigs suggested that the president should talk to some of McClellan's division commanders. Lincoln did, commenting to them that "if General McClellan did not want to use the army, he would like to borrow it, provided he could see how it could be made to do something." But the generals were little help. When Lincoln met with them again on January 13, a still pale and shaky McClellan rose from his sickbed to attend the meeting, which he was convinced was a conspiracy against him.

A few days later, in a meeting with the cabinet, McClellan again refused to reveal his plan of campaign and spoke of his conviction, steadily held now for several months, that the Rebels had twice as many men in Virginia as he did. This was the purest moonshine, but for McClellan it was practically an article of faith from which he never wavered throughout his tenure in army command. In fact, at this time he outnumbered the Confederate troops in Virginia by more than two to one. In retrospect, his constant insistence that he was outnumbered seemed almost intended to justify his fear of taking action. For the moment, any at rate, Lincoln had to be content with McClellan's assurance that at least he did have a plan.

Frustrated with his seeming inability to get action out of his generals and convinced from his study of the books on strategy that it would be a good thing to exert pressure on the enemy from multiple directions at the same time, Lincoln on January 27 issued General War Order Number One, directing that all the armies of the republic were to advance and attack the enemy on February 22, Washington's Birthday. On January 31 Lincoln added a further order specifying that on February 22, the Army of the Potomac was to advance against the Confederate army still encamped near Centerville. McClellan responded with a twenty-two-page letter explaining in detail why the Army of the Potomac should not advance any time soon. He did include in his letter, though, an explanation of his long-awaited campaign, a scheme for landing the army near the mouth of the Rappahannock River and moving in behind the Rebels at Centerville, trapping them. Lincoln doubted that the plan would really work, but, happy to be taken into the general's confidence at last, he deferred to the military professional and acquiesced in the army's remaining idle a few more weeks.

Less than one hundred miles away in Richmond, Jefferson Davis had his own problems that winter. After Beauregard's release to the press of his self-promotional report on the Battle of Bull Run, relations between the Creole general and the Confederate president had not been good. In the report, the general claimed that if only Davis had approved a plan he, Beauregard, had submitted before the battle, the Confederacy would have scored a virtually war-winning victory, but the plan had called for troops the Confederacy did not have. Beauregard aired this and other complaints to members of the Confederate congress, suggesting that if his ideas were given full play, he would shortly win the war. Hearing that Beauregard's nonsense had been repeated on the floor of the Confederate congress repeatedly taxed Davis's patience.

Relations between the president and Joseph E. Johnston had gone sour when that general discovered that in appointing the Confederacy's initial five full generals in September 1861, Davis had ranked him fourth, behind Adjutant and Inspector General Samuel Cooper and generals Albert Sidney Johnston (no relation) and Robert E. Lee. The last seemed to rankle Johnston particularly since he had spent his whole army career trying to get ahead of his West Point classmate Lee. Having used political connections to win a staff appointment as brigadier general in the U.S. Army just before secession, Johnston thought he had finally beaten Lee, and he believed that a Confederate law guaranteeing the same relative ranks in the Confederate army that officers had held in the U.S. Army would keep him ahead of his old West Point rival.

What Johnston had missed in the law was that his staff rank in the old army would not count toward his line rank in the new. Davis had read the law correctly and given Johnston his proper rank. Not accepting that, Johnston in mid-September wrote Davis a fifteen-page abusive letter concluding, "I now

General Joseph E. Johnston

and here declare my claim that, notwithstanding these nominations made by the President, and their confirmation by Congress, I still rightfully hold the rank of first general in the armies of the Southern Confederacy." Davis's reply was short and to the point: "I have received and read your letter of the 12th instant. Its language is, as you say, unusual; its arguments and statements utterly one-sided, and its insinuations are as unfounded as they are unbecoming." Relations between Davis and Johnston would henceforth be tense at best.

In the late fall of 1861, Beauregard and Johnston requested that Davis visit their headquarters and urged him vigorously to strip troops from other parts of the Confederacy in order to reinforce their army and enable them to take the offensive and win the war before the one-year enlistments of their troops expired. It would have been an extremely risky move elsewhere, with doubtful results in Virginia, and Davis was not prepared to make that gamble. He returned disappointed to Richmond, leaving his generals sullen and resentful. By midwinter Beauregard's troublemaking propensities had become so annoying that Davis arranged to have him transferred to the western theater of the war, where he would serve as second in command to Albert Sidney Johnston (West Point, 1826).

This other Johnston was perhaps the only man Davis admired more than he did Leonidas Polk. Sidney Johnston had been an upperclassman when Davis was a beginning student at Transylvania University in Lexington, Kentucky. Later Johnston had been an upperclassman when Davis was a plebe at West Point, and they had served together in the Mexican War. Johnston ever after remained for Davis the ideal of all that a soldier should be. In the wake of Polk's blundering away of Kentucky neutrality in September 1861, Johnston had arrived in Richmond from his previous post with the U.S. Army in California, and Davis had immediately assigned him to overall command of all of the Confederacy's northward-facing defenses from the Appalachians to the Great Plains.

What Davis failed to do was support Johnston with anything like adequate men or materiel. In part this was because Davis did not have anything like adequate numbers of men or amounts of materiel available, but in part it was because Davis had already begun to focus too much on the narrow but prestigious eastern theater of the war while giving less attention to the all-important heartland west of the Appalachians. Of the scant supplies of weapons that did become available during the fall of 1861, the lion's share went to Virginia.

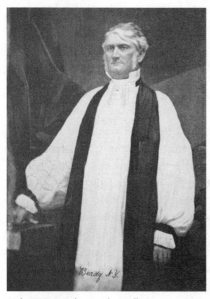

Bishop-General Leonidas Polk

General Albert Sidney Johnston

FORT HENRY

February 22, 1862, arrived, and the armies of the Union had not moved—with one exception. One Union army had already advanced in the days immediately preceding Washington's Birthday and had won what would prove to be two of the most significant victories of the war. That army belonged to Ulysses Grant. After the setback at Belmont, Grant had not given up his eagerness to get at the Rebels at Columbus, who soon numbered about ten thousand men. By early 1862, he had come up with a plan to drive southward up the Tennessee and Cumberland rivers and thus turn Columbus.

When Grant presented his plan to Halleck, the superior general rebuffed him so brusquely that Grant, still believing as everyone else did at that time that Halleck was a military genius, thought he must inadvertently have proposed something extraordinarily stupid. That was not the case. Halleck's rude dismissal of Grant's plan was not because it was a bad plan but because it was a good one, in fact, exactly the plan Halleck himself was contemplating. Nor did one need to be the country's leading military mind to see it. Several officers proposed it, and a woman in Maryland, after looking over a map, sent a letter to the government suggesting it. The question was not what to do but who could make it happen. Halleck wanted to be the one who did, but he wanted much more time for preparation first, thus his curt dismissal of Grant.

Throughout the war Grant would develop a pattern of being the man who accomplished things that others had only thought about doing. One reason was his persistence, usually aimed at the enemy but this time, of necessity, plied on his superior, Halleck. A couple of weeks later, he proposed his idea to Halleck again. This time the situation had changed enough to win Halleck's approval. Lincoln's General War Order Number One had reached Halleck's desk, and letting Grant off the leash for a few days might be a good way to satisfy the president and relieve the pressure. Then word arrived from Washington that a recently captured Confederate soldier had reported that Beauregard was coming from Virginia to Tennessee with fifteen regiments of troops. The Creole general was indeed on his way, but the part about the regiments was wrong. Beauregard did not have fifteen staff officers with him and no troops at all. Still, the threat that Confederate reinforcements were about to arrive and make future offensive operations much more difficult was the final prod Halleck needed to turn Grant loose.

Grant loaded his army, now grown to seventeen thousand men, into steamboats and set out from his bases at Cairo and Paducah on February 3. The next day the first elements of his force began landing on the banks of the Tennessee River several miles downstream from a Confederate outpost called Fort Henry. Begun during the days of Kentucky neutrality, Fort Henry was located near the river's northernmost point in the state of Tennessee. It was a poor location for a fort, but Kentucky was unavailable, and Tennessee planners wanted to protect as much of their state as possible. Worse, the fort had been under Polk's jurisdiction since the preceding summer, and Polk, with his fixation on Columbus, had accumulated most of his department's troops and both of its trained engineer officers at the Mississippi River stronghold, leaving Fort Henry undermanned and incomplete even after Johnston, who had been Polk's West Point roommate, sent him repeated orders to see to it that the fortifications on the Tennessee were in good shape. Now the poorly sited, incomplete, undermanned fort was all the Confederates had to prevent the deep penetration of the Confederate heartland via the Tennessee River.

After scouting the fort from a distance, Grant gave orders that the assault should take place at 10:00 a.m., February 6. His troops marched out of their camps that morning in high spirits but were soon dismayed to find that recent rains had turned the dirt roads of Tennessee into seemingly bottomless quagmires. Laboriously they waded on through the mud, dragging their artillery, caissons, and ammunition wagons, but when 10:00 came they were still far from their attack positions.

Cooperating with Grant's force on this operation was a squadron of four of the navy's new ironclad river gunboats under the command of Flag Officer Andrew H. Foote. Another of the navy's crusty, old seadogs, the tough, aggressive Foote was a stickler for precision. Grant had asked him to attack at 10:00 a.m., and that is exactly what Foote did, leading his boats into action with colors flying and guns blazing.

The gunboats were strange craft. Based loosely on the design of ordinary riverboats, they drew six to eight feet of water and were 175 feet long and a little more than fifty feet wide. A casemate, or box, covered nearly the entire deck space of each gunboat, enclosing its thirteen heavy guns and single, twenty-two-foot-diameter paddle wheel, driven by two steam engines mounted side by side in the vessel's shallow hold and capable of propelling the gunboat at a respectable eight knots. The casemate's sloping sides, along with the vessel's overall squat proportions, led nonplussed observers to nickname them, after their designer Samuel M. Pook, Pook's Turtles. The turtles' shells were only selectively strong and then only within limits—two and a half inches of iron plate forward, an inch and a half on the sides and the small

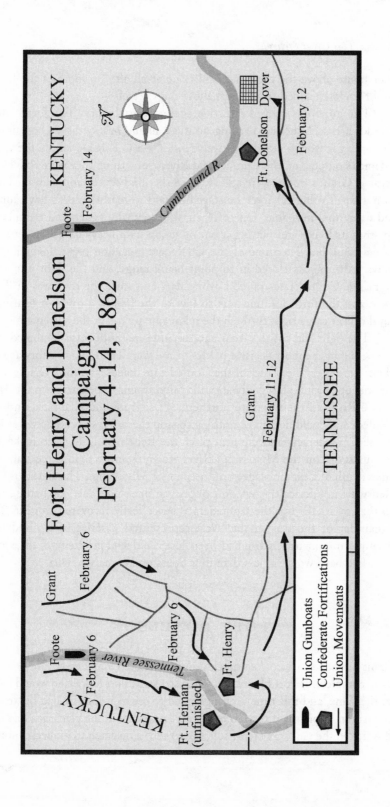

Fort Henry and Donelson Campaign, February 4-14, 1862

KENTUCKY

Cumberland R.

Foote
February 14

Dover

February 12

Ft. Donelson

Grant
February 11-12

TENNESSEE

Grant
February 6

Foote
February 6

KENTUCKY

Tennessee River

February 6

Ft. Heiman
(unfinished)

Ft. Henry

Union Gunboats
Confederate Fortifications
Union Movements

pilot house above the casemate, and none at all aft. No more of the heavy armor could be added to such a shallow-draft vessel.

The gunboats proved effective against Fort Henry. The fort's commander had seen the handwriting on the wall and hastily dispatched almost his entire garrison to march the twelve miles east to Fort Donelson, the Confederacy's outpost on the Cumberland River, something they were able to do because Grant's troops were still stuck in the mud several miles away. Then with a small volunteer force he stayed behind to man the fort's few cannon and delay the inevitable. One of their shots actually penetrated a gunboat, bursting its boiler and putting it out of action with heavy casualties, but the others came on. Then one of the Confederate cannon burst, mangling its crew; the gunboats closed in to point-blank range, and the fight was soon over. The Confederates raised a white flag, and since the river was in flood stage and the fort's location was so low to the banks, a rowboat bearing a naval officer came right through the main gate to accept the surrender.

The fight had cost less than 120 casualties on both sides combined. Yet it was one of the most decisive battles of the war. The Union victory at Fort Henry tore open the center of the Confederate defenses in the West, leaving the way open for Union gunboats and Union troops to penetrate up the Tennessee River all the way into northern Mississippi and Alabama, and the Confederacy could do almost nothing to stop them. West Tennessee was lost to the Confederacy, and the next place the Rebels could hope to make any serious stand on the Mississippi River was now more than three hundred miles south of Columbus, deep in the state of Mississippi. The Battle of Fort Henry did not decide the outcome of the war in a single day—no battle could do that by itself—but the Confederacy never really recovered from it. The remainder of the war in the West represented a series of Confederate attempts to win back what had been lost—and Union attempts to exploit what had been won—in less than four hours on February 6, 1862.

FORT DONELSON

Grant intended to follow up quickly and make the Confederate disaster even more complete. If Fort Henry had fallen so easily, Fort Donelson would likely do the same, and this time Grant planned to see to it that he had his troops in position in plenty of time to bag every last Rebel in the place as a prisoner of war. On the day Fort Henry fell, Grant sent a dispatch to Halleck informing him of victory and adding, "I shall take and destroy Fort Donelson on the 8th and return to Fort Henry."

It was not quite that easy. Heavy storms of rain, sleet, and snow swept across the Upper South for the next few days, rendering the roads once again impassable. By February 12 another sudden shift in the weather had brought clear skies and a warm sun that dried the roads and convinced many of Grant's soldiers on the march that day to throw away their overcoats as useless burdens, convinced as they were that spring had come in February here in the sunny South and that the war would be over long before autumn. By the morning of February 14 Grant had his army in place surrounding Fort Donelson, from the Cumberland River below (north of) almost to the river above the fort. All that remained was for Foote and his gunboats to go in and blast the Rebels into submission as they had at Fort Henry eight days before.

The situation inside Fort Donelson was considerably different than that inside Fort Henry had been, in part because of decisions Albert Sidney Johnston had made after the fall of Fort Henry. From his headquarters in Bowling Green, Kentucky, Johnston had realized that the ironclad gunboats opened a new chapter in warfare, making the rivers into highways of conquest for the side that owned them, and his side owned none. He assumed that Fort Donelson would not hold out much longer than Fort Henry had lasted.

From there, the logic of Johnston's decision was inexorable. He could not afford to abandon the fort without a fight because once it was in Federal hands, the Union gunboats would range up the Cumberland all the way to Nashville, cutting off his main body at Bowling Green. He needed a few days to get his troops back across the Cumberland at Nashville and continue the retreat southward. He did not want to sacrifice the garrison of Fort Donelson. He could not afford to lose a man unnecessarily if he was going to have a chance of retrieving Confederate fortunes in the West. He could not count on Grant to be slow again in surrounding the fort. So Johnston's only hope of both buying time and ensuring the garrison's escape would require inserting enough infantry into the fort to enable them to push the encircling Federals aside, break out, and rejoin the army somewhere south of Nashville.

The troops Johnston sent to Donelson were those he had on hand, close enough to reach the fort in time. There was a brigade under the command of Brigadier General Gideon J. Pillow, a Tennessee politician, political ally of the eleventh president of the United States, James K. Polk, and an ardent secessionist. A veteran of the Mexican War, Pillow was now serving as a political general in his second war. His past record did not inspire confidence—he had become notorious among U.S. officers in the Mexican War for having had his men construct a set of fortifications backward—but his brigade was available. Another available brigade belonged to another political general, former Virginia governor and U.S. secretary of war during the Buchanan administration, John B. Floyd. Widely suspected in the North both of financial graft while secretary of war and of deliberately transferring heavy cannon to southern arsenals on the eve of secession so as to make them easy pickings for the Rebels, he had been less effective for the Confederacy since he had put on its uniform, having contributed his part to the ongoing Confederate debacle in western Virginia.

Thus, Johnston sent what troops he could, and those included Pillow's and Floyd's brigades. By the time Grant arrived outside the fort, its defenders numbered about twenty thousand men. Floyd, as senior officer present in the fort, had the command. Grant's force outside the fort numbered about seventeen thousand.

The morning of February 14 dawned bitter cold. Another front had passed over during the night, rain turning to sleet and then to snow, several inches of it, and temperatures dropping into the low teens. Too close to the enemy to light campfires, the soldiers huddled grimly under the icy blast. At the appointed hour, Foote led the gunboats into battle, and soon troops all the way around the Union and Confederate perimeters, out of sight of the river, could hear the constant thunder of the big guns. Federals were confident, Confederates almost in despair. "The fort cannot hold out twenty minutes," Floyd wrote in a message to Johnston sent across the Cumberland as the gunboats closed in.

Then to everyone's astonishment, the Confederate shot and shell began to take their toll on the iron behemoths. The key difference was that Fort Donelson was located on a high bluff, giving its guns the ability to fire down at an angle onto the unprotected wooden decks of the gunboats. One boat after another went out of control, steering shot away or boilers burst, and drifted helplessly back down the river, still pounded by the Confederate guns until it mercifully passed out of range. The flagship's pilothouse took a direct hit, severely wounding Foote. Presently the last of the gunboats fell back down the river with heavy damage, and the fight was over. As the guns fell silent, stunned Union soldiers around the perimeter heard cheers starting in the Confederate positions near the river and running around the lines.

Grant took in stride the realization that his ground troops were going to have to take the fort with minimal help from the navy. He sent for additional troops from those he had left to garrison Fort Henry and settled down to prepare for either an assault or a siege. In the dark hours after midnight of another brutally cold night came a message from the wounded Foote asking if Grant could ride to meet him where the flagship and the other battered gunboats were tied up several miles below the fort. Though his message did not say so, Foote needed to explain to Grant that the fleet was going to have to withdraw to Cairo for repairs. Grant appreciated the voluntary cooperation of Foote, whose naval command had never been under Grant's orders. Eager to repay the flag officer's assistance, Grant agreed to go. He left no officer in command of his army but left strict orders with each of its three division commanders to remain in their positions and do nothing until he returned. One of the three was McClernand, a political general whom Grant had learned to distrust.

Grant was a general who devoted most of his thought to what he was going to do to the enemy and relatively little to what the enemy might be planning to do to him. He understood the value of momentum in warfare better than almost any other general on either side during the war, and he made a point of seizing and keeping it: "Get at the enemy as quick as you can. Hit him as hard as you can, and keep moving on." As long as he kept the momentum he was by far the most dangerous general of the war, but when something happened to halt his momentum, whether enemy action or the orders of a superior, he became vulnerable. The repulse of the gunboats had put Grant in such a situation.

Grant had been gone only a short time, and it was still dark when the numb and shivering troops on the right end of the encircling Union line, near the Cumberland on the opposite side of Fort Donelson from where Grant was riding away, saw darker shapes moving toward them from the direction of the fort. The Confederates were attacking. In keeping with Johnston's orders, having bought what they believed was enough time for Johnston's retreat from central Kentucky, Floyd, Pillow, and fellow brigadier general Simon B. Buckner (West Point, 1844) had arranged their breakout attack, reducing troops to a minimum on the northern perimeter to mass every available man for an assault southeastward, with the Cumberland River on their left.

The attack fell on McClernand's division and gradually by weight of numbers overwhelmed its regiments one by one from east to west, curling it back on Brigadier General Lew Wallace's center division. Wallace had previously sent only slight aid to McClernand because of Grant's orders to remain in place and do nothing, but his division was able to halt the Confederate offensive around midday.

From the point of view of the Confederate plan, the stand of Wallace's division was irrelevant. A yawning gap on the right of the Union line now left the way wide open for the entire Fort Donelson garrison to march out and take the road for Nashville and a reunion with Johnston's main body. Buckner, the only professional soldier among the top three in the fort, found Floyd on the battlefield and suggested the time had come to leave. Floyd agreed, but before he could issue the order for the withdrawal, Pillow found him. Flushed with victory, Pillow persuaded Floyd to cancel or postpone the withdrawal and order the troops back into the entrenched lines of the fort to rest and eat a meal. Pillow apparently thought the Yankees so badly whipped that the victorious Confederates could retire at their leisure.

A staff officer caught up with Grant as he was coming ashore after his conference on Foote's flagship and informed him that the army was fighting a desperate battle. Grant galloped back and arrived just as a lull was settling over the battlefield after Wallace's noon repulse of the Confederates. Sizing up the situation Grant decided the Rebels had attempted to break out and had failed to do so. "The one who attacks first now will be victorious," Grant told a staff officer. "The enemy will have to be in a hurry if he gets ahead of me." Grant gave immediate orders for an attack all along the line. On the center and right, Wallace's troops and some rallied units of McClernand's wrecked division drove back toward the positions McClernand had lost that morning, taking key ground.

On the Union right, Grant's old West Point professor, Brigadier General Charles F. Smith, led his division from the front, huge white mustache streaming over both shoulders. Smith forbade his men to stop and fire until they got inside the Confederate breastworks. The position was extremely strong, but the Confederate lines were thin because most of the troops there had been pulled away to take part in the breakout attack. Behind Smith's charismatic leadership the Union line surged up to the works. The color-bearer of the Second Iowa leapt over, and then hundreds of Federals followed, swarming over the breastworks and driving the Rebels back. Darkness and Confederate reinforcements brought their drive to a halt. The Confederates were men of Buckner's command hurrying back to their defensive positions after Floyd had ordered them to return to the fort.

That night the three Confederate brigadiers held a conference inside the fort. Buckner announced that the Yankees had possession of his lines and from their favorable position could overrun the entire fort at dawn. No option remained, he said, but surrender. Floyd said he dared not surrender; with the accusations leveled at his actions as secretary of war, the Yankees might hang him. Pillow said he would never surrender. A volunteer cavalry colonel named

Nathan Bedford Forrest came in and said a way out was still open, apparently unknown to the Yankees. It followed a road immediately along the bank of the Cumberland, and it would involve wading several hundred yards, "saddle-skirt deep," through an icy backwater. Buckner said if they did that, three-quarters of the men would die of pneumonia, and that would be immoral. It was their duty, he said, to surrender.

Floyd asked if he might turn the command over to Buckner and be permitted to escape personally. Buckner said he could if he got out before the white flag went up. "I turn the command over, sir!" said Floyd. "I pass it," said Pillow, his next in rank, and Buckner went to look for a bugler and a white flag. A disgusted Forrest led his own cavalry regiment out, along with quite a number of infantrymen who decided to tag along, clinging to the horses' stirrups when the water got deep. Floyd and Pillow found boats at the fort's landing—Floyd a steamboat on which he could take some of his men, Pillow an abandoned scow in which he could take a few staff officers as oarsmen. When Grant received Buckner's note asking for terms of surrender, he responded, on Smith's advice, "No terms except an unconditional and immediate surrender can be accepted. I propose to move immediately upon your works." Buckner, though grumbling about Grant's lack of chivalry, had no choice but to accept.

News of the victory thrilled the nation. With 12,392 Confederates heading north into Union captivity it surpassed Saratoga and Yorktown as the largest surrender ever on American soil. The intensity of the fighting was demonstrated by the fact that the 2,500 Union killed and wounded and the 1,500 Confederate were comparable to the numbers of killed and wounded at Bull Run (considerably more for the Union), though only about half as many troops had been engaged.

The capture of forts Henry and Donelson was enormously important and might almost be called the first turning point of the war. Up until that time, the Confederacy had had things pretty much its own way, but it never fully recovered from the loss of the forts. The twin February victories gave the Union control of the Tennessee and Cumberland rivers deep into what had been Rebel-controlled territory. Union gunboats, transports, and armies could range up the Cumberland all the way to Nashville and up the Tennessee all the way into northern Mississippi and Alabama. The Rebels could no longer hold positions along the Mississippi in the states of Tennessee or Kentucky because Union control of the Tennessee guaranteed the defenders would easily be turned and possibly trapped. Half the state of Tennessee passed to Union control, and the partial Confederate grasp on the state of

Kentucky was gone. Within weeks, Union troops would be poised on the edge of the Deep South states.

Grant became a national hero, and his demand for "unconditional surrender" gave a new meaning to his first two initials. Lincoln soon promoted him to major general of volunteers. The president did not fully realize it yet, but he had found a general who would fight and fight skillfully.

A WINTER OF
CONFEDERATE DEFEATS

Washington's Birthday came six days after the surrender of Fort Donelson and found the armies of the Union quietly encamped, though Grant's was resting from its earthshaking victories of that month.

In Richmond, the Confederacy had chosen this day, with its associations with the first president and father of his country, to inaugurate its first regular president, duly elected the preceding November in the glow of the Confederate victories of 1861. This of course was Jefferson Davis, the provisional president and only candidate for the regular presidency. The inaugural ceremony was anything but auspicious. A cold rain dripped sullenly out of a low, gray overcast. When the president's wife, Varina Howell Davis, asked one of the four black footmen who walked slowly beside the barely rolling presidential coach why they wore formal black suits and walked so slowly, he replied, "This, ma'am, is the way we always does in Richmond at funerals and suchlike."[1]

It certainly appeared that the Confederacy's funeral, if the southern slaveholders' republic should receive any such honor, would not be far off, for the disasters of Fort Henry and Fort Donelson, though by far the worst, had not been the only Confederate debacles in recent weeks. On January 19, a division of nearly six thousand Confederate troops under Major General George B. Crittenden (West Point, 1832), son of Union-loyal Kentucky Congressman John J. Crittenden, had attacked a smaller Union division of about 4,400 men under the command of Union-loyal Virginian George H. Thomas (West Point, 1840) at Logan's Crossroads in Kentucky.

It had been a sharp little fight on a foggy, rainy morning, with the Second Minnesota fighting it out with the Fifteen Mississippi with bayonets over a rail fence and the colonel of the German-speaking Ninth Ohio leading his men in a wild bayonet charge, shouting, "Close your eyes, boys, if it gets too hot for you." Felix Zollicoffer, a popular but very nearsighted Nashville news-

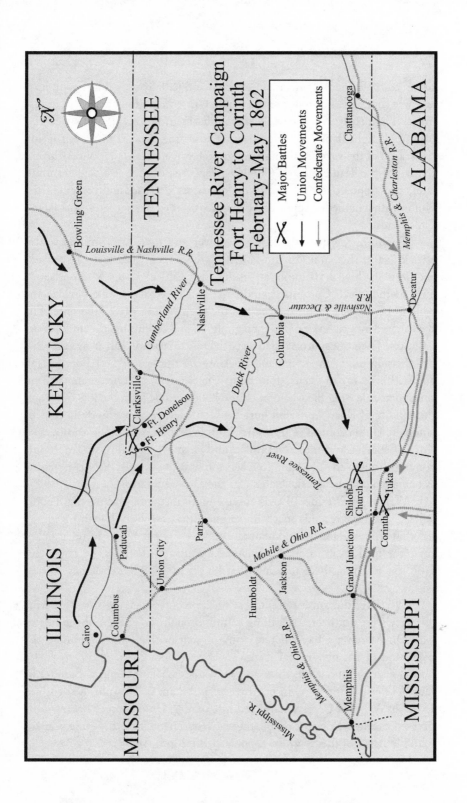

Tennessee River Campaign
Fort Henry to Corinth
February–May 1862

Major Battles
Union Movements
Confederate Movements

paper-editor-turned-Confederate-general, accidentally rode into Union lines and was shot. The Federals prevailed, and Crittenden's force retreated in disorder. The defeat would have been significant in destroying Albert Sidney Johnston's right flank had Buell been enterprising enough to exploit it and the season of the year propitious enough to favor such exploitation. As it was, the fall of the Tennessee and Cumber river forts, coming less than a month later, had ripped open the center of Johnston's defenses and presented the Union with a far better opportunity than that gained by the victory at Logan's Crossroads.

Then on February 8 Union sea power and its long amphibious arm struck again, this time on the North Carolina coast. A fleet of specially acquired shallow-draft gunboats under Flag Officer Louis M. Goldsboro entered the North Carolina Sounds, the narrow, shallow waters inside the band of barrier islands off the coast of the northeastern part of the state. The fleet chased away a few Confederate gunboats and suppressed the fire of shore batteries. Then transports landed a special ten-thousand-man army amphibious division under the command of Ambrose Burnside (West Point, 1847), and within less than twenty-four hours the 2,500-man Confederate garrison surrendered, leaving the island in Union hands. Aside from the loss of troops, the capture of Roanoke Island hurt the Confederacy by opening the way for complete Union control of the North Carolina Sounds and their shores, cutting off coastwise commercial traffic and closing a backdoor for materials coming through the blockade to reach the port of Norfolk, Virginia, via the Albemarle and Chesapeake Canal and the Dismal Swamp Canal.

Well might President Davis observe in his inaugural address that February 22, "We have recently met with serious disasters," but, though he admitted that "the tide for the moment is against us," he maintained nonetheless that "the final result in our favor is never doubtful." Perhaps, he suggested, God was teaching them to value their liberty by the high cost they paid to win it.

Whatever the cause and purpose of the Confederate disasters that winter, they were not over, and spring at first brought no change of the tide of war. On March 7 a Confederate army of sixteen thousand men under the command of Major General Earl Van Dorn (West Point, 1842) attacked a Union army of about ten thousand men under Major General Samuel R. Curtis (West Point, 1831) in northwestern Arkansas. Despite the death of Lyon at Wilson's Creek the preceding August, Union forces had steadily pressed Sterling Price's Confederate Missourians out of that state. Curtis, with his Army of the Southwest, pursued Price into Arkansas.

Retreating into Arkansas, Price's force again united with that of Ben McCulloch, reopening the previous year's questions about who should command whom. From far off Richmond, Jefferson Davis decided to fix the problem by assigning his fellow Mississippian Van Dorn to command both Price and McCulloch. Van Dorn had big plans. He would crush Federal strength in Arkansas and then march into Missouri. "I must have St. Louis," he wrote to his wife, "then huzzah!"

The first step was defeating Curtis, who had learned of Van Dorn's approach with a more powerful army and had taken up a strong defensive position along the valley of Sugar Creek. Van Dorn planned to march around Curtis, get behind him, and split his own army into two columns, one passing east and the other west of a landform called Pea Ridge and converging in an irresistible pincer movement on the Federal rear. In practice, however, everything seemed to go wrong. Curtis discovered Van Dorn's movement and turned his force in time to face him, stopping the two Confederate columns on either side of Pea Ridge and hindering their conjunction. McCulloch crept forward to reconnoiter the Union position in front of his column, and a Federal soldier shot him dead. Then Van Dorn discovered that the problem with being in the enemy's rear was that then the enemy was in his own rear. As a result his army ran low on ammunition with no good way of replenishing. The battle carried over to the next day, March 8, and ended with Curtis's Federals routing Van Dorn's Rebels. After the Union victory at Pea Ridge, Confederate forces would never again seriously threaten to gain control of Missouri but would henceforth struggle to maintain some hold on Arkansas.

The Confederacy suffered another, albeit less significant, setback later that month and even farther west. With authorization from Richmond, Confederate Brigadier General Henry Hopkins Sibley (West Point, 1838) had raised a brigade of Texas cavalry the preceding fall and marched it west in hopes of adding the western territories with their gold mines and possibly even Pacific coast harbors to the Confederacy. They got as far as Glorieta Pass, in the Sangre de Cristo Mountains of New Mexico, where on March 28, 1862, a smaller mixed force of U.S. Army regulars and Colorado and New Mexico territorial volunteers defeated them and turned back their expedition.

JOHNSTON PREPARES A RIPOSTE

Battles like Pea Ridge and Glorieta Pass, fought well west of the Mississippi River, were of tangential significance to the Civil War. If the Confederacy won the war and gained its independence, such battles would help decide what western lands the new slaveholders' republic might own, but nothing that happened out there was at all likely to decide the central momentous question of the war. That question might, by an off chance, be decided east of the Appalachians, but it was most likely to find its answer in the prewar heartland of America, the broad swath of country between the Appalachians and the Mississippi.

In the heart of that heartland during the Confederacy's bleak late winter of 1862, Albert Sidney Johnston made his plans for a counterstrike that he hoped would regain what had been lost at Henry and Donelson. He made no attempt to evade the criticism leveled at him in the newspapers for the twin debacles. "The test of merit in my profession," he wrote, "with the people, is success. It is a hard rule, but I think it right." He hoped to pass that test by means of the desperate counterattack he contemplated launching against Grant.

Despite his recent victories, Grant had had problems enough of his own of late. He had been eager to follow up on the successes at Henry and Donelson but could get little help from Halleck and no cooperation out of Buell. When he made a quick trip by steamboat to Nashville to talk to Buell, Halleck got wind of the visit and reprimanded Grant sternly. Then Halleck launched a full-scale offensive against his subordinate. He relieved Grant of command of his army and wrote to McClellan that Grant was acting without authorization, failing to send proper reports, and drinking. None of these things were true, and Halleck knew it. In the case of the last charge, drunkenness, Halleck was especially well informed. He had assigned a member of his staff, engineer Lieutenant Colonel James B. McPherson, to serve on Grant's staff, ostensibly to help Grant but really to report to Halleck on Grant's sobriety. McPherson had indeed helped Grant but had also reported quite truthfully to Halleck that Grant was firmly on the wagon. Halleck chose to lie to McClellan in order to undermine Grant. His probable motive was jealousy.

Grant might have remained sidelined and vanished from history save that his congressman, Elihu B. Washburne, once again went to bat for him to the Lincoln administration. Lincoln was inclined to give Grant the benefit of the doubt and may well have been canny enough to detect Halleck's jealousy in any case. He had Stanton order Halleck to explain the nature of his charges against Grant. Knowing that his allegations would never stand the light of day, Halleck backed down and reassigned Grant to command of what would come to be called the Army of the Tennessee.

By the time Grant resumed command, his army was encamped on the west bank of the Tennessee River at Pittsburg Landing, a two-house settlement at a steamboat landing about fifteen miles from the Mississippi line and twenty from the key northern Mississippi rail junction town of Corinth, where Albert Sidney Johnston was even then gathering his troops. Grant's orders from Halleck were to keep his army encamped idly at Pittsburg Landing until he could be joined by Buell's Army of the Ohio, marching overland from Nashville, and the Army of the Mississippi, which under the command of John Pope (West Point, 1842) had been cooperating with the navy in clearing away the Confederate defenders of the Mississippi who had already been turned by Grant's success on the Tennessee. When all three armies were in place, Halleck would come down to Pittsburg and take personal command for the final advance to Corinth. Above all, Grant was to do nothing that might bring on a fight with the Confederates—no aggressive patrolling, no forceful reconnaissance probes. The big battle was to wait until Halleck and all the troops were on hand.

Albert Sidney Johnston would no doubt have appreciated Halleck's orders if he could have known of them, but he did not intend to wait quite that long for the big battle. He had gathered in Corinth all the elements of his command east of the Mississippi—Crittenden's survivors from Logan's Crossroads, now no longer under Crittenden since that officer was facing court-martial for drunkenness on duty; Polk's Columbus garrison, having long since abandoned the fortifications Polk had kept them working on all winter; and Johnston's own main body, having marched all the way down from Bowling Green. Davis had hurried enough reinforcements from the rest of the Confederacy to bring Johnston's total force up to forty-four thousand men. The task before him was simple and extremely difficult. His best chance for reversing the tide of war in the West was to destroy Grant's Army of the Tennessee before Buell's Army of the Ohio or Pope's Army of the Mississippi could join it. Then, if his own army was still battleworthy, he could at least in theory turn on the two smaller Union armies and destroy them one after the other.

Johnston's army was composed of green troops, most of whom had never been in battle, and its units had never worked together before. Johnston wanted as much time as possible to train and organize it before leading it into battle. He therefore planned to wait until Buell, who was closer, had almost reached Grant. Then he would strike. On April 2 his scouts brought word that Buell was getting very close, perhaps only another day or two of marching from joining Grant. The time had come, and Johnston gave the order for his army to march the twenty miles to Pittsburg Landing the next day and attack Grant's army at dawn on April 4.

He assigned to his second in command, Beauregard, the task of composing the march orders. Beauregard and his chief of staff had a copy of Napoleon's order for the march to Waterloo and used it as a pattern, adapting it as best they could to the present troops and terrain. Their march order was much too complicated, especially for the army's woefully inexperienced troops and their equally green officers. Divisions and corps were to weave between each other on intersecting roads. The result, predictably, was chaos, with entire divisions getting lost and the army commander himself having to ride out in search of them. Eventually Johnston found all the pieces of his army, but there was considerable delay. Heavy rains occasioned further delay by turning the roads into mud. Johnston had to postpone the attack from the fourth to the fifth and then to the sixth.

By the evening of the fifth, Beauregard and most of the rest of Johnston's ranking subordinates strongly advocated aborting the operation and returning to Corinth since the element of surprise had almost certainly been lost. Johnston was adamant. "I would fight them if they were a million," he told a staff officer. In front of him was Grant's army with its back to the Tennessee River. "Tomorrow," Johnston grimly predicted, "we will water our horses in Tennessee River."

Alert Federals in the forward camps of the Army of the Tennessee, from sergeants all the way up to brigadier generals, had indeed detected the approach of Johnston's army and even exchanged shots with the Rebels in the days leading up to the battle, but Grant did not expect an attack. His headquarters were twelve miles downstream at the town of Savannah in order to make the earliest possible contact with Buell, whose leading elements on the morning of April 6 were still a full day's march from Pittsburg Landing. For the situation at the actual encampment at Pittsburg Landing, Grant was depending on Brigadier General William T. Sherman (West Point, 1840), the only professionally trained officer among the commanders of the five divisions encamped there. Since the camps of Sherman's division were among the farthest inland from the landing and Sherman said no significant Rebel force was nearer than Corinth, Grant took it at that.

In retrospect Sherman's stubborn refusal to believe a major Confederate army was nearby despite abundant evidence to the contrary brought in by members of his and a neighboring division seems incredible. Yet it was common for an army to experience harassment from light forces of the enemy. The question was whether heavy formations of the enemy lay behind the skirmishers one encountered, and the only way to find out was to probe forward aggressively, driving back the enemy's cavalry as well as his infantry skirmishers until encountering enough resistance to reveal that the enemy was present in force. It was just that sort of reconnaissance in force that Halleck had forbidden Grant and his officers to use, thus leaving them effectively blind to the approach of Johnston's army. They had to guess, and Sherman guessed wrong.

THE BATTLE OF SHILOH

Well before dawn on Sunday, April 6, Johnston's troops filed into their positions for the assault. Johnston's plan was based on the crude maps he possessed. The area where the Army of the Tennessee was encamped was a plateau about fifty feet above the level of the river, mostly wooded, cut near its edges with deep ravines, bounded on the north by the swampy bottomland of Owl Creek and its tributary Snake Creek and on the south by the equally swampy bottoms of Lick Creek. Johnston's maps showed the creeks running roughly from west to east, at right angles to the river, and this led him to assume that the Union line would run north and south and face west. In fact, the creeks ran from southwest to northeast, and the line of Union encampments ran more or less east and west, facing south. Johnston planned to place a large corps under Major General Braxton Bragg (West Point, 1837) on the right, with two smaller corps on the center and left and one in reserve. With this unbalanced formation he would strike heavily against the southern end of the Union line, turn it to the north, and then roll up Grant's army and drive it into a pocket formed by the swamps of Snake and Owl creeks.

Johnston let Beauregard handle the deployment of the troops for battle, and Beauregard arranged them differently, stretching each corps all the way across the battlefield and arranging the four of them one behind the other. It was the worst possible arrangement since it meant that as soon as successive corps moved up to help their comrades in front, their divisions and brigades would become mixed, and troops would be fighting alongside strangers and under officers they did not know. Johnston apparently discovered this after the troops were already in position. He was talking to Beauregard and other officers, who were once again trying to convince him to call off the whole thing, when firing broke out at the front. "The battle has opened, gentlemen," Johnston announced, "it is too late for us to change our dispositions."

What triggered the fighting was a Union patrol moving forward to investigate the suspicious sounds of movement in the woods in front of them. The fighting quickly became general and spread across the entire front as the Confederates launched their attack. On the Union left the completely green division of Brigadier General Benjamin S. Prentiss, an Illinois Democratic politician, fought for about an hour and then collapsed under the weight of Confederate numbers. Johnston, who was with the troops attacking Prentiss, interpreted this development in light of his imperfect maps and concluded that he had crushed Grant's flank and trapped him against the swamps to the north. "That checkmates them!" he exclaimed.

Not quite, but the collapse of Prentiss's division had certainly done the momentarily leaderless Union army no good. Johnston could have scored big gains by pursuing the fugitive fragments of Prentiss's division, but believing he faced no more threat in the direction they were fleeing (due north), Johnston diverted several brigades toward the west, where heavy firing could be heard through the forests.

That firing came from Sherman's division, holding the right end of the Union front line. After his poor showing in not anticipating the Confederate attack, Sherman was turning in the performance of a lifetime, rallying his troops and directing their defense of a low ridge on which stood a Methodist meetinghouse called Shiloh Church. He was slightly wounded and had several horses shot out from under him, but his men commented on his fierce but steady demeanor and calm, clearheaded instructions as key to their prolonged stand.

Grant had been about to eat breakfast at his Savannah headquarters when the sound of firing reached him from more than twelve miles away. He stopped with his coffee cup halfway to his lips, paused, set it down, and ordered his staff to join him on the steamboat that was kept tied up with a full head of steam, ready for his use. They raced up the river, pausing at Crump's Landing, halfway to Pittsburg, to alert Lew Wallace's division, which was encamped there. Wallace said he had heard the guns and had his men under arms. Grant instructed him to stand by for orders and then raced on up the river. Arriving at Pittsburg, Grant mounted up and rode to the top of the bluffs. The roar of battle that met him told him this was the big one. He immediately sent a messenger back downstream with orders for Wallace to march for the battlefield at once.

Back out on the fighting lines, Confederates had finally driven Sherman off Shiloh Ridge, but his division fell back in good order to the next ridge, where McClernand's division moved up to join him. Unfortunately the political general positioned his line incorrectly, weakening the fighting power of its veteran regiments. With the troops Johnston had diverted from the other end of the line, Sherman and McClernand were now facing almost three-fourths of the Confederate army, well over twice the roughly fifteen thousand men in those two divisions. The new position collapsed quickly, and the Federals reeled back another half mile or so. They rallied, and Sherman led them forward in a counterattack. The battle seesawed back and forth, with Sherman more often forced to give ground, but his division and McClernand's were holding the attention of the bulk of Johnston's army.

Between Sherman and the river, the divisions of William H. L. Wallace, a Mexican War veteran, and Stephen A. Hurlbut, another Illinois politician, moved into line, halting the renewed Confederate push on the Union left. Prentiss and a few of his fugitives fell in with the fresh troops in a position that ran between thickets along a country lane and through a peach orchard, pink with blossoms. Yet Grant now had no reserves left at Pittsburg, and his line was not long enough to touch the Tennessee River on its left. There a succession of rugged ravines, a single brigade of Union troops, and the artillery support of two timber-clad gunboats in the river were all that prevented the Confederates from pouring around Grant's left flank and cutting his army off from the landing.

With growing anxiety, Grant and his staff wondered where Lew Wallace was. In fact, he had taken the wrong road, perhaps through some failure in the communication of orders or from a misunderstanding of the situation on the battlefield. When subsequent couriers informed him of his error, Wallace proceeded at a steady but cautious pace that would have been very commendable for an ordinary march but was not at all the desperate rush the circumstances demanded. Grant never forgave Wallace.

Johnston's army was unevenly distributed. Heavy forces still pressed Sherman on the west end of the battlefield, though Johnston had pulled several brigades back to the east side, near the river, to strengthen the push against the surprisingly stubborn Yankees there. In the center, little more than a single Confederate brigade doggedly but vainly attempted to drive a brigade of Iowans out of a patch of thickets that came to be known as the Hornets' Nest.

Frustrated at the failure of his troops to dislodge Hurlbut's men from the peach orchard, Johnston personally rallied a regiment and led it halfway across the intervening cotton field in another charge. Turning back, he watched from the rear as his men swept on toward the peach orchard. To a staff officer he commented jubilantly about a Union bullet that had grazed the bottom of his foot, cutting his boot sole but leaving him unscathed.

"They almost tripped me up that time," he joked. He may not have realized it yet, but another bullet had torn through the back of his calf, slicing open a major blood vessel. Had the blood not been flowing into his intact boot, those around him would have seen a steady stream of it pouring to the ground. A few minutes later an aide found him reeling in the saddle and helped him to the ground in a sheltered spot. Minutes later he was dead. In his pocket was a tourniquet that could have saved his life. The time was about 2:30 p.m.

The Confederate attacks continued. The lone Union brigade in the brakes along the river finally gave way. Next in line, Hurlbut had to fall back, giving up the peach orchard. As he retreated, his division broke up in a confused stampede. More than two thousand of William Wallace's men, along with Prentiss and a handful of his, were cut off and captured as the Federal right collapsed. Wallace himself lay on the field, shot through the head.

Hurlbut's men rallied on a line of artillery Grant and his staff had put together on the last ridge overlooking Pittsburg Landing, and there Sherman's and McClernand's divisions joined them. The sun was dipping toward the western horizon as the Confederates prepared for one more attack, this one aimed at Grant's last possible line of defense. Lew Wallace's division was still slogging through the Owl Creek swamps. Buell's troops were struggling over roads almost as muddy on the east bank of the Tennessee, and even now his lead regiments were nearing the river, where steamboats would ferry them across to Pittsburg Landing. Grant's tired soldiers would have to receive the attack without the help of reinforcements. Then word passed along the Confederate lines that Beauregard had called a halt for the night. Grant had plenty of artillery, and his troops, though tired, were determined. He would probably have stopped a final push, but history will never know.

Grant's staff thought he would withdraw the army across the Tennessee during the night. Instead he made plans to strike back. When morning came on April 7, Grant's army, strengthened at last by Lew Wallace's division and three divisions of Buell's troops, went over to the attack and by afternoon had driven Beauregard's Confederates back through the abandoned and ransacked Union camps to about the place where the fighting had started the previous morning. With his army exhausted and near the point of collapse, Beauregard ordered a retreat back to Corinth. Grant's army was too spent to pursue.

The Battle of Shiloh was over. It introduced the country to bloodshed on a scale out of proportion to anything it had known before. Casualties had been almost exactly even, with the exception of the extra two thousand Federals captured late in the afternoon of April 6. Just over 1,700 men had been killed on each side, with another eight thousand Federals and eight thousand

Confederates wounded. The death toll from the two days of fighting along the Tennessee River quadrupled that of Bull Run and exceeded total U.S. battle deaths in the entire War of 1812 and Mexican War combined. Shortly before his death more than two decades later, Grant reflected on the events that transpired at Shiloh. "Up to the battle of Shiloh I, as well as thousands of other citizens, believed that the rebellion against the Government would collapse suddenly and soon, if a decisive victory could be gained over any of its armies." The two days of carnage along the Tennessee began to change his mind. Shiloh was a harbinger of the length and cost of the conflict that was then only just beginning.[2]

In the wake of the battle, Halleck arrived at Pittsburg Landing as planned and took command. The rest of Buell's and all of Pope's army arrived, swelling Union numbers there to more than one hundred thousand men. Halleck shelved Grant in a meaningless assignment as second in command, and Grant, who was receiving severe criticism in the newspapers for being surprised at Shiloh, contemplated resigning but thought better of it. Halleck advanced his ponderous army toward Corinth at a snail's pace, entrenching at the end of each day's short advance. Beauregard could find no way to stop him but did manage to get his army out of the path of Halleck's military glacier as it approached Corinth, leaving the Federals a hollow victory and a dusty and disease-ridden northeastern Mississippi rail junction town that they occupied May 30. By that time, the war was heating up on other fronts as well. On April 23, a U.S. Navy fleet ran the forts blocking passage up the Mississippi River from the Gulf of Mexico and the next day captured New Orleans without a fight, thus taking possession of the largest city and financial capital of the South. And in far-off Virginia, McClellan finally launched his grand campaign.

5

MCCLELLAN'S GREAT CAMPAIGN

MCCLELLAN'S PLANS
AND THE NAVAL BATTLE
OF HAMPTON ROADS

The winter months of 1862 saw Grant and Foote tear open the center of the Confederacy and advance into its heartland. That spring Albert Sidney Johnston first planned and then died trying to carry out his desperate effort to throw back the Yankees at Shiloh. All the while McClellan continued to plan and prepare for his grand offensive in the East. As the months passed without action in the East, Lincoln grew concerned. The Radical Republicans in Congress and their allies grew increasingly impatient. Among the most impatient were Secretary of War Stanton and the members of the Joint Committee on the Conduct of the War.

In response to Lincoln's General War Order Number One and his addendum singling out the Army of the Potomac and directing that it advance on the direct route to Richmond via the Rebel encampment near Centerville, McClellan had finally relented and revealed to the president his plan. He would land the army at the town of Urbanna, Virginia, he explained, near the mouth of the Rappahannock. From there it would march west along that river so as to come between Johnston and Richmond, cutting off the Confederate army and forcing its surrender. Then the Rebels would have to abandon Richmond. As McClellan saw it, this would win the war in one brilliant stroke with minimal bloodshed.

Lincoln reluctantly accepted McClellan's program, though he doubted that the plan would really yield such grand results. As he saw it, the Rebels were going to put up a scrap before they gave up Richmond or their cause. McClellan would have a battle to fight, whether he did it at Centerville or on the Rappahannock. Centerville was more convenient. Nevertheless, Lincoln acquiesced in the plans of the renowned professional soldier and allowed McClellan to continue with his preparations and leave the Army of the Potomac idle in its camps on Washington's Birthday.

Yet the president continued to have doubts about the way his dashing young general was running the army. For one thing, the Army of the Potomac now consisted of twelve divisions, too many for army headquarters to maneuver efficiently. The obvious solution was to organize the divisions into four corps, an arrangement first devised in France three-quarters of a century before. Napoleon had organized his army in four corps, and it had been one of the keys to his success. McClellan did not wish to do so because, he said, he wanted to see how his generals did in battle before he elevated four of them to the more responsible position of corps commander. It may not have entered into McClellan's motivation, but it was also a known fact that the army's senior generals were mostly Republicans, while the more junior division commanders were Democrats and McClellan favorites because their commander shared their political beliefs. These Democratic favorites would have to accomplish something in battle before McClellan could dare to promote them over their Republican seniors.

Of more sinister import, as time passed and McClellan did not move against the Rebels, some influential people in Washington began to question his commitment to the Union cause. Could it be that McClellan did not attack because he did not wish to see the rebellion crushed in a way that might damage the institution of slavery? And what of his Urbanna Plan? If it put McClellan between Johnston and Richmond, it would also put Johnston between McClellan and Washington—and a good deal closer to the latter than McClellan would be to the Rebel capital. Could that be deliberate? Lincoln did not quite share their darkest suspicions, but he did find the matter troubling.

On March 8 Lincoln met with McClellan and the division commanders of the Army of the Potomac. The generals supported McClellan's plan, and a somewhat reassured Lincoln continued his tentative support. He did, however, issue General War Order Number Two, stipulating that McClellan must leave in and around Washington enough troops to guarantee it against Rebel capture. The following day, without consulting McClellan, the president also issued an order organizing the Army of the Potomac into four corps and appointing its four senior generals, three of whom were Republicans, to command them. McClellan was disgusted at this interference with his genius, but he had no choice but to acquiesce.

Two days later came a further blow. Lincoln removed McClellan from the position of general in chief of all the Union armies. McClellan had previously held that job along with his position as commander of the Army of the Potomac. In removing McClellan as general in chief, Lincoln explained that in his campaign on the Virginia coast, McClellan would be far from Washington. Communications would have to go a long way around to reach him—down the Rappahannock, up Chesapeake Bay, and then up the Potomac. In addition, with the Army of the Potomac actively engaging the enemy, it would be better for McClellan to focus his attention on its operations. All of this was true, but removing McClellan as general in chief was certainly not a vote of confidence, and the general knew it. The Young Napoleon fumed and raged against Lincoln "the gorilla" in letters to his wife and conversations with his friends, but he could do nothing about it. This was in any case turning out to be an exceptionally bad week for "Little Mac," as his soldiers affectionately called him (behind his back).

On March 8, the same day that Lincoln had held his conference with McClellan and the other generals, the Confederacy had unveiled its long-rumored wonder weapon. When Virginia had seceded back in April 1861, rebellious Virginia militia had seized the U.S. Navy yard at Norfolk. The officer in charge of defending or evacuating the post had not done a very good job. His biggest blunder was failing to extract the most powerful ship in the yard—and one of the five most powerful in the U.S. Navy—the fifty-gun steam frigate *Merrimack*. Two hundred seventy-five feet long and thirty-eight and a half feet wide, the *Merrimack* displaced 3,200 tons and drew twenty-four feet of water. She had been laid up at Norfolk for the repair of her unreliable steam engine. When it became apparent that there would not be time to get her out of the yard before the Rebels took over, retreating U.S. forces set fire to her on their way out. Since she had been carrying no ammunition at the time, *Merrimack* burned down to the waterline and then sank.

The Confederates raised the hulk and began to rebuild her not as the graceful frigate she had once been but as something much more modern and deadly. The idea of putting iron plates on ships was not entirely new. Designer Samuel M. Pook and builder James B. Eads were by late summer 1861 working on the river gunboats that would later take Fort Henry. The French navy had seven years earlier built a class of armored flat-bottomed barges called floating batteries, self-propelled by steam engines at very low speed and designed for shore bombardment in coastal waters. In 1858 the French had laid down what would become the world's first ironclad oceangoing warship, *La Gloire*, commissioned in the summer of 1860. The British had commissioned their answer to *La Gloire* the following year, the nine-thousand-ton, iron-hulled monster *Warrior*.

What Confederate naval captain French Forrest and Lieutenant Catesby ap Roger Jones planned to make of the hulk of *Merrimack* was modest by comparison. Following plans drawn up by Lieutenant John M. Brooke, CSN, Forrest and Jones built a weather deck where the *Merrimack*'s surviving hull stopped at the waterline, and atop it they built a casemate extending most of its length and all of its breadth. The casemate's sides were made of twenty-four inches of oak and pine covered with four inches of iron and sloped steeply inward. Firing out through narrow gun ports in the casemate were ten heavy cannon. To her bow the builders affixed an iron beak for ramming. The resultant warship looked like a barn roof floating downriver in a flood. It was sluggish and hard to maneuver, and its theoretical top speed of nine knots was provided by the *Merrimack*'s condemned engine, which had not been improved by several weeks' immersion in salt water. The Confederates christened their new naval behemoth *Virginia*.

Word of what the Confederates were up to at Norfolk had leaked out, as such information almost invariably did during the Civil War, and the U.S. Navy Department had sought designs for ironclads of its own, finally selecting three. One was the big, bluff, 3,500-ton frigate *New Ironsides*. Another, USS *Galena*, was a seven-hundred-ton sloop of war with an experimental system of armor plates. The third was something absolutely revolutionary.

The work of Swedish American engineer John Ericsson, USS *Monitor* displaced one thousand tons and rode almost entirely below the surface so that its main deck, like the *Virginia*'s, was barely above the water. There the similarity stopped. Whereas *Virginia*'s deck was mostly taken up with its armored casemate, *Monitor*'s was empty save for a tiny, boxlike pilothouse forward and a squat, twenty-one-foot-diameter cylindrical turret amidships housing *Monitor*'s entire battery of two eleven-inch Dahlgren guns, the largest guns that had ever gone to sea up to that time. *Monitor*'s hull was made of five-eighths-inch iron but was out of reach of enemy shot below the waterline. Her turret was protected by eight inches of iron plate. A steam engine drove her at speeds up to eight knots by means of the marine screw Ericsson had invented. The world had never seen the like of her. The Navy Department had it doubts but agreed to acquire the craft, provided Ericsson committed himself to reimburse the full cost if his strange design proved a failure. Other critics noted skeptically that the vessel looked like "a tin can on a shingle."

The North's industrial superiority would soon make itself felt in the production of saltwater ironclads even as it already was out west in the building of the ironclad river gunboats. Parts for the *Monitor* were forged in nine different foundries and brought together to make the novel ship in only 120 days, while the *New Ironsides* and the *Galena* were still weeks or even months from completion. Yet the Confederates had the jump on Union builders with the *Virginia*, and the Rebel builders had had an engine, such as it was, as well as half a hull to begin with. In early March the hastily completed *Monitor* was still making a difficult voyage down to the Virginia coast from its birthplace in Brooklyn (*Monitor*'s low freeboard gave it questionable seaworthiness) when the Confederates at Norfolk decided the time had come for *Virginia* to make her debut.

On March 8 *Virginia* sortied from Norfolk under the command of Captain Franklin Buchanan and entered the body of water known as Hampton Roads, where the James River emptied into Chesapeake Bay and where Flag Officer Louis M. Goldsborough's North Atlantic Blockading Squadron rode at anchor. *Virginia* first attacked the sloop-of-war *Cumberland*, riddling her with shells that slaughtered her crew and covered her decks with gore and then ramming her while *Cumberland*'s own return fire bounced off *Virginia*'s sloping casemate, doing little damage. In the finest tradition of the U.S. Navy, *Cumberland*'s gunners kept firing as long as their guns were above water. One hundred twenty-one men went down with the ship. So too did *Virginia*'s iron beak, which had broken off in *Cumberland*, creating a slight leak forward in *Virginia*.

With *Cumberland* dispatched, *Virginia* turned next to the frigate *Congress*, whose commander, seeing the fate of *Cumberland*, attempted to maneuver his ship into water too shallow for the *Virginia* to follow. His trick backfired, however, when *Congress* herself ran aground. *Virginia* could not approach, but she could and did stand off and batter *Congress* with her guns. With scores of men dead on deck, including the commander, the senior surviving officer surrendered. Unable to take possession of his prize because of rifle fire from Union infantrymen ashore (part of the garrison of Fort Monroe, *Virginia*, which had remained in Union hands since the outbreak of the war and had recently been reinforced), Buchanan ordered his men to bombard it with red-hot shot, projectiles heated in a vessel's furnace and designed to set its opponent afire. They worked, and *Congress* burned on through the evening and well into the night before the flames reached her magazines and she exploded. One hundred ten men of the U.S. Navy were lost with her.

Next in line for destruction was USS *Minnesota*, one of the navy's five biggest frigates, of which *Merrimack* had been one in her previous life. *Minnesota* had been coming up to join the fight but had also run aground and looked like easy prey. The tide was falling, however, and *Virginia* could not close in to ship-killing range. Light was failing too, and *Virginia* had sustained various minor damage, none of it threatening but all adding up to a nuisance—here an iron plate loose, there a man wounded by fragments coming in through a gun port. The smokestack was riddled so that the boiler fires drew poorly, and the ship became even slower. There was also the leak where the beak had broken off. Buchanan himself was wounded, and his executive officer, Catesby ap Roger Jones, decided to take *Virginia* back to port, make temporary repairs, and come out to finish what was left of the Yankee fleet the next morning.

That night the *Monitor* steamed into Hampton Roads, still lit by the blazing *Congress*, and on orders from the senior naval officer afloat, anchored alongside the *Minnesota*. The next morning when the *Virginia* came out, *Monitor* stood out to meet her. For the next several hours the two ironclads blasted away at each other at close range, their sides sometimes actually touching, but neither ship's guns could pierce the other's armor, though each suffered minor damage. A shell penetrated the *Monitor*'s pilothouse, wounding her commander, Lieutenant John L. Worden. His executive officer took over and prepared to continue the fight, but by that time *Virginia* was retiring toward Norfolk.

Both sides claimed victory, but though Union losses had been greater, the U.S. Navy had achieved its strategic purpose at Hampton Roads, maintaining the blockade and containing the *Virginia*. Still, the continued existence of a weapon like *Virginia* presented problems for the Union, especially for McClellan, whose strategic ideas focused on approaching Richmond via Chesapeake Bay.

MCCLELLAN TARGETS THE
VIRGINIA PENINSULA

News of the Battle of Hampton Roads and the appearance of the *Virginia* complicated McClellan's strategic problems. So too did a simultaneous Confederate movement in northern Virginia. On March 9, the day the *Monitor* and the *Virginia* slugged it out in Hampton Roads, Joseph Johnston put his Confederate army on the retreat from its positions near Centerville and fell back all the way to the south bank of the Rappahannock. Though the retreat turned over several hundred square miles of northern Virginia to Union control and would have allowed McClellan's army to advance a good thirty miles closer to Richmond, if he had wanted to go that way, it completely destroyed his plan for a landing at Urbanna that would turn the Confederate position at Centerville and made it that much harder for McClellan to resist Lincoln's hints that he ought to adopt a direct overland approach to Richmond.

But resist he would. On March 13 McClellan got his corps and division commanders to agree to his new plan to land not at Urbanna but rather on the peninsula between the York and James rivers, using the Union enclave at Fort Monroe, scene of the recent naval battle. The *Virginia's* presence at Norfolk would make the operation riskier and preclude the kind of easy access up the James River that the U.S. Navy could otherwise have offered. Every misgiving that applied to the Urbanna Plan applied a fortiori to the proposed Peninsula Campaign, but with McClellan and his generals presenting a united front, Lincoln felt he had to accept their recommendation. After once again cautioning McClellan in writing about the absolute necessity of leaving adequate troops in the Washington area to ensure the security of the capital, Lincoln gave his approval to the general's new scheme. Four days later, on March 17, McClellan began embarking his troops at Alexandria, Virginia, for their short voyage down the Chesapeake to Fort Monroe.

Meanwhile, Union troops had advanced and temporarily taken over the abandoned Confederate camps before returning to their own bases in the Washington area. Newspapermen who accompanied the troops found a number of peeled logs, painted black and placed in gun embrasures in the Confederate fortifications to give the appearance to Union observers at a distance that the Confederates had more cannon than they actually did. These "Quaker Guns," as they were quickly dubbed in the press, suggested that McClellan had for months been held at bay by an enemy force of such extreme weakness that its cannon were mere wooden dummies. The logs became a subject of ridicule of McClellan in the public and especially among the Radical Republicans in Congress, who, according to their dispositions, became either increasingly contemptuous of the general's ability or increasingly suspicious about his allegiance.

Though Johnston's retreat had come as a severe blow to McClellan, it was not correspondingly welcome in Richmond. Johnston had enjoyed a sterling reputation in the prewar U.S. Army, and Davis prided himself as a former officer and secretary of war on knowing the best officers. He remained unshakable in his belief that Johnston possessed enormous skill, but he was becoming increasingly frustrated with that general's propensity for precipitate retreat. During the early days of the war, prior to Bull Run, Johnston had been stationed at Harpers Ferry and had bombarded Richmond with requests to be ordered to retreat. Recently he had started making noises about possibly having to abandon Manassas Junction and fall back behind the Rappahannock. Davis had admitted that such a step might become necessary, but he had counseled that Johnston make thorough preparations for any withdrawal so that valuable stocks of supplies and equipment would not be lost.

Johnston did the opposite, retreating suddenly and with no further warning to Davis or to the officers in charge of logistics. Immense stocks of baggage were left behind. Worse, the army abandoned mountainous supply depots that had taken the Confederate commissary department all winter to build up. Throughout the rest of the war the Confederate commissary department in Virginia never really caught up with demand after that loss. The last Rebel cavalrymen to pull out of the abandoned camps had orders to set fire to the supplies, and as the never-overly-well-fed Rebel soldiers turned their backs to the enemy and marched south, they were tantalized by the smell of sizzling bacon, wafting far and wide across the Virginia countryside from the burning supply depot. Davis was as disgusted as his soldiers, but he maintained Johnston in command and continued to believe he could do great things as a general if only he could be motivated to fight.

In reality, Johnston had begun to build a well-deserved reputation as the war's foremost retreater. Lacking nerve, he hoped for a grand battle in which his Rebel troops would man entrenched positions and cut down waves of blue-clad attackers. Unfortunately for the Confederacy, that fantasy never materialized. Johnston lacked the skill and audacity required to goad an opposing commander to order such an attack, and when his tactical dream failed to materialize, he continued to cede ground to the Union, both during the Peninsula Campaign and throughout the remainder of the war.

When Lincoln had relieved McClellan of duty as general in chief of all the Union armies, he had appointed no other general to fill that role. Henceforth he would do his best, with the aid of fellow lawyer, Secretary of War Stanton, to "boss the job" himself, as he put it. Two days later, Jefferson Davis had appointed Robert E. Lee to fulfill the role of general in chief, at least nominally, for the Confederate armies. Davis, who unlike Lincoln had an extensive military background, was confident that he could direct the war himself, but he wanted the assistance and advice of Lee, a former engineer officer whom Davis seemed to consider rather bookish and well suited to a desk job. Davis would have been well advised to rely heavily on Lee or another officer as a sort of chief of staff since he tended to attempt to micromanage the Confederate war effort in a way that proved detrimental both to it and to his own health.

So far, Lee was not having a very good war. He had served as Virginia's top general prior to its official incorporation into the Confederacy and had organized the Virginia forces, but that role had kept him on the sidelines while Beauregard and Johnston won laurels at Bull Run. Then Davis had assigned him to try to repair Confederate fortunes in western Virginia, but nothing could save the Confederate cause there, and Lee had returned to Richmond branded a failure in the press. His next assignment was to oversee and inspect the defenses of the Carolina and Georgia coastline. There too the task was more or less impossible, as the Federals with their naval superiority could make successful landings at almost any given place along the coast. Lee made the best arrangements he could before being called back to Richmond to take on the new role as what really amounted to a top adviser and assistant to the president in the direction of the war.

THE BATTLE OF KERNSTOWN AND THE BEGINNING OF THE PENINSULA CAMPAIGN

One hundred thirty miles northwest of where Lee was in Richmond and eighty due west of Washington, Major General Thomas J. "Stonewall" Jackson, of Bull Run fame, commanded a small division of about 3,500 Confederate troops in the Shenandoah Valley. Jackson had had a frustrating winter. An expedition he led to take the town of Romney, Virginia (now West Virginia), from the Federals had resulted in much suffering for his troops in the bitter cold. Some of his officers had complained to Richmond, triggering an order from Davis to withdraw from Romney and a corresponding threat from Jackson to resign. His friends had smoothed the matter over, and now Jackson was the Confederacy's man in the Shenandoah.

The Virginia iteration of the Great Valley of the Appalachians, the Shenandoah Valley comprised during the Civil War a curious feature of Virginia geography and culture. Bounded on the east by the Blue Ridge, on the west by the Alleghenies, and on the north by the Potomac, the Shenandoah

General Thomas J. "Stonewall" Jackson

was the breadbasket of Virginia, a land of agricultural plenty, faithfully maintained by thrifty, industrious farmers, many of whom were members of a pacifist German brethren sect who had migrated down the Great Valley from Pennsylvania. They gathered on Sunday mornings in plain, unadorned houses of worship, without steeples, and their insistence on baptism by immersion had led irreverent neighbors to nickname them Dunkers. Naturally the valley also had its share of Baptists, Methodists, and Presbyterians. It had fewer slaves than the rest of Virginia but was generally still committed to the twin causes of slavery and the Confederacy.

The valley had hitherto been a backwater of the war. In 1859 John Brown had done his part to help trigger the war at Harpers Ferry, at the extreme lower end of the valley (in the Shenandoah Valley, "lower" referred to the direction of the Shenandoah River, which flows generally southwest to northeast). Later Johnston had given Patterson the slip in the valley to get his troops to Manassas in time to help win the Battle of Bull Run. So far the valley had seen only minor fighting.

Now Jackson's orders from Johnston directed him to take action to prevent the Yankees from sending any more troops from northern Virginia down to the peninsula. Believing the area reasonably well pacified, Union commanders were indeed pulling units away to add to McClellan's massive army taking ship for the Chesapeake. In late March, Jackson got word that the Federals had pulled most of their troops out of the village of Kernstown, near

Winchester in the lower valley, about thirty miles from Harpers Ferry. Supposedly only a small Union rear guard remained at Kernstown, and Jackson decided that the situation offered him the perfect opportunity to carry out his orders by attacking and destroying the Union outpost there, forcing the Federals to halt their movement toward the peninsula and turn back to deal with him.

Jackson struck on March 23, but he was in for a surprise. His information had been wrong, and the Federals in Kernstown numbered nine thousand men under the command of Mexican War veteran Brigadier General James Shields. Jackson's badly outnumbered troops put up a game fight, but they had no chance of winning, and Stonewall had to retreat, something he very much disliked doing but had to continue for most of the rest of the month, falling back far up the valley. Despite the drubbing he had taken from Shields, Jackson had nevertheless succeeded in accomplishing his strategic goal. His aggressiveness at Kernstown convinced Lincoln that more troops were needed in that sector. He halted the movement of troops out of the Shenandoah, ordered others back to the valley, and began to contemplate anew the potential vulnerability of Washington.

As more and more units of McClellan's vast army arrived on the peninsula, it became increasingly obvious that the Federals were preparing a major campaign toward Richmond from that direction. McClellan may not have been the war's most aggressive general, but his strategic vision, in a narrowly military sense that ignored political realities, was nevertheless excellent. The presence of his army on the peninsula posed a desperate threat to the Confederate capital. Standing between McClellan and Richmond were about fifteen thousand Confederate soldiers under the command of Major General John B. Magruder (West Point, 1830). McClellan seemed the only military man in Virginia that spring who did not see that his massive army could have run over Magruder's corporal's guard any time it chose to do so. Magruder certainly saw it and frequently reminded the Richmond authorities of his—and their—danger.

Davis needed little reminder. On March 27 he called a conference at his residence, Richmond's Brockenbrough Mansion, so that he, Lee, Johnston, and current Secretary of War (the Confederacy's third) George W. Randolph could discuss the Confederacy's proper response to the threat. Of the four main participants in the conference, only Davis was not a Virginian. The discussion continued throughout the day and late into the night, sometimes growing passionate. Johnston believed that the correct policy was to withdraw Confederate forces all the way up the peninsula, virtually to the gates of Rich-

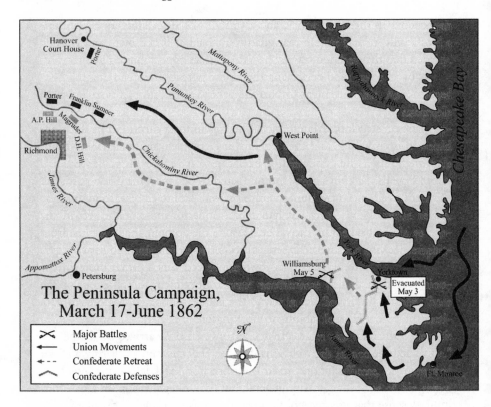

The Peninsula Campaign,
March 17–June 1862

	Major Battles
	Union Movements
	Confederate Retreat
	Confederate Defenses

mond, and there throw every soldier the Confederacy could possibly spare into a showdown battle while the enemy was as far as possible from his base of supplies at the foot of the peninsula.

Lee sensed in Johnston's proposal a willingness not only to retreat but also to give up Richmond in the name of saving his army. Lee disagreed vehemently, arguing correctly that Richmond must be held and that the place to do so was as far down the peninsula as possible. Beginning the process of stopping the enemy there would open the possibility for potential counterstrokes as the Federals worked their way slowly toward the Confederate capital. Davis had to consider that coming on the heels of a winter and spring of Confederate disasters from the Atlantic coast to the Tennessee River, the loss of Richmond might demoralize southern whites to the point of giving up the fight. Whatever his thinking, Davis sided with Lee and ordered Johnston to take his army to the peninsula and join Magruder near Yorktown, where a line of Confederate entrenchments spanned the peninsula, and there contest

The "White House of the Confederacy"—the official wartime residence of Confederate President Jefferson Davis.

every foot of ground with McClellan as the latter began his expected advance. Johnston returned sullenly to his command. As he later confessed, he had already made up his mind to retreat fairly rapidly up the peninsula and thus force his policy rather than Lee's on an unwilling Davis.

McClellan and most of his army were on the peninsula and preparing to advance by the beginning of April, but McClellan still had himself convinced that he was up against twice his numbers of Rebels. Where the Confederates would conceivably have found that many troops is a riddle to which Jefferson Davis would undoubtedly have liked to know the answer. Nevertheless McClellan remained convinced that only his superior skill could overcome the Rebel hordes and therefore that he must be very careful. His state of mind grew worse when on April 3 Lincoln informed him by dispatch from Washington that he had decided to withhold one of the four corps of the Army of the Potomac, McDowell's First Corps, for the protection of Washington.

Back when Lincoln had first approved the Urbanna plan, he had asked the generals what would be the minimum number of troops necessary to ensure the safety of Washington, and they had given him a figure. Lincoln had then stipulated to McClellan that that number of men needed to be in and around the capital. McClellan had agreed but had included in his count troops stationed in places like the Shenandoah Valley. They did perform a certain function for the protection of the capital, but they were not what Lincoln and the generals had had in mind. When Lincoln learned of McClellan's creative bookkeeping with troop strengths, he had decided to detach McDowell so as to make up the necessary minimum protection for Washington.

McClellan was already bitter about what he conceived as Lincoln's nonsupport and interference with his campaign, and this event made him more so. Ever afterward McClellan, along with his defenders down to the present day, argued that the loss of McDowell's forty thousand men was the undoing of the Peninsula Campaign. If not for that, Little Mac would insist, Richmond would have fallen and the war ended. To be sure, Davis, Lee, and other top Confederates dreaded the possibility that McDowell's command would join McClellan and rejoiced to see that it was staying in northern Virginia. Whether McClellan could actually have supplied an army as big as he would have had with McDowell's troops on the peninsula is open to question. As the campaign developed, the little more than one hundred thousand men whom McClellan did have there taxed the ability of his supply personnel and the single-track Richmond & York River Railroad to the utmost. Aside from that, as Lincoln was to learn to his sorrow, McClellan's invariable habit was to respond to reinforcements by claiming that his opponent had just received twice as many men and that he therefore was still unable to accomplish anything.

Two days later, on April 5, McClellan's grand army arrived in front of Magruder's Yorktown defenses. Johnston's troops were still not in the lines, and McClellan had the opportunity by an aggressive assault to sweep the defenders aside and drive into Richmond before Johnston or anyone else could stop him. That was not McClellan's way of doing things. He wanted to avoid bloodshed as much as possible—among his own troops because he seemed to love the army almost too much and among the enemy because he hoped to set up a compromise peace in which the Rebels would be assuaged, after their moderate military chastisement, and slavery would be saved. For him, avoiding casualties was also a matter of conceit. He would demonstrate his superior skill by deftly taking Richmond with negligible loss of life by means of the scientific methods of siegecraft. Therefore, with more than one hundred thousand men, he settled down to besiege Magruder's fifteen thousand men at Yorktown, and while the siege went on, Johnston's troops arrived from the Rappahannock and filed into the Confederate trenches, closing the possibility of a quick and easy victory.

Siegecraft was as close to a science as anything in warfare and seemed to offer a high probability of success if one had the material wherewithal to apply it. Its rules were well established and would not fail unless the besieged did something unexpected. It was an exercise in military engineering, and McClellan had been an engineer officer, second in his class at West Point, where engineering was the chief component of the curriculum. Thus, day after day McClellan's troops labored on their siege works, building the entrenched batteries from which the siege guns would pound the Rebels into submission. His numerical superiority rendered an elaborate siege unnecessary. Speed and overwhelming force would have trumped pick and shovel and allowed him to overrun the Yorktown works. Yet the safety promised by the science of siegecraft suited McClellan perfectly.

THE SIEGE OF YORKTOWN AND THE BATTLE OF WILLIAMSBURG

McClellan's progress was slow enough to stir serious discontent in Washington, where Lincoln wrote to his general assuring him of his continuing support but warning him of political realities. "You must act," the president admonished. Yet if the fear that McClellan would not act in timely fashion weighed heavy in one capital, the fear that he would act raised even more alarm in the other, where the danger of the Confederate situation seemed to grow by the day. By late April Lincoln had become satisfied enough with the safety of Washington to send some of McDowell's troops to McClellan via the Chesapeake and to allow McDowell with the rest of his force to advance directly south toward Richmond with a view to linking up with McClellan on the northeastern side of the Confederate capital. That would give McClellan a numerical superiority approaching three to one.

To make matters worse for Davis, the Confederacy also faced the danger that its army would disintegrate at the moment the enemy campaign against Richmond began in earnest. One year ago when each president had called for troops, the Confederacy had enlisted its soldiers for one-year terms. That had been an advantage when Union troops enlisted for only ninety days, but now the Union army had been reborn, larger than ever, of three-year volunteers, while the terms of enlistment of the Confederates were quickly running out.

Many of the troops had no intention of reenlisting, feeling that they had done their part and it was now someone else's turn to serve in the army. Besides, war appeared less exciting from the Richmond defenses than it had at enlistment rallies back home or even in the army on the eve of First Manassas. It was an attitude that could have killed the Confederacy. Even if enough other men had been available to refill the ranks, the Confederacy could not afford to lose its experienced soldiers.

The government had seen this crisis coming months before and had tried to head it off in ways that were not always wise. One had been to offer to allow troops to reenlist in other branches of the service or to reorganize their companies, electing new officers. The result was at least the temporary disorganization of a number of regiments in exchange for an entirely inadequate number of reenlistments. By early April the Confederate congress was ready to take the final radical step. On April 9 it passed the first national conscription act in American history, a remarkable exercise of central power on the part of a government whose post hoc defenders would claim had been contending for state rights and limited government. One week after its passage, Davis signed the bill into law.

The Confederate conscription law required military service of every white man in the Confederacy between the ages of eighteen and thirty-five while allowing a drafted man to avoid service if he hired a non–draft-eligible substitute to go in his place. The following week the Confederate congress passed additional legislation providing exemption from the draft for various classes of persons—those necessary to the war effort, such as employees in iron foundries, and those necessary to civilian life at home, such as physicians, druggists, ministers, and teachers. The exemption of educators led to a sudden significant increase in the number of small schools throughout the South.

The draft would eventually reach into many southern homes to snatch away men who had not previously enlisted, but its real targets were the men who were already with the colors. They too were subject to mandatory military service, and the army knew just where to find them. In effect, the conscription law extended their terms of service for the duration of the war. Many expressed bitterness at this in their diaries and letters. They seethed at the unfairness and the loss of freedom, but most remained in the ranks and would continue to fight fiercely in every battle. The soldiers were not the only ones whom the new policy rankled. Some southern politicians raised the hew and cry of the infringement of state rights and civil liberties, but they were in the minority. Most Confederates, including most members of the Confederate congress, were willing to put up with whatever infringements of state rights or civil liberty might be necessary in order to win the war.

McClellan was nearly ready to open fire with his heavy siege guns when on May 3 Johnston quietly withdrew his army from the Yorktown entrenchments and took up his retreat toward Richmond. Union troops entered Yorktown the following day. Once again both commanders in chief were dissatisfied, Lincoln that McClellan had delayed for a month in front of Yorktown and then let Johnston escape, Davis that Johnston had abandoned Yorktown before he had to and done so precipitously enough to lose more supplies and valuable cannon.

On a rainy May 5, elements of the pursuing Army of the Potomac bumped up against a rear guard of Johnston's army under Major General James Longstreet (West Point, 1842) near the old Virginia colonial capital at Williamsburg. The Confederates had previously built a chain of small forts across the peninsula there, though several of them remained incomplete, and the Confederate troops who were now to defend them were unfamiliar with their layout. In a confused battle fought partially in the woods; partially in plowed, muddy fields; and entirely in a steady drizzling rain, troops of two of McClellan's most aggressive division commanders, Joseph Hooker (West Point, 1837) and Philip Kearny, clashed with Confederate divisions under Longstreet and his West Point classmate Daniel H. Hill, an irascible North Carolinian who happened to be Stonewall Jackson's brother-in-law. Each side scored some small successes, and the Confederates withdrew at the end of the day, to the satisfaction of all concerned.

In the days that followed, Johnston, with his fifty-five thousand men, continued to retreat more rapidly than Davis would have liked, and McClellan, with just over one hundred thousand men, continued to follow more slowly than Lincoln would have liked. Much to Davis's chagrin, Johnston's retreat exposed the Confederate naval base at Norfolk. Much to Lincoln's chagrin, McClellan made no move to take it. So Lincoln and Stanton took a steamer down to the peninsula and, acting behind the front lines where McClellan's and Johnston's armies confronted each other, directed troops to make the necessary movements to take Norfolk. It was the simplest of military operations but was perhaps as close as any sitting U.S. president has ever come to directing military operations in the field.

The fall of Norfolk left the *Virginia* without a home. She had made a couple of sorties since the great battle of March 8 but only to try to lure the *Monitor* into engaging her on the Confederate side of the water. She had not again ventured among the Union fleet, now well prepared and supported by

Monitor. In that sense, the U.S. Navy had succeeded in containing her, but the Rebel ironclad had absorbed most of the navy's attention within the Chesapeake area, depriving McClellan of the naval gunfire support he had wanted. The capture of Norfolk removed this thorn in the side of the Union effort on the peninsula.

Weighted down with armor and with her main deck almost flush with the surface of the water, *Virginia* was not at all seaworthy. Her captain's choices were therefore to steam out into Hampton Roads again and fight to the finish, or else to abandon his ship and destroy her to prevent her falling into the hands of the enemy. James River pilots suggested a third possibility. If *Virginia* were divested of all her guns and much of her armor, she might be able to ascend the James to where Confederate forts just below Richmond offered at least temporary safety. He decided to try, but several miles up the river, the *Virginia* stuck fast, and it became clear that the James did not have enough water to float her even in her lightened condition. With Union forces approaching and no means of fighting them, the captain opted to abandon ship and set fire to the *Virginia.* Like her second victim, the *Congress,* she exploded when the flames reached her magazines, two months and three days after her combat debut.

JACKSON'S SHENANDOAH VALLEY CAMPAIGN

Jackson and his division were still out in the Shenandoah Valley. Johnston, who theoretically commanded all Confederate troops in Virginia, wanted him to come to the peninsula at once. That was in keeping with Johnston's overall concept that every available man should be concentrated in front of Richmond at the earliest possible day. In Richmond itself, Davis was letting Lee oversee the action in secondary areas like the Shenandoah Valley while he focused his own attention on the critical situation on the peninsula and his increasing frustration with Johnston's unwillingness to stand his ground and give battle to the enemy. Lee had a somewhat different concept from that of Johnston with regard to the proper use of Jackson's division. He would want it for the direct defense of Richmond eventually, but first he thought it might be of more service in the valley.

Jackson thought so too and had been arguing as much in his recent dispatches to Johnston and to the Richmond authorities. Because Johnston was busy on the peninsula and not always easy to contact, Richmond—and in this case that meant Lee—took a more active role in directing operations in the Shenandoah than would otherwise have been the case. In response to Jackson's claim that if left in the valley and reinforced he could accomplish major results for the cause of the Confederacy, Lee persuaded Johnston to modify his orders. The large division of Major General Richard S. Ewell was soon on its way to the valley and Jackson's command.

With Ewell's division and his own, Jackson launched one of the war's most famous campaigns of rapid maneuver. The Shenandoah Valley was threatened by Federals approaching from two directions. Jackson needed to remove those threats and then create a situation in the valley that would prompt Union authorities to divert troops away from the current offensive against Richmond. One threat was from a Union force under Brigadier General Robert Milroy, advancing through western Virginia and threatening to enter the valley through one of the gaps in the Allegheny escarpment. Milroy was the advance guard of the command of John C. Frémont. A powerful political general was not such an easy thing to get rid of, and often removing him from one theater of the war meant introducing him into another. After removing Frémont from Missouri, Lincoln had assigned him to the mountains of western Virginia, as perhaps the place he could do the least damage. Opposing the advance of Milroy's six thousand Federals were about 2,800 Confederates under Brigadier General Edward Johnson.

The other threat to Confederate control of the Shenandoah Valley was from the Union force under the command of Major General Nathaniel P. Banks, a political general who was a former Speaker of the U.S. House of Representatives and, more recently, governor of Massachusetts. He had been gingerly following Jackson's retreat up the valley since the Battle of Kernstown but had completely lost contact with the Rebel force. Having reached Harrisonburg, he informed Washington that Jackson had left the valley for good and requested that his own force be ordered to march to join McClellan outside Richmond where the real action was going to take place. Washington ordered away one of his two divisions but left him with the other to guard the now apparently empty Shenandoah Valley.

Jackson left Ewell's 8,500 men to watch the clueless Banks while with the rest of his command, now numbering 7,200 men, he marched into the Alleghenies to team up with Johnson against Milroy. They met the Yankees on May 8 near the village of McDowell, and though the Federals fought well and the Confederates took more casualties than their foes, Jackson was victorious. He pursued the retreating Federals a few miles and then turned back to deal with Banks, taking most of Johnson's troops with him.

Banks, who now had only about six thousand troops in his own command, found himself facing Jackson, who, together with Ewell, now had seventeen thousand. The Union commander began a rapid retreat northward down the valley with Jackson in hot pursuit. Banks turned and prepared to make a stand at Strasburg, but on May 23 Jackson outmaneuvered him and captured the Union outpost at Front Royal a dozen miles to the east, capturing seven hundred Federals and abundant supplies. With his position turned, Banks resumed his retreat down the valley to Winchester, another eighteen miles north of Strasburg. The day after the mishap at Front Royal, Lincoln canceled McDowell's orders to join McClellan and ordered him instead to march west for the Shenandoah.

With that, the most strategically important goal of Jackson's Valley Campaign had been accomplished. A major formation of Union troops had been diverted from McClellan's campaign on Richmond to the less strategically significant Shenandoah Valley. After the avalanche of Union victories in the West, the fall of Richmond might have been the additional push that was needed to topple the Confederacy by completing the demoralization of its people. The loss of the Shenandoah Valley would not have been helpful to the Confederacy, but the loss of Richmond could perhaps have been fatal.

Yet there were reasons why the capture of Richmond was very difficult to achieve. One was the Shenandoah Valley itself, which slanted from the remote hinterland of Virginia at its upper (southern) end to a place well within striking distance of Washington, Baltimore, and Harrisburg at its lower (northern) end. The valley was a vast granary for the Confederacy that could always provide supplies for Confederate armies passing through it or operating out of it and its eastern wall, the towering Blue Ridge, screened from easy observation of scouting Union cavalry on the piedmont whatever the Confederates might be up to inside it. Until something was done about it, the valley would provide an ever ready resource for skillful Confederate generals to overturn the best plans of their Union counterparts in Virginia.

Another reason why it was difficult to take Richmond was the proximity of Washington, which always had to be defended at all costs and where there were politicians, including the usually wise Lincoln, who might sometimes be baited into unwise interference in military operations in Virginia. And Jackson had baited Lincoln, not frightened him. The president was, as always, not prone to alarm about the safety of Washington, but he was enticed by the prospect of Jackson's army just eighty miles west-northwest of the national capital. His orders to McDowell were aimed not at saving Washington but at getting behind Jackson and trapping him. At the same time Lincoln issued those orders, he also ordered Frémont to march east. If all went well, McDowell and Frémont would meet in the valley somewhere south of Jackson, who would then be trapped. It was a promising prospect for the Union, but capturing Richmond would have been better.

Back in the valley, Jackson was not yet finished with Banks. Pursuing him to Winchester, Jackson attacked on May 25, breaking Banks's lines and driving his troops back through the town, where civilians, including a number of women, fired at them and pelted them with whatever objects they could lay their hands on. Losses in killed and wounded were about equal, three hundred Union to four hundred Confederate, but an additional 1,700 Federals were captured or missing. Jackson was in ecstasy, urging his men on to pursue the Yankees all the way to the Potomac.

They very nearly did. By May 29 advanced elements of Jackson's command were threatening Harpers Ferry, twenty-five miles northeast of Winchester and within sight of the Potomac. By that time it was clear that Union forces were closing on Jackson as Lincoln's trap threatened to snap shut. Jackson turned his troops south on May 30 and began a rapid march up the valley. His lead troops reached Winchester that night, but McDowell's advance guard was already in Front Royal, only a dozen miles from where the Valley Pike, Jackson's escape route, passed through Strasburg eighteen miles south of Winchester. Jackson's reputation now began to work for him. The commander of McDowell's lead division decided it would not be safe to advance any farther until the next division caught up and so called a halt at Front Royal while Jackson's army, covering prodigious distances each day, marched by a few miles away. Frémont performed with his accustomed ineptness, moving slowly and allowing Jackson to get past him as well.

Seventy-five miles southwest of Winchester, near the village of Port Republic, Jackson turned at bay and prepared to confront his pursuers. Frémont's troops were advancing from the north, McDowell's from the northeast. By controlling key bridges Jackson used two small rivers to keep his two enemies apart. On June 8 a portion of Ewell's division met Frémont's command in a blocking action at Cross Keys. Though Frémont outnumbered Ewell two to one, he advanced so tentatively that little serious fighting occurred. By nightfall Jackson felt confident that he had little to fear from Frémont and could bring all but a token force of Ewell's division over to Port Republic for his planned showdown with McDowell's lead division under Jackson's old Kernstown nemesis Shields.

On June 8, one month to the day after the Battle of McDowell, Jackson and Shields fought the Battle of Port Republic. Though a wizard of operational maneuver as he had just demonstrated over the course of the preceding month, Jackson was not always adept in tactics. He certainly did poorly in this battle, committing his troops piecemeal and without adequate reconnaissance. Troops on both sides fought hard. In the end, Jackson had more men available than did Shields and was able to force the Federals back. In this narrow victory, Jackson lost eight hundred men and Shields about one thousand.

The Battle of Port Republic marked the end of what was to become famous as Jackson's Shenandoah Valley Campaign, an operational masterpiece still studied by students of the art of war. Jackson's eighteen thousand men had marched hundreds of miles. Through excellent knowledge of the terrain, good intelligence of enemy strength and movements, and Jackson's ability to grasp quickly and accurately the operational situation and how he could make the most of it, his small army had defeated three separate enemy armies whose combined numbers totaled fifty-five thousand men. The strategic importance of the campaign lay in the fact that it had kept McDowell's command and possibly additional Union troops away from McClellan for several vital weeks.

FROM SEVEN PINES
TO THE SEVEN DAYS

By the time Jackson's Shenandoah Valley Campaign was at its height, McClellan's troops had reached the outskirts of Richmond. Union soldiers could see the spires of the Confederate capital's churches and hear its public clocks strike the hours. Davis seethed with anger at Johnston for his retreat into the very suburbs of the capital without giving battle to the enemy. To make matters worse, Johnston had not kept Davis apprised of his activities or plans. Like his old friend from prewar army days, George McClellan, he seemed to feel that the commander in chief had no right to know what the army was doing and what its commander planned. The president had ridden out to inspect the lines daily, much to Johnston's annoyance, and on one occasion would have ridden inadvertently right into Union lines had not Confederate soldiers flagged him down and warned him that, because of a retreat the previous evening of which Johnston had given him no word before or after the fact, he was actually about to proceed beyond the new Confederate lines. Davis applied heavy pressure on Johnston to persuade him not to give up Richmond without a fight. According to one account, Davis threatened that if Johnston would not fight for Richmond, he, Davis, would find a general who would.

At any rate, Johnston planned a May 31 attack on McClellan in which he hoped to take advantage of an important terrain feature near Richmond. Cutting across McClellan's position was a tributary of the James called the Chickahominy. Its valley amounted to a broad belt of swamp that troops, guns, caissons, and supply wagons could cross only with the utmost difficulty. The Chickahominy was particularly inconveniently located for McClellan since Richmond was on the south side of the Chickahominy but McClellan's supply line ran back to his right rear, on the north side of the swampy little river. That meant that in order to protect his supply line the Union general had to maintain a substantial force north of the Chickahominy and that in order to attack Richmond he had to place a large force south of that stream. Johnston planned to take advantage of that division of force by massing his own troops against the half of the Army of the Potomac that was south of the Chickahominy, betting that the difficult crossing of the swampy Chickahominy bottoms would prevent the other half of McClellan's army from coming to the aid of their comrades.

It was as good a plan as any he could have come up with, but its execution by the Confederate army was atrocious. Johnston assigned a key role in the assault to his senior division commander, James Longstreet, a man whose very demeanor seemed to inspire confidence among all those around him. Unfortunately Longstreet was headstrong and ambitious. Seeing that Johnston's plan called for him to attack under Johnston's direct supervision, he decided instead to shift his division to another part of the front where he could have independence. The movement threw the army into disarray and delayed the start of the attack for many hours. When it did go in, the attack was a confused mess. Late in the day Johnston rode to the front to try to sort it out and within the space of a few seconds was struck both by an enemy rifle bullet and by a shell fragment and carried off the field badly wounded. The Yankees would call this battle Fair Oaks after a location on the battlefield where their troops had done well. The Confederates would call it Seven Pines for similar reasons.

Davis and Lee had made the disturbingly short ride from Richmond to see the day's fighting. After Johnston's wounding, Davis looked up the army's second in command, Major General Gustavus W. Smith (West Point, 1842), but was dismayed to find him not at all posted on Johnston's plans and completely unequal to the occasion. As Davis and Lee rode together back into Richmond that evening, the president apparently reflected on the fact that the army would need a new commander. Its second in command was inadequate, and its third-ranking officer, Longstreet, had just turned in a dismal perform-ance. Yet the commander would have to be someone then present in the Rich-mond area since the army, with its back to the capital and a victorious enemy in front, would need his direction immediately. Turning to his companion, Davis announced that he would assign Lee to command of the army.

Lee took command the following day. Over the weeks that followed he went to work to get it back into fighting shape and put his stamp on it. He encouraged officers not to count battles as already lost on the basis of their inferior numbers but to apply themselves to overcoming such difficulties. In an apparent hint at where he planned to take the war, he named his new command the Army of Northern Virginia. By late June he was ready to launch an offensive of his own—and none too soon since McClellan had been edging ever deeper into the outskirts of Richmond and had to be turned back if the capital was to be saved.

Lee's plan was even more daring than Johnston's. McClellan had by this time increased the number of corps in his army to six by taking divisions from the Second, Third, and Fourth corps and using them to form the Fifth and Sixth corps for two of his personal favorites, Major General Fitz John Porter (West Point, 1845), who got the Fifth Corps, and Major General William B. Franklin (West Point, 1843), who got the Sixth. As the Army of the Potomac had edged closer to Richmond over the past month, more and more of the army had moved over to the south bank until only a single corps, the Fifth, remained on the north bank to cover the army's supply line, the Richmond & York River Railroad. That corps was Lee's target. He planned to reduce the Confederate defenders immediately in front of Richmond, facing McClel-lan's other four corps, to a bare minimum and mass almost all of his army, which would be reinforced by the addition of Jackson's command hastily summoned from the Shenandoah Valley immediately after the completion of its dramatic campaign there, against Porter's Fifth Corps near the hamlet of Mechanicsville. Davis was skeptical, but Lee won him over.

He planned to launch his attack at Mechanicsville on June 26. He got a scare when McClellan made a relatively minor push against the Richmond defenses on the twenty-fifth, but McClellan's push was a small affair aimed merely at seizing a few more yards of ground. Right on schedule, Lee opened his grand offensive the following day, with Davis and his staff on hand to observe. It was almost as bad a fiasco as Seven Pines. Jackson was supposed to open the offensive with an attack on Porter's exposed right flank, but the hero of Manassas and the valley inexplicably failed to get his troops into position. In

Lee's center, division commander Ambrose Powell Hill, West Point classmate of McClellan and unsuccessful suitor for the hand of the present Mrs. McClellan, got tired of waiting and launched his division straight against the entrenched Union defenders. This was the signal for the rest of Lee's army to join the assault, which it did. The result was a bloody repulse. Confederate losses were almost 1,500, while the Federals lost fewer than four hundred.

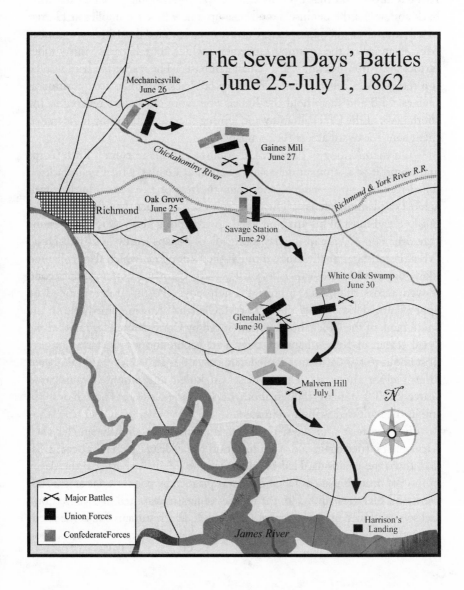

The Seven Days' Battles
June 25-July 1, 1862

If Lee had chanced to take a stray bullet and had died at Mechanicsville, he would have been counted as great a failure as Albert Sidney Johnston, but he survived and took up the offensive again the next day. Despite the Union victory on the twenty-sixth, McClellan was thoroughly cowed, convinced as usual that he was outnumbered at least two to one no matter how many men he had. He decided it would be impossible to defend the Richmond & York River Railroad and that his only chance was to abandon it, march his army back and across the peninsula, and take up a new base of supplies at Harrison's Landing on the James River, now available since the *Virginia's* demise. McClellan called the resulting movement, which took his army thirty miles farther away from Richmond, a "change of base." The rest of the world called it a retreat. McClellan ordered Porter to fall back five miles to a position at Gaines' Mill and there hold the Rebels one more day before retiring to the south bank of the Chickahominy and joining the rest of the army in its movement southeastward across the peninsula.

On the morning of June 27, Lee followed up the retreating Fifth Corps and found it in a stronger defensive position at Gaines' Mill. Again Jackson failed to come up to scratch, and again the rest of Lee's army hurled itself against the Union defenses. The result was even bloodier than the day before, but Lee had most of his army on hand, giving him a heavy numerical advantage over Porter. Late in the day a brigade of Texans led by John Bell Hood (West Point, 1853) finally broke through the Union line, which then collapsed like a breached levee. A division of the Sixth Corps and one of the Second moved across the Chickahominy to help cover Porter's retreat, aided by approaching darkness, but the rest of McClellan's army remained idle on the south bank of the Chickahominy, convinced by Confederate bluffing that the small screen of Rebels between them and Richmond was in fact a mighty host about to fall on them. Confederate casualties at Gaines' Mill numbered almost eight thousand. Union losses in killed and wounded numbered scarcely half that many, though another 2,800 Federals were captured or missing in the confused twilight retreat.

For the next four days, Lee, with an army only slightly smaller than McClellan's, tried again and again to cut off the Federals' path of retreat across and down the peninsula. Had he succeeded, he might have bagged the Army of the Potomac almost entirely, but he was plagued by poor or nonexistent staff work and had great difficulty getting his orders transmitted and carried out. Jackson continued in some strange sort of funk, and historians still argue about the nature and cause of his dysfunction that week. Extreme fatigue is as good a guess as any. Forced marches throughout the Shenandoah Valley and then on the way to Richmond probably exhausted Jackson. McClellan provided almost no instructions for his retreating army, busying himself with affairs well to the rear, preparation of the new supply base, and the like. His corps commanders coordinated the rearguard actions as best they could, and the troops fought stoutly on each occasion. Every day saw another battle. June 30 brought the climatic Battle of Glendale, as Lee's troops contended for a key crossroads whose possession would allow them to cut off the retreat of a major portion of the Army of the Potomac. Once again the combat was intense and lasted into the dusk. Casualties were about four thousand on each side, and the Federals succeeded in holding the vital crossroads.

Frustrated at his inability to trap McClellan in nearly a week of fighting, Lee on July 1 launched his army in another all-out frontal assault. This time the Army of the Potomac was arrayed along the military crest of gently sloping Malvern Hill, where massed Union artillery commanded a splendid field of fire. Again deficient staff work impaired Lee's control of his army. A Confederate attempt at a preliminary artillery barrage was a disaster, as well-aimed Union salvos silenced the Rebel batteries almost as quickly as they wheeled into position and opened fire. The infantry assault should have been canceled but went in anyway, with predictable results. When it was over more than five thousand Confederates lay scattered across the gentle, grassy slope. A Union officer surveying the field the next morning noted that "enough of them were alive and moving to give the field a singular crawling effect."[1]

The fighting that began with McClellan's minor push on June 25 and continued every day through the bloody finale at Malvern Hill came to be known as the Seven Days' Battles or just the Seven Days. They had produced bloodshed on a scale of which the nation had scarcely dreamed before. The Army of the Potomac, out of its total strength of 104,000 men, lost ten thousand killed and wounded and another six thousand captured. The Army of Northern Virginia, which started the battles with a strength of ninety-two thousand, suffered more than twenty thousand casualties, almost all of them killed and wounded, losses the Confederacy could not afford on a regular basis. Lee had failed in his effort to trap and annihilate McClellan's army, which was now securely ensconced around its base of supplies on the James River with naval vessels standing by to provide gunfire support. Yet in one week the scene of the fighting had shifted from the outskirts of Richmond to a point about thirty miles away. Additionally, Lee, though at a ruinous cost to his army, had established a towering reputation that would henceforth haunt the minds and inhibit the plans of every army commander he would meet—except the last one.

6

CONFEDERATE HIGH TIDE

LINCOLN TAKES A NEW GRIP

The Seven Days' Battles had powerful repercussions. Many things would change in their wake, and one of those was George McClellan's relationship with his government. The change could easily have been more sudden than it was. On the evening of June 28, in the midst of the Seven Days' fighting, McClellan had telegraphed the president reporting recent action and complaining bitterly, "I have lost this battle because my force was too small," blaming Lincoln and rejecting any personal responsibility, even though he had kept many of his troops idle. Then he added, "If I save this army now, I tell you plainly that I owe no thanks to you or to any other persons in Washington. You have done your best to sacrifice this army." War Department personnel who decoded the dispatch were aghast at the last two sentences and deleted them without even informing Lincoln of their inflammatory nature. The president never knew McClellan had written them and responded to the rest of McClellan's dispatch, "Save your Army at all events. . . . If you have had a drawn battle, or a repulse, it is the price we pay for the enemy not being in Washington."

Even though McClellan's most insulting sentences never reached Lincoln's eyes, the general's stock with the president was clearly falling. Lincoln had once said he would hold McClellan's horse if the general would bring victories, but it now appeared questionable that McClellan could do that. When Lincoln visited McClellan's camp at Harrison's Landing a few days after the end of the campaign, the general showed that he could be questionable in other ways as well. There on July 7 McClellan handed Lincoln a letter urging that the war should be fought only for the Union and not in any way to curtail much less eliminate slavery. Only the most limited of means should be used, as had been the case hitherto, treating Rebel civilians as if they were friendly civilians and not resorting to any of the harsh measures that were customary in time of war. McClellan further seemed to hint that if any other course were pursued, the army would not support it. This would have been going a bit too far, even for a general who had not just been beaten in a major campaign. As it was, McClellan's advice was just the opposite of the direction Lincoln was thinking of going and probably increased the president's skepticism about the wisdom of retaining him.

Firing McClellan outright would be politically risky. Instead of removing McClellan from the head of the army, Lincoln decided to remove the army gradually from under McClellan. Even before the beginning of the Seven Days' Battles, Lincoln had decided that the various Union troops operating in northern Virginia while McClellan was on the peninsula needed to be under a single commander. For that commander Lincoln looked to the West, where Union forces had scored one victory after another. The man he chose was John Pope, lately commander of the Army of the Mississippi under Halleck. Pope had snapped up several posts along the Mississippi that the navy had largely won for him and had participated in Halleck's hesitation waltz from Pittsburg Landing to Corinth.

Pope took over his new command on June 27, even as the Battle of Gaines' Mill was raging down on the peninsula. Christened the Army of Virginia, it consisted of McDowell's corps, which would never join McClellan outside Richmond, as well as Banks's hard-luck command from the Shenandoah Valley, and a third corps containing a relatively high proportion of German American regiments and commanded by none other than Franz Sigel, who had turned in a questionable performance at Wilson's Creek the preceding summer but was always a favorite of the typical German American soldier, who famously announced with pride, "I fights mit Sigel." All together Pope's new army counted fifty-one thousand men in its ranks. At any rate, Lincoln now had the option of transferring one unit at a time from McClellan's command on the peninsula to Pope's in northern Virginia, where Lincoln had always believed the true road to Richmond began.

Even while the Seven Days' Battles were still raging, it was becoming clear that, organize the troops how he might, Lincoln did not have enough manpower in uniform to conquer the Confederacy. He would need more, but issuing a call for enlistments at a time when public morale had just suffered the severe blow of McClellan's defeat in front of Richmond would be another politically risky move. Instead, Lincoln wrote a letter and gave it to Seward to take to northern state governors one by one in private discussions. "I expect to maintain this contest until successful, or till I die," Lincoln wrote, "or am conquered, or my term expires, or Congress or the country forsakes me; and I would publicly appeal to the country for this new force were it not that I fear a general panic and stampede would follow, so hard is it to have a thing understood as it really is." It would be helpful, Seward explained to each governor, if they would all sign an open letter, urging Lincoln to call on the states for more troops so that the Union armies would finally have enough men "to speedily crush the rebellion." The governors did so, and on July 1 Lincoln issued a call for three hundred thousand additional three-year volunteers.

This call summoned up another great surge of patriotic recruiting. More than half a million men had already enlisted out of a population of about thirty million, and the new call would dig deep into the nation's manpower reserves. Later that same month, Quaker abolitionist James Sloan Gibbons wrote a poem titled "We Are Coming, Father Abraham, Three Hundred Thousand More." In it Gibbons spoke for the new recruits, expressing their willingness to serve if their country needed them:

> We are coming, Father Abraham, three hundred thousand more,
> From Mississippi's winding stream and from New England's shore.
> We leave our plows and workshops, our wives and children dear,
> With hearts too full for utterance, with but a silent tear.
> We dare not look behind us but steadfastly before.
> We are coming, Father Abraham, three hundred thousand more!
>
> You have called us, and we're coming by Richmond's bloody tide,
> To lay us down for freedom's sake, our brothers' bones beside;
> Or from foul treason's savage grip, to wrench the murderous blade;
> And in the face of foreign foes its fragments to parade.
> Six hundred thousand loyal men and true have gone before,
> We are coming, Father Abraham, three hundred thousand more!

The poem first appeared in the New York *Evening Post* and was read to an enthusiastic crowd at a mass public meeting in Chicago. Luther O. Emerson, Stephen Foster, and others set it to music so that Americans were soon singing it to several different tunes.

Modern readers might be tempted to think Sloan guilty of sentimentalism with his talk of enlistees leaving their "plows and workshops" and their "wives and children dear." In fact, in many cases it was the simple truth. Regiments enlisted in this second great wave of patriotic enlistment tended to include a disproportionately high number of older men, in their late twenties or early thirties, married, with children. Their family responsibilities had held them back from enlisting the previous year. Now it seemed the country's need might demand even that sacrifice. In Newton, Iowa, farmer Taylor Pierce had a long talk with his wife, Katharine. She would have to operate the farm and care for their three children if he went, but she was willing. She would not have it said that her cowardice had kept her husband from serving the country in its time of need. As Taylor put it, "The rebellion could not be put down without the government got more help."

In Iowa City, Sam Jones also weighed enlisting. "Up to this time, I had not thought it necessary that I should go," he later explained. "I had had a feeling that those who were enlisting were doing it because they delighted in the public martial display of the soldier life; but a feeling came over me at this time that I was needed in the defense of my country." Could free government survive, he wondered, and would it require him to go and fight? His conclusion was, "We, the people, are the government." That decided it for him. "I made up my mind to be a soldier and fight for my country." Both Pierce and Jones became members of the newly recruited Twenty-Second Iowa Regiment.

Four hundred miles to the southeast, in the little village of Hope, Indiana, saddle and harness maker William Winters, like Taylor a father of three, had a similar talk with his wife, Hattie. She too agreed, and William joined the newly organized Sixty-Seventh Indiana Regiment. Five hundred miles to the northeast of Hope, near the Pennsylvania border in the western New York State town of Portville, Amos Humiston had much the same solemn discussion with his wife Philinda about how she would manage at home with their children, seven-year-old Frank, five-year-old Alice, and three-year-old Fred. The result was the same as those in the Taylor and Winters households and tens of thousands of others across the country, and Amos went off to join the new 154th New York Regiment. Of these four men, Taylor, Jones, Winters, and Humiston, only two would survive the war.

The women who remained at home, in both North and South, had to take on new roles and responsibilities in the absence of their husbands or other male family members, performing as best they could tasks that had previously been carried out by men. With very few exceptions the women did not see their new roles as a liberation, a revelation of their latent abilities, or anything else but a terrible burden that they had to bear for their families and for their country. Nineteenth-century American society recognized men and women as being fundamentally different and assigned different roles to them in keeping with their differing abilities and natures. The arrangement worked well, and very few people wanted to change it. Certainly, to judge by their surviving diaries and letters, scarcely any of the wives and sisters whom the soldiers left behind coveted the male roles of those who were away in uniform.

A few Civil War women were different, however, and seemed to covet the most thoroughly male role in that society, that of soldier. In some cases, a young, childless wife sought to accompany her husband to war by entering the army herself. Sometimes a young single woman sought the life of a soldier for reasons of her own. Enlistment physicals, if any, were cursory in the extreme, and a number of women, carefully disguised as young men, were able to find their way into the army. Of course, the law and army regulations, as well as the overwhelming majority opinion within society, held that the army was absolutely no place for a woman, and if her sex was discovered, dismissal was immediate. Some scholars argue that possibly as many as four hundred different women may have served for at least some time during the war, a number equal to about 0.01 percent of all Civil War soldiers.

The other twenty million or so women in America seemed to agree wholeheartedly with society's belief that soldiering was man's work. Sometimes young women sought to shame reluctant young men into doing their duty and enlisting. An able-bodied, single young man who was slow to join the company being organized in his hometown might well find a package, left for him by anonymous local young ladies, containing a hoopskirt and suggesting that, given his apparently nonmartial proclivities, the skirt might be appropriate attire. The message was clear: a real man did his duty, even if that meant fighting and possibly dying. Women stayed behind and kept the home fires burning.

As the new recruits flocked to the colors, the army could have gotten better use out of them if it had incorporated them into veteran regiments where the new men could learn the business of war with experienced soldiers alongside them. That was not how it was done. Troops were raised by states, as complete regiments, and each new regiment gave a governor additional opportunities to curry political favor by appointing its colonel and other field officers. The new recruits also felt more at home in new regiments, where everyone else was as green as they were, though that fact was not necessarily conducive to their advantage or safety in battle. Nonetheless, experienced regiments received only a trickle of recruits and grew smaller as the war went on, while most of the new men went into new regiments like the Twenty-Second Iowa, Sixty-Seventh Indiana, and 154th New York.

LINCOLN AND EMANCIPATION

The setback on the peninsula, even coming as it did at the end of a six-month string of Union victories in the West, showed that the war was going to be harder, more costly, and longer than most Americans had previously thought. Many Union policies, including Lincoln's own approach to the war, had been based on the idea that most white southerners were not deeply committed to the Confederacy and would not fight desperately to save it. Firm but gentle pressure from Union forces would bring these southerners to their senses. For that reason, Union policy toward southern civilians had been conciliatory, not treating them like rebellious civilians or even like civilians of an enemy country but rather like its own friendly civilians. This approach was most starkly on display when rebellious citizens of states claiming to be no longer part of the United States approached Union military commanders and demanded that they observe the Fugitive Slave Law by returning to them slaves who had escaped and fled into Union lines. During the first year of the war, Union officers had often complied with such demands, except when they were enterprising and principled enough to call the escapees contrabands and protect them or when Union soldiers, who were daily becoming less sympathetic toward slaveholders, succeeded in hiding the slaves.

The official policy of applying the Fugitive Slave Act even on behalf of people who were actively in rebellion against the government was intended both to assure white southerners that the government in Washington intended no social revolution such as immediate abolition of slavery would bring and that it was committed to respecting all of the property rights they claimed. That applied to food or draft animals that might be of great use to passing Union armies in the prosecution of the war, and it applied most strongly to the property rights white southerners claimed in their slaves. Just as a constitutional right to privacy was to become a code word for abortion rights in the late twentieth century, so a constitutional right to property had in the mid-nineteenth century become a shibboleth for the defense of slavery.

The first fifteen months of the war had demonstrated to Lincoln and to other perceptive observers, especially the common soldiers in the Union armies, that white southerners were deeply committed to both of the closely intertwined causes of the Confederacy and slavery. Indeed, Lincoln had learned to his dismay that even southerners who did not back the Confederacy still clung tenaciously to the institution of slavery and the white supremacy it protected.

Despite his having reversed Frémont's local emancipation proclamation the preceding year, Lincoln was—and had been since the day he took office—deeply committed to ending slavery as soon as he could do so in a way that would have a chance of surviving both politically and legally. He also hoped to accomplish his purpose with the minimum of painful upheaval to the country. Consistent with these goals, Lincoln hoped to persuade Congress to appropriate funds to compensate slaveholders for the emancipation of their slaves, and he hoped to persuade state legislatures to enact statutes for the gradual emancipation of the slaves within their borders. No one had ever questioned the legal right of a state legislature to take such action, and that would keep the matter out of the hands of the Supreme Court with its proslavery majority and rabidly proslavery Chief Justice Roger B. Taney.

For just these reasons Lincoln had been skeptical about other attempts to chip away at the edifice of slavery during the first year of the war. In August 1861 Congress had passed and Lincoln signed a Confiscation Act providing for the freeing of slaves actually used by the Confederate army for the building of fortifications and other warlike purposes. It was a start, but Lincoln doubted that it would stand up to constitutional scrutiny by the Supreme Court. In any case, it was cumbersome to implement and could never be expected to free very many slaves. When in April 1862, Major General David Hunter had issued an order freeing slaves within his command in the Union-held enclave on the southern coast, Lincoln had rescinded it as legally hopeless. Congressional bans on slavery in the District of Columbia and all U.S. territories, passed in April and June 1862, were positive steps, but Taney was already on record about the latter, and his views could be easily guessed about the former.

Lincoln's preferred approach to ending slavery started with the Union-loyal slave states. Lincoln hoped to persuade them to enact programs of long-term, gradual emancipation with congressionally funded compensation for slaveholders who had to give up their chattels. In order to achieve that goal and because he held the highly pessimistic view of race relations in a nonslave society that was widespread at that time, Lincoln also hoped to persuade freed slaves to accept colonization somewhere outside the United States. If the border slave states enacted gradual emancipation, owners were reimbursed, and freedmen left the country, states in the Confederacy would see that slavery could be given up without financial disaster or social upheaval and was therefore not worth fighting for. If slavery was not worth fighting for, there would be no reason to fight for the Confederacy. It was this belief that led Lincoln to imagine that Union military success, within the context of a conciliatory policy, would lead to the collapse of the Confederacy and the restoration of the Union. "We should urge it persuasively," he wrote in a March 24, 1862, letter to Horace Greeley, "and not menacingly, on the South."

He was destined to be disappointed on all counts. The border states indignantly rejected Lincoln's urging that they adopt gradual, compensated emancipation. Even Delaware, which had a tiny percentage of slaves and had never seriously considered secession, gave no consideration to the idea of the eventual emancipation of its slaves. If even Delaware would not entertain such a proposition, it clearly had little chance in any other state. Black Americans were understandably unenthusiastic about the prospects of leaving the country. Being in America, being at least prospective heirs to all its promise for the future, was the chief compensation they had for their and their ancestors' years of toil, and, as time was to show, it was no inconsiderable blessing but rather a boon sought eagerly in future generations by persons from every corner of the globe. They could hardly be expected to give it up willingly, and Lincoln, to his credit, would not see them go any other way.

Gradual, compensated emancipation and colonization were both clearly faint hopes by the beginning of the summer of 1862, and McClellan's retreat from Richmond during the last week of June, though militarily less significant than the events of the past six months in the West, was nevertheless the kind of high-profile, morale-raising event for the Confederacy that ruined whatever chances Lincoln may have had of applying overall military pressure on the Confederacy to the point that its populace began to doubt the wisdom of their decision for secession. The prospects for a short war, conciliatory policies, and voluntary emancipation all seemed to be fading to the vanishing point.

It was time to take a further dramatic step. Emancipation was not going to happen the easy way, was not going to happen at all, perhaps, unless Lincoln tried something new. As Lincoln himself put it two years later, "I felt that we had reached the end of our rope on the plan of operations we had been pursuing; that we had about played our last card, and must change our tactics, or lose the game!"[1] His answer was the Emancipation Proclamation. When he started writing the proclamation is something historians still argue about. Sources conflict.

He presented it to his cabinet for the first time on July 22. He began by explaining that he was not asking their approval on the policy. That was settled and was something that Lincoln said he owed to God. He said he was open to any suggestions they might have on the specific wording of the proclamation. The document he read announced that in all areas still in rebellion at the end of one hundred days, all slaves would be permanently free. He based the proclamation on his war powers as commander in chief. In that respect it differed from the Second Confiscation Act, which Congress had passed only a few days before. Lincoln believed his proclamation would prove more legally defensible. As commander in chief, Lincoln had the power to wage war against the nation's enemies, capture their ships, bombard their forts, shoot their soldiers—and take their slaves.

The cabinet members reacted with varying degrees of enthusiasm, but Secretary of State Seward had a practical suggestion. He approved of the proclamation, but Union forces had just suffered an embarrassing setback on the peninsula. If Lincoln were to issue the proclamation now, it would look bad. "It may be viewed as the last measure of an exhausted government," he explained, "a cry for help; the government stretching forth its hands to Ethiopia, instead of Ethiopia stretching forth her hands to the government." In short, as Lincoln later explained, it would sound like "our last shriek, on the retreat."[2] Lincoln had not thought of that, and the sense of it struck him forcefully. He agreed with Seward and put the draft of the Emancipation Proclamation into his desk drawer until the nation's armies should win a victory. It was to stay there longer than he expected.

POPE TRIES HIS HAND IN VIRGINIA

Another step that Lincoln took in order to achieve more satisfactory results in the war was to bring Henry Halleck to Washington as the new general in chief of all the Union armies. The post had been vacant since Lincoln had relieved McClellan of his duties on the eve of the Peninsula Campaign the previous March, and during that time the president himself had tried to provide central direction for the Union armies. Dissatisfied with the results of his own efforts, Lincoln now decided to bring in the learned Halleck, apparent architect of the Union's dazzling successes in the Mississippi Valley, whose troops called him, behind his back, "Old Brains." Lincoln issued his order promoting Halleck to Washington on July 11, and Old Brains formally took the reins of command on July 23.

By that time Pope had been in command of the Army of Virginia for almost a month. During that time he had made himself unpopular both with the enemy and with his own men. On July 10 Pope had issued an order dealing with hostile civilians and the guerrillas who sheltered among them, abusing the restraints of civilized war by using them as cover for waging their own war. Pope's order stated that henceforth civilians who engaged in acts of war or espionage against Union forces would be subject to the normal rigor of the laws of war, which prescribed summary execution in such cases. Local civilians would be held financially responsible for the depredations of the guerrillas who operated among them and whom they were presumed to harbor. Houses used as blinds from which to take potshots at Union troops would be destroyed. The Union army would live off the land, confiscating supplies it needed from the civilian populace.

In general Pope proposed to start treating Confederate civilians in the way that the laws of war prescribed for enemy rather than friendly civilians. His action was very much in keeping with the new turn Union policy was

General James Longstreet   General Henry W. Halleck

now taking, away from conciliation and toward a more pragmatic, hard-war approach, though at this time Pope could have known nothing of emancipation, Lincoln's ultimate hard-war policy. One did not have to be privy to White House cabinet meetings to see that white southerners had rejected northern attempts at conciliation and that nothing but stern, relentless war waging was going to end this conflict. The soldiers in the ranks of the Union armies probably knew it better than anyone else.

Nevertheless, Pope's order was controversial and came in for criticism by some northern Democrats, including McClellan and his cronies in the Army of the Potomac, who regarded it as a departure from their own highly civilized methods and a descent to waging war in manner reminiscent of Genghis Khan. Other strong critics of Pope's order included most Confederates who heard of it. Jefferson Davis called Pope's new policy "a campaign of indiscriminate robbery and murder" and directed that officers of Pope's army who fell into Confederate hands be treated as criminals rather than as prisoners of war. A furious Robert E. Lee reviled Pope as a "miscreant" and announced to a subordinate general, "Pope must be suppressed."

A few days after issuing his controversial order, Pope issued a proclamation to his troops intended to encourage and motivate them. "Let us understand each other," Pope wrote,

> I have come to you from the West, where we have always seen the backs of our enemies; from an army whose business it has been to seek the adversary and to beat him when he was found; whose policy has been attack and not defense. . . . I presume that I have been called here to pursue the same system and to lead you against the enemy. I am sure you long for an opportunity to win the distinction you are capable of achieving. . . . Meantime I desire you to dismiss from your minds certain phrases, which I am sorry to find so much in vogue amongst you. I hear constantly of "taking strong positions and holding them," of "lines of retreat," and of "bases of supplies." Let us discard such ideas. . . . Let us study the probable lines of retreat of our opponents, and leave our own to take care of themselves. Let us look before us, and not behind. Success and glory are in the advance, disaster and shame lurk in the rear.[3]

Pope's address hinted at the undeniable fact that the eastern Union armies had experienced little but failure while their western comrades had experienced almost nothing but victory. It also suggested that a spirit of defeatism and a feeling of inferiority toward the Rebels had infected the eastern forces, which was true, and it seemed to imply that western Union soldiers were better fighters than their eastern counterparts. That may have been true as well since the few regiments of western Union troops in Virginia were to compile a record as the Army of the Potomac's hardest fighters. But Pope's stating all of it in an order to his entire army was tactless in the extreme, and its possible truth, though unadmitted by those who resented it, made it rankle all the more. Thereafter, many of Pope's troops, as well as McClellan and his officers in the Army of the Potomac, seethed with hatred toward him.

As was shortly to become apparent, pronouncements about seeing "the backs of our enemies" in Virginia were best left to generals who could make good such boasts against Robert E. Lee. Pope began to advance along the line of the Orange & Alexandria Railroad, which led generally southwest from Alexandria, on the Potomac opposite Washington, through Manassas Junction, and on into the Virginia Piedmont. Banks and Sigel's corps joined him by marching southeast after crossing the Blue Ridge at one of its gaps. By early August Pope's army held the town of Culpeper Court House, south of the Rappahannock River, seventy miles southwest of Washington and about one hundred miles northwest of Richmond via the Virginia Central Railroad that joined the Orange & Alexandria at Gordonsville, about thirty miles farther down the Orange & Alexandria from Pope's position at Culpeper. Between Pope and Gordonsville was Stonewall Jackson with sixteen thousand Confederates, dispatched by Lee to impede the advance of "that miscreant Pope" and if possible begin the work of suppressing him.

On August 9 Pope's lead corps under Banks collided with Jackson in what came to be known as the Battle of Cedar Mountain. Banks drove forward aggressively, and at first it appeared that he might finally get the better of his old Shenandoah nemesis, who was not conducting the battle particularly skillfully. Tactics were not Stonewall's forte, but once all of his troops arrived on the battlefield, especially the large division of the hard-hitting A. P. Hill, Jackson had a two-to-one advantage in numbers and forced Banks to withdraw.

Theoretically Lee's position should have been a very dangerous one. With McClellan's army thirty miles southeast of Richmond and Pope's one hundred miles northwest of it, Lee should have been compelled to keep major forces guarding both directions. As Lee saw it, that was not the case. He had taken McClellan's measure during the Seven Days, and he believed he had little to fear from that callow young man. He therefore decided he could afford to leave only the smallest of forces to guard the peninsula approach to Richmond and take almost his entire army to suppress Pope. Davis expressed some misgivings about such an audacious course but allowed it out of confidence in Lee, whose reputation was fast becoming the rock on which all of Confederate morale and Confederate nationalism rested.

In fact, Lee's situation was even safer than he realized. On August 3 Halleck ordered McClellan to withdraw his army from the peninsula and transport it back up the Chesapeake to Alexandria for operations in northern Virginia. Unwilling to abandon his great campaign against the Confederate capital and perhaps sensing the movement as a first stage in the transfer of the units of his army, one by one, to Pope's Army of Virginia, McClellan protested the move and did not get his troops under way until August 14. For a prolonged period during mid-August, McClellan's army, the largest the Union possessed, would be in a position neither to threaten Richmond from the southeast nor to aid Pope on the Virginia Piedmont.

THE SECOND BULL
RUN CAMPAIGN

By mid-August Lee had joined Jackson north of Gordonsville along with the rest of the Army of Northern Virginia. Outnumbered, Pope fell back across the Rappahannock. Lee tried to move around Pope's flank, but the Union general skillfully maneuvered sideways to keep the river, swollen by recent rains, between himself and the larger Confederate army. For three days, Pope matched Lee move for move, and the frustrated Confederate general could get nowhere. Then on August 25 Lee dispatched Jackson with about one-third of the Army of Northern Virginia's infantry, together with Major General James Ewell Brown "Jeb" Stuart (West Point, 1854) and all of its cavalry, to swing wide and fast to the west of Pope's army, get behind him, and strike at his supply line, the Orange & Alexandria.

This sort of maneuver was what Stonewall did best, and Pope, who was apparently taking his own advice about looking "before us, and not behind," did not realize what was happening to him until Jackson's men on August 27 captured his supply depot at Manassas Junction. The ill-fed Confederates held high carnival amid the mountains of foodstuffs stockpiled there and then destroyed what they could not carry off. Jackson took up a strong defensive position along an unfinished railroad grade just west of the old Bull Run battlefield, overlooking the Warrenton Turnpike near the village of Groveton, and waited for Pope to react.

"Success and glory are in the advance, disaster and shame lurk in the rear," Pope had told his troops six weeks before. By August 27 it was clear to

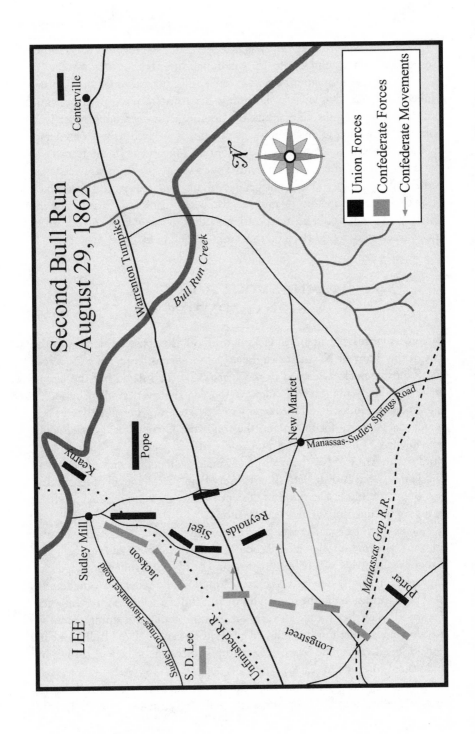

Second Bull Run
August 29, 1862

Union Forces
Confederate Forces
Confederate Movements

Centerville

Warrenton Turnpike

Bull Run Creek

New Market

Manassas-Sudley Springs Road

Pope

Kearny

Sudley Mill

LEE

Sudley Springs-Haymarket Road

Jackson

S. D. Lee

Unfinished R.R.

Sigel

Reynolds

Manassas Gap R.R.

Longstreet

Porter

Pope that at least Stonewall Jackson and a large segment of the Confederate army were lurking in the rear. Jackson's destruction of his supply line would have forced Pope to fall back in any event, but the aggressive Union general hoped that he could take advantage of the situation to trap and destroy Jackson's wing of the Army of Northern Virginia. Pope's withdrawal from the line of the Rappahannock necessarily released Lee to cross the river. This was exactly what Lee had intended to accomplish by Jackson's turning movement, forcing Pope back off the river and allowing Lee to get across it so that he could bring on a showdown battle with the outnumbered Union army somewhere north of it. He immediately put his large wing of the army, under the immediate command of Longstreet, on the march following Jackson's route to join Stonewall in the Union rear.

Pope mistakenly believed that Jackson was near Centerville and ordered his own army to concentrate on that place. As one of his divisions marched up the Warrenton Pike on the evening of August 28, Jackson decided it was time to attract Pope's attention somewhat more and gave the order for his troops to attack. Because the individual brigades of the Union division were strung out at long intervals, the fight that evening, which came to be known as the Battle of Groveton, pitted Ewell's division of Jackson's command, with 6,200 men, against little more than a single brigade of Federals, aided by a couple of regiments from the next brigade on the road, for a total Union strength of 2,100 men.

The Union brigade in question was the only brigade of western men fighting in Virginia, three regiments from Wisconsin and one from Indiana, under the command of Union-loyal North Carolinian John Gibbon (West Point, 1847), who had insisted that they wear the regulation dress uniform of the U.S. Army, with an almost knee-length uniform frock coat and a flat-topped, broad-brimmed black felt hat, encircled by a sky-blue wool hat cord and adorned with a small brass French-horn infantry pin in front and with the brim pinned up on the left side. The rest of the Union army preferred the more comfortable sack coat and kepi or forage cap, but Gibbon's boys soon learned to wear their regulation hats and coats with pride and gloried in being called the Black Hat Brigade until they earned another title.

On this August evening at Groveton, they faced what was for most of them their first combat and slugged it out at close range in the open field with Ewell's entire division, giving as good as they got. When darkness put a stop to the fighting, the battle had been a draw, and about one in every three men who had taken part in it was shot. Among the wounded was Ewell, whose shattered leg had to be amputated.

Once again Pope misinterpreted the intelligence he received, guessing that Jackson must have been in retreat from Centerville and that the clash with Gibbon's brigade had blocked his way. Jubilantly Pope concluded that he had Stonewall dead to rights and needed only to press on rapidly the next day and close in for the kill. He ignored other reports reaching him that day from the West. There an outlier of the Blue Ridge formed a range of hills known locally as Bull Run Mountain. The road Jackson had used to turn Pope passed through Bull Run Mountain at Thoroughfare Gap. That same August 28, Lee's own wing of the Army of Northern Virginia had pushed through the gap against the feeble resistance of a single poorly handled Union division. Bull Run Mountain had been the last obstacle in the way of Lee's reuniting with Jackson, which was now all but assured to happen within the next twenty-four to forty-eight hours, with ominous portent for the still oblivious Pope.

One bright spot in the outlook for Pope was that troops from the Army of the Potomac were finally beginning to join him, having come by ship up the Chesapeake from Harrison's Landing to Alexandria and then marched overland from there. Porter's Fifth Corps was on hand, as was the Third Corps under Major General Samuel Heintzelman (West Point, 1826). Two more corps, Franklin's Sixth and Major General Edwin V. Sumner's Second, had already landed at Alexandria, but McClellan would not let them advance to join Pope, citing vague concerns about their inadequate artillery and supply wagons. Less than three weeks earlier McClellan had written to his wife, "Pope will be badly thrashed within two days & . . . they will be very glad to turn over the redemption of their affairs to me. I won't undertake it unless I have full & entire control." Even as the battle was beginning in earnest on August 29 McClellan had advised Lincoln that it might be best "to leave Pope to get out of his scrape, and at once use all our means to make the capital perfectly safe."[4]

Beginning on the morning of August 29, Pope hurled his troops in one assault after another at Jackson's lines. The fighting was desperate, and sometimes Jackson's troops were on the verge of giving way, but each time they somehow rallied and held on. Lee, with Longstreet's twenty-eight thousand men, moved into position on Jackson's right, extending forward from the end of Jackson's line so as to threaten Pope's left flank. Union cavalry had brought reports of Longstreet's approach, but by this time Pope had made up his mind about the situation and was not going to be confused by facts. At first he refused to believe that Longstreet was present. Then he maintained that the larger Confederate force was on the field only for the purpose of covering the retreat of the full Confederate army, which he continued to insist was an ongoing effort.

When his assaults on the twenty-ninth failed to bring victory, Pope renewed his attacks on the thirtieth and continued them throughout most of the day. Finally, when Pope's army was exhausted and out of position from a day of fierce attacks that had once again come very close to success, Lee launched Longstreet's wing of his army in a giant flank attack that crumpled the left end of Pope's line. As the two armies struggled across the Bull Run battlefield where Union and Confederate had met thirteen months before, Henry House Hill once again became a key terrain feature, this time stubbornly held by Union troops to cover the retreat of the rest of the Army of Virginia northward across Bull Run. In the twilight, Pope's army made an orderly fighting retreat. It was a contrast with the undignified scramble of the previous summer, but it was still a retreat. Union casualties for the battle came to about ten thousand men, while Lee's losses were nearly as great at just over nine thousand.

Lee was by no means finished with Pope and sent Jackson swinging around the retreating Army of Virginia in another turning movement aimed at cutting Pope off from Washington and completing the destruction he had escaped at the Second Battle of Bull Run. Pope blocked Jackson in a September 1 clash at the hamlet of Chantilly. An inconclusive fight in the midst of a summer thunderstorm, Chantilly allowed Pope to complete his retreat to the fortifications around Washington. Lee had won a famous victory, but he had failed in his purpose of destroying Pope's army. Perhaps he could take comfort in reflecting that Pope was, in any case, "suppressed."

LEE MOVES NORTH

Lee's victories in the Seven Days and at the Second Battle of Bull Run had changed the momentum of the war in Virginia and shifted the scene of the fighting from the outskirts of Richmond north about one hundred miles to the outskirts of Washington. Of far greater importance, they had sent Confederate morale soaring, raised the Confederate image abroad, and discouraged the North. Lincoln sadly transferred Pope to Minnesota to deal with a Sioux uprising there, and with even greater sadness weighed the significance of reports he received that McClellan, Porter, and perhaps other officers of the Army of the Potomac had deliberately withheld needed support from Pope in hopes that he would experience a defeat. Porter would later be court-martialed and dismissed from the army for failing to obey one of Pope's attack orders during the battle, though the case would remain controversial for a generation and be overturned by the next Democrat to take the White House, Grover Cleveland, in 1886.

In having a desire to see Pope defeated, McClellan was, if anything, guiltier than Porter, but McClellan seemed to be, for the moment at least, indispensable. The army was dispirited, possibly too demoralized to fight effectively against an enemy whose aggressiveness seemed to know no respite. Lincoln believed that the only way to restore confidence and high morale in units of the Army of the Potomac was to restore them to McClellan's command. On September 2, Lincoln gave him command of all the Union forces in northern Virginia and Maryland. The three corps that had composed the Army of Virginia would henceforth be incorporated into the Army of the Potomac, to which the Ninth Corps was shortly added, fresh from its amphibious successes on the southern coast.

Lee's victories had affected foreign opinion as well and nowhere more than in Britain, where the government and many others within the landed gentry and wealthy mercantile classes had been none too well disposed toward the United States, which was their chief transatlantic rival and which the more perceptive of them could see was bound to surpass their country in power and greatness—if nothing happened to derail its growth. Now the British were closer than ever to outright recognition of Confederate independence. That summer U.S. ambassador to Britain Charles Francis Adams had learned that a ship under construction at the John Laird Sons and Company yard in Birkenhead was in fact intended for the Confederate navy. Acquired through the efforts of Confederate agent James Bullock, the vessel had been built in deep secrecy as hull number 290, a suspiciously sleek and powerful-looking bark-rigged ship with auxiliary steam power, then launched and christened the *Enrica*. Officials in the United States tried to get the British government to enforce its neutrality laws and seize the vessel, but before the British authorities acted, the mysterious *Enrica* had slipped out of port and rendezvoused at the island of Terceira in the mid-Atlantic with a Confederate supply ship that equipped her with eight cannon. With Confederate officers and a crew composed largely of Englishmen, she went into commission as the Confederate States Ship *Alabama*, a cruiser that would over the course of the next two years destroy millions of dollars worth of northern shipping. Historians still argue as to whether the British authorities deliberately dragged their feet in order to allow the *Alabama*'s escape from their waters, though after the war Britain paid the U.S. government an indemnity of more than fifteen million dollars. For now, though, the appearance of the Confederacy's swift new commerce raider served to underscore the apparently increasing British sympathy for the slaveholders' republic.

British leaders received news of the Confederate victories in Virginia that summer with delight. In the wake of Second Bull Run, Foreign Secretary Lord John Russell suggested to Prime Minister Lord Palmerston that the time had come for Britain to recognize the Confederacy and perhaps propose mediation with a view to restoring peace on the basis of Confederate independence. Palmerston was more cautious. He had heard that Lee was north of the Potomac, which if true was sure to bring a showdown battle. He told Russell they should await the outcome of that battle before acting.

Lee had indeed crossed the Potomac. After failing to trap Pope at Chantilly, Lee had decided to keep the momentum of his campaign going by swinging to the west of Washington and crossing into Maryland, with a view to possibly proceeding deep into Pennsylvania. He wrote to Davis, informing him of his plans and stating that he planned to cross the Potomac the next day unless contrary orders arrived from the Confederate president. Those would have had to have been already on the way since Lee's dispatch could not even have reached Davis before the first units of the Army of Northern Virginia began fording the Potomac near Leesburg on September 3.

By crossing the river east of the Blue Ridge and its northern extension, known somewhat perversely as South Mountain, Lee planned to keep up his threat to Washington, thus pinning Union troops down in its defenses. He then planned to march northwest and take control of the passes across South Mountain. These could be easily defended while his army cut off Washington's communication with the West via the Baltimore & Ohio Railroad and plundered the agricultural wealth of western Maryland and south-central Pennsylvania, living off the land and carrying away what it did not eat of the late-summer harvest. Also, Confederates had claimed since the beginning of the war that Maryland would eagerly join the Confederacy if not suppressed by Union troops. Some Marylanders certainly encouraged that view. A number of Maryland men had enlisted in the Confederate army, and some Maryland women had come south as refugees from Union rule, notably the beautiful and prominent Cary sisters of Baltimore, Jenny, Hetty, and their cousin Constance, who had sewn the first Confederate battle flag.

The Cary sisters also found a tune, "O Tannenbaum," to which James Ryder Randall's 1861 poem "Maryland, My Maryland" could be sung. Written in the wake of the Baltimore riot by a Marylander living in Louisiana, the poem called on citizens of the state to rise up and join the Confederacy:

The despot's heel is on thy shore,
Maryland! My Maryland!
His torch is at thy temple door,
Maryland! My Maryland!
Avenge the patriotic gore
That flecked the streets of Baltimore,
And be the battle queen of yore,
Maryland! My Maryland!

With eight more stanzas in similar vein, the song immediately became a
favorite all across the South, played by brass bands or sung by many a young

woman, accompanying herself on the piano, for the benefit of nattily uniformed young men about to depart for the seat of war. Various bands in Lee's
army played it as their units splashed through the shallow waters of the Potomac or marched northward into the Old Line State. This would be Maryland's chance to cast its lot with the Confederacy.

Lee believed he could remain in Maryland or in Pennsylvania for an
extended period with impunity because he reckoned that the Union army
around Washington was completely demoralized and would not be ready for
battle again for weeks if not months. If as reported McClellan was back in
command of that army, so much the better. Lee had taken McClellan's measure on the peninsula and believed he had little to fear from the Young Napoleon and certainly not anytime soon.

Lee hoped that his present campaign might be the last of the war. The
Confederacy was riding high after his recent victories, and even in the West,
Confederate armies had gone over to the offensive in Tennessee and Mississippi. Lee sent a dispatch to Jefferson Davis suggesting that with a Confederate army on northern soil, this would be a good time to call on Lincoln to
give up the war and grant Confederate independence. Davis thought more
like Palmerston, reckoning that a Confederate army north of the Potomac
guaranteed an impending showdown battle whose results both Lincoln and
the British would await before deciding their next move. To Lee's dismay,
however, Davis decided that the prospect of a battle leading to a political
settlement required his personal presence with the army and wrote Lee to say
he was coming. Lee did not want the president looking over his shoulder and
in a series of courteous but insistent dispatches succeeded in persuading Davis
that it would not be wise for him to hazard himself on the road between
Richmond and the army at this time.

The first disappointment for the Confederates was the chilly greeting
they received from the people of Maryland. Western Maryland, in which the
Army of Northern Virginia was now campaigning, was a land of relatively
few slaves and overwhelming allegiance to the Union. Only a few Marylanders hailed the Rebels' coming. If Lee's army was disappointed in the Marylanders, the feeling was mutual. Its ranks much diminished by battle losses,
as well as straggling by men exhausted or suffering from combat fatigue,
numbered only about thirty-eight thousand. After more than a year in an
army whose quartermaster department did at best an indifferent job of supplying new uniforms and accoutrements and after a summer of intense campaigning, the Confederate soldiers presented a ragged appearance, and one
Maryland diarist recorded that they were the dirtiest group of men she had

ever seen. The Marylanders had to admit, though, that Lee's men had a certain swagger about them.

A glitch arose in Lee's plan when the ten-thousand-man Union garrison of Harpers Ferry declined to evacuate when Lee's army passed north of it. Located where the Shenandoah River flows into the Potomac and then the Potomac passes through a narrow gap between the Blue Ridge and South Mountain, Harpers Ferry lies in a basin surrounded by high ground. No one could hold Harpers Ferry without holding that high ground. Lee's thirty-eight thousand men could fairly easily push the ten thousand Federals off the heights, trapping them in the basin of Harpers Ferry and compelling their surrender. That is why Lee had expected the Federals to pull out once he got well north of the Potomac. When they called his bluff and stayed put, Lee faced a difficult choice. To take the necessary high ground around Harpers Ferry, he would have to divide his army into at least three columns and send them marching by widely separated routes to come at Harpers Ferry from multiple directions. If McClellan moved aggressively toward him, Lee would be in a very dangerous situation with the components of his army so widely separated that they could not support each other and thus would be easy prey for the Army of the Potomac. Yet Lee could not afford to leave the Harpers Ferry garrison where it was since its presence in the lower Shenandoah Valley would interfere with his plans to have wagons haul at least some of his supplies from the valley via the excellent macadamized Valley Pike.

Lee believed he could trust McClellan not to be aggressive, and so on September 9, with his army encamped in and around Frederick, Maryland, Lee drafted Special Order Number 191, giving detailed instructions to his subordinates as to how the army should divide into four columns, three to march on Harpers Ferry by different routes and one to cover their rear against harassing Union cavalry from the direction of Washington by holding the passes of South Mountain. During the days that followed all went well for the Army of Northern Virginia as its separated components implemented Lee's plan. McClellan, who was under considerable pressure from Lincoln to do something about the Rebels north of the Potomac, advanced with uncharacteristic speed though still slow enough to give Lee plenty of time to carry out his plans. Thus, Lee's army marched northwest toward Harpers Ferry, and McClellan's, advancing from Washington, followed behind.

On the morning of September 13, some of McClellan's troops were resting in a field outside Frederick when two Indiana soldiers found three cigars lying on the ground, wrapped with a paper that, on further examination, looked important. History does not tell us what happened to the cigars, but

Harpers Ferry

the paper, which was a copy of Lee's Special Order Number 191, was quickly passed up the chain of command to McClellan himself, who read it and exclaimed, "Now I know what to do! Here is a paper with which, if I cannot whip Bobby Lee, I will be ready to go home." To Lincoln he telegraphed, "No time shall be lost. I think Lee has made a gross mistake, and that he will be severely punished for it. I have all the plans of the rebels, and will catch them in their own trap if my men are equal to the emergency."

Special Order Number 191 told McClellan that Lee's army was scattered and vulnerable and furthermore told him exactly where he could find its isolated parts. Since the order was already several days old, time was of the essence. A competent general would have put his army in motion at once. McClellan ordered the Army of the Potomac to wait eighteen hours and march the following morning, September 14.

Lee was stunned when scouts informed him that the Army of the Potomac was advancing aggressively toward the detachments he had left to hold three key gaps in South Mountain. Shortly thereafter he learned the reason why. A pro-Confederate civilian had actually been inside McClellan's headquarters when Special Order Number 191 arrived and brought word to Lee of the intelligence disaster. A quick investigation revealed the source of the leak. D. H. Hill's division had been operating with Jackson's command but still technically answered to Lee's headquarters. Both headquarters had copied the order to Hill, each not realizing what the other had done. Hill received only one of the copies, but when he confirmed that he had it, each headquarters assumed that all copies of the order were accounted for. The extra copy had somehow ended up wrapped around the cigars in the field outside Frederick.

Lee moved to salvage the situation, positioning his available troops to hold the passes of South Mountain. Most of his army had recently taken up its positions surrounding Harpers Ferry, and the only way they could quickly reunite would be through Harpers Ferry. If the Federal outpost held out several more days and if McClellan acted intelligently on the information he now had, Lee's situation would be dire.

THE BATTLE OF ANTIETAM

Prospects for the Army of Northern Virginia looked very grim indeed as Federal troops approached South Mountain that afternoon and, after several hours of cautious preparations, moved to assault the outnumbered Confederates. The heaviest fighting took place at Turner's Gap, northernmost of the three, where the National Road passed over the mountain and Lee had most of his troops. Watching Gibbon's Black Hat Brigade drive the defenders back toward the gap, McClellan is supposed to have exclaimed that the brigade was made of iron, giving it a new nickname, the Iron Brigade. Fighting continued at Turner's Gap for several hours, and the Confederates were just on the point of losing their last grip on the gap as darkness fell.

A few miles to the south, other Confederate forces successfully held Fox's Gap, but a few miles beyond that lay Crampton's Gap, where Confederate numbers had sufficed to provide only a few hundred defenders. McClellan protégé William B. Franklin, commanding the Sixth Corps, delayed for hours before launching an attack with overwhelming numbers that cleared the gap. With that, Franklin was in position to begin the destruction of Lee's army since he could have advanced toward Harpers Ferry, scarcely ten miles away, and made the fragmentation of Lee's army complete and irrevocable. Franklin was a true disciple of his mentor McClellan, however, and so, concluding that he was vastly outnumbered when in fact the exact opposite was the case, he halted and took up a defensive position.

Providence had already granted Lee a boon in the slowness with which McClellan had responded to the information in Special Order Number 191. Franklin's lethargy and caution was a second gift. After that, one thing after another seemed to go Lee's way. Confederate troops had to fall back from their positions on South Mountain that night, but McClellan kept his army almost stationary on September 15. Meanwhile, the Confederates had surrounded Harpers Ferry, and Jackson was presiding over efforts to capture the town and its garrison. Union commander Colonel Dixon S. Miles pulled almost all of his troops back into the indefensible town, virtually giving away the key high ground that overlooked it. Then on the morning of September 15 when Jackson launched his attack, Miles was so quick to order his command to surrender that he probably would have been court-martialed when Union forces next got hold of him had he not been struck and killed by one of the last artillery shells the Confederates fired before the white flag went up.

The surrender of Harpers Ferry gave the Confederates ten thousand Union prisoners and opened the way for the Army of Northern Virginia to reunite. Lee brought them together near the town of Sharpsburg, Maryland, about a dozen miles due north of Harpers Ferry, ten miles west of South Mountain, and a mile or two east of the Potomac, which here flowed from north to south. He deployed them facing east, toward South Mountain and McClellan's approaching army, on gently rolling terrain, with the valley of Antietam Creek in front of them.

Lee still had high hopes for victory, planning to repeat the successful formula of Second Bull Run. If it worked, he would lure McClellan into bloodying the Army of the Potomac in fruitless assaults and then conclude the battle with another devastating Confederate flank attack like the one with which Longstreet had ruined Pope on the plains of Manassas. The plan was audacious in the extreme. Lee's army was weakened by a summer of brutal campaigning and had been shedding stragglers steadily since it had marched north from Richmond. Worse, Lee's position, although presenting reasonable cover and good fields of fire, had key weaknesses. In front of it, Antietam Creek, with three stone bridges and several fords, offered only a minor obstacle to the enemy, while behind Lee's position, the Potomac was crossable at only one point, Boteler's Ford. Getting an army across Boteler's Ford would take hours, and if disaster befell his army, Lee would not be able to withdraw any substantial number of his troops via that ford before they were overrun and captured. Defeat on this field would be final for Lee and the Army of Northern Virginia.

Lee arrived near Sharpsburg on September 15 and began deploying the first units of his army, numbering about eighteen thousand men. The first elements of the Army of the Potomac arrived on the far side of the Antietam Valley that afternoon, and by nightfall virtually all of McClellan's troops were arrayed there. Thus, on the morning of September 16, Lee's eighteen thousand faced some ninety thousand Federals, and McClellan had the opportunity to crush the Confederate force at Sharpsburg and take it and its commander as prisoners. As Lee had apparently calculated, the Union commander hesitated. Convinced that Lee had one hundred thousand or perhaps one hundred fifty thousand men, McClellan spent the day studying Lee's position through a very large telescope mounted just outside the house he was using as his headquarters. While McClellan and his top generals took turns squinting into the eyepiece, most of the rest of Lee's army arrived from Harpers Ferry.

McClellan planned to push one wing of his army across Antietam Creek north of Lee's position and open the battle by having it attack southward between the Antietam and the Potomac. Union preparations on the evening of the sixteenth were obvious, and Lee had Jackson's wing of his own army positioned to meet the Union thrust. Action began at first light on the morning of September 17, about 5:30, and raged intensely on the northern end of the battlefield for the next five hours.

McClellan dissipated his advantage in numbers by committing his units piecemeal, one corps at a time, so that the Confederate defenders were able to shift to meet them. With the southern half of the battlefield quiet, Lee pulled troops out of line there to support Jackson on the left. Even at that, the Federals nearly broke through. The fighting raged back and forth, and the cornfield of a farmer named Miller changed hands as many as fifteen times and was left thickly strewn with corpses and with nearly every cornstalk cut down by bullets. By late morning the Federals on this front had reached their initial objective, a plain, whitewashed meetinghouse of a sect of German Baptists whom locals derisively called "Dunkers," but the Union attack was spent and could go no farther. Jackson, who realized that his line had several times that morning been within an ace of total collapse, attributed his successful defense to divine intervention.

About that time, fighting flared up in the center of the Confederate line, where a stray Union division had at first attacked by mistake. The Confederate position was extremely strong, but Lee and Jackson had left only the minimum defenders in their desperate quest to find every available man to hold the line near the Dunker Church. Both sides now fed reinforcements into the fight in the center, which focused on a sunken road—a dirt road eroded below surrounding ground level—that the Confederates used as a ready-made trench. One Union brigade after another attacked the Sunken Road until finally the Confederate line gave way. Longstreet, who commanded this sector, had no troops left to plug what was now a yawning gap in the center of his line. He had his artillery open fire on the pursuing Yankees and even assigned his own staff to man one of the guns after its crew had been shot down.

Though the troops that had captured the Sunken Road were fought out, McClellan had plenty of reserves and could have poured them into the gap, ripping Lee's army in two and completing its destruction. Franklin, whose Sixth Corps had not yet fired a shot in the battle, requested permission to advance and exploit the breakthrough, but McClellan refused. Sometime later, a division commander in the Fifth Corps, which had also been unengaged, suggested to McClellan that his corps ought to be ordered in. Overhearing the exchange, Fifth Corps commander Fitz John Porter cautioned McClellan, "Remember, General, I command the last reserve of the last Army of the Republic." This was errant nonsense, but it was good enough for McClellan, who left the Fifth Corps idle.

Meanwhile, on the southern end of the battlefield, Ambrose Burnside, with his Ninth Corps, was supposed to be diverting Confederate attention by crossing to the west bank of Antietam Creek. Here the Confederate line ran along the slope of a bluff that towered one hundred feet above the creek. Burnside was a highly intelligent, dedicated officer who on this day began giving the first indications that he was extremely inept at handling large bodies of troops on a battlefield. Although the creek was fordable in many places, Burnside focused his attention on a narrow, three-arched, stone bridge toward which he launched several attacks that either were broken up by the fire of a few hundred Confederates on the bluff or else veered off course and reached the wrong stretch of the creek. While Burnside strove earnestly but ineffectually for three hours to get his men across the waist-deep creek, McClellan dispatched a succession of increasingly insistent messages demanding action, and Lee drew off all but a handful of the units that had been guarding Burnside's front and shifted the troops to help hold his desperately hard-pressed left and center—exactly what Burnside was supposed to prevent.

Finally, around 1:00 in the afternoon, Burnside got a compact column of troops to charge straight across the bridge into the teeth of the Confederate fire. At almost the same time, one of his divisions found and used a ford

The stone bridge that took Burnside hours to cross at Antietam. Confederate sharpshooters occupied the hillside rising on the left-hand side of the creek, as viewed in this photograph. Courtesy of the Library of Congress.

about two miles downstream and flanked the Rebels. At last Burnside's corps streamed across the creek, formed its line atop the bluff on the west bank, and then had to wait in ranks for two hours while ammunition was brought up via the narrow bottleneck of the bridge. At last, at 3:00 p.m., the Ninth Corps swept forward and crushed the weakened right flank of Lee's line. Fleeing Confederates ran through the streets of Sharpsburg while Burnside's formation bore down not only on the town but also on Boteler's Ford, Lee's only line of retreat.

In the midst of their triumphant advance, the Federals were stunned when a new wave of Confederates struck their flank. A. P. Hill's division was the last of Jackson's troops to leave Harpers Ferry after processing the prisoners and booty there, and it reached the battlefield just in time to counterattack the Ninth Corps. Flanked, surprised, and further confused by the fact that many of Hill's Confederates were wearing Union uniforms captured at Harpers Ferry, the Federals fell back with heavy losses. They regrouped atop the bluffs and still outnumbered the Confederates in front of them, including

Hill's division, by a margin to two to one. Burnside, however, had had enough and ordered his corps to fall back to the east bank of the creek and assume the position in which they had started the day.

The guns fell silent. It was 5:30 p.m. More than 3,600 men lay dead on the field, a record that still stands for the largest number of Americans to die in battle in a single day. More than seventeen thousand others were wounded. The hours of darkness that night gave Lee the opportunity to use Boteler's Ford to retreat into Virginia, but he did not. Instead he kept his army on the battlefield the next day, daring McClellan to renew the assault and contemplating an attack of his own until Jackson tactfully showed him the impracticality of the idea. With an additional day's opportunity of trapping Lee's woefully outnumbered army with its back to the Potomac, McClellan did nothing. In the previous day's battle, he had committed scarcely two-thirds of his army, and he had nearly as many fresh troops left now as Lee had battle-weary men who could still stand on two legs. Yet McClellan remained convinced that somewhere behind the bluffs along the Potomac, another hundred thousand or so Rebels lurked, ready at any moment to swarm out and overwhelm his outnumbered Army of the Potomac. During the night of

Confederate dead at Antietam.

the eighteenth to the nineteenth of September, Lee reluctantly retreated across the Potomac into Virginia, marking the end of the campaign.

In military terms, the campaign had decided nothing. Lee's army had marched into Maryland, and it had marched back out again. No territory or resources had changed hands for longer than the few days the campaign lasted, and the relative strengths of both sides had remained the same. At most these fifteen days in September had revealed the resilience of the northern soldiers in returning to battle and fighting hard despite that summer's setbacks, and it had revealed the loyalty to the Union of the large majority of the citizens of western Maryland.

However, by forcing Lee to retreat across the Potomac much earlier than he had obviously planned, the Battle of Antietam had given Lincoln the victory he had been awaiting since July and with it the opportunity to issue the preliminary Emancipation Proclamation, thus opening a new chapter in the war.

7

LINCOLN TAKES
NEW MEASURES

THE EMANCIPATION
PROCLAMATION

On September 22, 1862, in the wake of what had been at least a strategic victory at Antietam, Lincoln issued the preliminary Emancipation Proclamation. In it the president announced that one hundred days from that date, January 1, 1863, all slaves living in areas then still in rebellion against the United States would be henceforth and forever free. The Emancipation Proclamation changed the immediate goal of the Union forces in the Civil War but not its underlying issues. The war had from the beginning been about slavery. Rebellious southerners had launched the Confederacy for the purpose of spreading and preserving slavery, while Lincoln had led the North in fighting to preserve the Union and constitutional government. Now the war would become as explicitly a contest about slavery on the part of the North as it had been from the opening shot, and before, on the part of the South.

The Emancipation Proclamation would also change the way the war was fought. Once it was issued, or at least once Lincoln's January 1 deadline had passed, there could be no more thought of conciliating the South. The trend to hard war, with southern civilians feeling all of the harshness conquered citizens usually do feel in a civilized war, would continue apace. Most white southerners would fight to the bitter end to preserve slavery and the system of white supremacy for which they thought it the only protection, and they would fight with renewed bitterness and intensity. Once the Union began recruiting black troops the following year, Confederate troops perpetrated a number of atrocities and massacres against them when they had opportunity. The war was becoming even more brutal than it had been up to now.

Reaction to the proclamation in the South was predictable. An outraged Jefferson Davis inveighed against the proclamation as "the most execrable measure in the history of guilty man" and announced that henceforth captured Union officers would not be treated as prisoners of war but would instead be turned over to state authorities for punishment as "criminals engaged in inciting servile insurrection." That threat was never carried out, possibly because the Union threatened retaliation on Confederate officers. Other white southerners denounced the proclamation in extreme terms. Confederate dentist and cartoonist Adalbert Volck depicted Lincoln as consorting with demonic spirits while writing the proclamation and contemplating with satisfaction imagined scenes of racial massacre.

Reaction among pro-Confederate northerners and even some Union-loyal Democrats was almost the same as that in the South. A regiment from southern Illinois, a part of the state where proslavery feeling ran strong, mutinied and had to be disbanded. In Virginia, McClellan was furious. To his wife he wrote, "I cannot make up my mind to fight for such an accursed doctrine." Nonetheless, at the urging of more level-headed fellow officers, he restrained himself and issued a very correct general order to the troops of his army, reminding them that "the remedy for political errors, if any are committed, is to be found only in the action of the people at the polls."

Abolitionists rejoiced all across the North, and a growing number of northerners who had never considered themselves abolitionists also applauded the proclamation as a necessary step toward winning the war. If slavery was trying to destroy the nation, one soldier wrote in a letter that was representative of the feelings of many northerners, then slavery needed to be destroyed. In the midterm elections that fall, the Republicans lost twenty-eight seats in the House of Representatives. Some of those losses may have been due to popular opposition to emancipation, but more were probably in response to disappointment with the apparent lack of progress in the war. Americans were and are notoriously impatient about such things. Placed in perspective, however, the Republicans' electoral losses did not amount to much anyway. They lost fewer seats in Congress than the party holding the White House usually lost in midterm elections during that era.

British reaction to the Emancipation Proclamation was complicated. After a long and arduous political struggle, Britain had abolished slavery in

Lincoln with McClellan (center left, facing Lincoln) after the Battle of Antietam.

all of its colonies in 1833, and since that time, Britons had come to pride themselves on their antislavery principles and feel rather superior to their American cousins on that score, as they did on every other. British leaders and much of the British press had for years sneered at the United States for its tolerance of slavery. During the first phase of the Civil War, British leadership could and did maintain that the Union cause was not the cause of freedom since the government in Washington did not have immediate emancipation as one of its direct war aims.

Now that had changed, and one would have expected to see the British government rally enthusiastically to the cause of freedom—if its prior strictures against the United States had been sincere. In fact, Prime Minister Viscount Palmerston and Foreign Minister Earl Russell were furious, ostensibly because they believed that the proclamation would incite slave revolt and massacres but perhaps because they resented losing their grounds for claiming moral superiority over the United States. At any rate, they came as close to leading Britain to war with the United States then as they ever did during the course of the war. Ultimately they did not dare to do so because of the tremendous outpouring of support for the Union among Britain's middle and lower classes. Henry Adams, son of the highly capable U.S. ambassador to Britain Charles Francis Adams, wrote, "The Emancipation Proclamation has done more for us than all our former victories and all our diplomacy." Though the Union cause had always been that of freedom, the Emancipation Proclamation made that fact clearly recognizable to the common man in Europe, and millions responded with enthusiastic approval. In vain, the haughty *Times* of London sniffed that the proclamation declared free only those slaves whom Lincoln had no ability to free and left in slavery all those whom he supposedly could have freed. The great majority of Britons recognized the proclamation's tendency as clearly as Jefferson Davis had.

From that time to this, some have wondered about the apparent discrepancy the *Times* mentioned. Lincoln declared free those slaves in areas still in rebellion—areas where he had no control. He left untouched those slaves in areas loyal to the Union—areas where one might assume that he did have the power to act. In fact, Lincoln's action was dictated by respect for law and fear of the federal courts, especially Roger B. Taney's Supreme Court. Lincoln did not want to violate the Constitution, and he believed that emancipation as an exercise of presidential war power, a hostile act aimed at subduing enemies who were waging war against the United States, was indeed constitutional. He also knew that if given a chance, Taney would strike down any action that impinged on slavery whether it was constitutional or not. An act of war by the president would not immediately land in the federal courts and so, unlike the Confiscation Acts, would not give Taney his chance. Of course, freeing the slaves by an exercise of presidential war powers meant that Lincoln did not, in fact, have the authority to free any slaves in areas not at war against the United States, the areas the *Times* had blamed him for neglecting.

When Lincoln at last issued the final Emancipation Proclamation on January 1, 1863, he therefore omitted from its application the non-Confederate slave states of Delaware, Maryland, Kentucky, and Missouri as well as the northwestern portion of Virginia, soon to become the separate state of West Virginia; the approximately half-liberated Confederate state of Tennessee; and several Union-occupied parishes of Louisiana around New Orleans. Of the three and a half million slaves in America at that time, only about twenty thousand actually experienced their official freedom on that day. These were contrabands who had fled into Union lines and were for the most part living in contraband camps in areas that were still technically regarded as war zones. These twenty thousand had not exactly liberated themselves, but they had cooperated in their liberation, as hundreds of thousands of their fellow slaves would do before the war was over. For slaves still behind Confederate lines on the first day of 1863 and for their masters, the Emancipation Proclamation was a declaration of war aims. A promise of what Union forces would do when they arrived. Slaves and slaveholders in the omitted areas could easily read the portents and see that once slavery was eradicated in the rebellious states, its lease on life elsewhere in the United States would be very short indeed.

THE KENTUCKY CAMPAIGN

None of this would become reality, however, if Union armies did not win the war, and even as Lincoln issued his September 22 preliminary Emancipation Proclamation, two major Confederate offenses were still in full swing west of the Appalachians in the strategically decisive heartland of the South. Even before Lee had started his abortive foray into Maryland, Confederate forces in the West had seized the initiative, and as of the time of Lee's retreat across the Potomac, the western Confederate forces were still pressing their offensives.

After capturing Corinth with his massive army at the end of May, Henry Halleck had dispersed his forces around West Tennessee and northern Mississippi with a view to holding the territory gained in the Union's successful spring campaigns in the West. He had dispatched Buell with about thirty thousand men to march east from Corinth, along the line of the Memphis & Charleston Railroad, repairing the railroad as he went and using it as a supply line. His objective was Chattanooga, Tennessee. A small, ramshackle town of perhaps two thousand inhabitants sprawling on the banks of the Tennessee River at the foot of 1,500-foot Lookout Mountain, Chattanooga was the gateway to the southern Appalachians. It sat at the eastern end of the gorge by which the Tennessee River plunged through the Allegheny Range, here known as the Cumberland Plateau, and from it railroads ran not only west to Corinth and Memphis but also northeast through Union-sympathizing East Tennessee to Virginia and southeast to Atlanta and the heart of Georgia. Taking it would be a first step toward Lincoln's long-desired goal of liberating the loyal citizens of East Tennessee, would seal off the most convenient line of rail communication between the Confederate eastern and western theaters, and would open the door for Union penetration into Georgia.

The task of defending Chattanooga fell to Confederate Major General Edmund Kirby Smith (West Point, 1845), who commanded the Confederate Army of East Tennessee. Smith's task was complicated by the fact that he

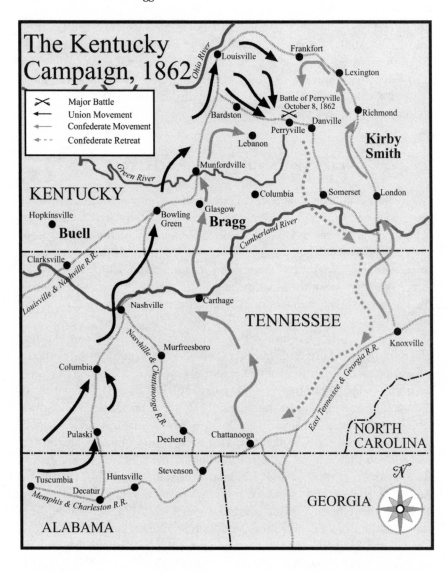

The Kentucky Campaign, 1862

✕	Major Battle
←	Union Movement
←	Confederate Movement
◄--	Confederate Retreat

also had to defend Knoxville, one hundred miles to the northeast, which seemed to be threatened by a Union division under the command of Brigadier General George W. Morgan. Morgan had been a West Point classmate of Smith's before dropping out because of bad grades. His force had recently driven some of Smith's troops out of Cumberland Gap and occupied that position sixty miles north of Knoxville.

Smith felt he had far too few men to defend against these two, widely separated threats and thought his situation almost hopeless. The only ray of hope for the Confederates in East Tennessee lay in the fact that Buell was advancing very slowly, partially because he was Buell and partially because Confederate guerrillas were swarming the countryside through which he was passing, wrecking the tracks of the Memphis & Ohio behind him as fast as his men could repair them in front and necessitating constant detachments to repair tracks and chase guerrillas. As typical guerrillas, the Rebel raiders sheltered among the civil population, finding comfort and supply there and shielding behind (and thus abusing) the immunity that civilized armies attempt to show toward civilians. Just as typically in such a situation, Union troops grew increasingly frustrated with the guerrillas' depredations and with the need to show restraint toward civilians, some of whom were undoubtedly collaborating with the bushwhackers who took potshots at them and waylaid their supply shipments. When Federal self-control slipped to the point that a Union brigade sacked the town of Athens, Alabama, a major scandal and federal government investigation followed. Nevertheless, at Athens, as on most occasions during the Civil War, the lives and persons of civilians remained safe, as the angry soldiers contented themselves with taking and destroying property.

Buell's slow progress across northern Alabama gave the Confederates time to react. The passive stance of the scattered Union forces Halleck had left in northern Mississippi placed no pressure on Confederate forces in that sector and thus left them available to counter Buell. The Confederate Army of Tennessee (not to be confused with Grant's Union Army of *the* Tennessee) had been encamped around Tupelo, Mississippi, since its retreat from Corinth. A few weeks after the retreat, Beauregard had granted himself an open-ended leave to recuperate at a southern Alabama health spa. Civil War commanding generals were not expected to take leaves, and this act was the last straw for Jefferson Davis, who promptly sacked Beauregard and replaced him with the army's second-ranking general, Braxton Bragg.

It was therefore to Bragg, as well as to the authorities in Richmond, that Smith appealed for help in stopping Buell's much larger force and saving Chattanooga. Richmond had no troops to send, and at first it seemed that Bragg was equally unable to help, faced as he was with Halleck's originally much larger Union army at Corinth. Desperate, Smith renewed his appeals, urging that if Bragg would bring his entire army to Chattanooga and operate from there, he, Smith, would be glad to serve as Bragg's subordinate in the campaign that would follow. Bragg outranked Smith, but since Smith had an

General Edmund Kirby Smith   *General Braxton Bragg*

independent command, the latter would not have been required by military law to obey Bragg unless the two were actually together at the same place. Smith was offering a higher degree of cooperation if Bragg would help him.

As the summer progressed, Bragg began to think this might be a good idea. The Union forces in front of him were spread out in garrisons holding West Tennessee and extreme northern Mississippi. They were obviously going nowhere, but he could get nowhere against them. He began to see that a rapid move to Chattanooga could do much more than just save the gateway to Georgia and East Tennessee. It could shift the whole momentum of the war in the region west of the Appalachians. Bragg decided to leave detachments in Mississippi to counter the two chief Union threats to the state. Sixteen thousand men under Major General Sterling Price would stay to watch the Federals in northern Mississippi, while about that many more Confederates would remain in the state under the command of Major General Earl Van Dorn, ready to counter Union efforts at taking the Mississippi River town of Vicksburg. After Farragut had taken New Orleans that April, he had taken his fleet up the river, captured Baton Rouge, and tried to take Vicksburg. There he had been joined by the Union river gunboat fleet—Pook's Turtles and their timber-clad consorts—which had defeated a Confederate riverboat fleet and captured Memphis in June. Only Vicksburg remained as a

Confederate outpost on the Mississippi, and Van Dorn was supposed to see that it held out.

With the rest of his force Bragg undertook the boldest strategic movement of the war to date. While his cavalry, artillery, and supply wagons proceeded across northern Alabama at a safe distance from Buell's plodding army, his infantry would board trains and ride the railroad to Mobile, Alabama, where they would transfer to a different railroad for the ride up to Chattanooga. It was the most significant use of railroads in the history of warfare up to that time, and it put Bragg's troops in Chattanooga in time to stop Buell, who was getting very close. As soon as the artillery and wagons arrived, the army would be ready to march northward into Middle Tennessee, turning Buell and threatening his supply lines.

Steamboats at the landing in Vicksburg.

Kirby Smith was delighted. While Bragg held Chattanooga and waited for his artillery and wagons, Smith took his own small army, reinforced with the largest division of Bragg's army, and marched north to deal with the small Union division at Cumberland Gap. Arriving in front of the gap, Smith sent a dispatch back to Bragg informing him that the Union position was too strong to attack and that he preferred going around the Federals by one of the other nearby gaps and entering Kentucky. Like Maryland, Kentucky was seen by Confederates as a slave state held in bondage to the Union only by the presence of Federal troops. That concept served as a powerful lure to Kirby Smith and a temptation for him to set aside his promises of obedience to Bragg as well as his strategic common sense.

The view that Kentuckians were awaiting only the appearance of a Confederate army to rise en masse and throw off the yoke of northern oppression had recently been reinforced by the exploits of the colorful and romantic Colonel John Hunt Morgan. In July, the Kentuckian Morgan had led his nine hundred Confederate horsemen on a daring raid into the Bluegrass State, capturing small Union detachments, including one Union brigadier general; damaging Union installations; destroying supplies; and leading the pursuing Union cavalry on a frustrating and fruitless chase. The enthusiastic reaction of Kentucky crowds, especially women, when Morgan's command rode through towns encouraged Confederate commanders like Kirby Smith to assume that tens of thousands of men in the state were only waiting for the opportunity to join the Rebel army.

Smith's planned lunge into Kentucky made political sense within the context of such assumptions, but it was not good military strategy since it would put Bragg and Smith too far apart to support each other and would leave Buell in their rear. It would work only if Kentuckians would rise en masse to help the Confederates drive out the Yankees. Despite Bragg's urging and Smith's own previous promise to obey Bragg's orders, Smith defied the higher-ranking officer and led his troops into the Bluegrass State.

Henceforth Smith's irresponsibility would control Bragg's movements during this campaign. When on August 28 Bragg finally had his wagons and artillery on hand and could begin his march northward from Chattanooga, he had to keep his army between Smith on the one hand and Buell's Union army on the other. To do otherwise would invite Buell to crush the two separate Confederate forces one at a time. Without Smith and the troops he had lent him, Bragg did not have men enough to fight Buell in Middle Tennessee, where he had hoped to stage the showdown battle of the campaign, and instead was forced by Kirby Smith's maneuver to advance his army into Kentucky as well, swinging north and west on the inside track of Smith's movement. Whether Bragg liked it or not, his whole campaign was now staked on the response of the Kentuckians. Hoping for the best, he brought along in his army's wagons twenty thousand extra rifles to equip the hordes of Kentucky recruits for whom he and other Confederates earnestly hoped.

As Smith advanced into Kentucky, he first passed through the hilly southeastern part of the state, an area where slave ownership was relatively rare and the people were generally hostile to the Confederate cause. As the march continued, his small army was happy to leave behind the rugged hill country and descend to what Smith called "the long, rolling landscape" that characterized the wealthy Bluegrass section of the state. Waiting for them there, near the town of Richmond, Kentucky, was an even smaller blue-clad force that Union authorities had hastily scraped together from inexperienced recruits who had responded to Lincoln's call for "three hundred thousand more." Smith's tough veterans defeated them easily, rounding up hundreds of prisoners and sending the rest fleeing in disorder from the battlefield. Then the Rebels advanced unopposed the remaining twenty-five miles and occupied Lexington, chief city of the Bluegrass region. Crowds of Kentuckians turned out to see and occasionally cheer them, especially women, who fluttered their handkerchiefs in greeting, but Smith thought that men were distinctly underrepresented among the spectators. Recruits were rare, but Smith's Confederates settled down to occupy the Bluegrass and requisition its abundant supplies.

Abandoned by Smith, Bragg was not strong enough to seek battle with Buell in Middle Tennessee, but he did outmarch Buell, beating the Federals to Kentucky and capturing a Union brigade that had been guarding the bridge over the Green River at Munfordville. Bragg's position at Munfordville put him squarely athwart Buell's supply line running back to Louisville. Buell could, if he chose, try to march around Bragg on one side or the other, but that would make his army vulnerable to Bragg's attack. If he chose to attack Bragg head-on at Munfordville, the Rebels, defending a strong position, would have even more advantages. It appeared that Bragg's skill and his troops' hard marching might win this campaign in spite of Kirby Smith.

One reason Buell moved so slowly was that he insisted on bringing with his army an unusually large number of wagons laden with supplies. Conversely, Bragg moved more quickly because his army traveled light and lived off the land. Encamped at Munfordville waiting for Buell to move, the Rebels soon exhausted local supplies. Kirby Smith was deaf to Bragg's pleas that he either join him at Munfordville or at least send some of the supplies his men were gathering in the rich agricultural district around Lexington. Buell, who still had adequate supplies, was in no hurry to move, and finally Bragg had to give up and march east to join Smith near Lexington. That cleared the way for Buell to advance to Louisville, where he received abundant reinforcements and supplies and could reorganize and refit his army.

While Buell was busy in Louisville, Bragg tried one last gambit to salvage the campaign. Little chance remained of defeating Buell in battle with the Confederate forces then in Kentucky, and pitifully few Kentuckians had enlisted during the campaign. Perhaps if Bragg could install a pro-Confederate state government at Frankfort, Kentuckians would feel more motivated to volunteer, and if they did not, a pro-Confederate state government was just the thing Bragg needed to help him implement the Confederacy's conscription law within the state. Richard Hawes, the Confederacy's shadow governor for Kentucky, had accompanied Bragg on the campaign, and in a formal ceremony at Frankfort on October 4, 1862, Bragg had him inaugurated.

No sooner had Hawes finished his inaugural address than the sound of artillery fire to the northwest alerted the small assembly of Confederate officers and pro-Confederate Kentuckians that a strong Union column was approaching the state capital from the direction of Louisville. Apprised by scouts that the Federals were too numerous to be turned back by the detachment of his own army at Frankfort, Bragg had to beat a hasty and ignominious retreat, together with the would-be governor, now returned to exile status after only a few hours in the capital city he claimed.

With Kentucky men of military age still avoiding Confederate ranks in droves, almost no hope remained for the success of the campaign, the central guiding concept of which—Kirby Smith's confidence that Kentuckians were eager to join the Confederacy—had been shown to be a delusion. Still Bragg was determined to try every possible alternative before giving it up. Buell was advancing from Louisville in several different columns on separate roads. Bragg saw an opportunity to attack and possibly destroy the Union column approaching Lexington. He ordered Kirby Smith to attack it head-on while Leonidas Polk, commanding Bragg's own army while Bragg exercised overall command of both forces, was to swing northwest and strike the Federals in the flank. The plan failed before it could begin as Polk became frightened and refused to obey Bragg's orders, forcing Bragg to call off Smith's attack. With that there was nothing left to do but abandon Lexington and begin retreating in a southeasterly direction.

As Bragg's forces pulled out of the Bluegrass region and fell back toward the southeast and Buell's separate columns continued advancing toward them from Louisville, Buell's main column collided with Confederate forces near the town of Perryville on October 8, about forty miles southwest of Lexington. Not realizing the size of the force in front of him, Bragg attacked. Buell, whose headquarters were a couple of miles behind the front, somehow did not hear the firing because of a rare phenomenon called an acoustic shadow, an atmospheric phenomenon in which very loud sounds that can be heard at long distances are nevertheless inaudible at medium distances. Unaware that a battle was in progress, Buell sent no aid to his frontline troops.

Buell had cultivated a climate of command in his army such that none of his subordinates who did know about the battle felt authorized to send help either. For that reason and because many of the Union troops were green, the Confederates experienced initial success, driving the Federals back as much as a mile in some places before more experienced Union troops arrived and made a stand. The Confederate success had been not quite sufficient to start a chain reaction that might have led to the collapse of Buell's larger army, and once the front was stabilized, the opportunity was past.

When Bragg that night learned the size of the Union force he was confronting, he resumed his retreat toward Tennessee. Buell made little effort to pursue and instead turned away and marched his army slowly to Nashville. The campaign was over, and neither side was satisfied. Kentuckians within the ranks of the Confederate army did not want to face the fact that their state had chosen not to fight for the Confederacy, so they blamed Bragg. Polk and Kirby Smith had performed poorly in the campaign, and they knew that Bragg knew it. So they blamed him too. Bragg was not adept at winning friends and influencing people, but even a skillful politician might have struggled to overcome the persistent campaign of undermining that would now be waged against him within the officer corps of his own army.

On the Union side, Buell's slowness and lack of aggressiveness was the object of contempt both among many of his subordinates and among his superiors in Washington. During the midst of the campaign, Lincoln had decided to replace Buell with Army of the Ohio corps commander George H. Thomas (West Point, 1840). That would have been a disappointment, since Thomas, though steadier and more competent than Buell, was nearly as slow. As it turned out, Thomas refused the proffered promotion, perhaps because he supported Buell's policies and perhaps because he did not want the responsibility of getting the army out of the mess Buell had gotten it into. Now with the campaign over and the Confederates having escaped back into Tennessee more or less unscathed, Buell's continued tenure in command of the Army of the Ohio was precarious.

IUKA, CORINTH, AND THE
HATCHIE RIVER

While Lee had ventured briefly into Maryland and Bragg and Kirby Smith had made their separate and poorly coordinated thrusts into Kentucky, a third simultaneous Confederate offensive had sputtered to an abortive start in northern Mississippi. Bragg had left Price there to watch the Federals at Corinth, Memphis, and other garrisons and had left Van Dorn in the central part of the state to watch the Union threat to Vicksburg. By late summer falling water levels in the Mississippi River had driven Farragut's ships back down to New Orleans, relieving the pressure on Vicksburg and freeing Van Dorn to join Price in an offensive that would support Bragg's efforts in Middle Tennessee and Kentucky. Together they would have about thirty-two thousand men and could pose a severe threat to Union forces in northern Mississippi and West Tennessee, who were already detaching troops to reinforce Buell.

Unfortunately for the Rebel cause, the Confederate command situation in Mississippi was as confused as it was in Kentucky. Just as Bragg outranked Kirby Smith but could not demand his obedience until their forces joined, so Van Dorn outranked Price but was similarly hamstrung by lack of authority to command him. Price proved as headstrong and uncooperative as Kirby Smith was proving at the same time in Kentucky. The Missourian wanted to drive northeastward toward Nashville. Van Dorn thought they should attack northwestward instead toward Memphis, and valuable time passed while letters went back and forth between them arguing the merits of their rival plans.

As Price maneuvered on his own, he reached the town of Iuka, less than ten miles from the Tennessee River in the northeastern corner of the state. Ulysses Grant, whom Halleck had left in command of the scattered Union forces in West Tennessee and northern Mississippi, had been following reports of Price's movements and believed he had a chance to trap the Missouri general at Iuka. Concentrating all the force he could spare from the many garrisons Halleck had required him to hold, Grant made plans to attack. William S. Rosecrans, who was then serving under Grant, told Grant that he knew the roads in that region and that it would be possible for him to lead an independent column to strike Price from behind at Iuka while Grant attacked with his main force in front. It was almost impossible to coordinate such widely separated movements in the Civil War, but Rosecrans assured Grant it would work, and Grant reluctantly agreed. Rosecrans moved slowly and took the wrong road, leaving Price an escape route. When on September 19 Price detected

Rosecrans's approach and attacked him, another of those strange acoustic shadows prevented Grant and those around him from hearing the sound of the guns and joining the battle from the other side. In the end, Price escaped.

Chastened by this close call, Price joined Van Dorn, and the two of them agreed to attack the Union garrison at Corinth. Hoping to deceive Grant about his intended target, Van Dorn marched his army as if to bypass Corinth and move into West Tennessee, then turned back to attack Corinth from the northwest on October 3. Grant was not fooled and had Rosecrans in place at Corinth, strongly reinforced, and with more Union troops on the way from Grant's other outposts. During the two-day battle, Rosecrans handled the defense poorly, and his troops suffered for it. Then when the Confederates nearly broke through his lines, Rosecrans panicked, galloping this way and that, cursing his men, declaring the battle lost, and ordering the burning of his supply wagons. Fortunately, the men in charge of his supply train were made of sterner stuff and ignored his order, while his frontline troops, many of them veterans of Fort Donelson and Shiloh, rallied and drove the Rebels back.

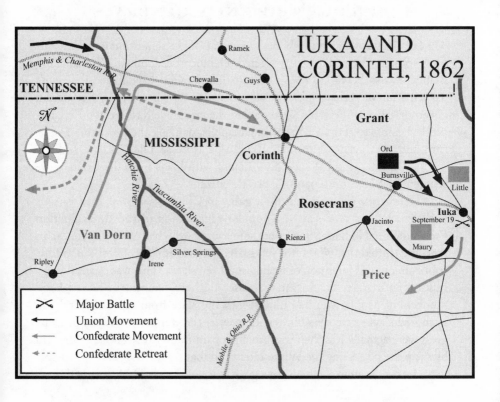

Grant had given Rosecrans strict orders to pursue the Confederates aggressively when they retreated from Corinth. Van Dorn's indirect approach to the town made him vulnerable to being trapped, and Grant intended to do it. He not only reinforced Rosecrans but also dispatched another column to cut off Van Dorn's crossing of the Hatchie River. These troops turned back the retreating Confederates on October 5, leaving Van Dorn at the mercy of Rosecrans's victorious army. But Rosecrans did not pursue. Only after Van Dorn had had time to find an alternate crossing of the Hatchie and get his battered army to safety did Rosecrans show any interest in following him. By then the opportunity was past. Van Dorn was in a strong position with a secure supply line, and any "pursuit" would have meant launching an entirely new campaign, something Grant was eager to do but for which he knew his army needed further preparations. He ordered Rosecrans to halt, and Rosecrans responded by complaining that Grant had prevented him from pursuing the defeated Van Dorn.

LINCOLN TRIES NEW GENERALS

The fall elections that year saw the Democrats make significant gains in Congress and elsewhere. The newly elected, Democratic-dominated Indiana legislature was so hostile to the war effort that it might have halted the state's participation or perhaps even considered secession. The doughty Republican governor Oliver P. Morton was equal to the crisis. He directed the Republican legislators to stay away from Indianapolis, denying the legislature a quorum and preventing it from transacting business. Then he ran Indiana without it, financing the state government with loans from the federal government and even from patriotic private citizens.

Democrats claimed that their gains in Congress as well as in various state legislatures represented a popular repudiation of the Emancipation Proclamation. No doubt there were some voters who had gone Republican in 1860 and shifted their votes two years later because of their opposition to Lincoln's announced intention of freeing southern slaves. This was especially significant in a state like Indiana, whose southern counties included large numbers of people who had moved into the state from Kentucky and still harbored slave-state sensibilities. However, the Republican losses in Congress were actually less than was usually lost in midterm elections of that era by the party possessing the White House. In that sense, they represented politics as usual, even in the midst of a great war, and a reasonably steady though by no means overwhelming degree of support for Lincoln and his war measures, including emancipation.

And if some Americans were not entirely satisfied with every measure Lincoln had taken in trying to win the war, Lincoln was foremost among them this fall. For the past fifteen months, since the summer of 1861, he had been placing his reliance on the most professional of professional officers to lead the nation's armies—McClellan, the rising star of the prewar army in the East; Buell, McClellan's protégé and less charismatic alter ego west of the Appalachians; and "Old Brains" Halleck, as his soldiers called him behind his back, author of books on the art of war, first in the Mississippi Valley and then in overall command in Washington. The results had been disappointing, to say the least.

McClellan had, in Lincoln's homely phrase, "the slows," and his operations had been so halting as to awaken in the minds of some serious people the suspicion that he was in fact a traitor who was trying to allow Rebel victory. After Antietam he had kept his army inert for weeks, doing nothing, while Lee's cavalry commander, Jeb Stuart, led the Rebel horsemen on a ride all the way around the Army of the Potomac. It was the second time he had done that since McClellan had been in command. When McClellan responded to one of Lincoln's many prods with the excuse that his army could not march at present because its horses were tired, an exasperated president replied, "Will you pardon me for asking what the horses of your army have done since the battle of Antietam *that fatigues any* thing?"

Finally, with painful slowness, McClellan began to advance into the Virginia Piedmont. His position forced Lee to try to cover both the Shenandoah Valley and the shortest route to Richmond—opposite directions from where McClellan was. By edging toward Richmond, McClellan was able to gain an advantageous position from which he had a shorter route to Richmond than Lee did. In the hands of an aggressive general, that position could have been Lee's undoing, but McClellan dawdled until Lee was able to recover and regain a position between him and Richmond. That was enough for Lincoln. On November 5 he relieved McClellan of command of the Army of the Potomac, replacing him with Ambrose Burnside. To Lincoln, Burnside's repeated insistence that he was not capable of commanding the army seemed like refreshing humility after McClellan's unwarranted boastfulness. Burnside had enjoyed success down the coast occupying places the navy had conquered, and he seemed like the sort of straightforward general who would fight instead of always dallying like McClellan.

By that time Lincoln had already run out of patience with Buell. After

General Pierre G. T. Beauregard   General Ambrose Burnside

Buell had tamely allowed Bragg to retreat unhindered and unpursued from his foray into Kentucky that fall, Lincoln relieved Buell from command of the Army of the Ohio on October 24. To replace him he tapped William S. Rosecrans, the victor of Corinth, though the soldiers who had served under him there could have given the president a different perspective if he had been able to sit down and talk with them. Rosecrans had enjoyed a measure of success under McClellan in western Virginia during the opening months of the war and more recently under Grant in Mississippi. Lincoln expected him to be an energetic and aggressive commander. Elevated to command, Rosecrans promptly renamed his army the Army of the Cumberland.

Lincoln had brought Halleck to Washington in midsummer 1862 to direct all the nation's armies, but Old Brains had proven a profound disappointment. Hesitant and afraid to give orders to generals in the field, Halleck had become, in Lincoln's words, "little more than a first-rate clerk." And, though Lincoln did not fully understand Halleck's role in the matter, Old Brains had left behind him in Mississippi a situation that added to the president's frustration. Halleck had dispersed the forces there into various garrisons so that it was hard to assemble a field army large enough to take the

Lincoln and McClellan in the camp of the Army of the Potomac after the Battle of Antietam.

offensive. He had also, throughout his command in the Mississippi Valley, reprimanded and threatened to remove Grant every time that officer had exercised initiative. The Union's best commander was thus little inclined to launch another advance and again risk Halleck's wrath. Lincoln did not understand this, but he did sense that the Union had lost momentum in the Mississippi Valley. To regain it, he was inclined to turn away from the West

General James Ewell Brown "Jeb" Stuart   General William S. Rosecrans

Point–trained professionals who had hitherto mostly seemed to lead the Union armies to strategically correct futility. Instead he looked to a political general, John A. McClernand.

Since the death of Stephen A. Douglas from pneumonia in 1861, McClernand had been Illinois's most influential Democratic politician, and having him in a general's uniform since about that time had served Lincoln's purposes by showing that this was more than just a Republican war. It served McClernand's purposes by giving him the opportunity to win military glory that might catapult him into the White House, as it previously had Zachary Taylor, Andrew Jackson, and George Washington. In speeches while home on leave, McClernand boasted that he was a born soldier, incapable of fear. In fact, he was a born politician, seemingly incapable of laying aside his constant angling for office even when called on to help fight the nation's most desperate conflict. He was a better general than most politicians, though that was not saying much, and he was a better politician than almost any other general.

After serving under Grant at Fort Donelson and Shiloh and having his division routed in both fights, McClernand had manipulated the governor of Illinois into finagling orders for him to go to Washington on state business.

McClernand's real business in the national capital was lobbying Lincoln for an independent command, and he pursued that goal relentlessly, accompanying the president on visits to McClellan's headquarters at Antietam after the battle. At last his efforts were successful, and Lincoln granted him special orders to raise an army and lead it down the Mississippi to capture Vicksburg, the Confederate stronghold that had defied Union efforts at the height of Federal success the preceding summer.

Lincoln wanted McClernand to help attract the recruits needed to meet the quotas of the midwestern states under the president's call for "three hundred thousand more." He was then to use his newly gained military experience to help organize and train the new regiments from his home state of Illinois and its neighbors and then, when they were ready, form them into an army and lead them down the river to Vicksburg. The president expected McClernand to worry less about the niceties of West Point form and instead take the fight aggressively to the enemy.

McClernand's new target lay squarely within Grant's geographic department, but Lincoln neither removed Grant nor informed him of the planned new operation. The president left Halleck, his "first-rate clerk," to write up McClernand's formal orders. Halleck might have been unnerved by Grant's daring aggressiveness, but he was appalled by McClernand's naive pretensions and shameless politicking. Halleck was a West Point man through and through, and he had also been both a businessman and a lawyer out in California before the war. The orders as he drew them up made clear that Grant would still command all personnel in his department, including McClernand; that Grant could make his headquarters wherever he chose in his department, including with McClernand; and that McClernand's expedition could include whatever troops Grant did not believe he needed for other operations in his department. McClernand, though a lawyer by profession, neglected to read the orders very carefully. Delighted with the prospect of an independent command out from under Grant, he hurried back to Illinois, where, instead of helping to recruit and train troops, he got married and contemplated with satisfaction his future military glory.

LINCOLN'S NEW COMMANDERS
LAUNCH THEIR WINTER
OFFENSIVES

One thing that was clear to each of the generals to whom Lincoln had given new army commands that autumn was that the president expected action. If

Lincoln had wanted the republic's armies to settle into winter quarters for the next several months, he could have left the former generals in command. They were more than adequate for that.

Burnside moved first. Lee's army was divided into two wings, guarding widely separated potential lines of Union advance. Burnside hoped to lunge between the two wings, cutting them off from each other and potentially from Richmond and forcing a battle in which he would hold all the advantages. When he shared his plan with Lincoln, the president said it would work if Burnside moved quickly. At first, he did. The Army of the Potomac marched on November 15 and two days later reached the Rappahannock River opposite the town of Fredericksburg, Virginia. Only a few hundred Confederate troops were on hand to dispute the crossing of Burnside's 130,000 Federals. Burnside had ordered the army's pontoons to be on hand ready for the construction of bridges across the Rappahannock, but through an administrative error, perhaps attributable to Halleck, the bulky, slow-moving pontoons were far away and would take two weeks to arrive.

Burnside's initial idea had been good, but when a problem arose he seemed incapable of adjusting to meet the challenge. Rather than changing his plan or seeking alternate means of crossing at least enough of his troops to hold the key high ground beyond Fredericksburg until the rest of the army could join them, he simply sat down and waited for the pontoons to arrive, and while he did, Lee united the two wings of his army and had more than seventy thousand men on the high ground southwest of Fredericksburg.

Burnside contemplated the several possible crossing points in the neighborhood and decided that what would surprise Lee the most would be a crossing straight into Fredericksburg, directly confronting Lee's strong position on a ridge called Marye's Heights, which paralleled the river about a mile beyond the town. Lee certainly was surprised, and even as Burnside's engineers on December 11 began laying the pontoon bridges opposite Fredericksburg, the Confederate general continued to doubt that his opponent could have blundered so spectacularly.

Lee left a single brigade of Confederate troops in the town to harass Union attempts to cross the river. As the engineers attempted to lay their pontoon bridges, Confederates hidden in the houses of Fredericksburg fired on them and drove them back from the riverbank several times. Confederate use of the town as a defensive position made it a legitimate target for the more than two hundred cannon Burnside had amassed on the high ground on his side of the river. They poured more than five thousand shells into Fredericksburg, substantially wrecking it but failing to drive out the stubborn

Confederates. Finally Burnside ordered a brigade to make a cross-river assault, using the pontoons as boats, and the Federals cleared the town of Rebels in bitter house-to-house fighting. The engineers quickly laid the pontoon bridges, and the rest of Burnside's army swarmed across the river. Once they got into the town-turned-fortress that no longer enjoyed the normal immunities of a civilian community, the Union soldiers took out their frustrations by adding a fair bit of vandalism to the damage Fredericksburg had already suffered from the shelling and close combat.

By the morning of December 13, Burnside was ready to launch his attack. He started with a diversionary assault a couple of miles down the river (which here flowed to the southeast). Here the Union attackers unwittingly struck a gap in Stonewall Jackson's line and made some initial gains before Jackson, who had more troops available than the small force Burnside had designated to make the diversion, mounted a counterattack and drove them back.

Around 11:00 Burnside's main effort got under way, with Union troops advancing straight out of Fredericksburg toward Marye's Heights. The Confederate line ran along the base of the heights, where a sunken road, edged by a stone wall, offered a ready-made defensive position that the Confederates had enhanced with a shallow trench. The Rebel infantrymen could stand almost completely concealed and shoot over the stone wall, while behind and above them, along the crest of the ridge, Confederate artillery fired over their heads. The long and very gradual slope in front of them provided an excellent field of fire, while just outside the edge of town a steep-sided drainage ditch, crossable at only a couple of points, funneled the advancing Federals toward the strongest section of the Confederate line, where riflemen two or three deep awaited them behind the stone wall. The sector was so narrow that only one brigade could advance at a time.

Burnside's grand attack thus degenerated into a series of brigade assaults one after the other, sixteen of them, right into the teeth of an impregnable defensive position. The Union infantrymen advanced bravely and were mowed down in rows until the survivors in each brigade could take no more of such mass suicide and dove to the ground seeking cover, sometimes behind the bodies of their dead comrades. Then the next brigade would advance to be butchered in turn, while the Confederates behind their stone wall suffered scarcely a handful of casualties. It was among the most one sided of the Civil War's major battles. Inside Fredericksburg, Burnside's dispirited troops took out their greatly enhanced frustrations in further damage to the property of the hapless but fortunately absent citizens of the town.

That evening Jackson urged Lee to attack and trap the Federals in Fredericksburg with their backs to the Rappahannock and only a few narrow pontoon bridges by which to escape. Lee demurred. He predicted that Burnside would order another day of fruitless assaults, bleeding the Army of the Potomac and further weakening it for the counterstroke he had in mind. In fact, Burnside, almost beside himself at the thought of the body-strewn slope outside of town, was contemplating putting himself at the head of his old Ninth Corps and personally leading a suicide attack the next morning. His subordinates talked him out of such a desperate move, and he sadly gave the order to begin the withdrawal to the northeastern back of the Rappahannock. The Battle of Fredericksburg cost the Federals 12,653 men killed, wounded, and missing, while Confederate losses were less than half that. Nevertheless, Lee, who still hoped in each major battle to annihilate the opposing army, was disappointed with the result.

So was Lincoln. "If there is a worse place than hell," he wrote, "I am in it." He had sacked the popular commander of the Army of the Potomac and replaced him with a general he hoped would act aggressively. Now that general's aggressive action had brought an embarrassing and bloody defeat in the still-stalemated but high-profile eastern theater of the war, where foreign observers and the heavy East Coast populace could not fail to take note of it. He tried to put the best face on matters in a public proclamation about the battle, but his optimism rang hollow. Morale plummeted in the Army of the Potomac, especially after Burnside's attempt at a January offensive ended in humiliating, if bloodless, failure when a multiday rain transformed Virginia's dirt roads into knee-deep troughs of mud, immobilizing the soaked and shivering Army of the Potomac before it could even reach the Rappahannock crossings. Less than a week later, Lincoln sadly decided to relieve Burnside.

THE UNION'S WINTER
OFFENSIVES IN THE WEST

Meanwhile, Lincoln's new command arrangements had, as he intended, produced aggressive action on the war's two other major fronts as well. The mere hint that offensive operations would now be welcomed rather than rebuked by Halleck had been enough to get Grant moving. Collecting together some of the forces Halleck had left scattered across West Tennessee and northern Mississippi, he formed a field army and in late November began advancing down the Mississippi Central Railroad into that state. He also directed Sherman, who had been commanding the Memphis garrison, to form a second column from the troops in and near that city and advance southeastward to rendezvous with Grant near Abbeville, Mississippi. Grant hoped that Confederate general John C. Pemberton, whom Davis had recently appointed to command the defenses of Mississippi, would challenge one force or the other and be caught in the closing Union pincers, but Pemberton fell back steadily in front of Grant, refusing to give battle.

Reluctant to continue stretching his own supply lines while pursuing the elusive Pemberton ever deeper into the interior of Mississippi and having learned, mostly through rumor, of McClernand's new assignment, Grant changed his plan of campaign. After seeking and receiving reassurance from Halleck that he still had full command of all troops in his department, Grant ordered Sherman to go back to Memphis and there collect all the regiments of new troops coming down from the Midwest in response to Lincoln's call the preceding summer for "three hundred thousand more." With his new army of thirty thousand men or so, composed both of veterans and of the new levies, Sherman was to board riverboat transports and travel down the river to Vicksburg. If Washington wanted a direct campaign against the Confederate Gibraltar of the West, as Vicksburg was already being called, he would provide it, led by the competent professional Sherman rather than the scheming politician McClernand. Meanwhile, Grant would try to keep Pemberton's main Confederate army occupied in northern Mississippi.

McClernand was still up in Illinois, delayed partially by festivities connected with his recent wedding and partially by a mistaken belief that he needed special orders from Washington in order to begin his river expedition. While he sent a string of whining dispatches to Secretary of War Stanton asking for such orders, Sherman, quite unbeknownst to McClernand, led McClernand's intended army down the Mississippi from Memphis.

Sherman and his men were in agreement with the new Union policy of hard war. It was no use, they believed, trying to placate the Rebels by waging the war with kid gloves—or, as Lincoln put it, "with elder-stalk squirts charged with rose-water." When Confederate snipers fired on some of Sherman's transports from a small settlement on the Mississippi shore, he had some of his men go ashore and burn the place to the ground. From now on, the conflict would be waged with all the rigor the laws of war provided.

Sherman's army reached its destination the day after Christmas and landed on the east bank of the Mississippi a few miles above Vicksburg. The army spent the next several days trying to advance against the Confederate fortress city. Confederate skirmishers, aided by a terrain of interlaced swamps

Grant's
Mississippi
Central
Campaign

TENNESSEE

Ft. Pillow
Jackson
Ft. Randolph
Bolivar
Memphis
LaGrange
Holly
Springs,
December 20,
1862
Corinth
Iuka
Grant
Van
Dorn's
Raid
Oxford
Tupelo

✕ Major Battles
◀ Union Movements
◀ Confederate Movements

Arkansas
Post

Grenada

ARKANSAS

Sherman
Chiclasaw Bayou
December 27-29,
1862
Vicksburg
Jackson
Meridian

LOUISIANA
Bruinsburg
Crystal Springs

Mississippi River

MISSISSIPPI

N

Port Hudson

Baton
Rouge

and bayous, slowed the Federals' progress. By December 29 they had come
within sight of the main Confederate line of resistance, strongly entrenched
on bluffs overlooking the meandering course of Chickasaw Bayou, a tributary
of the Mississippi. The terrain was worse than Fredericksburg, with the
bayou and its own numerous tributaries allowing the attackers to approach
only on narrow fronts in a couple of places. Sherman ordered an assault, but

it failed with a loss of 1,776 killed, wounded, and missing. Confederate losses were little more than one-tenth that many.

With rainy weather raising the river level and threatening to inundate his camps, Sherman ordered his troops back onto their transports. At this point, McClernand arrived, outraged at what he viewed as the abduction of his army and even more outraged that the plan he had advocated had already been tried and proven a failure. Pompous and insulting toward Sherman, whom he outranked, as well as Rear Admiral David D. Porter, who commanded the Navy's cooperating squadron, McClernand was nevertheless at a complete loss to know what to do next.

Sherman and Porter talked him into making a side expedition up the Arkansas River, 150 miles north of Vicksburg, where the Confederates had built Fort Hindman at a low bluff called Arkansas Post and were using it as a base from which to stage hit-and-run attacks on Union supply and communications along the Mississippi. The expedition's ironclad gunboats and thirty thousand ground troops might have been helpless against the unusual natural obstacles around Vicksburg, but Fort Hindman's 5,500 defenders had no such advantages. After a short, sharp fight on January 11, 1863, Porter's gunboats and McClernand's troops, led primarily by Sherman, captured the fort and almost its entire garrison, more than squaring the casualty ratio for the campaign. Indeed, with Union losses at Arkansas Post scarcely over a thousand men, the campaign's loss tally now tipped two to one in favor of the Union.

A few days later, Grant arrived to take command of the expedition in person. While Sherman had been experiencing frustration along Chickasaw Bayou and redemption, at least in a subordinate capacity, at Arkansas Post, Grant had been experiencing his own difficulties. After Sherman had departed for Memphis to begin his campaign down the river, Grant's army had advanced more slowly, continuing to move down the Mississippi Central Railroad in order to keep Pemberton occupied, and for a time it worked.

The situation had become a matter of acute concern to Jefferson Davis, who made a tour of inspection of the Confederacy's western armies during December. Joseph Johnston, who Davis had recently appointed overall Confederate commander in the West after his recovery from the wound he had suffered at Fair Oaks the preceding May, assured Davis that cavalry raids he was dispatching against Grant's supply lines would suffice to repel the Union offensive, but Davis remained unconvinced. Against the advice of Johnston and Bragg he ordered the latter to detach ten thousand men, about one-fourth of his infantry strength, and send them to reinforce Pemberton.

Before the reinforcements could arrive, Johnston's prediction proved true. A raid led by Nathan Bedford Forrest created confusion in West Tennessee. Worse, a second, more or less simultaneous raid under the command of Earl Van Dorn, who finally seemed to have found his niche as a cavalry commander, struck directly at Grant's forward base of supplies at Holly Springs, Mississippi, on December 21. The Union officer commanding the small garrison at Holly Springs proved to be a coward and put up very little fight. Van Dorn and his raiders destroyed the supplies and cut the railroad, putting Grant's army immediately on short rations, with no prospect of resupply. Continuing to push back Pemberton's army without a supply line would have been impossible, and Grant had no choice but to fall back on his rear-area bases in extreme northern Mississippi and West Tennessee. Though his troops had to take in their belts a notch during the trip, they staved off starvation at the expense of the farms and plantations in their path.

Pemberton was thus released to deal with Sherman and began shifting troops down to Vicksburg to meet the threat of the river expedition. The Battle of Chickasaw Bayou took place before most of them—or any of the troops from Bragg's army—could arrive near Vicksburg. As it turned out, none of them were needed since the position on the bluffs overlooking Chickasaw Bayou was all but impregnable against any attacking force, even with only a handful of defenders.

In mid-January a frustrated Grant arrived at the headquarters of the Mississippi River expedition, still embarked on steamboats, and Sherman, McClernand, and Porter briefed him on the failure at Chickasaw Bayou and secondary success at Arkansas Post. Grant faced a dilemma. Only from the interior of Mississippi could Vicksburg be approached with any hope of military success. Yet any approach through the interior of the state invited constant repetition of the kinds of raids that had derailed his recent push down the Mississippi Central. McClernand further complicated Grant's situation. Sherman, Porter, and other officers begged Grant not to leave the expedition in the not-so-capable hands of the ambitious political schemer. Grant knew he could not sack the president's special appointee—not yet, anyway—and he also knew that any plan that divided his force into two columns would give McClernand, as second-ranking officer, command of one of them. Grant therefore determined to unite his army and encamp it on the Louisiana side of the river just above Vicksburg, there to stay until he somehow found a way to get around the Confederate fortress city and its many natural barriers.

By that time the third of the Union's winter offensives had also run its course. Secrecy for military movements was a rarity in the Civil War, but few information leaks were as dramatic as the prompt publication by the *Chatta-*

nooga Daily Rebel of news that Jefferson Davis was transferring one-fourth of Bragg's infantry from the Army of Tennessee camps around Murfreesboro, Tennessee, to reinforce Pemberton in Mississippi. Among the *Rebel*'s most interested readers was William S. Rosecrans, who, though not a subscriber, received a copy in Nashville only a few days later. He immediately put his army in motion to attack Bragg's weakened force at Murfreesboro.

Confederate cavalry gave Bragg ample warning and slowed Rosecrans's advance so that it took several days for his Army of the Cumberland to cover the thirty miles to Murfreesboro. By the evening of December 30, 1862, the two armies confronted each other in battle formation straddling a shallow stream called Stones River, just north of town. That evening as the soldiers awaited the battle that was sure to open next morning, bands on both sides of the line took turns serenading the armies, who could clearly hear both the Rebel and the Union musicians. Finally, one of the bands struck up "Home, Sweet Home," and all of the others on both sides joined in as the soldiers sang along, concluding the concert with a poignant reminder of the American culture the contending forces shared.

Each commanding general planned to attack the other's right flank the next morning, but Bragg moved first, swinging wide to envelope the Union right. Suddenly plunged into a desperate situation, Rosecrans canceled his own attack and began shifting troops to shore up his hard-pressed right. There the Federals fell back, fighting furiously and leaving the battlefield littered with the dead of both sides. By late afternoon the right wing of the Army of the Cumberland had rotated back about ninety degrees and was desperately trying to hang on to the turnpike that ran northwestward toward Nashville and was the Army of the Cumberland's only line of supply and, if it came to that, of retreat. Rosecrans coped with the situation much better than he had the similar one at Corinth three months before. He maintained his composure and rode along his lines encouraging his men, who cheered him enthusiastically wherever he appeared.

Bragg was tantalizingly close to a victory that might cut off and trap the Army of the Cumberland but lacked the troop strength to finish the job. If he had still had those ten thousand men Davis had sent to Mississippi, things would have been different, but in that case Rosecrans might never have attacked in that time and place. As it was, Bragg had had to commit his reserve early in the day to compensate for a blunder by an incompetent division commander whom he had tried to remove months ago, only to be told by Davis that the man must stay. The attack suffered a further setback from the blundering of another of Bragg's subordinate generals who was intoxicated. Then when Bragg ordered the general commanding a large, unengaged division on his right to send troops for the final effort to crush Rosecrans's line, that general, a politician and former vice president of the United States, first refused, then forwarded the troops a brigade at a time, so that there was little prospect of using them for a concentrated mass assault.

On the other side of the lines, Rosecrans was well served by his subordinates, especially his senior corps commander, George H. Thomas, who held a key sector and proved to be a veritable rock in such a defensive role. When nightfall ended the fighting and Rosecrans consulted with his generals about what to do next, Thomas and others were strong in urging him to hold his ground, and so he did.

Bragg also decided to stay put the next day. It was the first day of 1863. In Washington, D.C., six hundred miles to the northeast, Lincoln issued the final Emancipation Proclamation, but on the battlefield on either side of Stones River, the two armies watched each other warily without engaging in further combat. On January 2 Bragg tried a limited assault to take a key piece of terrain from Rosecrans's Federals, but the attack turned out badly. That night, with his subordinates insistently urging him to retreat, Bragg finally gave up and ordered the Army of Tennessee to fall back behind a chain of hills called the Highland Rim, twenty-five miles to the southeast. The Battle of Stones River, or Murfreesboro as the Confederates called it, was over. Its percentage of casualties among the troops engaged, about one-third, would stand as the highest of any of the Civil War's many grisly encounters.

Rosecrans had won a victory by default and one that had gained him only a thirty-mile-wide swath of Tennessee countryside, but at this stage of the war Lincoln was happy to take any victories he could get. While discussing further operations in an exchange of telegrams with Rosecrans several months later, the president noted, "I can never forget, whilst I remember anything, that *about the end of last year,* and beginning of this, you gave us a hard earned victory, which had there been a defeat instead, the country scarcely could have lived over."[1]

8

"PEACE DOES NOT APPEAR SO DISTANT AS IT DID"

DISCOURAGEMENT AND DISCONTENTMENT ON BOTH SIDES

The winter offensives that Lincoln had sparked with his command shake-ups in the late fall of 1862 had run their course by mid-January 1863. In the high-visibility yet chronically indecisive eastern theater, Fredericksburg had been a spectacular fiasco. The two-headed monster of a command arrangement Lincoln had created in the Mississippi Valley had snagged a target of opportunity at Arkansas Post but had been stopped cold in its primary mission of taking Vicksburg and opening the Mississippi to midwestern commerce, a culmination that now seemed as distant as ever. In Middle Tennessee, Rosecrans had won a victory by staying on the battlefield longer than his opponent was willing to do, gaining a narrow swath of Tennessee countryside but bringing final Union triumph very little closer. Only in the Mississippi Valley, where Grant had taken command firmly into his own hands, was there any prospect of further offensive operations. Rosecrans's and Burnside's armies were firmly ensconced in winter quarters, and no progress could be expected from them for months to come, while Grant had encamped his army in front of Vicksburg but for the moment could find no way of getting behind the Confederate stronghold, where lay the only prospect of a successful assault.

It was all very discouraging—to Lincoln, to Union soldiers, and to the northern public. Disaffected members of the New Jersey legislature introduced resolutions complaining that the war was hopeless and the restoration of the southern states impossible. They called for an immediate end to hostilities and the opening of negotiations that could lead only to a permanent division of the country. Newspapers such as the *New York World* hewed to the same line, while newspapers in the South gleefully picked up and repeated such expressions of northern war weariness and defeatism. Demoralized or disloyal northern civilians sent copies of such negative newspaper articles to soldier acquaintances and relatives of theirs, down south in the camps of the armies in Louisiana, Tennessee, or Virginia. With the newspapers (or instead of them), they sent their own commentary on the current unwinnable war and the hopelessness of ever restoring the Union by force of arms. Some went so far as to urge the soldiers to desert and promise them protection and concealment if they should come back home now. A few radical opponents of the war actually visited the armies' camps in person to urge their friends to desert, though they risked arrest if discovered by most officers. Despite the officers' efforts, morale dropped still lower in the nation's armies among soldiers discouraged by the costly and seemingly fruitless campaigns that had closed out 1862.

On the other side of the lines, morale was, for the most part, correspondingly high. Confederate soldiers and civilians reveled in their armies' victories, especially the seemingly effortless triumphs of Robert E. Lee, whose fame was by now coming to rival that of his subordinate Stonewall Jackson. The latter had been a darling of the southern press and public since his exploits in the Shenandoah Valley the preceding spring, and now Lee took his place alongside him as one of the Confederacy's foremost heroes. Confederate morale and even the Confederate people's sense of nationhood were rapidly coming to center and rest on these two men and their ragtag but seemingly invincible army.

News from the Confederacy's other two major armies was generally encouraging if not quite as inspiring as that from Virginia. In Mississippi the Confederate commander was, it is true, the thoroughly uninspiring Pennsylvanian John C. Pemberton, but Vicksburg seemed as impregnable as ever, and Confederates enjoyed making jokes about Grant's ridiculously futile continued efforts at taking it.

The news from Braxton Bragg's army in Middle Tennessee was the least encouraging that winter. Not only had the Army of Tennessee given up another thirty-mile-wide swath of the state, but the army's high command was locked in unseemly bickering, with several of Bragg's subordinates determined never to forgive him for their own bad performances in the Kentucky Campaign. Bragg was anything but a politician, and his most glaring lack was his inability to win the hearts of his subordinates, though in several of their cases the efforts of the most gifted and charming of leaders would have been in vain. In the wake of the Battle of Stones River, a staff officer anonymously published a newspaper article accusing Bragg of retreating against the advice of his subordinate generals. This enraged Bragg since it was the exact opposite of the truth. He let it goad him into sending an ill-considered circular to all of his generals asking if they had counseled retreat after the recent battle and vaguely suggesting that he might resign if he did not have the confidence of his officers. All of them had to admit that they had indeed counseled retreat, but several, influenced by Bragg's bitter enemies Polk and Hardee, took the opportunity of assuring Bragg that he had no one's confidence and ought to resign at once.

Davis got wind of the affair and ordered Bragg's superior, Confederate western theater commander Joseph E. Johnston, to go to Bragg's headquarters at Tullahoma, Tennessee, and investigate the matter. Though Johnston's report was highly favorable to Bragg, Davis, perhaps influenced by his old West Point friend Polk, decided that Bragg needed to go. Johnston disagreed, and, besides, relations between Johnston and Davis were such that the general enjoyed few things more than thwarting the president's wishes. Johnston found excuse after excuse for disobeying Davis's repeated orders to relieve Bragg and take command of the Army of Tennessee himself until finally the campaigning season began. Johnston was needed in Mississippi, and Davis ordered him there, abandoning his effort to remove Bragg from command of the Army of Tennessee.

The Confederate public spent the winter for the most part in blissful ignorance of the fact that one of their three major armies was commanded by a man in whom the president had no confidence and whom the president had tried unsuccessfully to remove or that its high-command structure was so rife with personal animosities as to render that army almost incapable of concerted action. Through the winter and all the way through the spring season as well, the Union army facing Bragg's unhappy Army of Tennessee remained inert, doing nothing that might have taken advantage of the disarray in the Confederate high command.

That Union army was William S. Rosecrans's Army of the Cumberland. After his bloody victory by default at Stones River, Rosecrans's stock had soared in Washington, and Secretary of War Edwin M. Stanton had promised him whatever he needed in the way of supplies and equipment in order to get his army ready for a new advance. Stanton had not dreamed just how much supplies and equipment—and how much time—Rosecrans would believe he needed before he dared face the Rebels in battle again. While other generals, notably Grant, made use of what they had and got on with the war, Rosecrans for six months bombarded Washington with demands for mountains of supplies, hundreds of wagons, thousands of horses and mules, and a variety of new equipment, including the new seven-shot, magazine-fed Spencer Repeating Rifles to equip several of his regiments. Although he received virtually everything he requested, he nevertheless held his army idle in its camps around Murfreesboro while the nation's other armies launched campaigns and fought battles. Halleck, Stanton, and even Lincoln himself sent repeated messages prodding the reluctant general to fight, but throughout the first half of 1863 all were in vain.

GRANT'S NEW VICKSBURG CAMPAIGN

Meanwhile Grant tried every scheme he could think of to get his army around Vicksburg so as to have a fair chance in battle against its Confederate defenders. The steep bluffs on which Vicksburg perched represented the edge of Mississippi's interior plateau. South of Vicksburg the Mississippi River lapped the base of the plateau. North of the town it was the Yazoo River, angling down from the northeast, that ran along the foot of the bluffs. Between the Yazoo and the Mississippi and for a number of miles west of the Mississippi stretched the Mississippi Delta, with some of the South's richest cotton plantations ranging along the low curving forms of natural levies, formed by various streams and bayous and by former courses of the rivers themselves. Between the plantations lay dark cypress swamps and a maze of sluggish watercourses that scarcely seemed to flow in any direction at all.

Throughout the remainder of January 1863, as well as February and March, Grant's efforts were aimed at somehow getting his riverboat transport vessels, as well as the navy's river gunboats, into either the stretch of the Yazoo above Vicksburg or the stretch of the Mississippi below the town without their having to steam past the powerful Confederate heavy artillery batteries on both rivers at and near Vicksburg. Either stretch of either river would provide access to the interior plateau without suicidal assaults on prepared positions like those along Chickasaw Bayou.

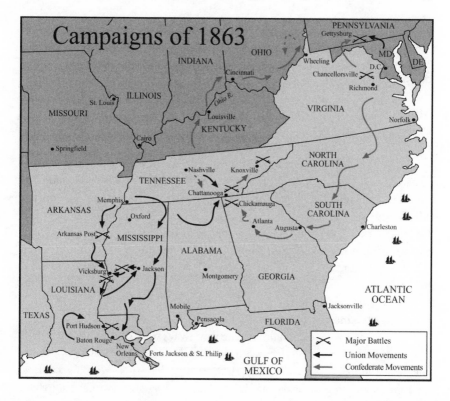

One interesting plan was based on the fact that Vicksburg lay on the outside edge of a bend in the Mississippi. The plan involved digging a canal across the tongue of land called DeSoto Point, located on the Louisiana shore on the inside of the bend. In theory this would allow access to the lower reaches of the Mississippi without running the gauntlet of the Vicksburg batteries. Lincoln, who in his youth had taken a flatboat full of midwestern crops down the Mississippi to New Orleans, was intrigued by the idea and followed its progress eagerly. The scheme called for digging a ditch of reasonable size across the bend and then for the river itself to take over and scour the ditch into a new and shorter channel, as it was wont to do even without any human assistance. Unfortunately, the upper end of the canal entered the river in an area of slack water, where erosion was unlikely. Ultimately, the river proved as perverse as ever, refusing to use the new channel offered by thousands of man-hours of Grant's soldiers' work.

Another plan involved opening the Mississippi River levy at Lake Providence, Louisiana, fifty miles upstream from Vicksburg. In theory this would make accessible a chain of interconnected swamps and streams, swollen by seasonal high water to just enough depth for the shallow-draft riverboats, so as to allow access to the Red River. The boats would then have easy steaming down the Red River to its mouth, about 130 miles below Vicksburg. Like the canal scheme, the Lake Providence undertaking promised access to the Mississippi, where it lapped the base of the state's interior plateau without exposing the boats to the guns of Vicksburg. Grant assigned one of his army's three corps to encamp at Lake Providence and work on clearing the cypress trees that clogged the proposed waterway, but after weeks of work, it became apparent that the boats would never be able to get through by that route.

Yet another plan called for cutting the Mississippi River levy on the Mississippi side at a place called Yazoo Pass, almost opposite the town of Helena, Arkansas, about 175 miles upstream from Vicksburg. This would allow the gunboats to pass into Moon Lake, thence into the Coldwater River, which would lead to the Tallahatchie, which at last would join with the Yalobusha to form the Yazoo. The fleet, followed by the transports, would thus have access to the Yazoo far above Vicksburg and could easily insert Grant's army onto the interior plateau of Mississippi.

It sounded simple enough, but the waterways were so narrow that details of sailors had to stand on deck with poles and push on the banks to get the sluggish gunboats to turn sharply enough to follow their winding courses. The gunboats' smokestacks brushed and banged against overhanging trees, sustaining damage while knocking loose a rain of snakes, lizards, opossums, and other arboreal creatures that fell to the decks and had to be swept over the side with brooms by other details of sailors. Scarcely able to advance at all through the swamp channels that passed for watercourses, the fleet finally encountered the Confederates at the junction of the Tallahatchie and Yalobusha rivers, where a detail of Pemberton's troops had erected a small fort made of cotton bales and armed with two cannon. The almost laughably small Fort Pemberton, as the Rebels called it, nevertheless proved to be enough to stop the gunboats since nature had almost stopped them already. The accompanying troops, surrounded by channels and even swamps too deep to wade, could do nothing to help. By mid-March it was clear that the expedition had failed and would have to withdraw.

About the time the Yazoo Pass Expedition stalled, Admiral Porter implemented a new idea for getting the fleet and transports into the stretch of the Yazoo between Fort Pemberton and Vicksburg. Only a few miles above Vicksburg on the Mississippi, a sluggish, narrow watercourse called Steele's Bayou led into the interior of the half-drowned delta country. Porter had heard that from it a series of interconnecting waterways led into the Yazoo. While a detachment of his gunboats was still involved in the Yazoo Pass Expedition, Porter led a squadron of his most powerful vessels up Steele's Bayou on March 16. Travel on the narrow, winding channels proved much like what the other boats had experienced on the previous expedition, with the added complication that sometimes willow withes in submerged thickets fouled the boats' paddle wheels, holding them stuck fast for hours until sailors could cut their way free.

Confederates felled trees across the channels both in front of and behind the fleet, hoping to trap and capture the vessels. It looked as if they might do just that when sniper fire drove Union sailors from the exposed upper decks, preventing them from clearing the logs or even steering the gunboats by the usual method, in these narrow waters, of pushing off the bank with poles. The sailors fired back at the snipers with their heavy cannon, while Porter made plans to abandon and blow up the vessels and lead the crews in trying to fight their way out through the swamps on foot if the situation became that desperate. He also asked a local slave who had joined his fleet to carry a message through Confederate-controlled territory to reach Major General William T. Sherman, whose supporting infantry of the Fifteenth Corps was several miles behind.

Major General William T. Sherman

Admiral David D. Porter

Using his knowledge of the area, the brave African American, whose name unfortunately no one thought to write down, evaded the Confederates and reached Sherman. The general acted with the energy that had already made him Grant's favorite subordinate. Quickly scraping together a relief force from scattered detachments that had been clearing away obstructions on the streams, Sherman, on foot, led it on a night march, sometimes wading swamps, to reach Porter's gunboats the next day. Although the operation was a failure, it displayed the excellent army–navy cooperation that made it possible for Grant even to think of trying to take Vicksburg. Porter, who was not actually subject to Grant's orders, had nevertheless been willing to take his gunboats into extremely narrow and hazardous waters in order to help Grant's effort succeed. Sherman did not let Porter down but extended himself and his troops to the utmost in order to get the navy out of its jam. Grant had actively fostered this sort of cooperation and mutual loyalty, and the strong team he had built augured well for ultimate success. For now, though, it was clear only that the Steele's Bayou route was impractical as a means of bypassing Vicksburg.

By this time Grant had come to the conclusion that the only practical way to get the gunboats and transports past Vicksburg was to run them down the Mississippi itself, directly under the guns of the Vicksburg batteries. When he approached Porter with his plan, the admiral agreed to try it but warned that the move would not be reversible. Once the gunboats had run downstream past Vicksburg they would not be able to return until Grant took the Confederate fortress city since the slow upstream run would be suicidal if the Rebels were still manning their guns on the Vicksburg bluffs. Grant agreed, and both officers began preparing their forces. The Army of the Tennessee began a slow and tortuous advance through the tangled swamps and back-channels of the delta country west of the Mississippi, building dozens of bridges and scores of miles of corduroy road (a road surfaced by saplings laid side by side to prevent wheeled vehicles from sinking into the mud).

Meanwhile, Porter prepared a squadron of his best ironclads to run the Vicksburg batteries on the night of April 16, 1863. With coal barges lashed to their sides to provide extra fuel in the remote lower reaches of the Mississippi, the gunboats moved out silently through the dark night, hoping to avoid detection by the Confederates on the bluffs. The Rebels proved too alert, and the heavy guns roared to life as the Union vessels moved into the difficult sharp bend of the river directly in front of the town. The sailors fired back as best they could with their own cannon while helmsmen struggled to keep the vessels on course through the treacherous eddies produced by the bend. For several minutes the roar of the guns was audible many miles away, but when the guns fell silent and the smoke cleared, Porter's fleet had successfully passed the batteries with only minor damage.

Six nights later army volunteers ran a group of leased transports past the batteries after civilian crews had balked at taking these frail, unarmed, and unarmored craft under the muzzles of the Confederate guns. The civilian boatmen's misgivings proved somewhat justified, as the Confederate gunners, without the hindrance of return fire, sank two of the transports and badly shot up the rest. Nevertheless, Grant's resourceful midwestern soldiers-turned-boatmen picked up their shipwrecked comrades, patched up the surviving vessels, and somehow got past the batteries with most of the flotilla intact and usable, ready to ferry Grant's army across the river south of Vicksburg.

While the gunboats and transports ran the Vicksburg batteries and Grant's army worked its way down through the swamps on the west bank of the Mississippi and prepared to cross the river, Pemberton remained confused. A simultaneous Union cavalry raid, which Grant had ordered for just that purpose, ranged virtually the whole length of the state of Mississippi, from the lines of Grant's rear-area forces near Memphis all the way past Jackson and down to where a small Union army under Nathaniel P. Banks was approaching the secondary Confederate bastion on the Mississippi River at Port Hudson, Louisiana. The expedition's commander, Brigadier General Benjamin Grierson, proved wily and resourceful in creating maximum disruption of Confederate rear areas while dodging all the troops that Pemberton dispatched to catch him. With his enemy thus distracted as planned, Grant prepared to launch his main campaign into the state of Mississippi.

On April 29, 1863, Grant's army landed on the east bank of the Mississippi River about forty miles below Vicksburg near the settlement of Bruinsburg and moved rapidly inland. The next morning his army defeated a detachment of Pemberton's Confederate army at Port Gibson. Rather than advancing straight north toward Vicksburg through a terrain of steep ridges and deep ravines, Grant moved northeast. On May 12 one of Grant's corps defeated another Confederate detachment near the town of Raymond. Two days later, Grant's troops marched into Mississippi's capital, Jackson, before turning westward to approach Vicksburg directly from the rear. On May 16 he met and defeated Pemberton's main field army at Champion Hill, about twenty miles east of Vicksburg. When Pemberton made a stand the next day at the main crossing of the Big Black River, Grant routed him again.

Mentally, Grant kept at least one step ahead of Pemberton, whose befuddled efforts at stopping Grant led to Confederate defeats in five consecutive battles as the campaign progressed through the interior of Mississippi. In a revealing measurement of the abilities of the rival commanding generals, Grant outnumbered Pemberton on every battlefield even though Pemberton had more troops in Mississippi than Grant did.

By May 18, Pemberton's army had taken refuge inside the fortifications of Vicksburg itself. Grant had made contact with the Mississippi River just above Vicksburg, reestablishing a short, secure supply line. His lines extended along the north and east sides of Vicksburg far enough to the south to cut off the Rebels there from receiving supplies and prevent them from escaping. In less than three weeks since landing in Mississippi, Grant had outmaneuvered Pemberton, won five battles, gained the advantageous position behind Vicksburg that had seemed impossible to reach, and bottled up the Confederate army in what was each day looking more and more like a trap. The campaign had been risky, and Grant had overcome both enemy resistance and incredibly difficult terrain. The result was an operational masterpiece that rivaled and perhaps exceeded Stonewall Jackson's spring 1862 Shenandoah Valley Campaign as the most brilliant of the war.

Even from the rear Vicksburg proved to be a very strong position, and

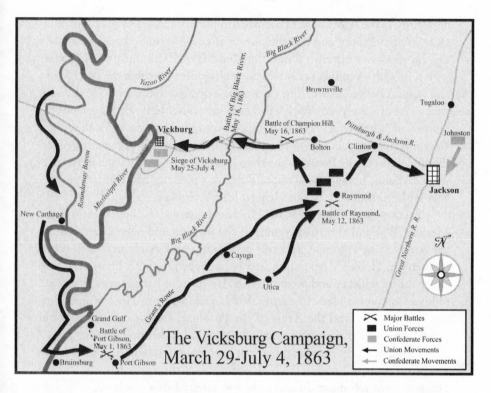

The Vicksburg Campaign,
March 29-July 4, 1863

Major Battles
Union Forces
Confederate Forces
Union Movements
Confederate Movements

Pemberton's demoralized soldiers found that within its heavily fortified lines they had a chance to stop the blue-clad soldiers who had chased them through Mississippi. Grant's all-out assaults on the city on May 19 and 22 both ended in bloody failure. Regretfully but with grim determination, Grant and his army settled down to a methodical siege, bombarding Vicksburg and digging their trenches ever closer so as to set up a final assault that would be guaranteed success. Meanwhile, Confederate soldiers and civilians inside Vicksburg went on short rations as supplies grew increasingly scarce.

THE CHANCELLORSVILLE CAMPAIGN

During the winter of 1863, while Grant had tried one plan after another to get at Vicksburg from a direction that offered hope of success, Lincoln had decided that the situation in Virginia required a new general there. Burnside's popularity in the Army of the Potomac had been dismally low since the debacle at Fredericksburg and had sunk lower after the abortive January offensive that his men were bitterly calling "the Mud March," after the onset of a rainy spell turned the Virginia roads into deep quagmires in which the army's guns and wagons bogged down. The discontent extended to the army's generals as well, most of whom were McClellan favorites still bitterly seething about the removal of "Little Mac," as the adoring troops called him. Some of the generals complained to Lincoln to the point that the president became convinced that the Army of the Potomac could no longer function with its present commander. Sadly, because he admired Burnside's modesty and dedication, Lincoln replaced him with Major General Joseph Hooker.

An 1837 West Point graduate, Hooker had served with distinction in the Mexican War and then had commanded a division and later a corps within the Army of the Potomac, generally performing well. Aside from that previous service, Hooker's reputation had been shaped by both his well-known penchant for whiskey and prostitutes and his habit of harshly criticizing each of his army commanders. In a letter that Lincoln wrote to Hooker on assigning him to command the Army of the Potomac, the president gently but firmly admonished the new commander that his undermining of his predecessors, particularly Burnside, had not been commendable and might well have created a spirit within the high command of the army that would make Hooker's own job more difficult. He also referred to a troubling statement Hooker had recently made to a reporter. "I have heard," Lincoln wrote,

> in such way as to believe it, of your recently saying that both the Army and the Government needed a Dictator. Of course it was not for this, but in spite of it, that I have given you the command. Only those generals who gain success can set up dictators. What I now ask of you is military success, and I will risk the dictatorship.[1]

Despite the concerns that had prompted Lincoln to write such a letter, Hooker's tenure in command of the Army of the Potomac began with much promise. He proved to be an able administrator, raising the army's morale as well as the state of its training and discipline. He also adopted an excellent plan for dealing with Lee as soon as spring weather dried Virginia's dirt roads. The plan was not unlike the scheme that Grant was simultaneously devising—and would simultaneously carry out—in the Vicksburg Campaign. Brigadier General George Stoneman (West Point, 1846) would lead the Army of the Potomac's cavalry on a raid deep into enemy territory to confuse Lee.

General Joseph Hooker

Then while part of Hooker's army continued to threaten Lee at Fredericksburg directly across the Rappahannock River, the bulk of the army would march upstream, cross the river, and march rapidly to get behind Lee and fall on him from the rear. That the campaign that followed took a much different course than Grant's Vicksburg Campaign was due mainly to the fact that Stoneman was not Grierson, Lee was not Pemberton, and, most of all, Hooker was not Grant.

On April 27, three days before Grant landed his forces on the east bank of the Mississippi, Hooker put his own army in motion and his troops began crossing the Rappahannock a number of miles above Lee's headquarters at Fredericksburg. The main body of the Army of the Potomac crossed the Rappahannock unopposed, marched south, and crossed the Rapidan, a tributary of the Rappahannock. Still they met no opposition, and Hooker could only assume that he had stolen a march on Lee exactly as he had planned.

Indeed he had, but that turned out to be almost the last thing that went right for Hooker. Stoneman's raid proved ineffective and accomplished nothing beyond depriving Hooker of most of his cavalry and thus of his means of discerning Lee's movements. By contrast, Jeb Stuart, leading Lee's excellent

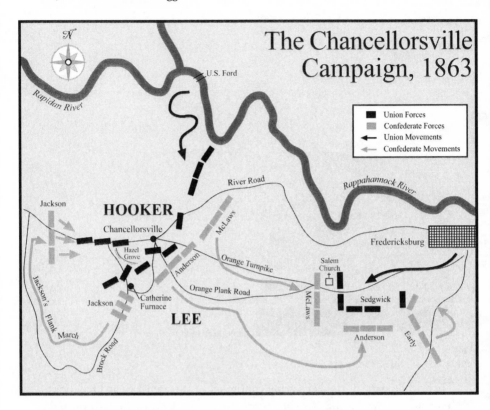

The Chancellorsville
Campaign, 1863

U.S. Ford

Rapidan River

■	Union Forces
▨	Confederate Forces
◀—	Union Movements
◀—	Confederate Movements

River Road

Rappahannock River

Jackson

HOOKER

Chancellorsville

McLaws

Fredericksburg

Hazel
Grove

Anderson

Orange Turnpike

Salem
Church

Jackson's Plank

Catherine
Furnace

Orange Plank Road

McLaws

Sedgwick

Jackson

LEE

March

Brock Road

Anderson

Early

cavalry, alerted the Confederate commander to Hooker's approach. Under cover of a dense fog, Lee withdrew most of his army from its positions around Fredericksburg, unnoticed by the large Federal corps of Major General John Sedgwick (West Point, 1837), which Hooker had left on the other side of the Rappahannock to threaten and hopefully to pin down Lee's main body. Leaving only a single reinforced division to watch Sedgwick at Fredericksburg, Lee marched with the rest of his army to counter Hooker's turning maneuver.

The main bodies of the two armies made contact on May 1, just as the Federals were about to emerge from a region of dense thickets and scrub forest known locally as the Wilderness of Spotsylvania, which stretched for a number of miles along the south bank of the Rapidan. Fighting erupted, and Hooker's troops were doing well when inexplicably he ordered a withdrawal into the heart of the Wilderness, where he ordered his army to take up a defensive position. Within the tangled underbrush of the Wilderness, the Army of the Potomac's two-to-one superiority in numbers was less significant, and its even more dramatic advantage in artillery meant nothing at all. Hooker's subordinate generals were stunned and confused, able to think of no reason why their army would choose to fight in a place like that, and, indeed, no reason existed except that Hooker had lost his nerve.

Hooker had boasted publicly all winter of what he would do when he finally got at the enemy. "May God have mercy on General Lee," he had blustered, "for I shall have none." Now, as for the first time his main army came to grips with Lee's, Hooker began to wilt. From his headquarters, located at a Wilderness crossroads called Chancellorsville, the rest of that day and throughout most of the next proceeded a stream of messages to his corps commanders, alternately urging them to assume strong defensive positions and to be prepared to pursue the enemy, who, Hooker asserted, must soon retreat. Hooker may have hoped that Lee would stage a doomed frontal assault like the one the Federals themselves had launched at Fredericksburg or, better yet, that the Confederate commander would see the futility of the situation and retreat without fighting at all. The Army of the Potomac's commander, who had always had a reputation for aggressiveness, now confused the advantages of the tactical defensive with the helplessness of complete passivity.

Feeding Hooker's wishful thinking that Lee would soon go away were reports on May 2 from one of his favorite generals, Third Corps commander Daniel Sickles. A Tammany Hall politician, Sickles had finagled a general's commission in the army when the war had broken out. His previous claims to fame had been a censure by the New York state legislature for escorting a notorious prostitute into its chambers and later an acquittal, on the nation's first-ever plea of temporary insanity, after ambushing and fatally shooting his wife's paramour. After Sickles had joined the army, he had gotten along well with Hooker since both men's tastes in recreation ran to whiskey and prostitutes. As the Army of the Potomac waited in its new defensive position in the depths of the Wilderness to see what its commander or the enemy would decide to do next, Sickles sent several dispatches to Hooker's headquarters claiming that, through gaps in the foliage created by the scanty local road network, he and his men had actually seen the Rebel army moving in retreat. Hooker ordered him to pursue, and Sickles probed forward and skirmished ineffectively with a Confederate column moving along one of the few, narrow woodland tracks in the area.

In fact what Sickles had seen and briefly encountered was not a retreat at all but one of the boldest offensive movements in American military history. Lee had thrown away the tactical rulebook, figuratively speaking, and for the second time in as many days had divided his army in the face of a much larger enemy force. This time Lee sent Stonewall Jackson with 70 percent of the Army of Northern Virginia's remaining available troops on a roundabout march along little-known roads that Jeb Stuart's cavalry, some of them local boys, had discovered, leading to a position squarely athwart the Army of the Potomac's right flank. There by the late afternoon of May 2 Jackson had, with much difficulty in the dense underbrush, deployed his twenty-eight-thousand-man corps ready to launch a flank attack on the unsuspecting troops of Hooker's flank, which Stuart had assured Jackson and Lee was "in the air," that is, not anchored on any natural feature such as a river. The Union officers, thinking the tangled thickets of the Wilderness impassable for a military formation, considered them a sufficient anchor.

Jackson struck at about 5:30 p.m., and the Union flank crumpled. Over the next two hours Jackson's men advanced two miles and took four thousand prisoners as one Federal unit after another struggled desperately to redeploy in the thickets and face the attackers, only to be engulfed and overrun by Jackson's yelling Rebels, beating their way steadily forward through the brush. By nightfall the Confederates had paused to regroup. Their success had been phenomenal, but a substantial part of Hooker's larger army still stood between Lee's and Jackson's separate Confederate forces, offering the Union commander the opportunity to inflict an annihilating defeat if he somehow regained his nerve.

Jackson hoped to forestall any such prospect and maintain Confederate momentum by launching a moonlight attack. With his staff he rode forward to see whether the new Union right was still "in the air" or whether the Yankees had succeeded in anchoring it to the Rapidan River. Jackson and his entourage completed their scout and turned back toward Confederate lines. As they approached along the narrow track between the darkened woods, nervous pickets (outpost guards), several hundred yards down the battle line from them, exchanged a few shots, a common occurrence when the armies lay only a short distance apart at night. This time, as was also not usual, the outburst of firing by the pickets set off a general volley that rolled along the main battle line for several hundred yards as jittery soldiers fired blindly into the darkness whence they suddenly suspected the foe might be approaching. Caught only a few dozen yards downrange, Jackson's entourage was riddled. Several officers fell. Jackson took a bullet in the right hand and another in the left arm. The latter was a serious wound that shattered the bone not far below the shoulder and necessitated amputation. The surgeons did not consider his injuries life threatening, but Jackson was out of the fight. Command of his wing of the army fell to cavalry commander Jeb Stuart.

With his ablest general down and the larger Union host standing between the still-severed wings of his own army, Lee was in a very dangerous position despite the dramatic success his troops had enjoyed during the final hours of daylight. That night, however, Hooker came to the rescue by withdrawing his troops to a tighter defensive perimeter, opening the way for Lee to reunite his army. Instead of counterpunching, the Union commander called for help from Sedgwick, still back at Fredericksburg with a single corps. So the next day Sedgwick brushed aside the Confederates at Fredericksburg and struck out to join Hooker, approaching from Lee's rear. Lee left a small force to watch Hooker's still-enormous army and with the bulk of the Army of Northern Virginia turned and pounced on Sedgwick while Hooker remained cowed and inert. The lone Union corps did well to escape back across the river.

Lee then turned his attention back to Hooker. Hooker's withdrawal to form a tighter perimeter had given up a clearing of high ground that formed one of the only decent artillery positions in the Wilderness. From that vantage point the usually inferior Confederate artillery had a heyday, pounding the Federals around Hooker's headquarters at Chancellorsville. A shell hit one of the porch columns of the Chancellor house while Hooker was leaning against it, leaving the Union commander stunned and confused, though his subsequent conduct of the battle was no worse than before. Beaten back from the Chancellorsville clearing by relentless Confederate attacks and bombardment, Hooker had his men take up another line still farther to the rear and finally ordered a retreat across the Rapidan, ending what would be known as the Battle of Chancellorsville.

The battle would go down in history as the greatest achievement of the Lee–Jackson partnership. It was also the last. Like thousands of Civil War soldiers, Jackson suffered the amputation of a limb, in his case the left arm. His recovery progressed well for several days, but then pneumonia set in, and Jackson died a week after the battle. His loss crippled the previously superb command system of the Army of Northern Virginia and was a severe blow to Confederate morale.

Yet although the Battle of Chancellorsville would be studied and celebrated for more than a century to come, the clash in the Virginia Wilderness had accomplished nothing beyond killing and wounding some thirty thousand men and persuading Fighting Joe Hooker to take his army back to the camps it had left when the campaign started. No territory changed hands for more than a few days, and when the campaign was over the Confederacy was no closer to victory than it had been before, unless that victory could be brought by means of attrition, a dubious proposition by which the Confederacy could only hope to counter the Union's greater numbers with its own supposedly greater devotion to its cause. Like every other battle in the eastern theater of the war up to that time, Chancellorsville had been a bloody but ultimately indecisive clash, full of heroism and mighty feats of arms but offering little realistic chance of changing the course of the war.

LEE MOVES NORTH

It was different in the West. There the Union forces, chiefly those under Grant's command, were steadily draining the life out of the Confederacy, not through attrition but rather through well-conceived operations with increasingly skillful and confident troops within a theater of the war that, unlike Virginia, offered the Union genuine opportunities to inflict serious strategic damage on the Confederacy. Almost each western campaign thus far in the war had cost the Confederacy territory, population, agricultural production, transportation facilities, and sometimes even some of the South's scarce industrial capacity. By late spring 1863 it was becoming increasingly clear that unless something could be done to break Grant's grip on Vicksburg, he would soon deliver the most damaging blow yet by capturing the fortress town and its thirty-thousand-man garrison and cutting the Confederacy's already tenuous connection with its trans-Mississippi states of Arkansas, Louisiana, and Texas, with their abundant supplies of beef, leather, and other commodities much needed in the rest of the Confederacy, especially by its armies.

How to do this was a question much on the mind of Jefferson Davis and his advisers that May. As Grant's lightning campaign through Mississippi began to unfold disastrously for the Confederacy, Davis had ordered Joseph Johnston to the state, but the western theater commander proved little help. By the time he arrived in Mississippi, Grant was already between him and Pemberton. Thereafter Johnston had assembled a small army from troops in the area and reinforcements Richmond sent him, but he held his force north of Jackson and did nothing. Davis and Secretary of War Seddon sent him reinforcements from Bragg's army and from the Atlantic and Gulf coasts until Johnston had about thirty thousand men. They begged him to move aggressively against Grant, but Johnston demurred, claiming that he had only twenty-three thousand men and urging Richmond to send him enough troops to make success certain.

In this situation Davis and his advisers considered sending Lee and/or some of his troops to Mississippi. One proposition they entertained was sending Longstreet's corps, most of which had been in North Carolina on detached duty during the Battle of Chancellorsville. Lee, not surprisingly, disagreed. Instead, in conference with Davis and the cabinet in Richmond, he advocated an operation that he and Jackson had been planning since that winter for carrying the war into Pennsylvania as soon as the army's artillery horses had eaten enough spring grass to regain their strength. They were ready now, and Lee wanted to go north. The summer heat and diseases of the lower Mississippi Valley would, Lee claimed, force Grant to give up his siege of Vicksburg and retreat north. The general was persuasive, and, after long discussions, both cabinet and president agreed. Lee's army would remain intact and would march north while the Confederates in Mississippi would fend for themselves.

Lee began his movement on June 3, shifting units of his army successively west along the south bank of the Rappahannock while its rear guard continued to confront Hooker across the river at Fredericksburg. By June 8, two of Lee's three corps had reached the neighborhood of Culpeper Court House, Virginia, about thirty-five miles northwest of Fredericksburg. The next day, Hooker, suspicious that the Rebels were in motion on the other side of the river, launched his cavalry, under Major General Alfred Pleasonton (West Point, 1844), on a reconnaissance-in-force across the Rappahannock. The result was the Battle of Brandy Station, the largest cavalry fight of the war.

The chief duties of Civil War cavalry were gathering information about the enemy army and preventing enemy cavalry from gathering information about one's own. Stopping Pleasonton's probe was therefore the duty of Jeb Stuart and his Confederate cavalry. Stuart and his troopers had enjoyed great success thus far in the war, partially because southern culture made it easier to raise effective volunteer cavalry there than in the North, partially because Stuart was a flamboyant but highly effective commander, and partially because the Army of the Potomac's cavalry had been saddled with commanding generals like McClellan, who had kept the army sitting still while Stuart literally rode circles around it. He had done so twice thus far in the war.

By June 1863, the situation was changing. The Yankee troopers had been steadily gaining skill and confidence and were now more or less the equals of Stuart's horsemen and more numerous. Pleasonton was no Stuart, and

Hooker was certainly no Lee, but the two Union officers now managed to give the Union riders a fair shot at Stuart's troopers. Stuart himself unwittingly helped by being preoccupied with a grand review of his cavalry he had staged the day before for the admiring ladies of Culpeper. Pleasonton's probe took him and his riders completely by surprise. The result was a daylong battle of galloping horses and swinging sabers. Stuart finally drove back Pleasonton's squadrons but not before being forced to call on Confederate infantry for assistance. The appearance of those gray-clad foot soldiers on the battlefield at Brandy Station tipped Lee's hand and gave Pleasonton the information for which he had come. Such military information is only as good as the analysis of the general who receives it, in this case, Hooker.

In the century and a half that has passed since the Civil War, some historians have criticized Lincoln for being too ready to sack a defeated general. If anything, Lincoln was too patient with the succession of generals who commanded the Army of the Potomac. Hooker's case is an example. He had lost his nerve the moment his army had contacted Lee's at Chancellorsville, but Lincoln had patiently allowed him a second chance. Now as the evidence indicated Lee was moving north, Hooker showed once again that he lacked the nerve to come to grips with the renowned Confederate general and his army. First he misinterpreted the news of Brandy Station. Then he hesitated, unwilling to accept the situation that was developing in front of him. When Lee's lead corps reached the Shenandoah Valley and turned northeast toward the Potomac, it was no longer possible to mistake the Confederate general's purpose. Hooker responded by coming up with a series of plans, each of which involved having someone else, perhaps a subordinate with a corps or two, deal with Lee while Hooker and the main body of the Army of the Potomac went elsewhere, perhaps to Richmond. Lincoln wisely rejected Hooker's schemes, one after another, reminding his general that Lee's army and not Richmond was the proper target and urging him to strike aggressively at that army while it was stretched out and vulnerable during its northward march.

Hooker demurred, but he did put his army in motion, marching north to stay between Lee's army on the west and Washington on the east. The long-suffering soldiers of the Army of the Potomac had to put in hard marches, sometimes thirty miles or more in a day, in order to make up for their general's late start. By late June, Lee's army had entered south-central Pennsylvania through the Cumberland Valley, an extension of the Shenandoah Valley north of the Potomac. The Rebel army's lead elements, following the northeasterly curve of the valley, were approaching Harrisburg. Hooker demanded that Washington give him control of the Harpers Ferry garrison and, when his superiors rejected his demand, requested to be relieved of command, assuming that Lincoln and Halleck would not dare to remove the commander of the Army of the Potomac with Lee deep in Pennsylvania and a major battle in the offing. They dared. Hooker had not realized how low his stock had sunk in Washington. Lincoln, on June 28, replaced him with Fifth Corps commander George G. Meade (West Point, 1835).

That same day Lee also received a nasty shock, learning for the first time of Hooker's northward marches and of the Army of the Potomac's consequent presence only a few dozen miles from his own. That information came from a spy, not, as it should have, from Jeb Stuart, Lee's chief of cavalry and de facto chief of intelligence. Lee had hitherto assumed that his opponent's army was still deep in Virginia since Stuart had brought him no word of its movement.

That was Stuart's duty, but he was by this time far out of position to perform it. Stung by the embarrassment of Brandy Station, Stuart had

General George G. Meade

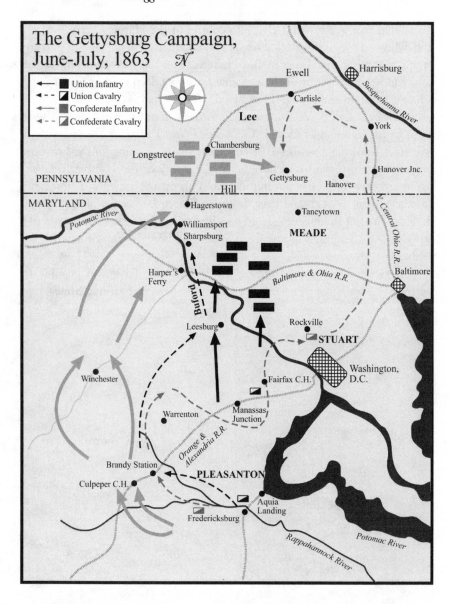

The Gettysburg Campaign, June-July, 1863

Legend:
- Union Infantry
- Union Cavalry
- Confederate Infantry
- Confederate Cavalry

PENNSYLVANIA

MARYLAND

Harrisburg

Ewell

Carlisle

Lee

York

Chambersburg

Longstreet

Hanover Jnc.

Gettysburg

Hanover

Hill

Hagerstown

Taneytown

Williamsport

Sharpsburg

MEADE

Harper's Ferry

Baltimore & Ohio R.R.

Baltimore

Buford

Leesburg

Rockville

STUART

Winchester

Fairfax C.H.

Washington, D.C.

Warrenton

Manassas Junction

Orange & Alexandria R.R.

Brandy Station

PLEASANTON

Culpeper C.H.

Aquia Landing

Fredericksburg

Rappahannock River

Potomac River

Susquehanna River

N. Central Ohio R.R.

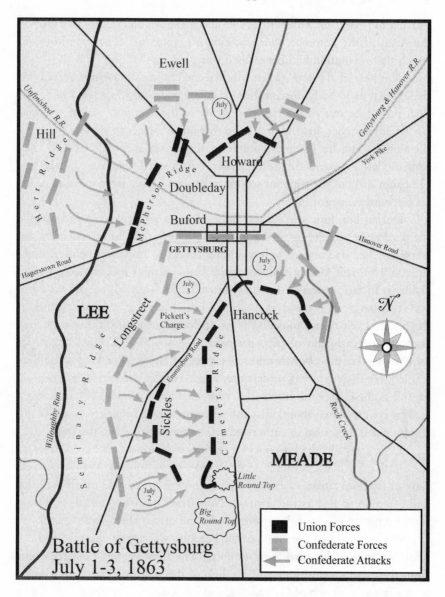

Battle of Gettysburg
July 1-3, 1863

Union Forces
Confederate Forces
Confederate Attacks

decided to stretch his orders from Lee and make another daring ride around the Army of the Potomac, thus restoring his reputation. The superiority on which that reputation had been based was gone forever now, and the newly confident blue-clad riders successfully screened Stuart's horsemen away from the Federal main body, forcing him to take a wide outside track. On top of that, just as he started his ride, the Army of the Potomac started its rapid northward marches, forcing him to go that much farther to get around it. By the time he and his troopers completed the circuit and rejoined Lee, they were too late to provide the reconnaissance he needed. Lee had to make this campaign without the superior scouting that had been a large measure of his own previous superiority.

During late June the various units of Lee's army were spread out for the purpose of plundering the Pennsylvania countryside. At the outset of the campaign Lee had issued high-sounding orders to his troops admonishing them not to treat Union civilians as the Union armies had treated Virginia civilians. In fact, however, Lee fully intended his army to live off the land, and its behavior in Pennsylvania differed little from that of Union armies in the South. Lee's troops took all the food, clothing, shoes, and livestock they could find, occasionally offering payment, at gunpoint, in Confederate paper money they knew to be worthless but more often simply taking what they wanted. On their superiors' orders they burned bridges, railroads, and depots, as well as the Caledonia Ironworks, whose owner, Thaddeus Stevens, was a leading congressional abolitionist and advocate of racial equality. Some of the troops added their own unauthorized acts of vandalism along the way.

Lee's army also had a policy of seizing and carrying off into slavery in the South every black person it encountered—man, woman, or child, escaped slave or freeborn citizen of Pennsylvania. Those who received timely warning and could do so fled as the Army of Northern Virginia approached. Those who did not or were too slow were caught and driven along under guard.

On learning that the Army of the Potomac was nearby, Lee ordered the scattered units of his own army to unite. The most centrally located point from their various positions and the hub of the south-central Pennsylvania road net was the town of Gettysburg, and Lee's orders directed his troops in that direction with a view to uniting at nearby Cashtown. The concentration of forces was nearing completion when, on the evening of June 30, Lee approved a request from one of his division commanders who wanted to take his division—one of nine infantry divisions in Lee's army—and probe toward Gettysburg the next day.

THE BATTLE OF GETTYSBURG

Early on the morning of July 1, that division, under the command of Major General Henry Heth, encountered Union cavalry near Gettysburg. The blue-jacketed troopers fought a skillful delaying action until the Union First Corps arrived and handed Heth a severe drubbing. By that time it was mid-morning, and Lee had arrived from Cashtown along with most of the rest of the Confederate Third Corps. Almost simultaneously the Confederate Second Corps, still marching to join Lee's main body after having threatened Harrisburg, approached Gettysburg from the north while the Third Corps faced it from the west. Shortly after noon the Confederates recognized and made the most of this opportunity to strike the Union defenders of Gettysburg from two directions.

Despite the arrival in the meantime of the Union Eleventh Corps, the Federals were badly outnumbered. Lee's seventy-five-thousand-man army was divided into three corps plus cavalry and artillery, while Meade's eighty-six-thousand-man force was composed of seven corps plus the usual artillery and cavalry. Thus, Lee's corps averaged twice the size of the Union formations of the same name. The more numerous Confederates dróve the Yankees through the town of Gettysburg, capturing many along the way. The surviving Federals took refuge on a hill that overlooked the town from the southeast and was known, because of the presence of the municipal cemetery, as Cemetery Hill. Lee ordered Second Corps commander Richard S. Ewell to continue the attack against the bluecoats on the hill if he thought he could do so without too much trouble. Ewell did not think so, and he was almost certainly right. The hill was a strong defensive position, held by a substantial number of well-led troops. With Ewell's decision not to press the attack, the day's fighting ended.

Meade, who arrived on the battlefield well after nightfall, had not done particularly well that day. The day before he had decided to concentrate his own army in a defensive position just across the Maryland line some miles to the south along Pipe Creek and had sent an order for such a movement to each of his corps commanders. The orders had not yet reached the commanders of the First and Eleventh corps before their troops became involved in the fighting at Gettysburg, but they did reach the other five corps commanders in time to make them hesitant and uncertain about whether they should march to join the fighting at Gettysburg, of which couriers informed them and which some could hear in the distance, or whether they should march as ordered toward Pipe Creek. Meade did not adequately clarify the situation until it was too late to help his hapless troops at Gettysburg. Indeed he seemed as uncertain as any of his corps commanders, remaining thirteen miles away at Taneytown, Maryland, throughout the day and sending various subordinates to direct the fighting at Gettysburg. During the evening, however, and through the course of the night, four more of Meade's corps arrived at the Union position south of Gettysburg.

Thus, on July 2 Meade had six of his seven corps and Lee eight of his nine divisions present to continue the fight. The remaining troops of each side would arrive later that day. Before they did, Lee renewed his attack. Hoping to repeat the success of Chancellorsville, he sent Longstreet with three divisions on a roundabout march to strike at the Union left flank while Ewell attacked the Union right flank with three more divisions. As it turned out, Lee had received incorrect information about the location of the Union left, but by the time Longstreet reached that neighborhood, late in the afternoon, the Union commander in that sector, Daniel Sickles, had, in violation of Meade's orders, moved his troops to a vulnerable position.

Longstreet struck, and intense fighting raged for hours around landmarks that would later be famous: a peach orchard, a wheat field, a boulder-strewn hillside the locals called Devil's Den, and a higher hill they called Little Round Top. Meade sent reinforcements steadily throughout the evening and almost blundered by pulling too many troops away from his opposite flank. A subordinate talked him into leaving at least a minimal force to guard the right, and this proved fortunate when in the last minutes of twilight Ewell struck there. In confused night fighting the Federals on the right managed to hold on to most of their positions, as had those on the left.

Still determined to build on the success he had won in the first day's fighting, Lee planned to attack again on July 3. Since he had tried both Union flanks and found them strong, he reasoned that the Union line must be thin in the center, along a gentle fold of ground that ran south from Cemetery Hill and was called Cemetery Ridge. Longstreet, with three new divisions in place of the exhausted ones he had used in the previous day's fight, would attack there. Simultaneously, Ewell would renew the attack on the Union right that had seemed promising as darkness closed in the night before. His troops would assault Federals on a wooded eminence called Culp's Hill. While those two attacks struck the Union center and right, Stuart, who had finally arrived with his weary cavalry late on July 2 to a frosty reception from Lee, would lead his troopers on a ride far around the Union right flank and into the rear of the Army of the Potomac so as to strike the center of the Union line from the rear while Longstreet was assaulting it from the front.

Confederate dead on the Gettysburg battlefield.

As events played out on July 3, Lee's Napoleonic plan went badly awry. The Federals on Culp's Hill, now reinforced, preempted Ewell with a pre-dawn attack of their own bent on regaining the positions they had lost the night before. Ewell's lines surged forward in their own attack, and several hours of fighting followed. By mid-morning Ewell's troops were fought to a frazzle, and the Union right flank remained solidly in possession of Culp's Hill. Meanwhile, Longstreet, who disagreed with Lee's plan of battle, had moved slowly and was not ready to launch his assault on the center. Shortly after noon Longstreet's cannon unleashed a preparatory bombardment. Stuart launched his ride to swoop down on the Union rear, but before his squadrons could get close they were met and turned back by Union cavalry under the command of a twenty-three-year-old newly promoted brigadier general named George Armstrong Custer.

On the other side of Cemetery Ridge, the Confederate preparatory bombardment lifted, and Longstreet's three divisions of infantry advanced in the long, straight ranks that were the standard fighting formations of the Civil War. The open farmland of the shallow valley between the armies gave a rare opportunity of viewing eleven thousand men in such formation, and it was an impressive sight. Long-range Union artillery tore at the Confederate lines as they marched steadily forward. Then when they were about three hundred yards from the Union lines, the batteries opened up on them with canister, and the Union infantry added their rifle fire, mowing down hundreds of attackers.

The Confederates pressed on to within a few yards of the Union line and in one place actually drove it back a few yards, several hundred gray-clad soldiers stepping over the low stone wall the Federals had held in that sector and occupying a small copse of trees that was the only landmark in that open stretch of ridge. Then Union reinforcements surged forward and overran them, sending the rest of the Confederate attackers stumbling back toward their starting point three-quarters of a mile away. Longstreet's grand assault, often called Picket's Charge, after one of the three division commanders, was over.

So too was the Battle of Gettysburg, though the participants were not yet aware of the fact. Lee expected that Meade would counterattack. He did not, and the armies spent the next day at a standoff. During the days that followed, as Lee retreated back to the Potomac and especially when he and his army were temporarily trapped on the north side of the flood-swollen river, Lincoln desperately hoped that Meade would follow up his victory with an aggressive pursuit that trapped and destroyed the Army of Northern Virginia. Instead Meade followed cautiously and paused long enough for Lee to get across the Potomac, much to Lincoln's disgust. Meade had his reasons. He had been in command scarcely more than a week, and his army had taken severe losses, including three of its seven corps commanders. Lee's army, though beaten, would still have fought well on the defensive. Lincoln's frustration was understandable since decisive results seemed to beckon, but, as usual in the eastern theater of the war, those results remained just out of reach.

Curiously, in view of all this, Gettysburg stands in the popular imagination as the great decisive battle and turning point of the war. In fact, it was nothing of the sort. It was not even a turning point within the indecisive eastern theater of the war. Militarily it was just one more bloody and inconclusive clash of the armies, full of sound and fury and acts of sublime heroism on both sides but bringing the end of the war not one day closer.

From the time Lee took command of the Army of Northern Virginia at the end of May 1862 until the time Grant took over direct operational supervision of the Army of the Potomac at the beginning of May 1864, a complete deadlock existed on the war's eastern front. During that time, everything south of the Rappahannock and Rapidan rivers was Confederate territory and everything north of those streams Union. From time to time one army or the other would strike its tents and make a foray into the other's territory. A bloody battle might result, as had been the case at Antietam, Fredericksburg, Chancellorsville, and Gettysburg, or the armies might maneuver around each other in a menacing minuet without coming to the point of mass bloodletting, as was to be the case with the lesser-known Bristoe Station and Mine Run campaigns in the second half of 1863. Either way, when each campaign was over the armies returned to the positions they had held before it started. In those six campaigns Lee had crossed the Rappahannock on the offensive three times, and his enemies had crossed it on three of their own offensives, and the results, other than several tens of thousands of men killed or wounded, was to demonstrate that with the present commanders and relative sizes of armies an almost perfect balance existed. Lee could not remain north of the Rappahannock, and his enemies could not remain south of it.

The only difference with the Gettysburg Campaign was that Lee's army returned to Virginia with many new horses and several months' worth of a much-needed supply of food that it had plundered from the civilian population of Pennsylvania. It also brought along perhaps a hundred or so Pennsylvanians of African descent whom it had kidnapped and carried south to be sold into slavery. It is ironic in the extreme that Confederate propaganda, both during the war and since, succeeded in establishing as fact the myth that Lee's noble soldiers left civilians and their property untouched during their march to immortality at Gettysburg, in contrast to the blue-clad "Yankee vandals" in their marches through the South. The real contrast was that the "Yankee vandals" did not kidnap civilians.

DECISIVE UNION VICTORIES IN
THE CONFEDERATE HEARTLAND

While the Gettysburg Campaign took its ultimately indecisive course in the East, momentous events were taking place in the Mississippi Valley. Day after day Grant's siege lines pressed closer and closer to the Vicksburg defenses until by the first days of July they were in many places within a dozen yards or so of the Rebel parapet. Twice during the siege Union troops tunneled under the Confederate fortifications and set off massive powder charges, hurling men and guns through the air, along with the logs and earth of which the fortifications had been constructed, and leaving yawning craters where stout bastions had been. Each time, Confederate reserves moved up to hold the line and prevent a Union breakthrough. Yet as Grant's approach trenches crept ever closer and food inside the city grew ever scarcer, it became increasingly clear that a coordinated Union assault would soon strike the entire Confederate perimeter at the same time and that Pemberton's troops would have little or no chance of stopping it. The gray-clad defenders could not know it, but Grant had set July 7 as the day for the assault.

It never came to that. On July 3, as Pickett's division was preparing for its march to immortality half a continent away at Gettysburg, Pemberton requested surrender negotiations. Grant agreed to accept the capitulation of Pemberton's thirty thousand troops and then to parole them, a practice common during the war up to that time. Prisoners would give their parole—their word of honor—that they would not take up arms again until they had been officially exchanged by the release of an opposing soldier from prison or from his own parole. It was, quite literally, an honor system for prisoners of war, and the amazing thing was that it had worked up until that point in the conflict. Captured soldiers were thus spared the misery of months or years cut off from family in an enemy prisoner-of-war camp, while the captors were spared the burden of transporting and maintaining them. The system could work as long as each side, especially the one with more paroled prisoners, placed the value of honor above the value of the military advantage that might be gained by the early release of its troops. That situation ended with the enormous surrender at Vicksburg. Confederate authorities promptly and illegally returned the thirty thousand men to duty without exchange. With that, the parole system was over since Union commanders could not henceforth trust the Confederates to keep their word. As a result, prisoner-of-war populations began to grow steadily on both sides.

The surrender ceremony at Vicksburg took place on July 4 as Lee was beginning his retreat from Gettysburg. Three days later, having heard of Vicksburg's surrender, the subsidiary Confederate bastion at Port Hudson, Louisiana, surrendered to besieging Union forces under Nathaniel P. Banks. The twin victories severed the Confederacy from its trans-Mississippi resources and reopened the river as an artery of Union commerce, enabling Lincoln to note in a speech a few weeks later, "The Father of Waters goes again unvexed to the sea."

Meanwhile another Union army had scored a significant success within the Confederate heartland. In a nine-day campaign in late June and early July, Rosecrans's Army of the Cumberland, after months of urging by the authori-

Ulysses S. Grant

ties in Washington, had finally moved and had maneuvered Bragg's Army of Tennessee almost out of the state whose name it bore, all the way from Tullahoma, near the center of the state, back to Chattanooga, a handful of miles from the Georgia line. Bragg, handicapped by dissension among his subordinate generals almost to the point of mutiny, was unable to counter effectively. The campaign produced no major battle and only a few relatively minor clashes between small detachments. Yet, though it was less significant than Vicksburg, it was much more significant than Gettysburg since it transferred thousands of square miles of formerly Confederate territory firmly and permanently into Union control, inflicting a severe loss on the Confederacy in agricultural production, recruitment, and morale. In one sense, however, the Tullahoma Campaign was more like Gettysburg than Vicksburg. It left the defeated Confederate army intact and able to fight another day, as the Federals would learn with sorrow three months hence during the bloody Chickamauga and Chattanooga campaigns.

Nevertheless, the Union armies had scored major victories on all three main fronts of the war, along the eastern seaboard at Gettysburg, in Tennessee in the form of the Tullahoma Campaign, and most significantly at Vicksburg, where Grant's victory had secured the Mississippi Valley under Union control. In a letter to be read at a public rally in Illinois that August, Lincoln

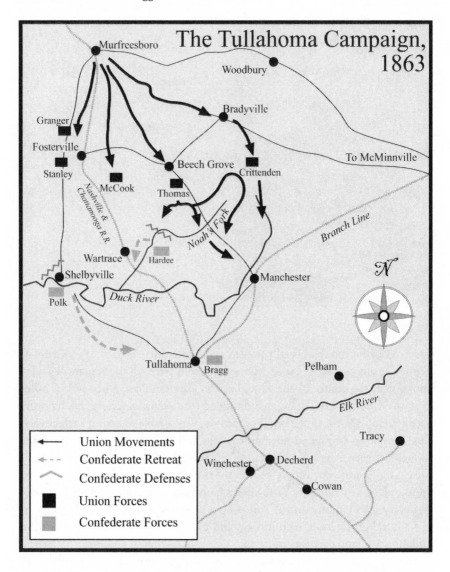

The Tullahoma Campaign, 1863

reviewed the recent victories and those who had fought to achieve them. Then he concluded, "Thanks to all. For the great republic—for the principle it lives by, and keeps alive—for man's vast future—thanks to all. Peace does not appear so distant as it did. I hope it will come soon, and come to stay; and so come as to be worth the keeping in all future time."[2]

9

"THE UNFINISHED WORK"

STRESSES AND TURMOIL ON THE
CONFEDERATE HOME FRONT

As the war entered its third year in the spring of 1863, civilian populations on the home fronts felt its pinch with ever increasing sharpness.
In the South, the effect of the war was felt not only in the absence in the
army of more than one third of the region's white male population but even
more directly in the growing shortage of food, especially in urban areas and
near the fighting fronts. This was ironic because the South was an overwhelmingly agricultural region. At the outset of the war, Jefferson Davis had
appealed to planters to shift from cotton to food production, but most had
thumbed their noses at his request since cotton was a more lucrative crop.
Indeed, if it could be run through the Union blockade on one of the sleek,
fast, purpose-built blockade-running vessels that British shipyards were soon
turning out, cotton offered bigger profits than ever in the markets of Europe.
Yet despite the continued devotion of vast acreages to the white fiber, the
South still produced enormous amounts of food, amounts that should have
been adequate to feed its people. Why then was hunger stalking significant
segments of its population?

One reason was the lack of transportation to move the food from where
it was grown to where it was to be consumed. Although the South's rail network had grown rapidly during the 1850s, it was still fragmented and partial.
Very few trunk lines carried rail traffic from one southern region or state to
another. Most of the South's railroad tracks had been laid down with a view

to carrying cotton and other produce from interior areas to ocean or river ports whence it could be shipped to the markets of the world. Few of these small rail systems connected with each other, and it would have done little good if they had since many had incompatible gauges (width between rails), and thus their rolling stock could not move on another railroad's track.

The war made the South's railroad transportation system worse. Each side tore up the other's railroad tracks when it could reach them. Sometimes retreating Confederate forces tore up their own tracks to prevent advancing Federals from using them for supply lines. Sometimes the Confederate government disassembled a section of track in order to use the iron rails for the construction of ironclads, few of which, like the *Virginia*, were completed before the Federals could seize them and none of which enjoyed even the *Virginia*'s brief success. The iron that plated their incomplete forms or that lay stacked beside the dry dock awaiting application might well have served the Confederacy better as rails. Thanks to the shortage of transportation, food tended to stay in the agricultural districts where it grew rather than finding its way in sufficient amounts to the cities and fighting fronts where the need was greatest.

Further exacerbating the difficulty southern city dwellers faced in attempting to purchase food was the impact of the Confederacy's method of financing the war. Americans (with the exception of some politicians) have never liked taxes, and during the nineteenth century they reliably voted for the sort of small government that is consistent with a low-tax, high-prosperity economic regime. Wars are expensive, and not the least of the curses they bring on a society is the growth of that society's own government. What the government consumes or redistributes, the people must provide, whether they do so in taxes or by other means. Since the Confederate government never mustered the political will to impose the taxes necessary to finance a fraction of its war effort and since it was not very successful in obtaining foreign loans, it depended on printing presses churning out thousands upon thousands of Confederate banknotes.

The result was massive inflation, as the Confederate government sucked more and more of the value out of the money that remained in all of its citizens' pockets, bank accounts, or mattresses. As prices soared, southerners condemned sellers as war profiteers. As holding cash became more and more obviously a path to economic ruin, smart businessmen tried to store their wealth in commodities instead, and the public labeled them hoarders and speculators, the worst kind of war profiteers. Preachers and editors published laments at how such economic practices revealed the lost virtue of the southern people, who now seemed to put personal gain ahead of devotion to their newly minted country, but in fact the culprit was their own government's economic policies, which made such practices unavoidable for anyone trying to escape economic ruin.

Meanwhile, hardship steadily increased throughout the South and with it discontent. On April 2, 1863, that discontent flared up into open unrest. In Richmond on that day a large mob composed mostly of women began breaking into shops and helping themselves not only to food but also to clothing, shoes, and even luxury items such as jewelry. Some of the rioters were armed, and shopkeepers remembered particularly one large and forceful woman and the large and menacing Colt dragoon revolver with which she threatened them while she and others ransacked their stores. As the mob worked its way through the business district, the city militia battalion arrived, and so did Jefferson Davis.

The Confederate president climbed atop a wagon near where the militiamen stood in line, nervously fingering their rifles. In a brief speech, Davis urged the rioters to return to their homes. Then he added, "You say you are hungry and have no money; here, this is all I have," and with that he threw all the coins in his pocket into the crowd, which remained standing, sullenly glaring at president and militia. Finally, Davis announced that if the street were not clear in five minutes he would order the militia to open fire. He then pulled out his pocket watch and quietly watched the seconds tick off. Not until he had instructed the commander of the militia detachment to order his men to load their weapons did the crowd begin to filter away, but before the five minutes were up, the street was empty of rioters.

As ominous as this so-called Richmond Bread Riot was, its grave portent was heightened by similar outbreaks of civil unrest and looting that sprung up in several cities in Georgia and North Carolina. Clearly the strains of war were beginning to tell on southern society. Although suffering may have been more intense and was certainly more visible in the cities, it was present in the countryside as well. A large portion of the white male population was in the army, and many a farm was left to the efforts of a wife and such of the children as were old enough to wield a hoe. In many cases, the families left behind had been unable to raise sufficient crops, and their food supplies were dwindling.

Since the Confederacy was literally years behind in paying its troops, the soldiers had nothing to send their families back home. In this situation, a steady stream of letters began to reach the Confederate War Department from wives requesting furlough or discharge for their husbands so that the men could come home and help their families get in a crop. To have acceded to such pleas would have been to begin the dissolution of the Confederate armies, and the authorities not surprisingly declined. As the war progressed and the hardship became more acute, such letters increasingly came not to Richmond but to the soldiers themselves in the field, wives urging husbands to obtain leave if they could or come home without leave so as to save their families from starvation.

The fact that so many of the South's white men were in the army was another sign of the long reach and considerable power of the central Confederate government in Richmond in defiance of the concept of state rights. The Confederacy had been well in advance of the Union in imposing national conscription, and its version of the draft was more rigorous and sweeping than the northern version, demanding the service of every man, with the exception of certain protected classes and skills, between the ages of eighteen and thirty-five. Later the upper limit of the draft was raised to forty-five. Men of ordinary means complained bitterly about the "twenty-slave rule" that exempted large slaveholders from duty in the ranks, and state-rights purists, such as Georgia Governor Joe Brown, raged against the draft as a violation of the principles of federalism and constitutional government. Davis and the Confederate congress were undeterred, but in some regions of the South, draft resisters gathered in large bands and withdrew into the hills, woods, or swamps, there to bid defiance to Confederate authority. Well-advised draft enrollment officers did not venture into such areas.

CONSCRIPTION AND DISSENT ON THE NORTHERN HOME FRONT

The situation in the northern states was far different than that in the South, and although hardship might be felt in some families, particularly those whose breadwinners were in the army, the economy overall was booming. Yet despite abundance, the North also experienced significant social unrest during 1863. The causes of the turmoil included war weariness, unwillingness to be drafted, and disagreement with the cause of emancipation. War weariness affected all regions equally, but resentment of the draft and resentment of emancipation were closely related and combined to produce powerful effects in specific localities.

Discontentment with conscription stemmed both from an unwillingness to fight—at least to fight for the cause of emancipation—and also from the perceived inequity of the rules Congress had laid down for the administration of the draft. Out of the usual processes of compromise and legislative pulling and hauling had emerged an Enrollment Act in March 1863. The law required every man between the ages of twenty and forty-five to register (enroll), and then, provided that a federally established quota of recruits did not volunteer within a given congressional district, the draft would go into effect in that district and make up the difference. The congressmen had thought to soften the impact of the draft by providing two remarkably ill-conceived safety valves. A man who did not wish to serve had the option, if drafted, of hiring another, undrafted man to go in his place, thus securing permanent immunity from conscription. Naturally, such substitutes were bound to become expensive, so in order to keep the price within someone's idea of reasonable bounds, the law also provided that a drafted man could pay the government a three-hundred-dollar commutation fee and go free but only until his number came up again in a future round of conscription, if it ever did.

Rarely was the law of unintended consequences more starkly on display than in this legislative masterpiece. The three-hundred-dollar commutation price was still far out of reach of an unskilled laborer, for whom that sum might represent an entire year's wages or more. Substitutes were even more expensive. The wealthy could purchase exemption, while the working man had only the choice of fight or flight (to Canada). This led to unrest and complaints (similar to simultaneous grumblings in the Confederacy) that the conflict was "a rich man's war and a poor man's fight." Instead of mollifying public annoyance with the draft, the commutation and substitution provisions became the focus of the discontent.

In most districts, diligent efforts by local authorities succeeded in meeting the recruiting quotas. This was usually accomplished by offering large bounties for recruits, payable on enlistment. Most (though by no means all) of the recruits thus gained were the dregs of society, and many turned out to be bounty jumpers, enlisting in one locality for a large cash payment, then deserting as quickly as possible to enlist in another town for another large bounty, repeating the process over and over until they either amassed a fortune or else were caught and placed before firing squads. They, as well as the substitutes whom wealthy draftees hired, were of at best dubious value to the army, as were the conscripts who actually did find their way into the ranks. The latter made up only a small percentage of the total numbers mustered into service since the impact of the draft lay primarily in spurring "voluntary" recruitment. However, its net yield was but a small trickle of good soldiers among hordes of nearly worthless substitutes, bounty jumpers, and conscripts.

In some areas, resistance to the draft was more intense and could flare up into violence. This was true in localities where popular opposition to the cause of emancipation ran high. In such districts men angrily announced that they would not fight for the African Americans, to whom they referred with disparaging epithets. Regions of particular resistance to the draft included the Ohio River valley in the southern parts of Ohio, Indiana, and Illinois, but the furor was most intense among the Irish immigrant population that made up most of the lower class of New York City.

When in the summer of 1863 a renewed round of conscription was about to go into effect in the city, the Irish population launched the war's most violent urban riot. For several days mobs ran rampant through the streets, killing policemen and African Americans and burning buildings, including an orphanage for black children. In order to quell the riot, authorities finally had to bring in several regiments of troops from the Army of the Potomac. Some officials had doubts as to whether the citizen-soldiers would actually fire on their rioting fellow citizens in the streets of New York. The veterans of Gettysburg had neither doubts nor hesitation in mowing down those whom they saw as traitors who were stabbing the Union cause in the back while the more honest Rebels attacked it in front. The arrival of battle-hardened troops quickly brought peace to the streets of New York.

Northern opposition to the Union cause could take more outwardly respectable forms than the raging mobs in the streets of New York. A large faction of the Democratic Party in the North denounced the war as wicked, foolish, and a failure to boot. These "Peace Democrats," also known as "Copperheads," controlled the Indiana legislature and had considerable political strength in other states as well, and they criticized the war and obstructed measures for its support as much as they could. Indiana's Republican governor, Oliver P. Morton, showed considerable determination and creativity in order to keep his state contributing to the Union war effort.

Sometimes Union authorities lost patience with the Copperheads. After Ambrose Burnside's unhappy tenure in command of the Army of the Potomac, Lincoln had assigned the earnest but inept general to command the Department of the Ohio, duty which at that point in the war involved mostly the administration of a rear area including several midwestern states. On April 13, 1863, Burnside issued General Order Number Thirty-Eight, stating that he would not tolerate the "habit of declaring sympathies for the enemy."

Eighteen days later, former congressman Clement L. Vallandigham defied the order.

Vallandigham had reached Congress in 1857 after narrowly losing the 1856 election in his district but then persuading the Democratic majority in Congress to seat him in place of his victorious Republican opponent. As an incumbent he had won the next two elections by the thinnest of margins. When the Civil War began, Vallandigham, a virulent racist and enthusiastic backer of slavery, had denounced the Union cause and voted against every single bill for the support of the armed forces. In the 1862 elections, despite the country's dissatisfied mood that had given the Democratic Party additional seats in Congress, the voters of western Ohio had swept Vallandigham out of office in a landslide. Nevertheless, the renegade Ohioan was one of the foremost leaders of the Copperhead movement and coined its slogan, subsequently repeated with various mutations, about maintaining the "Constitution as it is and the Union as it was."

In a major public speech on May 1, 1863, the newly unemployed former congressman denounced "King Lincoln" and called for his ouster from the White House. The war, Vallandigham complained, was not for the Union but for the freedom of the slaves and therefore not worth fighting. Several days later Burnside had Vallandigham arrested for violation of General Order Number Thirty-Eight. In response, a Copperhead mob turned out and burned the offices of Dayton's pro-Republican newspaper, the *Journal*, rival of the pro-Vallandigham Democratic *Empire*. A military tribunal tried and convicted Vallandigham for violation of Burnside's order, sentencing him to two years' imprisonment. A federal district court upheld the validity of the military trial and conviction, as did the Supreme Court, several months later. Meanwhile, Lincoln decided to commute Vallandigham's sentence to banishment to the Confederacy. If Vallandigham wished to side with the Rebels, to the Rebels he would go, where he could, if he were man enough, shoulder a musket and fight for the beliefs he had been espousing for many months.

Instead, after Union troops had seen him through the lines under flag of truce in Tennessee, Vallandigham traveled to the coast and left the Confederacy on a blockade-runner to Bermuda, whence he took ship for Canada. Arriving in Windsor, Ontario, he declared himself a candidate for governor of Ohio in the election that fall, calling for Ohio to secede from the Union if Lincoln did not at once recognize Confederate independence. The Ohio Democrats gave him their nomination, while the Republicans nominated staunch "war Democrat" John Brough. The result was an overwhelming landslide victory for Brough. Subsequently, Vallandigham reappeared in Ohio, showing up at a number of public events, but the authorities ignored him.

Meanwhile, Burnside had had a run-in with another prominent Copperhead. Wilbur F. Storey, the virulently Copperhead editor of the *Chicago Times*, enraged Burnside by his paper's unrelenting hostility to the Lincoln administration and the Union war effort. On June 1 Burnside issued an order stating, "On account of the repeated expression of disloyal and incendiary sentiments, the publication of the newspaper known as the *Chicago Times* is hereby suppressed." An immediate furor arose, and Lincoln revoked Burnside's order.

MANEUVERING AGAINST THE ENEMY, LATE SUMMER, 1863

Meanwhile, back on the fighting fronts, the late summer of 1863 saw lulls in both regions that had been the scenes of heavy action during the late spring and early summer. In the Mississippi Valley, Grant's army consolidated the vast gains of the Vicksburg Campaign, and the authorities in Washington diverted a significant portion of Grant's strength, the Thirteen Corps, to Bank's Department of the Gulf.

As Grant later noted ruefully, the troops were sent where they could do the least good. He would have liked to have resumed the offensive with a drive against Mobile, but Lincoln and his advisers in Washington were eager to establish a Union presence in Texas, where the French emperor Napoleon III was in process of setting up a subservient regime under the rule of puppet emperor Maximilian, a clear violation of the Monroe Doctrine. In theory, Napoleon would be impressed by the arrival of Union troops in the vicinity of the border and would abandon his Mexican adventure. As it turned out, all such efforts, like any other plans that placed troops under the command of the dismal Banks, were doomed to failure. The quickest way to get the French out of Mexico would be for the United States to triumph over the rebellion and then turn its undistracted attention to Maximilian and his French master.

The other sector that had seen heavy fighting during the early summer was the eastern theater, where Lee's Pennsylvania gambit had failed at Gettysburg. Though somewhat reduced in numbers, Lee's army was in a much better state of supply than it had been at the beginning of the summer thanks to the abundant booty it had plundered from the Pennsylvania countryside during the Gettysburg Campaign. On the other side of the lines, Meade was cautious as ever. Lee was first to take the offensive again, moving deftly around Meade's flank and marching north to threaten Washington as well as Meade's supply line. Cautiously but with equal deftness, Meade fell back, denying Lee the advantage he had sought. Hoping to catch and damage Meade's army as it withdrew, A. P. Hill, commanding Lee's Third Corps, struck incautiously at a Union column near Bristoe Station, Virginia. A brief reconnaissance would have revealed far more Federals present than Hill had imagined and in a very strong position. Hill's corps suffered a bloody repulse, and Lee, seeing that the campaign would accomplish nothing, ordered his troops back to their camps south of the Rapidan and Rappahannock. Thus, for a fifth time since the eastern armies had established themselves on opposite sides of those rivers, an offensive foray by one side or the other had ended in a failure that left the strategic situation in Virginia unaltered.

On the central fighting front, in Tennessee, where William S. Rosecrans's Army of the Cumberland faced Braxton Bragg's Army of Tennessee, the situation was much different. Early summer there had brought no heavy fighting but rather the almost bloodless maneuvering of the Tullahoma Campaign, by which Rosecrans had expelled Bragg from Middle Tennessee. Handicapped by the near-mutinous state of his top generals, Bragg had fallen back all the way to Chattanooga, almost on the border with Georgia, while Rosecrans had halted his advance near Winchester, on the opposite (northwestern) side of the Cumberland Plateau.

Lincoln, Stanton, and Halleck had been almost at the end of their patience with Rosecrans over his six-month delay between the Battle of Stones River and the Tullahoma Campaign. When that campaign halted without a major battle and with Bragg's army still intact, their annoyance began to grow once again. Rosecrans insisted on halting his army until its state of supply and equipment was once again as perfect as he could make it. Six weeks passed, and it was August 16 before the Army of the Cumberland once again marched out of its camps to follow up its previous advantage against Bragg.

While Rosecrans had used the six-week midsummer lull to refit his army, the Rebels too had been busy. For months a coterie of influential Confederates had been urging that the Confederacy's best strategy was to concentrate its strength in the center for a decisive, war-changing blow that would crush Rosecrans and begin the unraveling of the Union's effort to restore the southern states to their allegiance. Rosecrans's success in the Tullahoma Campaign, with its inherent threat to Chattanooga, finally galvanized the government in Richmond into acting on that plan. Davis overruled Lee's objections and ordered James Longstreet with two divisions of his First Corps of the Army of Northern Virginia to reinforce Bragg for a counterstroke against Rosecrans.

By the time Longstreet's detachment got under way, Union troops under Burnside, now leading a one-corps Army of the Ohio, had advanced from Kentucky and captured Knoxville, Tennessee, cutting the direct rail connection between Virginia and Chattanooga. Longstreet's troops therefore had to ride the trains all the way down the East Coast and then back north through Atlanta to join Bragg. This delayed their arrival until the second half of September, but their presence, along with that of various reinforcements Davis ordered to Bragg from other corners of the Confederacy, would raise the Army of Tennessee to nearly seventy thousand men, its greatest ever numerical strength and enough to claim a moderate advantage over Rosecrans's Army of the Cumberland.

The reinforcements were not with Bragg when on August 16 Rosecrans launched his new campaign. As usual, the Army of the Cumberland's commander had prepared meticulously, and his plan demonstrated how powerful a factor it was to be allowed to choose the time and place of action. Although his army had to cross several formidable barriers, Rosecrans's possession of the initiative turned each of them to his advantage. The first barrier was the Cumberland Plateau, and immediately behind it lay the broad Tennessee River. For Bragg the problem was that the plateau was a barrier sufficient to prevent cavalry reconnaissance—especially reconnaissance directed by Bragg's rather mediocre cavalry commanders—but nevertheless contained more gaps than his army could possibly hold in strength. As Bragg put it, "A mountain is like the wall of a house full of rat-holes. The rat lies hidden at his hole, ready to pop out when no one is watching."

Complicating the problem for Bragg was Burnside's possession of Knoxville and potential threat to move down the Tennessee Valley and link up with Rosecrans, a threat so severe that Bragg simply could not afford to permit it. He had to play Rosecrans strong to the northeast of Chattanooga even at the expense of leaving a weak side to the southwest of the town, where a Federal passage of the mountains and river would be less immediately disastrous. In the end, that was exactly where Rosecrans made his move, feinting elaborately upstream of Chattanooga, then pushing his army quickly across mountains and river below (southwest of) the town. By the time Bragg learned of Rosecrans's advance, the Army of the Cumberland was already across the Tennessee River and pressing east toward the final barrier, the long ridge known as Lookout Mountain. Towering as much as 1,400 feet above the surrounding terrain, Lookout extended several score miles southwest from Chattanooga, where it loomed over the town, across the northwestern corner of Georgia and well into Alabama. Surmounted by a rocky escarpment known as the palisades, Lookout could be crossed only by tortuous mountain roads and then only where gaps in the palisades allowed passage.

Once again the initiative and the corresponding advantage belonged to Rosecrans. Moving his army in three widely separated columns to take advantage of as many far-flung gaps, the Union commander made it impossible for Bragg to discern the exact points of advance until it was too late to counter. With that, Rosecrans had successfully turned Bragg's position in Chattanooga, threatening his supply line back toward Atlanta and putting him in immanent danger of being trapped against the Tennessee River just as Pemberton had allowed Grant to trap him against the Mississippi at Vicksburg four months before. Bragg was too canny to let that happen, so he took the only other option and put his army in retreat southward out of Chattanooga.

While one of his three corps moved in and occupied the key rail junction town, Rosecrans, traveling with his center corps twenty-four miles to the south, stood atop Lookout Mountain and observed the long cloud of rising dust to the south of Chattanooga that could mean only that Bragg was in retreat. Rosecrans's reaction was to pursue, and he ordered all three of his corps—the Twenty-First at Chattanooga, the Fourteenth with him twenty-four miles to the south, and the Twentieth another eighteen miles farther south—to press eastward as rapidly as possible and tear into the flanks of the fleeing Rebel column.

The problem with all this was that Bragg's army was not fleeing. The wily Confederate had shifted south twenty-five miles from Chattanooga to the town of La Fayette, Georgia, in order to escape Rosecrans's trap, but he and his army were as yet far from defeated. On the contrary, the Rebels were at bay, looking for an opportunity to strike at their tormentors—and the long-awaited reinforcements were beginning to arrive. By pressing his campaign beyond Lookout Mountain, Rosecrans was following the pattern he had set after the Battle of Corinth eleven months before, trying to exploit momentum he did not have. This time, however, Grant was not on hand to stop him.

As Rosecrans pressed forward, Bragg soon found the opportunity he sought. On the evening of September 9, scouts brought him word that a Union division had crossed Lookout Mountain via Stevens Gap, twenty-four miles south of Chattanooga, and descended the west slope into a side valley known as McLemore's Cove. If Bragg could have written the orders on which this column of Federals was marching, he could not have arranged the situation any more favorably for himself and his army. The Union division was temporarily isolated from its comrades still atop the mountain but only an easy ten miles from Bragg's main point of concentration at La Fayette. Confederate forces found themselves perfectly positioned to strike the Federals simultaneously in the front and flank with overwhelming force. Better still, McLemore's Cove was open to the northeast, thus easily admitting Bragg's flanking column, but the cove was closed on the south, forming a cul-de-sac as if perfectly designed for trapping overaggressive Yankees.

Bragg immediately issued the orders that should have brought his army clamping down like the jaws of a nutcracker on the front and flank of the Union division, and over the next day and a half he reiterated them with increasing emphasis—all to no avail. Once again the dysfunctional high command of the Army of Tennessee came to the aid of the advancing Federals. Two of Bragg's generals, Daniel Harvey Hill and Thomas C. Hindman, balked; produced a string of excuses; and finally refused to carry out Bragg's orders. The Federals, who were in fact the vanguard of the Fourteenth Corps, finally discovered their danger and withdrew unscathed to the crest of Lookout. Too many of the Army of Tennessee's generals had in their self-seeking combined to convince each other and many of their comrades that Bragg was so hopelessly incompetent that any order he gave had to be a disastrous mistake just because he gave it. The result in McLemore's Cove had been the loss of what one of Bragg's staff officers described as an opportunity "which comes to most generals only in their dreams."[1]

Yet even with the opportunity in McLemore's Cove gone, Bragg's position was still amazingly good. With his army concentrated around La Fayette and steadily increasing as reinforcements arrived, he was closer to each of Rosecrans's three separate corps than any of them was to one of the others. Centrally located and with good roads at his disposal, Bragg could strike at Union columns too weak to meet his massed troops and too widely separated to support each other. On September 12 Bragg accordingly issued orders for his troops to strike the isolated Twenty-First Corps, which had been moving south from Chattanooga as Rosecrans's left wing. Again a Confederate general, this time Leonidas Polk, refused to carry out Bragg's orders, and the opportunity went begging.

Over the course of the next week Rosecrans, at last aware of his danger, strove to draw his columns together and reunite his army, sidling the Twenti-

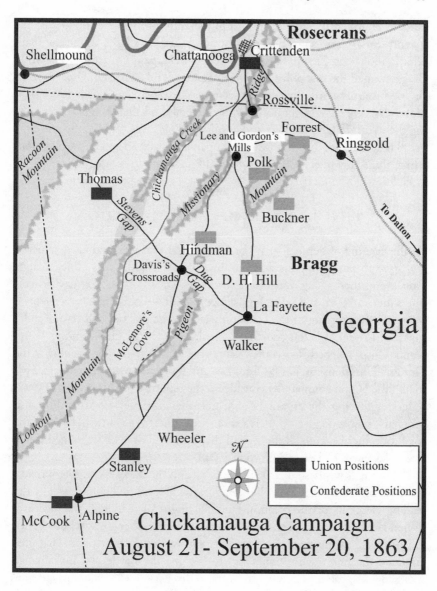

Chickamauga Campaign
August 21- September 20, 1863

eth and Fourteenth corps northward to join and ultimately leapfrog past the Twenty-First Corps's position near Lee and Gordon's Mill, where the main Chattanooga–La Fayette Road crossed Chickamauga Creek. Meanwhile Bragg awaited the rest of his reinforcements and did some sidling of his own, sliding his army north opposite Rosecrans's. If Bragg could move faster than his adversary, he could get north of the Federals and then lunge west, blocking their path to Chattanooga and positioning his army to drive the outnumbered bluecoats southward toward the open maw of McLemore's Cove, from which the Army of the Cumberland could not hope to escape.

THE BATTLE OF CHICKAMAUGA

By the evening of September 17, Bragg believed that goal had been achieved and gave the order for his army to advance westward, cross Chickamauga Creek, and then swing south to destroy the Federals. The next day his columns met stubborn and skillful resistance from Rosecrans's cavalry screen and managed the crossing of the creek only late in the day but still several miles north of Rosecrans's left (northern) flank. As George H. Thomas's Fourteenth Corps reached Rosecrans's temporary headquarters that evening at the Gordon-Lee Mansion, not far from Lee and Gordon's Mill, after a hard day's march the Union commander considered the reports from his cavalry of Confederates forcing the crossings of Chickamauga Creek north of him and ordered Thomas to give his men a short break and then get them back on the road for a night march all the way to the farmstead of a settler named Kelly, five miles north of Lee and Gordon's Mill.

Thomas's weary soldiers stumbled through the darkness on rough roads, less than half lit by the smoky light of occasional fence-rail bonfires set by the leading elements of the column, but their night of marching was decisive. When the battle opened the next morning, September 19, the Fourteenth Corps was as far north as any major element of Bragg's army, and what precipitated the first clash of what was to become the Battle of Chickamauga was Federals probing eastward from the Kelly Farm and encountering Confederate cavalry guarding the flank and rear of Bragg's army as it faced south ready, as Bragg supposed, to drive the Army of the Cumberland into McLemore's Cove. A day of confused but intense fighting followed as Rosecrans shifted more and more troops north to support Thomas and Bragg turned unit after unit of his army and sent them driving to the west rather than to the south. With a dense forest canopy extending over most of the battlefield, both commanders could often do little more than order their arriving divisions to march toward the sound of the firing.

The day ended with the Army of the Cumberland holding its own, including the vital Chattanooga–La Fayette Road and Dry Valley Road, both giving access to Chattanooga. Rosecrans met with his generals that night and announced that he would not retreat the next day but would keep the left wing as strong as possible while the right wing continued to draw in on the left. Bragg too was determined to continue the fight the next day. That night he received further reinforcements, bringing his total strength to sixty-eight thousand versus Rosecrans's sixty-two thousand, minus the losses of the first day.

Less auspiciously, Bragg's reinforcements also included James Longstreet. Convinced that he was the Confederacy's greatest general, Longstreet had found it galling enough serving under his imagined inferior Lee. He was incensed at having to serve under Bragg and doubly so when Bragg let a little thing like a battle distract him to the point of sending no welcoming party to meet Longstreet at the nearest railway stop, Catoosa Platform. When Longstreet finally arrived at Bragg's headquarters late that night, Bragg felt compelled to reorganize his army in the middle of the night, midway through a major battle, in order to give Longstreet a command befitting his seniority if not his self-image. Bragg divided his army into two wings, the right under Polk, the left under Longstreet. The right would lead off the attack "at day-dawn," and then the assault would extend farther and farther to the left until the whole army was engaged. They would bend back the Union left and drive the Army of the Cumberland into McLemore's Cove.

Once again the Army of Tennessee's high command malfunctioned. Polk, whose wing was to open the attack, failed during the night to notify his subordinate commanders that an attack was even scheduled, so when day dawned on the morning of September 20, the units of the Confederate right wing were out of position and completely unprepared for action. Instead of making haste to remedy his lack of preparation, Polk took a leisurely breakfast. After more than three hours and several increasingly irate messages and finally the personal intervention of the army commander, the assault finally began around 9:30 a.m., though it was still badly coordinated.

During the interval between the time the attack was supposed to have gone in and the time it finally did, the Federals in front of it, belonging to George Thomas's very heavily reinforced Fourteenth Corps, made use of the time to build log breastworks. Such improvised field fortifications were coming into increasingly wide use during the course of 1863. They changed the whole equation of battle, multiplying the defenders' strength by a factor of three or more. Polk's stumbling assaults broke in slaughter in front of Thomas's breastworks.

Noon was approaching when Longstreet's turn came. With more time to prepare, he had (whether by accident or design is unclear) arranged the eight brigades of the center of his wing in a column of attack five brigades deep on a two-brigade front and had aimed it at the Union right center, where the two-brigade division of Brigadier General Thomas J. Wood held the line.

At least, Wood was supposed to hold that sector of the line. In fact, at the moment Longstreet advanced, Wood's brigades were not in line. Longstreet and his Confederates could not have known it, but a misunderstanding had occurred at Rosecrans's headquarters about the actual arrangement of the Army of the Cumberland's units. Rosecrans, who thanks to his nervous nature had in recent days been unnecessarily depriving himself of rest and nourishment, became confused and, thinking a gap existed in his lines, ordered Wood to march his division to a different part of the field and close the gap. In fact, no gap had existed—until Wood pulled his brigades out of line in obedience to Rosecrans's order. And just then, before Union officers could remedy the sudden disruption of their army's line, Longstreet's column of attack roared through the gap, splitting the Army of Cumberland in two within minutes.

Following up his success, Longstreet drove the severed right wing of the Army of the Cumberland off the battlefield after short but bitter fighting, but the defeated Federal units were able to withdraw via the Dry Valley Road behind the cover of Thomas's still-intact left wing. While still holding his lines on the left, Thomas was able to use his reserves and some rallied formations from the Union center to cobble together a line on a chain of hills blocking any Confederate advance northward in pursuit of the retreating Union right. There he held on through hours of intense fighting until retreating on Rosecrans's orders late in the evening. Rosecrans sent the orders from Chattanooga, to which he had fled shortly after Longstreet's breakthrough.

THE BATTLE OF CHATTANOOGA

Chickamauga was the first Confederate victory in the western theater of the war, but it was not the decisive victory the Confederacy had needed and on which it had gambled in weakening other regions to reinforce Bragg. Because it had been the Union right that broke, while the left wing held firm, the battle offered Bragg no opportunity for exploitation or pursuit. Thomas's wing, reinforced by now with much of the rest of the Army of the Cumberland, continued to cover the retreat, taking a strong defensive position so that any attempt by Bragg to advance toward Chattanooga would have ended in slaughter. So too would any Confederate attack on the heavily fortified Union lines just outside the town of Chattanooga, into which Rosecrans had withdrawn his army within little more than twenty-four hours after the end of the fighting in the valley of Chickamauga Creek. Then Rosecrans transformed the situation into one that did, after all, offer decisive results to Bragg.

The Army of the Cumberland was still full of fight, but its commander was a beaten man. His army in Chattanooga depended for its supplies on the road and rail corridor via the Tennessee River Gorge downstream from the town, yet Rosecrans ordered his troops to withdraw without a fight from the high ground that commanded that route. That high ground was the northern extremity of Lookout Mountain, towering 1,400 feet above Chattanooga and, more important, dominating the Tennessee River, which lapped the toe of the mountain. Confederates on Lookout and in the adjoining Lookout Valley to the west of the mountain could prevent supplies from reaching the bluecoats in Chattanooga via boats on the river, wagons on the road that hugged its bank, or trains on the railroad track that ran beside it. Bragg advanced in the days after the Battle of Chickamauga, occupied the high ground, and placed Rosecrans's army in a state of siege almost as severe as that which Grant had successfully laid to Pemberton's army in Vicksburg a few months before. Rations were soon desperately short in the camps of the Army of the Cumberland, and the army's horses and mules died in droves from starvation.

In Washington, Rosecrans's defeat at Chickamauga had aroused concern. His behavior after the battle, acting, in Lincoln's words, "confused and stunned, like a duck hit on the head," excited consternation, especially on the part of the excitable secretary of war. Lincoln and Stanton quickly made arrangements to send relief to beleaguered Chattanooga. They dispatched two corps of the Army of the Potomac, the Eleventh and Twelfth under the command of Joseph Hooker, by rail as reinforcements, and, far more important, they assigned Grant to take overall command of all Union forces west of the Appalachians and to go to Chattanooga at once and set the situation there to rights.

Grant arrived in the town on October 23 via the same route that was bringing the Army of the Cumberland its thin trickle of supplies, a rough track that made a sixty-mile roundabout trip through the mountains. Arriving cold and wet in a howling storm after the long, muddy ride, Grant received a chilly welcome from Thomas, who on Grant's orders had recently assumed command of the Army of the Cumberland in place of Rosecrans. Thomas sympathized with Rosecrans and resented having to take orders from Grant. Undeterred, Grant set to work to break the siege. First, he ordered his old lieutenant Sherman, now leading Grant's former command, the Army of the Tennessee, to bring four divisions of the victorious veterans of Vicksburg across northern Alabama and southern Tennessee to join the force around Chattanooga.

Then Grant implemented a plan to reopen the supply line into Chattanooga through the Tennessee River Gorge. Part of the scheme had been developed by Rosecrans's staff before his relief, but Rosecrans had not thought the time right for implementing it. Grant excelled at recognizing good plans and making them happen. In a skillfully executed night assault, Union troops descended the Tennessee by boat and seized key terrain in Lookout Valley, aided by the fact that Longstreet, who commanded the Confederate troops in this sector, had devoted only a tiny fraction of his available force to holding that vital position. The detachment that had come west from the Army of the Potomac, commanded by former Army of the Potomac commander Joseph Hooker, then moved in from the railhead at Bridgeport, Alabama, and linked up with the Federals who had taken Lookout Valley, strengthening the Union grip on the Tennessee River Gorge. With that, the "Cracker Line," as the Union soldiers called it, was open, and supplies, including the ubiquitous hardtack "cracker" that was the mainstay of the Union soldier's diet, began to flow into the town in vast amounts.

This changed the entire operational equation around Chattanooga and throughout the western theater of the war. From holding a stranglehold on the Army of the Cumberland in Chattanooga, Bragg had gone literally overnight to simply sitting in front of a fully supplied opposing force that now outnumbered his own. He immediately ordered Longstreet to gather his forces and counterattack to regain Lookout Valley and reestablish the siege, but that general, who had seemed so impressive in Virginia when Lee had told him what to do, blundered again, using only a couple of brigades and managing the fight so badly that the attack fizzled almost as soon as it got started.

Few options remained open to Bragg. A frontal assault on the fortified lines around Chattanooga would play directly into Grant's hands. Retreating toward Atlanta was unacceptable to the Confederate government. Waiting passively in place to see what Grant would do promised to be as disastrous a policy for Bragg as it had been for Pemberton a few months before. A move westward to turn Grant's right flank would take the Confederates directly into the path of Sherman's oncoming force.

That left only a move to the northeast to turn Grant's left flank. It would be risky, of course, but so was everything else Bragg could do. It would require getting rid of Burnside's small Union force at Knoxville, but Burnside was known not to be one of the more formidable Union generals. Besides it would open the way for a turning movement that might repeat the northward campaign that had shifted the scene of conflict all the way into Kentucky the preceding year, and it would also reopen the direct rail connection to Virginia. Lee had been clamoring for the return of Longstreet's detachment, and Davis usually listened to Lee. Bragg, for his part, was more than willing to part with Longstreet, at least, after that general's recent performances. Using Longstreet's divisions to clear East Tennessee as the first phase of the army's turning movement would thus have the added benefit of getting Longstreet away from Chattanooga and of getting his troops halfway back to Virginia and thus pleasing the Confederate government in Richmond.

So Bragg ordered Longstreet to take his detachment up the Tennessee Valley to Knoxville, destroying or driving off Burnside's force. Burnside proved as unskillful as expected, and Longstreet had an opportunity of trapping the Union force before it could fall back into the Knoxville defenses. Longstreet, however, matched Burnside blunder for blunder and let the Federals escape. Then he settled in for an inept siege of Knoxville.

By November 24 Grant's preparations at Chattanooga were complete. On that day, Sherman's command made a river crossing above the town and moved quickly to take up a position threatening Bragg's right flank on the northern end of Missionary Ridge, a six-hundred-foot-high landform on the east side of Chattanooga. By nightfall Sherman's troops were poised to advance against Bragg's flank on the ridge. Simultaneously, Hooker's command successfully stormed Lookout Mountain, pushing back the Confederate left flank to Missionary Ridge so that Bragg's entire line ran along the ridge.

Sherman opened the ball the next morning with his attack on the Confederate right, which Grant was counting on as his main blow. The mountainous terrain around Chattanooga was new to both armies and to their commanders, and the massive terrain features had much different tactical effects than did analogous features in the gently rolling terrain in which they had previously fought. Ridges like Lookout Mountain had proved surprisingly vulnerable to direct assault. Now Missionary Ridge turned out to be a much stronger position against a flank attack than anyone had previously imagined. That factor, along with the presence of Bragg's best division commander, Major General Patrick R. Cleburne, on the Confederate right was enough to stop Sherman's assault in its tracks.

Grant had anticipated subsidiary pushes from Hooker against the Confederate left flank at the other end of the ridge and from Thomas, with the Army of the Cumberland, against the enemy's center. Grant had not expected much from these efforts beyond diversion of the enemy, and so far they had not delivered even that. Hooker's attack against the south end of Missionary Ridge was delayed by an unbridged creek on the way there, and Thomas showed no inclination to make so much as a threatening movement on his front.

Grant's headquarters were near the center of the line, and so in mid-afternoon he approached Thomas and asked if he thought it would be a good idea to threaten the Rebel center. Thomas, who was scrutinizing the Confederate line through his field glasses, ignored Grant, though he could hardly have failed to hear him. Some minutes later Grant simply ordered Thomas to advance his army and take the first Confederate line of rifle pits, which was at the base of Missionary Ridge. Some time later when the Army of the Cumberland still did not advance, Grant again prodded Thomas, who lamely explained that he had given the order but did not know why it was not being carried out. Finally, late in the afternoon Thomas's army did advance, though he had neglected to see to it that his division commanders knew their objective. Some units thought they were driving for the top of the ridge, others that they were to stop after taking the first Confederate line at its base. Still others had no idea where they were to stop.

Fortunately for Thomas's men, the Confederate entrenchments at the base of the ridge were lightly manned, and about half of the units in them had orders to retreat after two volleys. Their hasty departure was demoralizing to the remainder of the Confederates on that line, who had no idea of any such orders. Thus, the first Confederate line fell easily into Union hands. Confusion then reigned in Union ranks as some units started immediately up the ridge and others halted uncertainly. Eventually, division, brigade, and even regimental commanders, recognizing that their troops were taking heavy fire from the crest of the ridge, made the decision to advance, and all five attacking divisions went up the slope, though now in very ragged formation.

Like Lookout Mountain the day before, Missionary Ridge proved surprisingly vulnerable to direct attack, its steep slope and rugged folds providing much cover for advancing attackers. Eager to avenge their defeat at Chickamauga, Thomas's troops pressed doggedly upward and broke the Confederate line in several places virtually simultaneously. At almost the same time, Hooker finally got his troops onto the south end of the ridge, adding to the Confederate discomfiture. Resistance quickly collapsed, with all of Bragg's army in headlong flight except for Cleburne's still-resolute division, which covered the rest of the army's retreat much as Thomas's command had done for the Army of the Cumberland after Chickamauga. That, along with the rapid approach of night, precluded effective pursuit and allowed Bragg's army to escape, minus several thousand prisoners and several dozen cannon left in the hands of the exultant Federals.

YEAR'S END, 1863

Up in Knoxville, Longstreet heard of Bragg's defeat and made an attempt to storm a key Union fort near the city. Like almost everything Longstreet did during his western sojourn, the attack was woefully mismanaged and developed into a resounding failure. Grant, in the wake of his Chattanooga victory, dispatched Sherman and his hard-marching troops to deal with Longstreet. As Sherman's troops neared Knoxville, Longstreet broke off the siege and retreated northeastward into Virginia. Never again would Longstreet or any large detachment of troops from the Army of Northern Virginia serve in the war's western theater, and never again would the Confederacy make such a concerted effort to turn the tide of the war in this decisive theater and regain all that it had lost since the debacles at Fort Henry and Fort Donelson.

Grant's resounding victory at Chattanooga capped a six-month period of dramatic Union successes including the culmination of the vast and complicated Vicksburg Campaign as well as victories at Gettysburg, Tullahoma, and Chattanooga with only the temporary setback of Chickamauga. In response to these encouraging developments, pointing to eventual restoration of the Union and an end to slavery, Lincoln issued a proclamation establishing November 26 as a nationwide day of thanksgiving to God. This nationalized a holiday that had been traditional for many years in the New England states as well as in some of their western progeny. Peace did not seem as distant as it had only a few months before.

On November 19 Lincoln had delivered "a few appropriate remarks" (so read the note inviting him to speak) at the dedication of a new National Cemetery at Gettysburg, established to accommodate the many thousands of Union dead from the preceding summer's battle. In one of the most eloquent speeches ever made in the English language, Lincoln explained in clear and forceful language and with striking brevity why the North was fighting and why it must fight on to final victory. "Four score and seven years ago," the president began, referring to the writing of the Declaration of Independence,

> our fathers brought forth on this continent a new nation, conceived in liberty and dedicated to the proposition that all men are created equal.
>
> Now we are engaged in a great civil war, testing whether that nation, or any nation, so conceived and so dedicated, can long endure. We are met on a great battle-field of that war. We have come to dedicate a portion of that field, as a final resting place for those who here gave their lives that that nation might live. It is altogether fitting and proper that we should do this.
>
> But, in a larger sense, we can not dedicate, we can not consecrate, we can not hallow this ground. The brave men, living and dead, who struggled here, have consecrated it, far above our poor power to add or detract. The world will little note, nor long remember what we say here, but it can never forget what they did here. It is for us the living, rather, to be dedicated here to the unfinished work which they who fought here have thus far so nobly advanced. It is rather for us to be here dedicated to the great task remaining before us—that from these honored dead we take increased devotion to that cause for which they gave the last full measure of devotion—that we here highly resolve that these dead shall not have died in vain—that this nation, under God, shall have a new birth of freedom—and that government of the people, by the people, for the people, shall not perish from the earth.[2]

10

FROM THE RAPIDAN
TO THE JAMES TO
THE POTOMAC

THE WAR ENTERS
ITS FOURTH YEAR

The year 1864 dawned amid high hopes in the North. The victories of the preceding six months made final triumph seem within reach before another new year dawned. In Grant, Lincoln had finally found the general he felt confident could see the conflict through, and the northern people shared their president's confident expectations for quick and decisive battlefield victories as soon as the drying of the South's dirt roads made it possible to open the campaigning season again that spring. With Grant in mind, Congress recreated the rank of lieutenant general, which previously only George Washington had held (Winfield Scott had ranked as a brevet, or honorary, lieutenant general). After satisfying himself that Grant had no ambitions for the 1864 presidential election, Lincoln nominated him for the rank, and Congress promptly gave its approval. Grant was now the highest-ranking Union general, and Lincoln formally appointed him as general in chief of all the Union armies. President, Congress, and public eagerly awaited the coming of spring and Grant's devastating new campaign.

Surprisingly, Confederates also looked with confidence to the resumption of active campaigning in the spring of 1864 despite the string of defeats with which they had finished out the year 1863. This curious state of mind

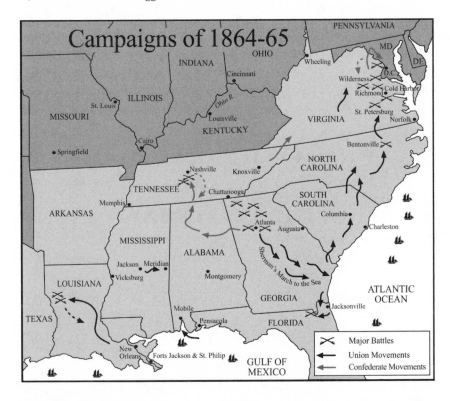

sprang in part from their own residual belief in their inherent superiority to northerners and in part from focusing on a number of Confederate victories in minor battles during the winter and early spring of 1864. Rebels could point with pride to their side's dramatic, if strategically relatively insignificant victories over secondary Union expeditions or garrisons at places like Olustee, Florida; Sabine Pass, on the Texas–Louisiana line; Fort Pillow, Tennessee; or Mansfield, Louisiana. Confederate forces had also held on to Charleston, South Carolina, including a battered but still defiant Fort Sumter, despite the Union's joint army–navy expedition to take it, including several ironclad warships and several thousand ground troops. These victories all put together did not equal half the strategic importance of a single Vicksburg or even a single Chickamauga, but they sustained white southerners in the sublime confidence that they were bound to win the war in the end.

Adding to Confederate optimism was the fact that Lincoln was up for reelection in the fall of 1864. There was never any question of postponing or canceling the election. The northern voters were going to have the chance, in the middle of a war for the nation's survival, to express—and enforce—their opinion as to whether that war should continue. If, as seemed likely, a "peace Democrat" won the Democratic presidential nomination, the election might well become a referendum on the war. If the Confederate armies could thwart Union plans for 1864 and exact heavy punishment in doing so, the northern electorate might become demoralized enough to choose a candidate who would give up the war and accept Confederate independence. As events were to prove, both Union and Confederacy entered the fourth year of the war with far more optimism than was warranted.

The war was changing. The fight at Fort Pillow, in which Confederate cavalry raiders under the command of the unorthodox but highly successful Nathan Bedford Forrest captured a minor Union garrison on the Mississippi River, also marked a disturbing trend toward more violence in the war. Almost nothing enraged white southerners more than the presence of tens of thousands of newly freed African Americans in the ranks of the Union armies. Since the first black soldiers had donned the blue a year before, Confederates had voiced many threats, both formal and informal, of what they would do to black soldiers and their Union officers. President Davis himself had decreed that captured black soldiers would be treated not as prisoners of war but as recovered slaves, and their white officers, if captured, would be turned over to state authorities for disposition under the laws governing the incitement of slave rebellion—an offense punishable by death. Lower-ranking Confederates, from brigadier down to private, penned in letters and diaries and shared with each other their more straightforward threat to take no black prisoners at all. Their attitudes are revealing about the racial motivations of Confederate soldiers.

The case of Fort Pillow became an early example of the fulfillment of these threats. There attacking Confederate troops killed black Union soldiers as they attempted to surrender and killed some who apparently had successfully surrendered a few minutes before. It was one of the most famous but far from the only case of such behavior on the part of Confederate troops, who went almost mad with rage at the sight of black men in blue uniforms bearing arms against their former masters. This new element of brutality raised the overall level of violence in the war, as black and sometimes white Union troops learned of the Confederate massacres and sometimes carried out small-scale, unauthorized retaliation, especially in the heat of battle.

Confederate policy toward black Union soldiers added to the horrors of war in another way. Since official Confederate policy regarded captured black soldiers not as prisoners of war but rather as slaves to be returned to bondage, the Confederacy refused to exchange such captured blacks. Union authorities, particularly Grant, believed themselves obligated to protect the rights of every man wearing the uniform of the United States. They therefore maintained that no exchanges could take place unless both black and white soldiers were released without discrimination. On top of this, the parole system was already in bad shape after the Confederacy had returned to the ranks, without exchange, the paroled prisoners of Pemberton's army surrendered at Vicksburg.

By the beginning of heavy fighting in the spring of 1864, parole and exchange had ceased completely. As prisoners were taken, they went into prisoner-of-war camps that had been designed for far smaller numbers of men and a system that had never foreseen such a massive prison population. The Confederacy had difficulty feeding its own troops, and the prisoners penned up by the tens of thousands in open stockades like that at Millen, Georgia, or the infamous Andersonville prison in the same state had a much lower priority. Camping in one place for an extended period, whether prisoners or not, was statistically the most dangerous thing Civil War soldiers did since the stationary camp promoted the spread of the war's most efficient killers, disease germs. In the prison pens of the South, disease raged among populations weakened by malnutrition, adding to the horrors of the last year of the war. The only war crimes trial arising from the Civil War ended in the hanging of Andersonville commandant Major Henry Wirz.

Aside from the increasing brutality of the war due to Confederate reaction to black soldiers and the resulting breakdown of the exchange system, the conflict had a momentum of its own in moving toward increasing destructiveness. Each side would show itself in 1864 and 1865 even more willing to destroy the property of enemy civilians than had been the case the year before, as the citizens of Chambersburg, Pennsylvania, and Columbia, South Carolina, along with many others, were to experience. Guerrilla warfare was another aspect of the conflict that tended to increase its violence and decrease restraint. As Confederate fortunes waned and more of the South came under Union control, guerrilla activity increased. The guerrillas hid among the civilian population and drew their sustenance from it, thus making it a target of Union retaliation. Guerrillas were also more likely to ignore the laws and customs of war, as when Confederate guerrilla leader William Quantrill and his men massacred the male population of the Unionist Kansas town of Lawrence. By the final weeks of the war, guerrillas and even regular Confederate cavalry harassing Sherman's advance through the Carolinas were routinely murdering Union soldiers who fell into their hands.

PREPARATIONS AND PLANS FOR
THE 1864 CAMPAIGN

Leaders on both sides knew that the coming campaigns would require the largest armies they could possibly raise. For the Confederacy this simply meant continued enforcement of its conscription law, which included the indefinite extension of every serving Confederate soldier's term of service. On the Union side it was more complicated. The system of raising new troops continued, with local recruiting quotas and the threat of conscription to follow if districts did not make their quotas. The special problem for the Union was that it was still committed to honoring its contracts with the soldiers who in the spring and summer of 1861 had enlisted for three-year terms. Those men's terms would expire during the campaigning season of 1864, and they made up nearly half the Union army and were among its best and most experienced troops. The Union could not afford to lose all or even most of them, but neither Lincoln nor Congress would ever have approved the Confederate expedient of simply extending all terms for the duration of the war.

The only solution was to persuade the veterans, who could no longer have any illusions about what war and soldiering meant, to reenlist voluntarily. For that purpose, the government offered a number of inducements. Any man who reenlisted received a four-hundred-dollar bounty in addition to whatever bounty his home state and town were offering for recruits at the time. He would also receive a thirty-day furlough as well as an extra chevron on his uniform sleeve, marking him as a "veteran volunteer." If a specified percentage of a given regiment reenlisted, that regiment could keep its organization and its regimental number. That last provision added group solidarity as a motivating factor and also supplied an additional motivation for officers to encourage their men to reenlist since only through the survival of the regiment could the officers keep their commissions.

Ultimately a very high percentage of veterans in the Union's western armies—the Army of the Tennessee, the Army of the Cumberland, and the Army of the Ohio, clustered near Chattanooga under Sherman's command—chose to reenlist. Among these seasoned and confident western soldiers, reenlistment rates approached 100 percent, a testimony to the Union fighting man's devotion to see the Union preserved and slavery abolished. By this time, Union soldiers clearly understood that preserving the Union and ending slavery were one and the same. Yet, while many may have enlisted in 1861 bent on nothing but preserving the Union, those reenlisting in 1863 and 1864 knew that they were fighting for the cause of emancipation.

Within the Army of the Potomac, where soldiers had experienced a procession of dismal commanders and much less success, reenlistments ran about half that rate. New levies, often composed of the worst offscourings of the slums and dockyards, would have to make up the difference within the Union's fighting force in Virginia.

When Grant assumed overall command of the Union armies, Sherman urged him to maintain his headquarters in the western theater, correctly pointing out that that region had been and would continue to be the scene of the war's really decisive fighting. Grant, however, was far more politically astute than Sherman would ever be, and he recognized that politics required him to go east and pitch his headquarters tent with the Army of the Potomac. Northern public opinion expected it, counting on Grant to be the man who would finally whip Lee, and only by staying in Virginia could Grant neutralize political pressures on the operation of the Army of the Potomac, pressures that would, if left unchecked, allow Lee to use the politicians' fears for Washington to disrupt Union arrangements—as the wily Confederate had done before.

Grant thus would accompany the Army of the Potomac, which would remain under Meade's command, somewhat to that general's own surprise. As Grant explained to Meade before the campaign started, his army's objective was to be Lee's army—not Richmond or any other strategic location. "Wherever Lee goes, you will go also." In Grant's reckoning, once Lee's army was destroyed, he could have all the strategic locations he wanted. Yet the Army of the Potomac would march toward Richmond nevertheless not because the city itself was Grant's chief objective but in order to force Lee to stand and fight. In Grant's scheme of things, Richmond was to serve the purpose of an anvil. The Army of the Potomac would be the hammer that would pound Lee's army.

But Grant's plan for the spring and summer of 1864 called for much more than just another On-to-Richmond campaign. While the Army of the Potomac advanced to hammer Lee against Richmond, two smaller Union armies would threaten the Rebel capital simultaneously from both east and west, forcing Lee to divide his attention and possibly his army. To the northwest of Richmond, Grant's orders called for General Franz Sigel to lead a new Army of the Shenandoah up the valley of that name, threatening the breadbasket of Virginia and potentially its direct line of communications with the trans-Appalachian states. At the same time, Grant wanted General Benjamin Butler to lead his Army of the James up the river of that name to approach Richmond from the east, posing an immanent threat to that city both directly and by threatening its rail connections to the Deep South through the town of Petersburg, twenty-five miles to the south.

Nor were Grant's plans for success in 1864 limited to the narrow and perennially deadlocked fringe of the continent between the Appalachians and the Atlantic. West of the mountains lay Grant's old command, the Military Division of the Mississippi, now under Sherman. Grant's most trusted lieutenant was to lead the combined armies of the Tennessee, the Cumberland, and the Ohio, one hundred thousand strong, in a campaign across north Georgia from Dalton toward Atlanta with the assigned goal of hammering the Confederacy's Army of Tennessee in the same way Meade, under Grant's direct supervision, would be pounding the Army of Northern Virginia. As in Virginia, Grant planned for the trans-Appalachian theater a secondary campaign that could distract and weaken the Confederate army there while Sherman went in for the kill. General Nathaniel P. Banks, commanding the Department of the Gulf, was to lead his army, including two corps of Grant's old Vicksburg veterans, in a drive to capture the Confederacy's last major Gulf Coast port at Mobile, Alabama. When Grant explained to Lincoln his plans for the coming summer's campaign, the president grasped the concept at once and summed it up in one of his colorful midwestern expressions: "Those not skinning can hold a leg."

The great nineteenth-century Prussian general Helmut von Moltke once quipped that no plan survives contact with the enemy but is said to have added that luck is the residue of good planning. So it turned out for Grant in 1864, but not before a number of disappointments altered his plan and made his task more difficult. Banks, Butler, and Sigel were the purest of political generals, chosen by Lincoln at the outset of the war not so much because he thought they could win victories—though he hoped they might—as because he believed he needed to secure the support of their constituencies. Those constituencies were northeastern Republicans, northeastern Democrats, and German immigrants, respectively.

Hitherto in the war each of these three political generals had given ample evidence of his military incompetence, but Grant, always sensitive to Lincoln's political needs, chose to try to work with them. He hoped that Sigel would finally make good use of his prewar training in the Prussian army to wage a successful campaign that would at least neutralize the Shenandoah Valley, but the hapless German general blundered to defeat there in the May 15 Battle of New Market, at which the corps of cadets of the Virginia Military Institute fought as a battalion in the victorious Confederate army commanded by former U.S. vice president and 1860 southern Democratic presidential candidate John C. Breckinridge.

Butler's failure was even more disappointing because his campaign had offered so much more potential. The approach from the east via the James River had always been the best way to get an army to the vicinity of Richmond. Even McClellan, obtuse as he could be, had seen that much, although he had missed the political and strategic problems that could beset a Union general who made that route his main approach to the Rebel capital. Grant hoped that with Sigel taking the Shenandoah Valley away from Confederate strategists and Meade, under Grant's direct supervision, keeping Lee busy, Butler could strike a blow at the seat of both the rebellious government and Confederate supplies in Virginia that would at least hamstring Lee in the midst of his fight to the death against the Army of the Potomac. Grant also hoped that Butler might turn out to be the kind of politician in uniform that he had encountered in the western theater with his Army of the Tennessee, where Democratic politician John A. Logan and Republican politician Frank Blair were competent and hard-hitting military commanders, and, just in case Butler lacked military expertise, Grant made sure his two top subordinates, Tenth Corps commander Quincy Gillmore and Eighteenth Corps commander William F. Smith, were highly regarded professionals to whom Grant hoped Butler would leave much of the direction of the operation.

Each of Grant's hopes for the James River Campaign was dashed in succession. Butler seemed to see the campaign as his ticket to military glory and insisted on being a hands-on commander. In that role he performed as ineptly as top brass on both sides had every reason to fear from their political generals by this stage of the war, and Gillmore and Smith were no help with their hesitant, confused, and conflicting counsels.

After throwing a serious scare into the Confederate government by approaching an almost defenseless Richmond and then threatening what would have been an equally devastating blow against Petersburg, Butler hesitated long enough to allow the Rebels to pull together a scratch force scarcely more than half the size of his own thirty-thousand-man Army of the James. This force was under the command of Pierre G. T. Beauregard, recently transferred to Virginia after successfully defending Charleston, South Carolina. Beauregard attacked Butler's army and drove it back into a peninsula called Bermuda Hundred, formed by the confluence of the Appomattox and James rivers. Butler was safe there, only a few miles from Richmond and its vital southern rail connection, and his army could receive its supplies via the river, but the Confederates were able to build a relatively short line of fortifications across the neck of Bermuda Hundred and keep Butler bottled up there, where his army had no chance for further offensive operations and posed relatively little threat to the Confederacy.

In the western theater Grant's plan to get his subordinate generals either to skin or to hold a leg, as Lincoln put it, met with even more complete failure. Early that spring, before Grant became general in chief, Banks, with the approval of Lincoln and Halleck, had taken his army up the Red River into the heart of Louisiana. The authorities in Washington hoped Banks's expedition would present the French emperor Napoleon III with the sobering prospect of an impending Union presence in Texas and thus prompt him to curtail his current expansionist adventure in Mexico, where French troops were working on establishing a puppet regime. The Union government also hoped that Banks would be able to liberate large amounts of cotton, for lack of which the textile mills of the Northeast faced the prospect of idleness.

As it turned out, cotton was the only thing the expedition gained. After a slow progress up the Red, Banks blundered to defeat at the Battle of Mansfield and then retreated back down the river, nearly losing Porter's gunboat fleet to falling water levels as the Confederates diverted much of the river's flow for that purpose. A resourceful army officer with experience moving felled logs down Wisconsin streams designed wing dams that raised the river's depth in the channel enough to allow the valuable ironclads to escape, but by the time Banks returned to the Mississippi it was too late to launch a campaign against Mobile or to return the corps of Sherman's army that he had borrowed. Grant and Sherman were not impressed, and neither, presumably, was Napoleon III.

GRANT AND LEE IN THE
VIRGINIA WILDERNESS

The failures of the political generals left Grant and Sherman to carry out the spring offensive with the Union's two major armies without the help of the peripheral operations Grant had planned. Fortunately Grant and Sherman enjoyed a warm rapport and complete and well-founded trust in each other. Sherman later wrote to Grant describing his confidence during this campaign, "I knew wherever I was that you thought of me, and if I got in a tight place, you would come, if alive."[1]

On May 4, 1864, both Sherman's army group in Georgia and Meade's

Army of the Potomac marched out of their camps, Grant accompanying the latter. The two campaigns that began that day took different shapes both because of the differing approaches of Grant and Sherman and because of the differing personalities of their opponents. Lee, combative as ever, met Meade's army almost immediately. Grant had hoped to push rapidly through the tangled second-growth thickets of the Wilderness before making contact, but Lee met him there on May 5, not far from where the wily Rebel and Stonewall Jackson had humbled Hooker the year before. Jackson was not in the Wilderness this May, however, and neither was Hooker.

Instead of pulling back on first contact with the enemy as Hooker had done the year before, Grant drove straight at Lee. Intense fighting raged in the thickets the rest of that day, and the next morning, May 6, Grant launched a renewed attack that crumbled Lee's line and threatened to break the Army of Northern Virginia in two. As Lee personally attempted to rally his troops and all seemed lost, two fresh Confederate divisions arrived on the battlefield: Longstreet's troops, which had missed the first day's fighting while marching up from their camps some distance from the rest of the army. At the head of Longstreet's column was the hard-hitting Texas Brigade. As the Texans formed a line of battle in preparation for launching a counterattack, Lee in desperation rode his horse into position to lead the charge. Appalled, the Texans began shouting, "Lee to the rear!" and, crowding around his horse, finally turned its head and led it to the rear. Officers and men promised the general they would drive the Yankees back if only he would retire to a place of relative safety. Reluctantly, Lee did so. The Texans, joined by the rest of Longstreet's corps, were as good as their word and halted the Union offensive after hours of bloody fighting.

On the other side of the lines, Grant had to contend not only with Lee and his army but also with the bad habits and defeatist attitudes ingrained in the Army of the Potomac since its inception under McClellan. Toward midmorning that day a distraught general rushed up to Grant's headquarters group exclaiming that he had seen all this before and knew just what Lee was going to do next, with the implication that it would mean disaster for the Army of the Potomac. Grant had heard enough of this sort of talk. "Oh, I am heartily tired of hearing about what Lee is going to do," he barked. "Some of you always seem to think he is suddenly going to turn a double somersault and land in our rear and on both our flanks at the same time." He sent the general back to his command with the admonition not to spend so much time thinking about what Lee was going to do to them but instead to start thinking about what they were going to do to Lee.[2]

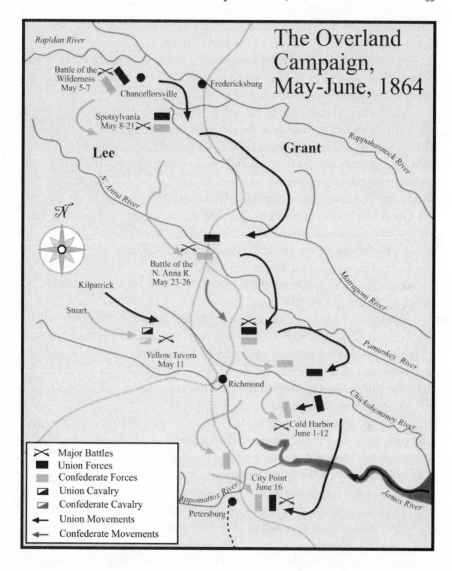

The Overland Campaign, May-June, 1864

In fact, later that day Lee did launch successive attacks against both of Grant's flanks. Each scored some limited local success, but after falling back a short distance the experienced Federals halted their Confederate pursuers and established firm new defensive positions. The thickets that had aided the Rebels by masking their movements proved a hazard as well. As Longstreet that afternoon attempted to regroup his command in order to follow up the initial success of his attack on one of the Union flanks, some of his own troops, hearing the headquarters group approaching through the dense underbrush, fired blindly, giving Longstreet a severe neck wound and killing or wounding several of his key subordinates. Lee's most experienced corps commander would be out of action for months.

Meanwhile Grant, true to his word, wasted little time worrying about Lee's efforts and slugged away at the Army of Northern Virginia with attacks of his own. By the end of the second day's fighting, the result of this clash between the war's two most successful commanders was a draw, though the Union, with the larger number of troops it had in the Wilderness, had suffered correspondingly more casualties. Grant could afford this. Lee could not, but Grant had no intention of winning the war by attrition by pushing both armies into the meat grinder of battle until his was the only one left. As Grant's Vicksburg campaign clearly demonstrated, the tenacious Union general favored maneuver over human erosion. Nevertheless, if that was the only advantage he could gain from the Battle of the Wilderness, as it came to be called, he would grimly take it and keep moving on.

Rather than keep feeding the meat grinder in the tangled forests of the Wilderness, Grant decided to slide eastward around Lee's right flank and seize the crossroads hamlet of Spotsylvania Court House, which would put him between Lee and Richmond. If the move succeeded, Lee would have to fight the more powerful Army of the Potomac at a severe disadvantage. Grant put his army in motion on the evening of May 7.

For the private soldiers in the Army of the Potomac, with their extremely close-up perspective on the battle they had just fought, the combat of the past two days did not seem all that much different from that of Chancellorsville or any of the other bloody and indecisive defeats the army had suffered at Lee's hands during the past two years. As the column marched away from the positions it had held in the still-smoking Wilderness, the men remained uncertain as to whether they had won or lost and whether their march was an advance or a retreat. The answer came when the head of the column approached a crossroads where it had to turn either north or south. As the lead regiment reached the crossroad, its officers turned it south, away from the Potomac and retreat and toward Richmond and an ultimate victory that many of the marching men would not live to see. Despite the prospect of another immanent bloody meeting with Lee's army, the men of the Army of the Potomac waved their caps and cheered at the realization that they had fought a battle and were still advancing.

The private soldiers of the Army of the Potomac had never been the problem; under McClellan, Burnside, Pope, or Hooker they had always been ready for hard fighting. But that night's march demonstrated that the army's command and staff still made it the clumsy instrument McClellan had forged in the camps around Washington in the fall of 1861. Two and a half years of futility had reinforced the cautious, deliberate habits of the officers who maneuvered the army. As an organization it had never developed the quick, supple efficiency of Grant's old Army of the Tennessee. In the case of the present movement from the Wilderness to Spotsylvania, the cavalry that was supposed to lead the march somehow did not arrive in time, and the supporting infantry was slow in coming up.

As always, Lee was quick to make his opponents pay for such sloppy performances. With the aid of excellent intelligence from his chief of cavalry, Jeb Stuart, the Confederate commander correctly anticipated Grant's target and quickly put his own troops on the march. The Army of Northern Virginia moved with the speed Grant had come to expect from his own troops out west but was frustrated to find he could not obtain from the Army of the Potomac. The result was that by the time blue-clad troops arrived in force in the vicinity of Spotsylvania Court House, they found solid Rebel lines blocking their path.

The Rebels had entrenched, as both Union and Confederate troops were by this stage of the war quick to do both here in Virginia and down in Georgia. Any place a unit of infantry halted for more than a couple of hours, the troops dug trenches and felled trees to make obstructions (abatis, as they were called in the military parlance of the time) out of their tops and added their trunks to their breastworks. The practice had begun in relatively isolated cases in late 1862 and had spread throughout 1863. By 1864 it was virtually universal. Breastworks multiplied the already heavy advantage of the defender. A well-dug-in defending force could now be reasonably confident of repulsing several times its number of attackers and inflicting ghastly casualties while doing so, a fact that did much to shape the conduct of the 1864 campaigns in both Virginia and Georgia.

Grant brought the Army of the Potomac up against Lee's extensive Spotsylvania breastworks and struck at them to make sure the Rebels were truly present in strength. They were, as the Union soldiers paid the price in casualties to find out. The frustration was bitter at Grant's headquarters and those of the Army of the Potomac. Meade blamed the Army of the Potomac's new cavalry commander, Philip Sheridan, whom Grant had snatched from a division command in the Army of the Cumberland and brought with him to put some drive and fire into the eastern army's horse soldiers. Sheridan said it was Meade's fault for hamstringing his command and detaching much of its strength with assignments like shepherding supply wagons. Turn him loose with all his cavalry, he said, and he would whip Jeb Stuart. Both Meade and Sheridan were known for their irascibility, and the interview was a stormy one. The seething Army of the Potomac commander referred the matter to Grant, complaining of Sheridan's preposterous boast that he could whip the legendary Stuart. To Meade's surprise and disgust, Grant responded wryly, "Did Sheridan say that? Well, he generally knows what he is talking about. Let him start right out and do it."[3]

So on May 9 Sheridan took his ten thousand troopers and set out southward, directly toward Richmond, marching in a column that sometimes stretched as long as thirteen miles. Among his goals were tearing up the railroad behind Lee and threatening Richmond, but both of these were for the purpose of accomplishing the expedition's chief goal: gaining a showdown with Jeb Stuart and whipping him. That showdown came two days later, six miles outside of Richmond, near a derelict inn called Yellow Tavern. Stuart met Sheridan with 4,500 men, and a four-hour battle ensued. When it was over, Sheridan's squadrons had succeeded in brushing past the Confederate horsemen who had tried to block them, but, more importantly, Stuart had taken a .44-caliber pistol bullet in the abdomen and died the next day. Sheridan wisely chose not to challenge the stoutly built Richmond fortifications, even lightly manned as they were. Instead he rode to Butler's nearby lines at Bermuda Hundred to rest and resupply his command before riding back to rejoin Grant on May 24. The raid had deprived Grant of cavalry scouting for two weeks but deprived Lee permanently of the services of Stuart, perhaps the best scouting cavalry commander of the war and already a legend throughout the South.

THE BATTLES OF SPOTSYLVANIA COURT HOUSE AND THE NORTH ANNA RIVER

Meanwhile back at Spotsylvania Court House, Grant continued to probe for weaknesses in Lee's position. During the course of May 10, units of the Army of the Potomac made local assaults on several sectors of Lee's heavily entrenched lines. Most were dismal failures, but one showed promise. A young colonel named Emory Upton believed he knew how to defeat the ubiquitous entrenchments. Arranging twelve picked regiments one behind the other, he had them charge full speed toward the Confederate breastworks without pausing to fire. As he hoped, this overwhelmed the defenders of a narrow section of entrenchments, and his attacking column broke through. The assault ultimately failed, however, because of the difficulty of exploiting a breakthrough once made.

Grant was intrigued by Upton's effort. The sector the colonel's column had struck looked particularly vulnerable, a protruding bulge, or salient, in the Confederate line that the soldiers had nicknamed the Mule Shoe because of its shape. It allowed a large concentration of Confederate cannon there to get a crossfire on Union troops approaching either end of Lee's line, but it was itself vulnerable to direct attack, especially if that attack converged from all sides of the salient. That was exactly what Grant planned to do, using Upton's tactics with a whole corps instead of a mere twelve regiments. The army spent May 11 in preparation.

The attack went in as scheduled in the predawn hours of May 12. For once Lee had guessed wrong about what an opponent would do next. Thinking that the quiet on the eleventh portended a Union withdrawal, perhaps in preparation for another lunge to the east, Lee had begun to pull his army back in preparation to sidle east himself to counter Grant's presumed next move. The first step was pulling the cannon back out of the Mule Shoe. Their crews had just limbered up and pulled out of their emplacements when Grant's massive assault sent the twenty thousand men of the Army of the Potomac's Second Corps storming over the breastworks, capturing four thousand defenders; their division commander, Major General Richard Johnson; and the cannon, whose crews did not have time to unlimber again and fire.

As with Upton's attack two days before but now on a much larger scale, the assaulting force struggled to overcome the disorganization generated by its successful advance. While its officers strove to untangle its ranks and get it moving forward again, Lee rushed Major General John B. Gordon's division into the Mule Shoe to plug the hole in his line. Once again in desperation Lee moved into position to lead the charge personally, but his troops would have none of it, again shouting, "Lee to the rear," as the Texans had done six days before and refusing to advance until he had drawn back to safer ground.

With their army commander out of the way, Gordon's men surged forward and struck the disorganized Yankees of the Second Corps, driving them back to the breastworks. Determined to hold the gains they had made, the Federals pushed back, and a frenzied hand-to-hand struggle raged across the breastworks, Federals on one side, Confederates on the other, the two lines standing within arm's reach of each other, shooting, bayoneting, and clubbing with a ferocity that seemed scarcely human. As both sides pressed reinforcements to the embattled section of parapet, the battle raged on for hour after hour. Tens of thousands of rifle bullets hissing past their intended targets mowed down the foliage just behind the lines and whittled through the bolls of trees a foot thick, while enough of the bullets found their marks to pile bodies two or three deep or more for scores of yards on either side of the breastworks. Near the center of the disputed barricade, the breastworks made a sharp corner, and that feature gave its name to this particular part of the Battle of Spotsylvania, which would thereafter be remembered as the Bloody Angle.

Almost incredibly, the fighting around the Bloody Angle continued throughout the daylight hours of May 12 and then through most of that night, amid pouring rain, until by 3:00 a.m., May 13, Lee's troops had completed a new line of breastworks across the base of the Mule Shoe, sealing off the sector for which the Federals had fought for almost twenty-four hours. The Confederate survivors of the fight at the Bloody Angle then fell back to the new line, leaving Grant's troops in possession of the Mule Shoe, now a smoking, steaming wasteland of churned mud, shredded foliage, and thousands of corpses, some of them almost trampled into the mud.

The result was far from what Grant had intended. Hitherto in the war his generalship had been reminiscent of a swordsman who had defeated his opponents by lightning rapier thrusts. Now the weapon in his hand, the Army of the Potomac, seemed less like a precision sword than a heavy club. There was no denying these eastern soldiers would fight with ferocity and die with sublime courage, but the army's staff and command echelons never seemed to get the knack of Grant's style of warfare. The result was the drawn-out Battle of Spotsylvania with its appalling casualties.

Grant probed hard at Lee's lines on May 18, and Lee returned the favor the following day. Each learned at some cost that the other was still holding his entrenched lines in more than ample force to slaughter any number of attackers. Grant was reluctant to continue the sort of massive bludgeoning match the campaign had become and still hoped to win a decisive battle rather than grind his foe down by attrition. Accordingly, on the night of May 20, Grant put his army in motion, once again swinging to the southeast in hopes of turning Lee and forcing the Army of Northern Virginia into a stand-up fight in open country.

Once again Lee reacted quickly, putting his own army on the march the following day and on May 22 took up and entrenched a strong position behind the North Anna River, once again blocking Grant's advance but twenty-five miles closer to Richmond. The Army of the Potomac arrived the next day, and two of its corps reached the southern bank of the North Anna River, one near Jericho Mill and the other ten miles or so downstream near Chesterfield Bridge. Moderate fighting flared on both fronts. On the twenty-fourth, however, the Army of the Potomac's center found the river strongly defended near Ox Ford and was unable to force a crossing.

In response to the successful Union crossings on the twenty-third, Lee had arranged his army in a sprawling, upside-down V with only the point and a brief segment of the western leg touching the river near Ox Ford. This left the Army of the Potomac in three separated segments—one south of the river on the upstream side of Lee's entrenchments, another south of the river on the downstream side of Lee's entrenchments, and the third north of the river in the middle. River crossings by pontoon bridge made large troop movements between these segments difficult. In theory, Lee, who had recently received nine thousand reinforcements comprised of troops released by the failure of Butler's and Sigel's offensives, could mass his forces against either end of Grant's line with a heavy local advantage in numbers, while Grant would have difficulty reinforcing or withdrawing those isolated corps.

During the Civil War, such theoretical advantages rarely translated to reality, and the North Anna was no exception. Lee was sick in his tent, and of his experienced corps commanders, Hill was also sick, Longstreet was still out of action with his Wilderness wound, and Ewell was breaking down under the stress of the preceding three weeks of campaigning. Hill and Ewell were still on duty but functioning very poorly. From his cot, Lee was unable to give sufficient direction to Longstreet's less experienced replacement to carry out such a mass attack. Whether such an assault would truly have been decisive is doubtful. Such efforts almost never were, and had the attackers found the Federals entrenched, as was likely, the advance would likely have been short and bloody.

THE BATTLE OF COLD HARBOR

After weighing his options, Grant decided to swing his army to the left yet again. His lead units stepped off just after nightfall on May 26. This time Grant's target was the crossroads of Cold Harbor, another twenty-five miles or so to the south-southeast of the North Anna battlefield and only about ten from Richmond, on the Gaines' Mill battlefield, where McClellan and Lee had fought the third of the Seven Days' Battles almost two years before. Yet again, Lee detected Grant's move and countered by retreating to meet him. Union and Confederate cavalry sparred with each other repeatedly as they screened and scouted in front of their armies and reached Cold Harbor on the last day of May. The rival horsemen struggled for control of the cross-roads, fighting dismounted as cavalry almost always did in this war when combat grew severe. Each side looked eagerly for the arrival of its supporting infantry, the arm of the service that did most of the heavy fighting.

The Confederate foot soldiers were first on the scene, but when on the morning of June 1 the lead division of gray-clad infantry made its bid to drive off the Union cavalry, its attacks were piecemeal and poorly coordinated. The Union troopers, fighting not only dismounted but also entrenched, stood them off until the blue-clad infantry could come up and take over, securing a stalemate around Cold Harbor. By this point in the campaign, although a steady stream of reinforcements hurried on by Richmond had replaced almost all of the troops Lee had lost since fighting had opened in the Wilderness almost four weeks before, the Army of Northern Virginia had nevertheless lost a good deal of its offensive edge, largely because of the attrition among its experienced leaders, from regiment and brigade commanders all the way

Grant at his headquarters at Cold Harbor.

up to generals commanding corps. Henceforth when Lee tried to take the initiative, he would find his army almost as clumsy a weapon as Grant had found the Army of the Potomac from the campaign's outset.

Grant sensed the diminished offensive power of Lee's army and also noticed that even when the Army of the Potomac had occupied a vulnerable position straddling the North Anna, with a corps isolated on either flank, the Confederates had not attacked. He drew the conclusion that the opposing army was on its last legs. "Lee's army is really whipped. The prisoners we now take show it, and the actions of his Army show it unmistakably. A battle with them outside of entrenchments cannot be had."[4]

With that thought in mind he ordered a quick attack on the evening of June 1, but the commanders of the Union assault divisions had had little time to reconnoiter the enemy's position or to arrange their own troops. The result was failure. Much as he had at Vicksburg in late May the year before when a similar quick attempt to take advantage of momentum and storm the city had failed, Grant ordered thorough preparation and a full-scale assault. While Grant's subordinates made their preparations, Lee's engineers laid out and his soldiers constructed the most elaborate line of fortifications yet seen in Virginia. Meade, to whom Grant had entrusted the task of preparing and reconnoitering for the attack, did not see to it that his subordinates made adequate reconnaissance of the intricate new defenses.

When the time for the big push came at 4:30 a.m., June 3, many Union soldiers were grimly pessimistic about their chances. The army did not yet use dog tags, and whether a casualty's family would ever be notified of his death usually depended on whether comrades of his own company—and thus usually from his own hometown—found his body and wrote to his loved ones. Now in the faint hope that some other kind soul might perform that last kindness for them, many of the soldiers wrote their names and home addresses on slips of paper and then pinned those slips to the backs of their uniform jackets.

When the attack went in, many units did not press it home with much vigor. Especially in the sectors that had experienced repulse on the evening of June 1, troops went to ground before reaching the prime killing range of the Confederate rifles. Elsewhere along the front, the Federals pushed forward doggedly. In the Second Corps sector they even scored a brief local success, taking a few of the advanced Confederate trenches before Rebel artillery and counterattacking Rebel infantry drove them out. The end result was the same, and when the firing slowed down and the smoke cleared somewhat, it was obvious that the Army of the Potomac had made no dent in Lee's lines.

Grant ordered a halt shortly after noon. The attack had cost the Army of the Potomac somewhere between 3,500 and 4,000 men. For the rest of his life, he regretted having ordered the June 3 assault, as he did the May 22, 1863, assault at Vicksburg, but as Lee too had learned from hard experience, sometimes the only way to know that a major assault would not work was to try one.

Action along the front settled down to desultory sniping and artillery bombardment. On June 5 Grant sent Lee a note by flag of truce suggesting an informal two-hour truce to recover the dead and wounded from between the lines. Lee's reply insisted that the truce be a formal one, which would, in the military etiquette of the time, amount to a tacit admission by Grant that Lee had defeated him in a major battle—a small propaganda coup and a point of pride for the Confederate general. Grant was naturally reluctant to gratify his enemy in this way or do anything else that might hurt Union morale in what was already becoming a difficult campaign season, with its heavy casualties and lack of the immediate dramatic success that many had unreasonably expected. Yet after some further exchange of stiff notes, he finally concluded that there was no other way to help his wounded men. The formal truce took place on June 7, by which time it was already too late for most of the wounded lying between the lines. Union morale continued to erode both inside the Army of the Potomac and on the home front, where some were already beginning to criticize Grant, little more than a month into his first major campaign as general in chief.

GRANT'S PETERSBURG GAMBIT AND EARLY'S RAID ON WASHINGTON

Grant could see clearly that although the Army of Northern Virginia might have lost some of its previous operational verve on the offensive, it was more than ready and able to fight defensively behind breastworks, and Lee had it firmly positioned so that that was all it needed to do in order to fulfill its primary mission of protecting Richmond. Grant had reached a tight corner from which no further left-handed turning movements could bring the Army of the Potomac closer to the Confederate capital so as to threaten it and force Lee to fight on terms other than his own. After several days' consideration, Grant determined to undertake a bigger and bolder turning movement than any he had yet made in Virginia. It would not take the Army of the Potomac closer to Richmond but farther away, but in doing so it would pose a still greater threat to the Confederate capital.

Grant's plan was to break contact with Lee's army and swing to the left again, cross the James River, and march against the town of Petersburg, Virginia. Located on the Appomattox River about thirty miles south of Richmond, Petersburg was the railroad hub on which depended the food supplies both of Richmond and of Lee's army. There the Weldon Railroad, coming up from the south, joined the Southside Railroad, angling in from the southwest, and their combined freight rode a single set of rails the final thirty miles north to Richmond. If Grant could take Petersburg, Lee would have to give up Richmond. The movement began on the night of June 12 and ran smoothly. Grant's army crossed the James River on a 2,100-foot pontoon bridge Union engineers had built. Lee suspected nothing, and his army remained in its entrenchments around Cold Harbor.

The Confederate general too had been thinking during the week that had followed the doomed Union assaults. Despite his army having fared better in the fighting at Cold Harbor, Lee was grim about the long-term prospects. "We must stop this army of Grant's before he gets to the James River," he told his subordinate General Jubal Early. "If he gets there it will become a siege, and then it will be a mere matter of time."

To stop Grant, Lee decided to try a method that had worked against other Union commanders in 1862. He dispatched Early, now in command of the Second Corps of the Army of Northern Virginia in place of Ewell, to march west and enter the Shenandoah Valley. The valley was a natural advantage for the Confederacy. A Confederate army in the valley could relatively easily screen its movements from normal Union cavalry reconnaissance by holding the limited number of passes over the Blue Ridge, on the valley's eastern edge, and as long as that army was in the valley it could draw its rations from the well-stocked granaries and smokehouses of that rich farming country. The valley slanted from southwest to northeast, so that a Confederate army that marched all the way to its northern end would emerge ninety miles northwest of Washington, well positioned to threaten Baltimore, Harrisburg, or the national capital. Lee hoped that Early's foray might draw troops away from Grant's army and put political pressure on Washington to sue for peace.

In 1862 Stonewall Jackson's operations in the Shenandoah Valley had created alarm in Washington and baited Lincoln into diverting troops from McClellan when that general had been approaching Richmond over the same ground where Grant's troops had attacked during the first week of June. Lee

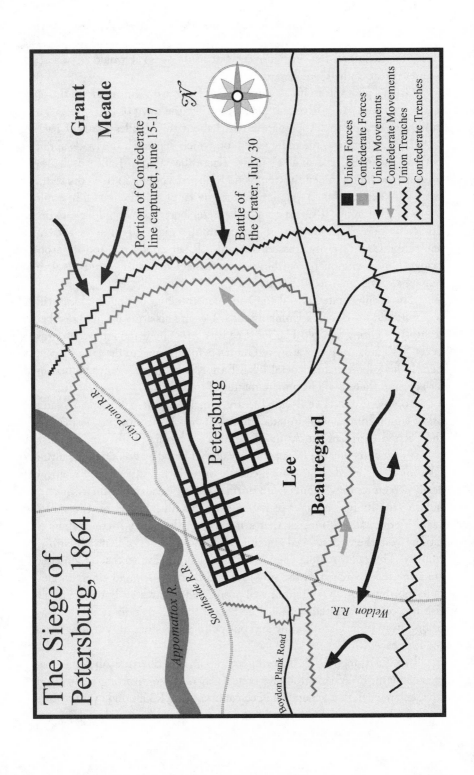

The Siege of
Petersburg, 1864

Grant
Meade

Portion of Confederate
line captured, June 15-17

Battle of
the Crater, July 30

N

Petersburg

Lee

Beauregard

Appomattox R.

City Point R.R.

Southside R.R.

Boydon Plank Road

Weldon R.R.

Union Forces
Confederate Forces
Union Movements
Confederate Movements
Union Trenches
Confederate Trenches

hoped that Early could launch a raid that would accomplish at least as much. Besides that, Union General David Hunter was operating with a small force in the Shenandoah Valley, and Lee hoped Early would be able to put a stop to that.

While Early's troops marched west, Grant's marched south. His leading elements reached Petersburg on June 15 to find the city defended by only very scant Confederate forces, part of the small command under Beauregard that had been holding Butler bottled up in Bermuda Hundred. The Union troops swarmed over the fortifications ringing Petersburg, but as the outnumbered Confederates desperately tried to form another line and dig in even closer to the town, the commander of the leading Union corps, afraid he might have misunderstood his orders, halted his troops. Beauregard used every hour's delay to bring up more troops and entrench those he had. By the next day, Grant and Meade were on the scene and ordered renewed attacks, but the Army of the Potomac was worn out and bled white by the past six weeks of fighting. Its troops did not attack with the same drive and élan they had shown in the Wilderness and at Spotsylvania. Despite a continued heavy Union preponderance in numbers, a series of poorly coordinated, halfhearted assaults over the following three days failed to break through the growing numbers of Confederate defenders and their increasingly stout second line of fortifications.

Since the Federals had first appeared in front of Petersburg, Beauregard had sent one urgent message to Lee after another, apprising him of the situation and begging him to send troops. Lee had remained steadfastly incredulous. So skillful had been Grant's departure from Cold Harbor and march south that although Lee had been expecting Grant to move against the James River and knew that the Army of the Potomac was not present at Cold Harbor, he still could not believe that the Federals had already reached and crossed the James and were threatening Petersburg. The truth finally began to dawn on him during the night of the seventeenth to the eighteenth of June, and before daylight he dispatched two divisions to reinforce Beauregard. Even with these additional troops, Beauregard faced long odds at Petersburg, but the tenacity of his troops, the enormous advantages of the entrenched defensive, and the sluggishness and lack of aggressiveness by the battle-weary Army of the Potomac combined to prevent a Union capture of the vital rail junction.

With the rest of Lee's army rapidly filing into the new inner line of Petersburg fortifications and removing all further prospect of taking the place by storm, Grant settled down for a quasi siege of the city and its northern neighbor Richmond. He could not cut off the flow of food into the two cities, but he could press his entrenchments ever closer to the Confederate defenses, pounding them day after day with siege artillery and constantly stretching his lines westward around the south side of Petersburg to threaten the two rail lines that had now become the last lifelines of the Confederate capital. Grant had wanted to avoid such a siege because it would be long and trying on Union morale. Lee had hoped to avoid a siege because he knew that in military terms its only possible outcome would be his defeat—provided that Union morale and political will remained steadfast.

Meanwhile out in the Shenandoah Valley, Hunter's troops had been living off the land and causing consternation and outrage among the populace by acting as if they were in enemy territory in the midst of a hostile civilian population. On June 11, Hunter ordered the Virginia Military Institute burned as well as the house of former Virginia governor John Letcher, who had issued a proclamation calling on civilians to wage a guerrilla war against Hunter's forces. By June 18, as Hunter approached Lynchburg, Early was on hand with his corps. Reinforced by the remnant Confederate forces that had been operating in the valley, Early's command was strong enough to convince Hunter to withdraw. The Union general retreated with his force into the Allegheny Mountains of West Virginia, leaving the Shenandoah Valley wide open for Early.

Early marched his command down the Shenandoah Valley and on July 5 began crossing the Potomac into Maryland. The next day, as the tail end of his column was completing its crossing of the river, Early's vanguard took Hagerstown, Maryland, and demanded that the municipality pay twenty thousand dollars or be burned. The townsmen paid up. In Washington, seventy-five miles to the southeast, consternation reigned, as officials made hurried preparations to defend the city. Since Grant had pulled nearly all of the garrisons out of the forts around the national capital to reinforce the Army of the Potomac, the city was vulnerable. Halleck's frequent telegrams had kept Grant apprised of the situation, and the latter now decided he would have to detach troops from the Army of the Potomac to meet the threat. One division of the Sixth Corps pulled out of its trenches around Petersburg; marched down to the James River landing at City Point, Virginia, where Grant had recently established his main staging base and forward supply depot; and from there went by steamboat to Baltimore.

On July 9 Early's men marched into Frederick, Maryland, scarcely fifty miles from the capital, where they demanded and received the sum of two hundred thousand dollars to leave the city standing. About ten miles southeast of Frederick, the road to Washington crossed the little Monocacy River. On the far bank of the Monocacy waited a force of just under six thousand Federals, inexperienced militia stiffened by the Sixth Corps division Grant had first dispatched north. The force along the Monocacy was under the command of Major General Lew Wallace, who had disappointed Grant at Shiloh and would later go on, while serving as governor of the New Mexico Territory after the war, to write a novel titled *Ben Hur*. On this day Wallace had the unenviable task of delaying Early's march. He did not know whether the Confederate general's target was Washington or Baltimore, but he had to stall him long enough for reinforcements to reach those cities. At the Battle of the Monocacy he accomplished just that, delaying Early for most of a day, although his militia was routed and his more experienced troops had to make a fighting retreat.

On July 11 Early's troops swarmed into the suburbs of Washington. In Silver Spring, Maryland, they burned the house of U.S. Postmaster General Montgomery Blair. Pressing on, they arrived within range of the Washington fortifications, where they skirmished for several hours. By this time the defenses were manned no longer by government clerks and soldiers in the final stages of recovery from wounds or sickness but rather by the sturdy veterans of the Sixth Corps, the two remaining divisions of which Grant had dispatched from City Point as the reports from Washington had grown more dire.

Early's troops could accomplish nothing against powerfully built fortifications, strongly held by experienced soldiers, and so after exchanging fire for several hours, they retreated, though not before Lincoln himself had visited a frontline fort and observed the fighting. The president showed great curiosity and perhaps a desire to share at least a small taste of the experience of battle into which it had been his duty to send so many men. According to one account, a junior officer a short distance down the line, not recognizing the tall man in civilian suit and stovepipe hat placidly gazing over the top of the parapet, had shouted, "Get down, you fool." Lincoln seemed to smile quietly to himself and, after a final look at the battlefield, stepped down to a place of greater safety.

Early's small army marched west again, back toward the Shenandoah Valley. Early detached a force to stop by the south-central Pennsylvania town of Chambersburg and demand a ransom of one hundred thousand dollars in gold or five hundred thousand dollars in U.S. currency. When the unfortunate townsmen, who had been plundered by Lee's army the year before, could not come up with the money, the Confederate officer commanding the detachment had much of the town burned. Confederate troops also went out of their way to find the house of Republican newspaper editor Alexander McClure, on the north side of town, away from the other fires, and burn it too.

As Early's army had marched away from Washington, the Confederate general had profanely boasted to one of his officers that he thought he had badly frightened Lincoln, whose head and stovepipe hat above the Union parapet none of the Confederates seems to have recognized. In that much Early was clearly mistaken. The chief purpose of the raid that had taken the Rebels within sight of Washington had been to create within the Union government and high command sufficient alarm to force Grant to break off the siege of Richmond and Petersburg and hurry the Army of the Potomac back toward its namesake river to save the national capital. Lincoln had sufficient confidence in Grant to leave military matters largely, if not quite entirely, in that general's capable hands, and Grant did not scare easily. He had detached just enough troops to guarantee the security of Washington and in just enough time to get there. It would still be necessary to find a way to deal with Early, who hovered annoyingly with his army in the lower (northern) Shenandoah Valley, but the siege of Petersburg and Richmond ground on unabated.

11

THE ATLANTA CAMPAIGN

FROM DALTON TO THE ETOWAH

Simultaneous with the Army of the Potomac's offensive that Grant supervised in Virginia, Sherman launched an offensive of his own with the Union's three prime western armies—the Army of the Cumberland, under the command of Major General George H. Thomas; the Army of the Tennessee, under the command of Major General James B. McPherson; and the Army of the Ohio, under the command of Major General John Schofield—about one hundred thousand men in all. On the same May 4 that the Army of the Potomac crossed the Rapidan on its way to encounter Lee in the Wilderness, Sherman's armies began to advance from their camps around Chattanooga. They made contact with main-body Confederate forces on May 7.

Except for the absence of Robert E. Lee on this front, the challenge facing Sherman in North Georgia was even more daunting than the tangled Wilderness and the succession of rivers that lay in front of Grant in Virginia. Three significant rivers lay athwart Sherman's path: the Oostanaula, the Etowah, and the Chattahoochee. Between them high, sometimes craggy ridges barred the way. Across all this Sherman would have to depend for all his supplies on a single-track railroad, the Western & Atlantic, which ran from Chattanooga to Atlanta. Even north of Chattanooga his supplies would still have to travel down a single set of rails all the way from Louisville, Kentucky, three hundred miles farther north, and almost the whole route, from the depots at Louisville to the rear areas of Sherman's armies, would be within

271

striking range of raiding Rebel cavalry who had already demonstrated their propensity for tearing up tracks. Sherman had small garrisons in blockhouses guarding key bridges and trestles and had pre-positioned spare parts and repair crews to keep the trains rolling and the hardtack reaching the haversacks of his soldiers. An important element of Sherman's genius was his skill at logistics, the business of keeping his army supplied.

The first obstacle Sherman would have to negotiate was steep and rugged Rocky Face Ridge, lying across the Western & Atlantic and stretching many miles on either side. Sherman's opponent, Confederate General Joseph E. Johnston, had entrenched his army, named the Army of Tennessee but not to be confused with the Union Army of the Tennessee, along this seemingly impregnable position with its greatest strength flanking the gap through which the Western & Atlantic crossed the ridge, a deep declivity the locals called the Buzzard Roost. Johnston devoutly hoped Sherman would hurl his

A Union track repair crew in Tennessee.

troops against it so that he could slaughter them. Johnston had not, however, taken the trouble to reconnoiter the southwestern reaches of Rocky Face, where a winding narrow valley called Snake Creek Gap pierced the ridge and emerged only a few miles from the Western & Atlantic fifteen miles behind Johnston's position and about five miles north of where the railroad crossed the Oostanaula River at the little town of Resaca.

Sherman did know about Snake Creek Gap. Among this remarkable general's many striking qualities were a strong memory and a sharp eye for terrain. As a junior officer back in the 1840s Sherman had been stationed in North Georgia and had ridden all over these hills on army business. The consequence was that in this campaign in the Deep South, the Union commander knew the terrain better than his Confederate opponent. Sherman planned to turn Johnston's powerful position on Rocky Face Ridge by sending the Army of the Tennessee through Snake Creek Gap while the Army of the Cumberland and the Army of the Ohio feigned an all-out frontal attack.

Sherman had won all of his Civil War success thus far in the Army of the Tennessee, and he had taken over command of that army when Grant had moved up to command of all of the western armies the previous autumn. Now that Sherman in turn had taken over command of the all the western armies, he still had great confidence in his old outfit, which he knew would march fast, strike hard, and overcome most natural obstacles. Sherman planned for the Army of the Tennessee to debouch from the gap and tear up the Western & Atlantic well behind Johnston's army, then pull back slightly and assume a strong defensive position. With his supply line broken, Johnston would have to retreat. As he did so the Army of the Tennessee would fall on his flank, and the rest of Sherman's forces would crash down from the north to complete the destruction of Johnston's army.

Commanding the Army of the Tennessee now was thirty-six-year-old Major General James B. McPherson. An Ohioan like Grant and Sherman, McPherson had risen from childhood poverty to graduate first in the West Point class of 1853, and in the Civil War he had risen rapidly in rank. Suave, polished, handsome, and genial, as well as genuinely concerned for the welfare of his men, the young general was as popular with his troops as he was well liked by his superiors. McPherson seemed nearly perfect in every way, and if he had any fault as a general it may have been that his perfectionism did not allow him to feel comfortable in situations that were not completely within his control.

On May 9, as five hundred miles to the northeast Grant's and Lee's armies were taking up their positions outside the Virginia hamlet of Spotsyl-

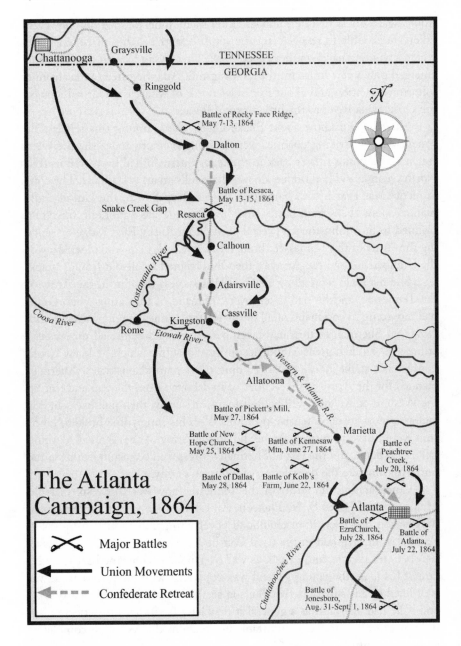

Graysville

TENNESSEE

Chattanooga

GEORGIA

Ringgold

Battle of Rocky Face Ridge,
May 7-13, 1864

Dalton

Battle of Resaca,
May 13-15, 1864

Snake Creek Gap

Resaca

Oostanaula River

Calhoun

Adairsville

Coosa River

Cassville

Kingston

Rome

Etowah River

Allatoona

Western & Atlantic R.R.

Battle of Pickett's Mill,
May 27, 1864

Battle of New
Hope Church,
May 25, 1864

Battle of Kennesaw
Mtn, June 27, 1864

Marietta

Battle of
Peachtree
Creek,
July 20, 1864

Battle of Dallas,
May 28, 1864

Battle of Kolb's
Farm, June 22, 1864

The Atlanta
Campaign, 1864

Atlanta

Battle of
EzraChurch,
July 28, 1864

Battle of
Atlanta,
July 22, 1864

Chattahoochee River

Major Battles

Union Movements

Confederate Retreat

Battle of
Jonesboro,
Aug. 31-Sept. 1, 1864

vania Court House, McPherson, in his first independent operation as an army commander, led the Army of the Tennessee through Snake Creek Gap undetected by Johnston and with all the speed and resourcefulness Sherman had expected. He emerged from the gap and was approaching Johnston's vital Western & Atlantic supply line before he encountered the enemy and then only light forces guarding the Confederate rear. His lead elements were within half a mile of the tracks and driving the enemy easily when McPherson became worried and ordered his troops to fall back, leaving the railroad intact. Brilliant as he was, McPherson had assumed his enemy was equally perspicacious and therefore reasoned that Johnston must be about to descend on him with most of the Confederate Army of Tennessee. McPherson kept his Army of the Tennessee entrenched in a strong position in the mouth of Snake Creek Gap for the next two days, while Johnston finally learned of his dilemma and hurried troops south to confront McPherson and protect the Confederate line of communication and retreat.

Sherman was deeply disappointed at the failure to cut Johnston's communications and gently chided McPherson that he had lost the opportunity of a lifetime. Nonetheless, adjusting to the partial failure of his plan, Sherman took his other two armies around via the route McPherson had taken so as to come up behind the Army of the Tennessee at the mouth of Snake Creek Gap and support it in a much more powerful move to cut the Western & Atlantic.

Meanwhile, because of Banks's failure in the Red River Campaign and consequent failure even to launch the campaign Grant had ordered against Mobile, Confederate Lieutenant General Leonidas Polk was free to bring nineteen thousand Confederate reinforcements up from central Alabama, arriving in Resaca just in time to secure the town and with it the Oostanaula River bridge. Johnston made good his escape from Rocky Face Ridge and fell back twenty miles to confront Sherman with more than sixty thousand men in extensive entrenchments anchored on the Oostanaula below Resaca and stretching in a long arc across the western and northern sides of the town. Heavy skirmishing, sometimes escalating to battle intensity, occupied the next two days as Johnston hoped once again that Sherman would send his troops to their deaths in hopeless frontal assaults, and Sherman again declined to oblige him.

Instead, Sherman had a brigade of the Army of the Tennessee stage a cross-river assault upstream from the Confederate entrenchments on the north bank. There Johnston had posted fewer defenders. Even at that the river crossing was difficult, with teams of soldiers lugging heavy boats down to the bank under fire and then rowing across the Oostanaula to storm the Confederate lines. The rest of the Army of the Tennessee quickly followed, and Johnston was turned again. Rather than risk being trapped on the north bank by Sherman's Federals seizing the crossing from the south side, the Confederate general once again put his army in retreat. His troops crossed the Oostanaula during the predawn hours of May 16 and burned the railroad bridge behind them. Sherman's expert and well-equipped railroad repair crews got to work immediately and soon had supply trains rolling into Resaca and ready to proceed southward in the wake of Sherman's now rapidly advancing armies.

Johnston's army marched steadily southward, as the Confederate general looked for a defensive position he liked. Sherman followed with his three armies spread out on three different roads, five to ten miles apart. The great host could march more rapidly that way, and the formation offered Sherman the chance of bringing one of the side columns crashing down on Johnston's flank if the Confederates were to turn and "show fight," as the Civil War soldiers put it.

In fact, under Richmond's nearly constant prodding to turn and fight, Johnston decided to do just that. He believed he saw an opportunity of catching the Army of the Ohio, smallest of Sherman's armies, isolated on the Union left near the town of Cassville. He positioned Hardee's corps to screen off Sherman's other two armies and massed Hood's and Polk's corps to fall on Schofield's single-corps army. With preparations complete, Johnston issued a grandiose proclamation to his troops, to be read aloud to every regiment in the Army of Tennessee, expressing confidence that God was supporting the Confederate cause and the intention of leading the army in an offensive that would crush its enemies.

Then events took an unexpected turn. Sherman's armies possessed the intangible advantage of momentum. A brigade of Thomas's Army of the Cumberland had missed its road some miles to the north and had veered out of the column and far out to the Union left, behind the route of Schofield's Army of the Ohio. On realizing his mistake, the commanding officer of the errant brigade had decided not to backtrack but rather to keep his men tramping south and seek roads that would angle back to the southwest and reunite him with the main column.

As Hood's corps, on the Confederate right, waited to spring the ambush on the unsuspecting Schofield, Thomas's wandering brigade bumped into the rear of Hood's right flank. Hood had a reputation for all-out aggressiveness, and it was that reputation that had won him his present assignment, as Davis had hoped the young Texan's relentless combativeness would counterbalance Johnston's excessive caution and propensity for retreat. But Hood had won his reputation in old Virginia, and the Yankees back there had seemed to belong to a different breed, not the kind that suddenly appeared on one's flanks and rear just when one was expecting to flank them. Hastily Hood redeployed to defend his flank and sent word to Johnston that, threatened as he was, he now could not take part in any attack. Shocked, Johnston called off the offensive.

Meanwhile, the commander of the off-course Union brigade, taking stock of the mass of Confederate troops his advanced units had spotted ahead, decided that perhaps a little backtracking might be in order after all. Thus, Confederate reconnaissance turned up nothing on Hood's flank, but by that time the day was well spent, and Sherman's separate columns were converging in front of the Confederate position. Johnston met with his corps commanders to try to sort out the situation. Hardee urged that they once again stand their ground and dare Sherman to assault their position, but Hood and Polk claimed that their positions were indefensible, enfiladed by Union artillery, and that the best course of action was to attack the enemy the next day, though by now the temporary local advantage in numbers that had initially lured Johnston to attack was long gone. Johnston weighed his generals' advice and decided to split the difference and retreat.

On May 20 the Army of Tennessee once again turned its back to the enemy and marched southward, this time crossing the Etowah, while some of the Confederate soldiers wept openly in their disappointment and the abandoned citizens of towns like Cassville and Kingston fled in confusion or waited in mute astonishment for whatever a Yankee occupation might bring. Already Johnston's retreats had uncovered not only the towns along the Western & Atlantic but also those that lay downstream along the southwest-ward-slanting rivers in the Confederacy's infant military-industrial complex in northwestern Georgia and northern Alabama. Union troops had recently taken possession of Rome, Georgia, with its vital iron mills and cannon foundries.

FROM THE ETOWAH TO
THE CHATTAHOOCHEE

Two of the three river barriers were now behind Sherman, but the highest and steepest of the ridges lay just ahead, and Johnston was heading for the narrow defile where the railroad crossed the highest of them, Allatoona Pass, determined to establish the most formidable defensive line he had yet placed in Sherman's path. Once again Sherman's knowledge of the North Georgia terrain stood him in good stead. Aware that Allatoona Pass would be impregnable, he chose not to approach it at all but rather to undertake his boldest turning movement thus far in the campaign. Loading the supply wagons with as much hardtack as they could carry, he cut loose from the Western & Atlantic and struck out due south while the tracks angled off to the southeast toward Allatoona and the eagerly waiting Johnston. Sherman hoped to swing wide around Johnston's left (western) flank and, if Johnston did not react promptly, reach the Chattahoochee in less than a week, trapping the Confederate Army of Tennessee.

Johnston, however, was alert this time and quickly swung his own army west to meet Sherman. On May 26, the same day that up in Virginia Grant decided there was little more to be gained on the North Anna lines and launched the turning movement that would take the Army of the Potomac to Cold Harbor, Sherman's and Johnston's armies made contact south of Pumpkin Vine Creek, along a line stretching from Dallas, Georgia, on the west through New Hope Church to Pickett's Mill on the east. On that day and the next, Sherman launched corps-sized probes at the latter two places, finding the Confederates entrenched and suffering more than a thousand casualties in each of the two encounters. Johnston surmised that Sherman's vigorous testing of the eastern end of his defenses might mean that Sherman's own lines were thin at their western end and ordered William B. Bate's division to test the hypothesis on May 28. Bate's men suffered a repulse that differed only in scale from the rebuffs Sherman's men had received at New Hope Church and Pickett's Mill.

Days of heavy skirmishing followed, with neither side gaining much of an advantage and conditions made still more miserable by steady rain. With rations running low, Sherman needed to get back to the railroad, so he tried another turning movement, this time lunging east and passing Johnston's right flank. Again Johnston was quick to react and June 9 was in position again astride the Western & Atlantic, blocking Sherman's road to Atlanta. Yet despite Johnston's success in blocking Sherman's sidelong moves, each one had brought him a little closer to his goal. The net effect of his zigzag from the Etowah River bridge west to Dallas and then back east to the railroad had been to move the Union forces fifteen miles closer to Atlanta and, most significantly, past the impregnable defensive position at Allatoona Pass.

By now Sherman's armies had reached Big Shanty (the present-day town of Kennesaw) ninety miles from their starting point at Chattanooga and only twenty-five from Atlanta. Ahead of them, however, lay another ten miles or so of terrain only marginally less forbidding than the range they had bypassed around Allatoona. Johnston's Confederates held a line anchored on the heights of Brush Mountain with a bulge in the center to include Pine Mountain, from which Rebel officers could survey every move Sherman's forces made. Despite the progress of his armies, the red-bearded Union general was frustrated that he had not been able to trap Johnston's army or bring it to battle in the open field. On June 14 as he studied Pine Mountain through his field glasses, he was annoyed to see a cluster of gray-clad officers on the mountaintop serenely scrutinizing his positions. "How saucy they are," he exclaimed in disgust, and turning to a subordinate he ordered him to have a battery open up on the summit and at least make the cheeky Rebels take cover.

The Union gunners already had the range. Indeed, the main goal of Union operations for the day or two before had been to find artillery positions from which the crest of Pine Mountain could be taken in crossfire and made untenable. How close they had already come to doing so was demonstrated by the identities of the officers Sherman had seen, though he could not have recognized them at that distance. Hardee had recommended to Johnston the evacuation of the mountain, and the two had come to survey the terrain in person, with Polk tagging along. The Union gunners' first round was a near miss, and Johnston ordered the group to scatter and take cover. A second shell exploded closer still as Johnston and Hardee scurried for safety and Polk paced solemnly away with the dignity befitting a lieutenant general and an Episcopal bishop. The third round struck him squarely, killing him instantly.

Later that day, Union signalmen intercepted a Confederate wigwag message from the mountaintop summoning an ambulance to retrieve Polk's remains, and the next morning Federal skirmishers probed forward to find that the Rebels had abandoned Pine Mountain. Sherman wrote with grim satisfaction in a dispatch to Washington that day, "We killed Bishop Polk yesterday and made good progress today." The bishop-general's death was a blow to Confederate morale, especially within the Army of Tennessee and in the Confederate White House, off in Richmond, where Jefferson Davis, the admiring underclassman of Polk's West Point days, lamented the loss as one of the worst that had befallen the Confederacy. White southerners had viewed the presence of a bishop among the leaders of their armies as evidence of the holy nature of their cause. Northerners had seen the prelate's service as a sacrilege in the causes of slavery and rebellion. Whatever the moral impact of his Confederate career and sudden death, Polk, by his incompetence and stubborn willfulness as a general, had done much damage to Rebel fortunes west of the Appalachians, in the heartland of the South, where the decisive action was taking place. Thus, the shot Sherman's gunners had fired produced mixed results.

Using the same methods that had persuaded the Rebels to relinquish Pine Mountain, Sherman, by stretching his line around one flank or the other and taking up advantageous artillery positions, succeeded in prying the Confederates out of several other segments of their line. Yet to the Union commander's heightened frustration, his nemesis Johnston merely pulled his line back a few miles to an even stronger position anchored by Kennesaw Mountain. This time it seemed no amount of hitching and sidling would give Sherman the leverage he needed to dislodge Johnston from his lofty defenses. Sherman surmised that if Johnston had stretched his smaller army as far as Sherman's larger forces had yet stretched, the Confederate line must be fatally thin somewhere, perhaps in the sector that included Kennesaw, where the natural strength of the position might have convinced the Confederate general he could afford to do so. A Union assault had driven this same Confederate army off of Missionary Ridge the preceding November. Perhaps it would work again. In any case, Sherman thought his repeated turning movements were becoming too predictable.

The attack went in on June 27. While elements of the Army of the Tennessee feinted against Johnston's right and Schofield's Army of the Ohio did the same on the Rebel left, one corps of the Army of the Tennessee assaulted the Confederate entrenchments on Kennesaw, and one corps of the Army of the Cumberland hit Johnston's lines in the sector next door to the mountain. Both assaults ended in bloody failure before mid-morning.

The factor that Sherman had underestimated was the magnitude of the multiplying effect of the elaborate entrenchments both sides were routinely building this summer. Given the weapons technology of that era, the entrenchments made the tactical defensive all but invincible to anything less than a five- or six-to-one superiority in numbers by the attacking force. The Battle of Kennesaw Mountain, as it came to be called, would go into the history books as Johnston's greatest victory and Sherman's worst blunder. As a set-piece defensive battle fought from entrenchments, it was characteristic of the Confederate general; as an ill-advised assault, it was out of character for his Union counterpart. The cost in casualties, about three thousand Union to about one thousand Confederate, was lower and less lopsided than most failed major assaults of the war. In Virginia that spring and summer, it would have been just another day of campaigning, but it stood out in Georgia because Sherman preferred other methods, and Johnston, happy in his entrenchments, let him use them.

Indeed, even as the assaults on the Kennesaw lines were running their bloody course, Schofield was finding that with Johnston's attention focused on defending the Confederate center, the Army of the Ohio was able to pass around his left flank, several miles southwest of the scene of that day's heavy fighting. In that sense, even the Battle of Kennesaw Mountain was a Union success, as Sherman shifted the Army of the Tennessee—his "whiplash," as he called it, because of this army's tactical flexibility and lightning speed— around to that end of the line to exploit Schofield's success and turn the Kennesaw Mountain line.

Once again, as throughout the campaign to this point, Johnston faced the choice of either retreating or taking the offensive against Sherman in a battle in the open field. As before, Johnston chose retreat. Tramping down the back slopes of Kennesaw Mountain and their other positions along the line, the Confederates marched through Marietta under the eyes of its dismayed civilian population and took up a position several miles south of the town, near the hamlet of Smyrna, Georgia. Again Sherman threatened Johnston's flanks, and again the Confederate retreated, this time to a semicircle of very strong fortifications on the north bank of the Chattahoochee River, covering the Western & Atlantic bridge. Johnston had had his chief engineer officer direct the construction of these works in advance and hoped from this position to be able to pose an insurmountable threat to any attempt Sherman might make to cross the river either upstream or down.

It proved a vain hope. Sherman, who in this campaign was demonstrating himself to be the war's master of turning movements, successfully turned Johnston again, this time using Schofield's army and crossing the Chattahoochee upstream from Johnston's fortifications. Johnston, with his back to the river and in danger of being cut off should Schofield move in behind him on the south bank, quickly made his retreat, falling back behind Peachtree Creek, a tributary of the Chattahoochee. As in his previous retreats starting all the way up at Dalton, Johnston made the movement skillfully, but Johnston's excessive willingness to retreat and surrender territory had previously hurt the Confederacy both in Virginia and in Mississippi and was part of the reason for the critical situation it now faced in Georgia.

Johnston's army was backed up almost into the suburbs of Atlanta, and Peachtree Creek was the last natural obstacle left to defend. From hills on the north bank of the Chattahoochee, Sherman's men could see the city toward which they had been marching and fighting for the past two months. The next time Sherman successfully turned Johnston, the Confederate general's options would be either battle in the open field, as Sherman had been seeking throughout the campaign, or else the abandonment of Atlanta.

DAVIS SEEKS A
FIGHTING GENERAL

Far off in Richmond, Jefferson Davis was deeply dissatisfied with the course of the campaign thus far. Back in the spring, before Sherman's advance started, Davis had wanted Johnston to launch an offensive of his own, turning Sherman and perhaps finally recovering the vast territory and strategic advantage that the Confederacy had lost in its heartland. The president had offered to reinforce Johnston heavily if the general would undertake such a program. Johnston had refused every suggestion of offensive action but had insisted that Davis ought to send him the reinforcements anyway. When Sherman had advanced, Davis had indeed reinforced Johnston, ordering Polk to join him with his nineteen thousand, virtually the entire force that had been defending Alabama. Yet Johnston had still fallen back in the face of Sherman's repeated turning movements, and despite almost constant skirmishing and the occasional repulse of a Union assault or two, the Confederate general had attempted nothing like the kind of all-out battle that might have had the potential, if all went well, to destroy Sherman's force or compel it to retreat.

Though more than five hundred miles away, the Confederate president had kept close track of the campaign through various sources of information. Johnston's reports, as was typical of that general, were relatively uncommunicative and gave no clue at all as to what Johnston might be planning in order to stop Sherman, but their very datelines, each progressively closer to Atlanta, told the story. Davis heard more about it from Georgia politicians, who were by now bombarding him with complaints and demands for a change of command in their state as more and more of their constituents passed under Union control or fled southward as refugees. Davis also had a source within the high command of the Army of Tennessee. Hood and Davis had become personally acquainted during the former's convalescence in Richmond after his Chickamauga wound. Throughout the campaign in Georgia that spring and summer, Hood had sent Davis a steady stream of letters, reporting on operations in the kind of detail Johnston would not provide and presenting events—and his own performance—as he wished the president to perceive them.

Throughout the campaign Johnston's dispatches to Richmond touted a single remedy for the situation in Georgia, and that was that the Confederate high command should send Nathan Bedford Forrest and his division of cavalry from Mississippi into Middle Tennessee, there to cut Sherman's supply line. Davis rejected the proposal every time. Forrest was needed to protect Mississippi from Union forays, and besides, Johnston had his own cavalry and should send them to break the railroad in Tennessee. Johnston's assertion that he could do nothing and that someone else ought to win the war for him was by this time all too familiar to the Confederate president. Johnston, for his

The Atlanta railroad depot.

part, claimed that he needed his own cavalry and could not spare them for the raid he wanted Forrest to make.

Sherman had, since before leaving Chattanooga, been concerned about the possibility of Forrest raiding his supply lines. Besides leaving small garrisons in blockhouses at key bridges and culverts along the railroad and prepositioning repair crews and replacement parts for the tracks, Sherman had also arranged for Union expeditions, larger than Forrest's command, to launch raids into Mississippi. Their goal was to destroy Forrest if possible but at all events to keep him busy in Mississippi. Major General Samuel D. Sturgis had led the first such venture, but he proved woefully inferior to Forrest in cunning and mental toughness. On June 10, while Sherman was facing Johnston's lines on Pine, Brush, and Lost mountains, the wily Confederate scored his greatest tactical masterpiece, trouncing Sturgis at the Battle of Brice's Crossroads near Tupelo, Mississippi. Sherman was disgusted when he heard the news, but as far as he was concerned even a tactical fiasco like Brice's Crossroads was a strategic success if it kept Forrest in Mississippi and off his supply line in Tennessee. If necessary, Sherman could afford to send one such expedition after another for Forrest to thrash, as long as the ruthless Confederate stayed in Mississippi to do the thrashing.

For a second Mississippi expedition Sherman tasked Major General A. J. Smith commanding one of the corps of Sherman's old Army of the Tennessee veterans that Banks had taken with him on his Red River Expedition. Smith's competence and the hard-fighting skill of his troops had saved Banks from an even worse disaster in Louisiana. Now that that dismal campaign was at last over, Smith and company were available for other duty, and Sherman ordered him to go find Forrest and whip him. Smith did just that, getting the better of the Confederate raider and inflicting heavy casualties on his force at the July 14 Battle of Tupelo. Smith's supply situation required him to return to his base immediately after the battle, without completing the destruction of Forrest's command, but when Forrest tried to harass Smith's return march the next day, one of Smith's doughty midwestern soldiers shot the Confederate general in the foot, inflicting a minor wound but compounding Forrest's frustration. Unlike Sturgis's expedition, Smith's had been both a tactical and a strategic success.

By that time, with the Army of Tennessee on the outskirts of Atlanta, Davis's patience with Johnston was nearing an end. He had every reason to believe that the general would, within the next few weeks, abandon Atlanta with no more of a fight than he had put up during any of his other pauses in the long retreat from Dalton to the Chattahoochee, apparently content that despite whatever disasters had befallen the Confederacy on his watch, he was not to be blamed. Davis was well aware of the enormous transportation and manufacturing importance of Atlanta to the Confederacy and of the city's even greater significance to the morale of both sides, and he was not willing to allow it to be given up the way Johnston showed every indication of being about to do. He sent a pointed telegram to Johnston demanding that the general spell out his plans for the defense of the city "so specifically as will enable me to anticipate events," a clear indication that Davis expected Johnston to take the initiative against Sherman.[1] Johnston replied that he was so badly outnumbered that he could do nothing but stand on the defensive and react to the enemy's movements. This was exactly what he had been doing all the way down from Dalton, and every reaction had been a retreat.

Davis dispatched Braxton Bragg, who had by then become his top staff general in Richmond, to travel to Atlanta to investigate the situation and possibly replace Johnston with either of the Army of Tennessee's two senior corps commanders, Hood or Hardee. Hardee's near-mutinous behavior had helped to undermine Bragg during that general's tenure in command of the Army of Tennessee, and he had turned down command of the army the preceding December. His army nickname, Old Reliable, was probably more of a commentary on the low average quality of the generals in the Army of Tennessee than it was a testimony to Hardee's merits. Nothing in his career suggested him as a candidate for leading the kind of desperate fighting that was now going to be necessary if Atlanta were to be saved.

Hood was just the man for desperate fighting. The tall, tawny-bearded Texan had graduated forty-fourth in the fifty-two-man West Point class of 1853 and had turned thirty-three years old during the campaign down from Dalton. He had first ridden to fame in the second year of the war as commander of the Texas Brigade of the Army of Northern Virginia, Hood's Texas Brigade, as some still called it, renowned as the hardest-hitting unit of Lee's army. From there Hood had risen to lead a division and suffered at Gettysburg a wound that paralyzed his left arm. Promoted to corps command and transferred to the Army of Tennessee in time for Chickamauga, Hood had taken a bullet in the right thigh that had necessitated amputation just below the hip. He now had to be helped into the saddle and strapped there to ride, but no one would ever question his combativeness. Queried by Davis as to Hood's fitness to take the reins of the Army of Tennessee now with its back to Atlanta, Robert E. Lee responded that Hood was "a bold fighter, very industrious on the battlefield, careless off."[2]

Both Davis and Bragg believed that Hood was the man they needed for

General John Bell Hood

the present crisis or at least the best man they could get at the moment. On July 17 Davis sent orders by telegraph relieving Johnston of command and appointing Hood in his place. Hood's letters to Davis over the preceding three months had helped to undermine Johnston with the president, but ultimately Johnston had been the author of his own downfall by refusing to risk a battle that might mar his reputation and by showing concern only for ensuring that everyone knew that the bad results achieved on his watch were not his responsibility. Whatever Hood's intentions might have been in writing his letters, he was appalled to learn that he had been thrust into the command with the army backed up against Atlanta. First individually and then in concert with his two fellow corps commanders, he appealed first to Johnston to ignore the order, at least temporarily, and then to Davis, via telegraph, to rescind it. Neither complied, and Hood found himself irrevocably in command of an army in desperate circumstances.

THE BATTLES OF PEACHTREE CREEK AND ATLANTA

After several days of rest along the banks of the Chattahoochee, Sherman's armies advanced once more toward Atlanta. Thomas's Army of the Cumberland approached the city directly from the north, while McPherson's Army of the Tennessee, again playing its role as Sherman's whiplash, swung wide to the Union left to strike the Georgia Railroad near Decatur and then approach Atlanta from the east. Schofield's Army of the Ohio advanced between its two larger partners, maintaining contact with both by its skirmishers. As had been the case most of the way from Dalton to the Chattahoochee, the Army of the Tennessee would be turning the Rebels, threatening to cut an important line of communication between Confederate forces in Georgia and Virginia.

As the movement was in progress, Sherman learned of the change of commanders on the Confederate side. He was not familiar with Hood, but his subordinates were. Thomas had been one of Hood's instructors at West Point, and McPherson and Schofield had been his classmates there. The latter had even been his roommate and had coached the academically challenged future Confederate general through some of his more difficult mathematics courses. Hood was a fighter, the three generals assured Sherman, "bold to rashness" and very likely to attack someone at the first opportunity. Sherman was pleased. Johnston's repeated slippery retreats had prevented Sherman from coming to grips with the Rebel host in Georgia on any but the most disadvantageous terms, with the Confederates firmly ensconced behind impregnable breastworks that Johnston obviously longed for Sherman to assault. True, Johnston had fallen back all the way to Atlanta in order to avoid any different sort of encounter with Sherman, but the result had been to deny Sherman the opportunity of fulfilling Grant's orders to hammer the Army of Tennessee. Now, with Hood in command, Sherman was confident he would be able to get a stand-up fight out of the Rebels.

At about the same time Sherman was learning of Hood's accession to command, Hood was learning that Sherman had turned him again. Like Johnston with each of Sherman's turning movements, Hood now faced the choice of either fighting or retreating, but unlike Johnston, Hood never had the chance of retreating without giving up Atlanta. The necessity of the situation, the president's obvious expectations, and his own nature all dictated Hood's next move. The questions were where and when he would strike.

Hood's answer came at 4:00 on the afternoon of July 20 in the form of an all-out assault of the Army of the Cumberland, which at that time had just finished crossing to the south bank of Peachtree Creek. Hood hoped to catch Thomas in the act of crossing the creek, giving the Confederates a numerical advantage against the part of the Army of the Cumberland already on the south bank and catching the Federals before they could dig entrenchments. It might have worked if it had been launched several hours earlier, and Hood had meant it to be. Confederate armies, by law, never had enough staff officers, so that it was always difficult for a commander to translate his ideas into action, often requiring him to invest much personal attention in preparations.

When Davis sought Lee's advice about replacing Johnston with Hood, Lee had characterized Hood as being "careless" off the battlefield, and the fiery Texan's lack of attention to detail was no doubt exacerbated by his crippling wounds. To make matters worse, Hood had to depend much on Hardee, his only experienced corps commander. Hardee was uninspired at the best of times, but at this time he was in an extended sulk over having been passed over in favor of his junior, Hood, for command of the army. At Peachtree Creek he was more than usually slow in getting his troops into position. The result was an attack that was several hours late. The Army of the Cumber-

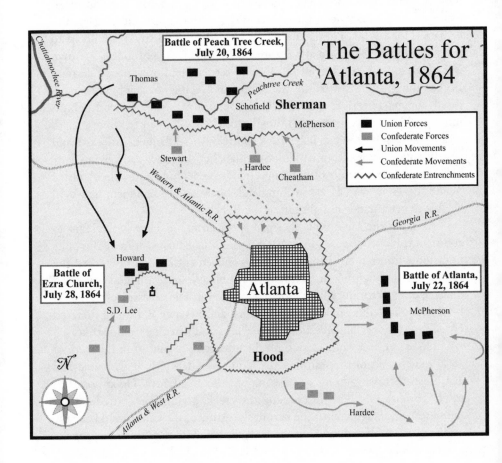

The Battles for Atlanta, 1864

Battle of Peach Tree Creek, July 20, 1864

Battle of Ezra Church, July 28, 1864

Battle of Atlanta, July 22, 1864

Union Forces
Confederate Forces
Union Movements
Confederate Movements
Confederate Entrenchments

land was already united on the south bank of the creek, and much of it was entrenched. Where it was not, the Confederate attackers scored a few temporary local successes before being driven back by Union counterattacks. Where the defenders were already behind breastworks, the attack made no headway at all. When the firing stopped that evening, Confederate losses totaled 4,796 men, while Thomas's casualties were scarcely more than one-third that many.

Sherman's turning movement continued apace the next day, with the Army of the Tennessee gaining the railroad east of Atlanta and then pushing westward toward the city, driving the Confederate defenders before them. With the failure of his first offensive, Hood faced again the unpleasant choice of either attack or retreat, with the latter meaning the abandonment of Atlanta. Again Hood chose to fight. During the thirty-six hours after the fighting had stopped along Peachtree Creek, Hood hastily shifted his troops through the city from the north side to the east for a blow against McPherson. Doing the hardest marching was Hardee's corps, which had been the most heavily engaged at Peachtree and now had the assignment of marching all the way around McPherson's left (southern) flank to hit the Army of the Tennessee in the rear. Hood was trying to make war the way he had seen Lee and Jackson do it in the Army of Northern Virginia. His plan for the attack on McPherson was very similar to what Lee and Jackson had done to Hooker at the Battle of Chancellorsville. Hardee would attack the Federals in flank and rear while the rest of the army, save for light forces detailed to hold the lines in front of Thomas and Schofield, would attack the Army of the Tennessee in front.

Across the lines, Sherman believed Hood had gotten all the aggressiveness out of his system in the July 20 assault along Peachtree Creek and would shortly retreat and abandon Atlanta. The Union general's chief concern now was the possibility that Lee in Virginia might send reinforcements to Hood. Grant had recently telegraphed to warn that in the deadlocked situation on the Petersburg front he could no longer guarantee that Lee could not do so, and everyone remembered Rosecrans's painful discomfiture at Chickamauga the preceding fall, in large part due to the arrival of troops detached from the Army of Northern Virginia. To forestall the repetition of such an event, Sherman wanted the Georgia Railroad, the most likely avenue for the approach of troops from Virginia, thoroughly destroyed for many miles east of Atlanta. On the morning of July 22, he decided that the single cavalry division he had working on that task of destruction was not going to be enough, and he told McPherson that he wanted an entire corps of the Army of the Tennessee, the Sixteenth, assigned to the job.

McPherson thought otherwise. His skirmishers had advanced that morning and found that although the Confederates had pulled back from some of the more advanced positions on his front, they were still present in force, well dug in, and showing no signs of being ready to evacuate Atlanta. Furthermore, McPherson believed his old classmate Hood was going to attack again, soon, and against the Army of the Tennessee's exposed left (southern) flank, where McPherson proposed to post the Sixteenth Corps. Sherman was unconvinced, but he liked and respected McPherson and so agreed to let him keep the Sixteenth Corps on his left flank until midday and then, if nothing happened, to dispatch it on the track-wrecking mission.

Midday came and no attack from Hood. McPherson with a number of his officers was sitting in the shade of a grove of trees. Some were finishing up lunch while McPherson prepared to write an order shifting the Sixteenth Corps from flank protection to railroad destruction. Just then firing broke out on the army's flank and rear, exactly where McPherson had predicted. The rapid crescendo of the sound indicated a major assault, and McPherson hastily rode off to inspect his lines. The Sixteenth Corps was just where it needed to be, and it stopped the first onset of the Confederate flanking attack. Between the Sixteenth Corps and its neighboring unit to the right, the Seventeenth Corps, was a gap in the Union line, and as McPherson reconnoitered and issued orders to bring up reserves to plug it, Confederate attackers swarmed through the gap and fatally shot the Union general.

The action that would come to be called the Battle of Atlanta was the largest and most hotly contested of the several clashes around the city. Hardee's flank march was a hard one for his battle-weary troops, and once again, this time with a better excuse, they were late in getting into position. That was the reason the attack had not come when McPherson had predicted. Now with its commander dead, the Army of the Tennessee felt the full weight of the Confederate attack, both in front and via the gap in its line, against its flank and rear.

Hood had indeed succeeded in doing something very much like what Lee and Jackson had done to Hooker at Chancellorsville, but Lee and Jackson had not been up against the Army of the Tennessee. Organized by Grant and seasoned by two years of hard but successful campaigning, the army refused to believe it could be beaten. Its new commander, in place of the fallen McPherson, was a striking contrast to the badly frightened Hooker of Chancellorsville. Major General John A. Logan, commander of the Fifteenth Corps, was an Illinois politician in uniform. Nicknamed "Black Jack" by his men because of his swarthy complexion, Logan combined adequate military

The Ponder House, on the outskirts of Atlanta, became first a haven for Confederate sharp-shooters and then a target for Union artillery.

acumen with an amazing ferocity and an even more amazing ability to infuse his own fighting spirit into the men he commanded.

Throughout the remainder of the day the men of the Seventeenth Corps fought both front and rear, leaping from one side of their breastworks to the other to direct their fire against whichever threat seemed most pressing at the moment. Only when the Confederates succeeded in achieving a simultaneous coordination of their attacks were they able to push the stubborn Federals on the left of the Seventeenth Corps out of their breastworks, while the corps' center and right held firm. The left pivoted back so that the corps' line formed an angle with its apex on a key piece of high ground the soldiers called the bald hill. The focus of repeated desperate Confederate assaults, the Union's hilltop position held.

A mile north of the bald hill, Confederate attackers made use of a brush-choked railroad cut to penetrate and break the lines of the Fifteenth Corps, once again threatening the Army of the Tennessee with destruction. The

Federals rallied, however, and Logan himself arrived from the other end of the battlefield at the critical moment to shouts of "Black Jack! Black Jack!" from his men. The Union counterattack swept the Confederates back out of the Union position, securing that sector. The firing continued around the bald hill until nightfall obscured the targets, but Hood's attack had clearly failed. Casualties in the Army of the Tennessee came to 3,641, including McPherson, while Confederate losses totaled 8,499.

STALEMATES IN GEORGIA
AND VIRGINIA

After the Battle of Atlanta Hood's army drew back into the fortifications ringing Atlanta. Sherman's turning movement had worked insofar as it had achieved the destruction of the Georgia Railroad east of Atlanta, and it had induced Hood to come out and fight twice. It had not destroyed Hood's army, though it had resulted in total casualties amounting to about a quarter of his strength. It had also failed to drive Hood out of Atlanta. The Confederates still had a railroad running into the city from the southwest and with it could supply their army in Atlanta.

This railroad Sherman immediately proposed to cut, and he gave the order to his old whiplash, the Army of the Tennessee, though bloodied by its recent fight and having lost a much loved commander in McPherson. The army would pull out of the positions it had fought for in the recent battle and swing around behind Schofield's and Thomas's armies in a long, counterclockwise march around the city from its southeast side to its southwest, where Sherman hoped it could cut the railroad somewhere between Atlanta and the hamlet of East Point, where the railroad forked into two diverging lines. During the march the army received a new commanding officer. Sherman appreciated Logan's fine service, but he believed the commander of the Fifteenth Corps lacked the expertise to handle the entire army. The job therefore went to thirty-four-year-old Major General Oliver O. Howard, who had graduated fourth in the West Point class of 1854. Howard had lost his right arm in the 1862 Peninsula Campaign, commanded the unlucky Eleventh Corps at the Battle of Gettysburg, and more recently had served as a corps commander in the Army of the Cumberland.

Sherman rode with Howard on July 28 as the Army of the Tennessee passed beyond Thomas's right flank and marched down the west side of Atlanta. As they heard firing flare up near the head of the column, Howard, remembering Hood from their West Point days, observed that the Confederate general was about to attack again. Sherman demurred. Hood would hardly dare to attack them again, he thought. But Howard was right. The Rebels were advancing in force for the third time in eight days. While Sherman rode back to get reinforcements started on their way from his other two armies, Howard quickly got his lead corps, Logan's Fifteenth, into line along a low ridge that ran roughly perpendicular to his route, crossing the road near a Methodist meetinghouse called Ezra Church. The soldiers had no time to entrench or to build up proper breastworks and had to content themselves with throwing together a few fence rails and whatever else they could find for protection in the few minutes before the Confederate attack struck.

Faced with yet another of Sherman's turning maneuvers, Hood had indeed chosen fight rather than retreat. After the battles of Peachtree Creek and Atlanta, Hardee's corps was fought out and needed rest, so Hood gave this attack to his other two corps, both of which had been engaged at Atlanta though less intensely than Hardee's. The corps commanders, Stephen D. Lee and Alexander P. Stewart, both had good records at lower ranks but were new to the job of directing a corps in battle. Hood's orders called for them to take up a specified position in front of Sherman, blocking his flanking movement and forcing him to attack. When the Confederates approached their assigned position, however, they found that Howard had just occupied it. Faced with this situation, Stewart urged that they follow the spirit of the orders and take up a different position, farther back, but Lee, who was the senior of the two, insisted that they would just have to attack and drive the Yankees out of the position Hood had assigned to them.

The fighting began in mid-afternoon, and the Confederates launched wave after wave of assaults against Logan's line without making any gains at all. By evening when the fighting sputtered out, the Confederates had lost some three thousand men, while Logan's corps, the only one engaged on the Union side, had suffered little more than one-sixth that many. The skill of the Union generals and their soldiers, the inexperience of the Confederate generals, and Hood's inability to supervise personally the movements of his army had all combined to produce one of the most lopsided battles of the entire campaign.

Hood had accomplished at least one thing by the movement that resulted in the Battle of Ezra Church: he had compelled Howard to stop short of Atlanta's last railroad lifeline. Over the days and then weeks that followed, Sherman tried to stretch his line far enough down the west side of Atlanta to reach the railroad southwest of the city, while Hood extended his entrenchments and stretched his lines farther and farther to counter him. In some ways the situation was similar to what Sherman had faced when his armies were stalled in front of Johnston's mountaintop positions north of Marietta. The stout fortifications of Atlanta now served the place of Brush, Pine, and Kennesaw mountains. Without letting go his grip on his railroad supply line, Sherman could not extend his lines far enough to get to the railroad behind Hood, who, having the inside position, always had a shorter distance to cover. Both sides were unwilling to assault the other's breastworks, and Sherman, with his three armies stretched to the utmost, could not make another turning movement that might force Hood into a fourth stand-up fight. As July gave way to August, the situation around Atlanta was a stalemate.

Back in Virginia the situation around Richmond and Petersburg looked much the same, as Grant strove to stretch his own lines around the south side of the latter city, reaching for the rail lines that fed Lee's army. A late-June probe toward the Weldon Railroad, easterly of the two leading into Petersburg, ended disastrously when Lee aimed a counterstrike and the Union troops in the operation fought poorly, ran away, or simply surrendered. The loss of fighting spirit and leadership in the Army of the Potomac was more obvious than ever. Some divisions had taken more casualties than they had had members when they marched into the Wilderness scarcely four weeks before. They continued to exist thanks to the steady influx of replacements, many of them draftees, bounty jumpers, or other poorly motivated recruits, but they were not the same fighting forces they had been.

Late July saw another Union effort to break the deadlock around Petersburg. A colonel who had been a mining engineer in civilian life hatched a plan to run a mine shaft more than five hundred feet to reach a Confederate fort and blow it up from below, opening a gap that attacking Union troops could exploit. Military engineers were familiar with the concept but judged the distance to be wildly impractical. To their surprise, the colonel and his regiment, with minimal support from army headquarters, succeeded in building their tunnel and planting four tons of gunpowder under the Confederate fort.

The mine lay within the sector of Burnside's Ninth Corps, and Grant ordered Burnside to follow up the explosion of the mine with an all-out assault. Burnside selected and trained one of his divisions, composed entirely of black troops, to lead the attack. When Meade learned of the plan, he insisted that another division lead the way. If the blacks went first, he thought, they might take heavy casualties, and northern public opinion might think the former slaves had been deliberately sacrificed. Burnside appealed to Grant, who backed Meade. So Burnside had his other division commanders draw straws for the honor. The worst of them drew the short straw, made no effort to prepare his troops or instruct his officers, and spent the morning of the attack getting drunk in a bomb shelter in the rear.

While he did, the mine blew with spectacular effect, and then his division advanced and dissolved into confusion. The Confederates recovered and launched a counterattack, which proved successful despite the advance of Burnside's other divisions, including the black one, to join the attack. Driven back into the crater itself, the attackers suffered appalling casualties before some of them could escape back to Union lines. As at Fort Pillow and other places during the last year and a half of the war, the incident degenerated into a racial massacre, as Confederate troops refused to take black prisoners and instead shot down or bayoneted men who had ceased to resist. Grant later sadly described the event, known as the Battle of the Crater, as "the saddest affair I have witnessed in the war."

Thereafter Grant continued to slug at Lee's positions, alternating right jabs direct at Richmond north of the James with roundhouse swings beyond his left flank aimed at taking and holding a section of the Weldon Railroad, which he succeeded in doing late in August. Confederates subsequently carried supplies around the breach via a thirty-mile detour in wagons. It was a painfully slow and difficult way to get the cargoes to the city, but what it did bring in helped to eke out what the single remaining railroad, the Southside, could carry. Meanwhile, the drumbeat of Grant's operations continued, another every few weeks, each testing the remaining strength of Lee's lines or stretching them a little farther in the direction of the final railroad.

WAR ON THE POLITICAL FRONT

While Grant strove to tighten his grip on Richmond and Petersburg and Sherman did the same with Atlanta, Lincoln was fighting a war on a different front. This was an election year, and the Union cause could lose at the polls much more easily than on the battlefield. Even within his own Republican Party the president did not enjoy unanimous support. Radical Republicans, the party's vanguard on issues of emancipation and civil rights for the newly freed slaves, were dissatisfied with Lincoln's caution about the potential political and legal pitfalls that lay in the path of goals that he largely shared with them.

Those among the Radicals who were most dissatisfied with Lincoln but despaired of denying him the Republican nomination for another term chose instead the quixotic alternative of launching a third party. A convention of the most discontent of the Radicals met in Cleveland, Ohio, on May 29, styling itself the Radical Democracy Party. On May 31 the four hundred or so delegates in attendance gave their presidential nomination to the 1856 Republican candidate and more recently failed general John C. Frémont. In his June 4 letter of acceptance, Frémont stated that he would step down as candidate if the Republicans nominated someone other than Lincoln.

The Republican convention met in Baltimore that same first week of June, styling itself the National Union Party in hopes of attracting the votes of war Democrats. To strengthen the appeal to members of the Democratic Party who supported at least the war to restore the Union, the Republicans set aside Lincoln's first-term vice president, Hannibal Hamlin, in favor of Tennessee senator and occupation governor Andrew Johnson, the only senator from a seceding state to keep his seat in the Senate and remain loyal to the Union. Johnson was a lifelong Democrat and admirer of Andrew Jackson. Lincoln was, of course, renominated by a resounding majority, drawing 494 of 516 votes on the first ballot. The rest went for Grant but promptly switched to Lincoln to make the nomination unanimous. In his own acceptance letter, written June 9, while Grant's army still lay before Cold Harbor, Lincoln wrote, "I have not permitted myself, gentlemen, to conclude that I am the best man in the country; but I am reminded, in this connection, of a story of an old Dutch farmer, who remarked to a companion once that 'it was not best to swap horses when crossing streams.'"[3]

The part of the Democratic Party that the Republicans did not succeed in drawing into the National Union Party—and it was much the larger part—was increasingly dominated by the so-called peace Democrats, who had never sympathized with the war or its purposes, least of all emancipation, and were now more determined than ever to bring it to an end at once, without freedom for the slaves and, perhaps, without even the preservation of the Union. They met in their own convention that August in Chicago, where the Republicans had joyously nominated Lincoln four years before, and adopted a platform, written by Clement Vallandigham, that called the war a failure and demanded an immediate cease-fire along with the opening of negotiations with the Confederate government. Some of their prominent leaders advocated that the reunion negotiations should include a constitutional convention to make whatever changes might be needed in that venerable document to satisfy slaveholders that their peculiar institution would be safe forever under a new Union and constitution. Whatever followed in the wake of a Democratic victory would almost certainly not be "the Constitution as it is and the Union as it was."

In a stroke of cynical political genius, the Democratic delegates chose as their presidential nominee George B. McClellan. The general was still tremendously popular with the soldiers of the Army of the Potomac and perhaps with other elements of the population as well. As a general, he would, by his presence at the top of the ticket, somewhat counteract the impression the platform would naturally create that the party was lacking in patriotism, fortitude, or both. Indeed, upon accepting the nomination McClellan wrote a public letter, more or less repudiating the platform on which he had just agreed to run. The political professionals who ran the Democratic Party were not concerned. Once elected, McClellan would be politically beholden to them and compelled to adopt at least some of their policies, even if his protestations against the platform were more than just campaign rhetoric. The convention that nominated him had announced that Vallandigham would be his secretary of war.

As the campaign progressed, Lincoln had to deal with practical difficulties presented on both sides, by those who believed he was prosecuting the war too vigorously and with too much concern for the freedom and rights of blacks and those who believed he was displaying exactly the opposite fault. The Radical Republicans in Congress found a way to make Lincoln's summer difficult by challenging him for control of Reconstruction, the process by which the rebellious states were to be restored to their proper relationship to the nation as a whole and to the national government.

The process of Reconstruction had begun as soon as Union armies had made their first strides in reconquering Rebel states. Lincoln had directed the establishment of loyal state governments in the Union-held areas of Tennessee, Virginia, and Louisiana. In order to encourage the citizens of the rebellious states to rally around the new governments and withdraw their support from the Confederacy, Lincoln in December 1863 issued a proclamation on Reconstruction, containing what came to be called his "Ten Percent Plan." Lincoln's program offered a lenient, gentle return for the Union's erring southern citizens. At its heart was a provision that as soon as a number equal to 10 percent of a state's 1860 voters took an oath henceforth to be loyal to the Union, those who had taken the oath could participate in the formation of a loyal state government.

The challenge from the Radical Republicans came in the form of the Wade-Davis Bill, introduced the preceding December and passed by Congress on July 2. Its entire approach to Reconstruction contrasted sharply with Lincoln's. Whereas the president believed the rebellious states had never left the Union and needed only to be restored to their proper practical relationship with it, the Radical Republicans, including the bill's sponsors, Senator Benjamin Wade of Ohio and Congressman Henry Winter Davis of Maryland, maintained that the states claiming to be part of the Confederacy had committed "state suicide" or were "conquered provinces." Either way, they were to be administered by the national government until they met stringent requirements for readmission as states. The Wade-Davis Bill stipulated that a southern state could form a loyal state government when a majority, not 10 percent, of its total number of 1860 voters took an "Ironclad Oath," swearing that they had never voluntarily supported the rebellion. Under those terms, no Confederate state could have formed a government without a great deal of perjury—unless it extended the vote to black former slaves, virtually all of whom could have taken the Ironclad Oath with complete honesty.

Although the bill's provisions were in many ways reasonable and just (and included much that was later incorporated into the Fourteenth Amendment to the Constitution), it clashed with Lincoln's ideas not only by claiming congressional rather than presidential authority over the process of Reconstruction but also by making it more difficult to entice wavering southerners to abandon their rebellion and return their allegiance to the United States, as had been Lincoln's goal in issuing the Ten Percent Plan. It also posed a threat to the Union-loyal governments Lincoln had already established in the Union-held sections of Louisiana, Arkansas, and Tennessee. Since Congress had adjourned for its summer recess a few days after passing the bill, Lincoln was able to give it a "pocket veto" by simply declining to sign it. He later issued a statement explaining that the Wade-Davis Bill offered a fine plan of Reconstruction for any southern state that might choose to adopt it, but he did not wish to make it the only available choice. As usual, Lincoln was balancing justice against practicality. The war continued in all its fury, and to the president even a bit of excessive leniency might be acceptable if it could still the guns sooner while preserving Lincoln's two nonnegotiable goals of Union and emancipation.

The Radicals were furious. On August 4, the sponsors of the bill issued a manifesto denouncing Lincoln, and the next day Horace Greeley's *New York Tribune* printed it. Wade and Davis denounced Lincoln in strident language, complaining of presidential encroachment on the powers of Congress as if the Constitution had said nothing at all about the veto power. Wade and

Davis accused Lincoln of ruling the country as a despot and trying to use Reconstruction to set up his own reelection.

As for Horace Greeley, he was finding additional ways to make Lincoln's reelection more difficult, with the assistance of Jefferson Davis. In early July, while Early's Confederates were rampaging through Maryland and bearing down on Washington, Greeley informed Lincoln that he had received a missive from two men in Niagara Falls, Ontario, purporting to be agents of the Confederate government with powers to negotiate a peace settlement. Greeley made an emotional appeal to Lincoln to follow up this contact. Professing to know that the Confederate people universally longed for peace, Greeley "ventured to remind" the president "that our bleeding, bankrupt, almost dying country also longs for peace—shudders at the prospect of fresh conscription, of further wholesale devastations, and of new rivers of human blood." This was entirely in keeping with the severely defeatist tone of Greeley's editorials of late.

Lincoln realized that the affair offered precisely no chance at all of bringing about peace with reunion and emancipation, his minimum terms, and that if the men actually were agents of the Confederate government, their mission was merely to depict Lincoln as a warmonger who would not accept a reasonable peace agreement and further to demoralize the northern people into giving up the war and voting for McClellan. Wisely, the president replied, "If you can find any person anywhere professing to have any proposition of Jefferson Davis in writing, for peace, embracing the restoration of the Union and the abandonment of slavery, whatever else it embraces, say to him he may come to me with you."

This was not what Greeley expected, and he tried to beg off in a letter complaining that the Rebel envoys were unlikely to show him their credentials, much less share with him their terms. "I was not expecting you to send me a letter," Lincoln wrote in reply, "but to bring me a man, or men." To sound the matter to its bottom, Lincoln dispatched one of his private secretaries, John Hay, to carry his letter to Greeley and then accompany Greeley to Niagara Falls to meet with the purported Confederate agents. To Greeley, Lincoln added, "I not only intend a sincere effort for peace, but I intend that you shall be a personal witness that it is made."

Quite unwillingly, Greeley accompanied Hay to the Canadian border, and together they found that the Confederate agents had no peace proposals to make or any intention of serious negotiation. Not surprisingly, the pair was hardly on its way back to Washington before the rumor was abroad that Lincoln had turned down a perfectly reasonable peace proposal. Lincoln would have liked to counteract the rumor by publishing excerpts of his correspondence with Greeley, but to this Greeley would not agree unless his own defeatist outburst was published as well. Lincoln thought it best to forbear and endure the rumor.

With the Republican Party splintered by the defection of the Radicals and Lincoln denounced as a despot by Republican congressmen while the editor of the nation's most-read newspaper tried to make the president look like a warmonger who would not accept peace even though the enemy was supposedly eager for it, the prospects of Lincoln's reelection looked grim. Meanwhile the Democrats appealed to the country's war weariness while at the same time running a famous and popular, once-idolized general for president.

Much more important than all of this, however, was the continuing stalemate on both major military fronts, in Georgia and Virginia. Hopes for quick and easy victory had been far too high that spring, and the casualty lists from Virginia had been far too long ever since the campaign started. Now with both of the Union's major fighting forces seemingly stalled short of their objectives, national morale sank to perhaps its lowest ebb of the war. Trained military men who understood strategy might recognize that Grant and Sherman had their opponents pinned down and that final victory was, as Lee himself realized, only a matter of time, but the public back home, knowing little of strategy and only what newspapers like Greeley's told them about the war, could see only futility amid ongoing slaughter.

The Confederate military situation was desperate, with no hope of survival unless the Union tired of the fight and gave up, but by the dog days of August, it was looking more and more as if that was exactly what the northern electorate would do. McClellan might claim that he would continue the war until the Union was restored, but nearly everyone else in the country, both North and South, seemed to understand that a vote for McClellan was a vote for peace with neither Union nor emancipation and that such would follow his accession to office, almost regardless of whether McClellan wished it or not.

By August Lincoln himself, one of the most astute politicians of his day, believed the prospects of his own reelection were very dim. On the twenty-third of the month, Lincoln wrote, "This morning, as for some days past, it seems exceedingly probable that this Administration will not be re-elected. Then it will be my duty to so co-operate with the President elect, as to save the Union between the election and the inauguration; as he will have secured his election on such ground that he cannot possibly save it afterward." He folded the sheet of paper and placed it in an envelope, then sealed it. Later that day, he produced the envelope at a cabinet meeting and asked each member of the cabinet to sign across the flap of the envelope without knowing what was inside. Apparently Lincoln hoped that after losing the election, he might, by displaying the statement to McClellan with proof that it was dated from before the election, gain the cooperation of the president-elect in securing the political support necessary for an all-out effort to win the war before inauguration day. Yet if the nation had voted for McClellan and thus voted to give up the war as lost, further efforts to win it would have been desperate indeed.

Then on September 2 a telegram arrived from Sherman: "Atlanta is ours and fairly won."

12

LAST CHANCES FOR
THE CONFEDERACY

FROM JONESBORO
TO CEDAR CREEK

By late August, Sherman had realized that he simply could not stretch his lines far enough to the southwest to cut Hood's railroads. Nor would a cavalry raid suffice since horse soldiers on a raid in enemy territory could rarely afford to stop in one place long enough to make a thorough job of destroying the tracks. Nothing would suffice but getting a major force of infantry onto the tracks, and, since the trench lines could not stretch that far, the force that struck the railroad would have to cut loose from the rest of his armies, as well as its own supply lines, in order to make the raid.

It was one of Sherman's greatest strengths as a general that when the situation in front of him required bold action, he took it. So he drew up a plan to leave only a single corps, Major General Henry W. Slocum's Twentieth, astride the tracks north of Atlanta, maintaining the Union hold on the Western & Atlantic. Sherman would lead the remaining two corps of the Army of the Cumberland, plus all of the smaller Army of the Tennessee and Army of the Ohio, in a broad turning maneuver, casting loose of supply lines and all connection with Slocum to pass around the west side of Atlanta and reach the vital railroads directly south of the city.

The plan worked exactly as Sherman had hoped, and all three of his armies made firm lodgements on and across the railroads before the Confederates could react in force. Belatedly Hood discovered Sherman's purpose and moved to counter him, dispatching Hardee with two of his three corps south to the railroad town of Jonesboro, twenty miles south of Atlanta, where the Army of the Tennessee had made its lodgement on the Macon & Western, the easterly of Atlanta's two remaining rail lines. On August 31 Howard's troops repulsed the Rebel assault more easily than they had at the battles of Atlanta and Ezra Church the month before. The next day, September 1, the Federals went over to the attack and routed Hardee's large detachment. That left Hood with little choice but to retreat and give up Atlanta.

Sherman occupied the city the next day without making much effort to catch and capture Hood's retreating army, but a well-developed killer instinct was not among the red-bearded Ohioan's many strengths as a general. He was content, for now, with Atlanta and for good reason. Sherman's capture of the city was exactly the sort of major, tangible progress that the northern voters needed in order to be assured that the war was not, as the Democrats claimed, a failure. It is possible that Lincoln would have won the election that November, even if Sherman had not taken Atlanta first. It is also possible that even if Lincoln had lost the election the Union might have won the war anyway, either before or after McClellan's inauguration. Yet the best, almost the only remaining Confederate hope of independence lay in Lincoln's defeat and McClellan's election to the presidency, and after Sherman took Atlanta, Lincoln's reelection was all but assured.

In the wake of Sherman's victory, other Union victories seemed to cluster during the late summer months. Some had preceded the capture of Atlanta but had gone relatively unnoticed amid the prevailing northern gloom at the apparent continued futility of Union efforts in front of Richmond and Atlanta.

On June 19 the day of reckoning had finally come for the Confederate navy's notorious CSS *Alabama*. The sleek commerce raider had been built in Britain under a false name, taken to sea, armed, and commissioned into the Confederate navy on August 24, 1862. Her twenty-four officers hailed from the Confederate States, but her 120-man crew was a motley collection from the seafaring nations of the world, most being British. Over the next twenty-two months the *Alabama* had roved the Atlantic, Pacific, and Indian oceans, hunted by a total of twenty-five Union warships. She had captured sixty-six U.S. merchant vessels worth millions of dollars, burning most of them. She had also sunk a smaller Union gunboat in battle.

Alabama was in harbor at Cherbourg, France, where her captain, Raphael Semmes, had tried and failed to get the French authorities to ignore their nation's neutrality and allow him the use of their dockyards to overhaul

General Sherman inside the captured fortifications of Atlanta.

his vessel, when on June 14, 1864, the USS *Kearsarge* arrived and stood off the harbor entrance, obviously awaiting the *Alabama*. Five days later Semmes took his vessel to sea, and the two fairly evenly matched men-of-war fought the most spectacular ship-to-ship battle of the conflict, watched by thousands on the French shore. In a little more than an hour, the *Kearsarge* sent the *Alabama* to the bottom, ridding the seas of the greatest nuisance and threat to Union trade.

A little less than seven weeks later the U.S. Navy had scored another success, this time in American waters. On August 5 the old sea dog Farragut, in his wooden flagship *Hartford*, had boldly led his squadron of ironclads and wooden ships into Mobile Bay past two powerful Confederate forts. One of his most powerful ironclads, the monitor USS *Tecumseh*, struck a mine (then called a torpedo) and went down, but the rest of Farragut's ships got through. Inside the harbor they met the CSS *Tennessee*, the most powerful ironclad the Confederacy ever built, and pounded it until it surrendered. With that, the Confederacy's only remaining major Gulf Coast port was closed beyond hope of further use by blockade-runners. Union presence in the bay posed a constant threat of further offensive action against the city of Mobile itself.

Additional Union successes followed close in the wake of Sherman's capture of Atlanta. After Early's raid on Washington, the Confederate had withdrawn into the lower (northerly) Shenandoah Valley and there had remained as a continuing nuisance to Union operations in Virginia, with an ongoing threat to make another lunge toward Washington or Baltimore. Dissatisfied with the apparent inability of the Union generals in that area to see Early off for good and all, Grant assigned Sheridan to take two divisions of his cavalry and take command of all of the Union forces operating against Early and unite them into a hard-hitting Army of the Shenandoah that would neutralize both Early and the valley whose name it bore. Sheridan's

Confederate Cabinet Member and Senator   Admiral David G. Farragut
Howell Cobb of Georgia

new army would include the Federals previously operating in West Virginia under Major General George Crook as well as the Sixth Corps and the Nineteenth Corps, the latter recently transferred to Virginia from the Department of the Gulf, where it had soldiered grimly through Banks's dismal Red River Campaign.

Sheridan took over his new army in early August and took several weeks preparing his force and feeling for Confederate weak points. Though badly outnumbered, Early seemed to believe he had little to fear from Sheridan. He found out otherwise when on September 19 the new Union commander attacked the Confederates near Winchester. In the war's third battle to take its name from that town, the opposing forces slugged it out in a daylong fight. Then as the Rebels began to fall back under heavy Union attacks, the Union cavalry came thundering down on the Confederate flank, turning the retreat into a rout. Early's army survived though badly battered and suffering the loss of experienced officers such as Major General Robert E. Rodes, one of the Army of Northern Virginia's most aggressive division commanders, who was killed in the fighting.

Early fell back twenty miles to the vicinity of Strasburg, where he took

Phil Sheridan (left) with several of his officers. Seated at right is George A. Custer.

up a strong position with his right flank anchored on the North Fork of the Shenandoah and his left on Fisher's Hill. Sheridan followed aggressively and again engaged the Confederates on September 21. After heavy skirmishing that day and the next morning, Sheridan, at Crook's suggestion, launched a flank attack that crumbled the Confederate line. Defeated again—and more soundly than before—Early retreated all the way up the valley, another eighty miles to the vicinity of Waynesboro. This left virtually the whole length of the Shenandoah Valley open for Sheridan to begin to implement the second part of the instructions Grant had given him when assigning him there.

For three years the Shenandoah Valley had been the granary of Virginia, and its thriving farms had provided food for Confederate armies passing through it on their way to gaining positions of leverage over the Union forces operating east of the Blue Ridge. In the spring of 1862 it had been Jackson's small army throwing a scare into Washington by its sudden move down the valley. That fall Lee had planned to draw supplies through the valley to support his invasion of Maryland. In the summer of 1863, the valley once again provided food for Lee's army as it marched through on its way to invade Pennsylvania. A year later, Early had made use of the valley in the same way for the raid that took him to the outskirts of Washington and forced the diversion of the Sixth Corps from Grant's operations around Petersburg. In each case the agricultural abundance of the Shenandoah Valley had enabled Confederate commanders to operate without the constraints of logistics—the laborious task of supplying an army in the field—that would otherwise have slowed their movements and limited their reach. Thus, in the strange ways of war, it was the idyllic farms and rich harvests of the Shenandoah Valley that had made possible things like the appearance of Early's army on the doorstep of Washington and the burning of Chambersburg.

Now Grant was determined to put a stop to that, at least until the next year's harvest came in. "Eat out Virginia clean and clear," he had ordered Sheridan, "so that crows flying over it for the balance of the season will have to carry their own provender." With Early having abandoned the lower hundred miles of the valley, Sheridan was now free to carry out that order, and he did his best. He later reported that during the first two weeks of October his troops slaughtered thousands of cattle, sheep, and hogs and burned "2,000 barns filled with wheat, hay, and farming implements" as well as "over seventy mills filled with flour and wheat."

It sounded like a great deal, and if one happened to own one of the targeted barns or mills, it was a severe loss. Yet it was far short of a total devastation of such an abundant farming district. For the most part, the Yankees did not burn houses. Furthermore, letters and diaries reveal that for most inhabitants of the valley, life went on in its accustomed way, with the usual round of dances and other celebrations, and farmers were taking wagon loads of grain to market only weeks after the passage of Sheridan's army. No evidence exists that anyone starved, either in the Shenandoah Valley or anywhere else in the South, outside of prison pens such as Andersonville. Like other instances in which Union forces struck at Confederate logistics during the final year of the war, "the Burning" of the Shenandoah, as it came to be called, grew larger in legend than in life, as passing generations exaggerated its destructiveness with each retelling.

Throughout Sheridan's operations in the valley, as in other Union campaigns in the South, valley residents, though often frightened at the approach of the enemy, were in fact quite safe in their persons, as the killing or injuring of noncombatants was all but unheard of. Rapes were as rare as elsewhere in the presence of the armies of either side, a rate that compared favorably to that of most major cities. Indeed, as nineteenth-century mores dictated, women enjoyed immunity even when they demonstrated hostility to Union troops. Such hostility was most often verbal, but even when a woman swung a broom at a foraging bluecoat, the result was usually that the assailed soldier ducked and his buddies laughed.

When civilians became combatants, however, the situation was quite different. Men who implicitly claimed immunity as civilians when large numbers of Union troops were present but then bushwhacked isolated soldiers forfeited not only that immunity but also any right to be treated as prisoners of war. If captured, they could, under the laws of war, face summary execution. Their actions also exposed the surrounding neighborhood to greater destruction of property. When on October 3 Sheridan learned that his engineer officer, Lieutenant John R. Meigs, had been murdered by bushwhackers near the village of Dayton, he ordered the burning of every house within a five-mile radius but relented and canceled the order after his troopers had torched only about thirty houses and barns. Confederate guerrilla leader John S. Mosby and his troopers continued to be a constant thorn in Sheridan's side.

While Sheridan's men strove to destroy the valley's usefulness for future Confederate offensive operations, Early planned a comeback. He marched his army, somewhat recovered from its previous drubbings, down the valley until he neared the town of Strasburg. Sheridan's army was encamped just north of Strasburg, along Cedar Creek, a tributary of the North Branch of the Shenandoah River. In a well-conceived plan for a surprise flanking attack,

Early marched his troops through the night of October 18 and struck the Union left out of the dawn mists the next morning. Crook's contingent folded quickly under the surprising onslaught, and the Nineteenth Corps, in the center, gave way after a somewhat harder fight. On the Union right, however, the Sixth Corps was able to rally and hold its ground. Early was delighted nonetheless as the fugitives of the two routed Union corps streamed down the valley toward Winchester in retreat. He was confident that the Sixth Corps would soon follow its comrades to the rear without his having to hurl his thinned gray ranks against it in potentially costly attacks.

Sheridan had not been present for the early morning fight. He had traveled to Washington to confer about future operations and had been on his way back to the army. He was in Winchester that morning, twelve miles from the battlefield, when the sound of the guns reached him. Mounting his large black stallion Rienzi, Sheridan galloped southward along the Valley Pike toward Cedar Creek. He began to meet stragglers heading the other way. The men recognized the small general on the big horse and cheered wildly, but Sheridan roared for them to turn around and march back toward the enemy. And they did.

Arriving on the battlefield around 10:30 a.m., Sheridan found the Sixth Corps steady and Early apparently not inclined to press his advantage. Sheridan spent the middle hours of the day getting his army back in order and then at 4:00 p.m. launched an assault that crushed Early's army, recapturing the eighteen guns the Union had lost in the first phase of the battle and taking twenty-five more that had belonged to the Confederates that morning. For the Confederate infantry, what had started as a battle ended as a footrace to escape the pursuing Federals. Early retreated far up the valley with what was left of his command, but it would never again pose a threat to Sheridan or anyone else, and the Confederacy would never again make use of the Shenandoah Valley.

THE ELECTION OF 1864

The Union victories in the English Channel and at Mobile Bay, Winchester, Fisher's Hill, Cedar Creek, and, above all, the capture of Atlanta cut the ground out from under the Democrats' claim that the war was a failure and could never be won. On the contrary, Union forces were striding toward victory with seven-league boots, and the Confederacy's days were clearly numbered. This had been true for some time, but the fall of Atlanta focused the public's attention and brought the progress of the war into perspective so that its trend became unmistakable even for civilians who understood little of military affairs.

The month of September also brought political developments that made McClellan's chances for the presidency appear noticeably slimmer. John C. Frémont and others among his new Radical Democracy Party had been appalled by the Democratic Party platform with its promise to save slavery and tepid hopes of saving the Union. Frémont did not like Lincoln but knew he would like McClellan even less. In mid-September he arranged a deal with Lincoln. Lincoln dropped from his cabinet Postmaster General Montgomery Blair, whom the Radicals despised, and Frémont withdrew from the presidential race. With Frémont gone, Lincoln's chances of reelection rose still higher.

The presidential election of 1864 was the first to occur while the nation was in the midst of a major war, and the very fact that it came off as scheduled and that the government allowed the people what amounted to a referendum on the conflict that had been raging for the past three and a half years was a major triumph for self-government and a testament to the resilience of what Lincoln had called "the Great Republic." The fact that the election was taking place during wartime also meant that for the first time in the nation's history a significant percentage of the eligible voters were in the army. Soldiers in the field had never before voted in U.S. elections, but for 1864 most of the northern states passed laws enabling them to do so. In Indiana the Democrats controlled the legislature and stubbornly refused to allow soldiers to vote anywhere except in their home counties. Lincoln hinted in a letter to Sherman, whose armies included most of the state's regiments, that it would be helpful if he could furlough as many Indiana soldiers as possible without jeopardizing military operations. In the lull that followed the fall of Atlanta, Sherman, who fully sympathized with Lincoln's desire not to see the Hoosier soldiers disenfranchised, furloughed them en masse.

Sherman also furloughed two of his best corps commanders. Both Frank Blair and John A. Logan had been politicians before the war, though neither was a political general in the purest sense of the term. Blair was the brother of fired Postmaster General Montgomery Blair, and Logan had been a Democrat before the war. Now both returned to their home states, Blair to Missouri and Logan to Illinois, to campaign for Lincoln.

When election day came, Lincoln garnered just over 2.2 million votes to McClellan's 1.8 million. Lincoln's 55 percent share of the popular vote borders on being a landslide. The wide distribution of his support throughout the loyal states turned that margin into a major electoral landslide, with Lincoln receiving 212 electoral votes to McClellan's 21. The Democratic candidate captured his electoral votes in his home state of New Jersey, plus the border slave states of Delaware and Kentucky. Otherwise, Lincoln's statewide margins of victory were under five percentage points only in New York, Pennsylvania, and Connecticut.

Notably, while 55 percent of the voters nationwide chose Lincoln, 78 percent of Union soldiers did so. As it turned out, their votes did not decide the election, as Lincoln would have won even without them. Yet it was significant in another way. Cynical historians write as if all wars are decided and directed by politicians who carefully keep themselves out of harm's way while herding the unwilling masses to their deaths as cannon fodder, and there were those on both sides of the Mason-Dixon Line during the Civil War who looked at the Union and Confederate draft laws and complained that the conflict was "a rich man's war and a poor man's fight." Yet the overwhelming majority of Union soldiers, men who by then knew firsthand what war meant and who would bear the burdens and losses of its continuance, announced with their votes that this was their war and their fight and that they believed the causes of Union and emancipation were worth pressing on to final victory, cost what it might.

A victory for McClellan in the election of 1864 might or might not have led to Confederate independence, but such an event was the Confederacy's last realistic hope of survival beyond the meager few months that its dwindling armies might be able to keep some fragment of its claimed territory out from under the boots of blue-clad soldiers. Lincoln's victory meant that Confederate defeat, with the attendant restoration of the Union and abolition of slavery (a constitutional amendment abolishing slavery throughout the entire United States had already passed the Senate and was pending consideration in the House), was as certain as nearly any future event could ever be in the course of human affairs. The Union was now committed to prosecuting the war more vigorously than ever, if need be until at least 1867 if not 1869, and the Confederacy could not hope to survive even to the earlier of those dates.

SHERMAN IN ATLANTA

All that remained now was to convince the people of the Confederacy that the end was at hand for their slaveholders' republic and that they ought to give up and accept it. The question was how many more men would have to die or be maimed before that end arrived.

In Virginia, Grant's and Lee's armies continued to face each other from their trenches stretching from the north side of Richmond, down the east side of Richmond and Petersburg, and around to the south of Petersburg. Fighting flared every few weeks as Grant either reached farther west across the south side of Petersburg or jabbed at Lee's lines either north or south of the James River to force the Confederate general to keep every sector of his line manned, thus hamstringing Lee's efforts to match Grant's repeated grabs for Petersburg's one remaining southern rail connection, the Southside Railroad, southwest of town. Elements of the battle-weary Army of the Potomac turned in several strikingly poor performances in these operations, but with each passing month Grant weakened and stretched Lee's army and fastened his own grip more tightly than ever on it and on Richmond and Petersburg.

In Georgia, once the euphoria of capturing Atlanta had worn off, Sherman experienced several weeks of frustration as he tried to hold what he had gained and figure out what to do next. His biggest problem was one that had plagued him all the way down from Chattanooga, and that was his reliance, for every hardtack cracker and piece of salt pork his men ate, on a single set of rails leading all the way back to Louisville. The problem was worse now not only because the distance was longer than it had been at any time during the campaign but also because, at least as it appeared initially, Sherman would have more mouths to feed. As was typical when a southern city fell under Union control, the Confederates left behind a population of thousands of noncombatants, including many families of Confederate soldiers, who were thus destitute. Rather than see them starve, Union officers in places such as Nashville, Memphis, and New Orleans had provided them regular rations. Thus, the northern taxpayer got to pay not only for the feeding and maintenance of the nation's army but also for the feeding of a large number of the families of those bearing arms against the nation.

Sherman was determined that it would be different in Atlanta, and so on September 7 he ordered the evacuation of the remaining civilian population of the city either south into Rebel lines if they chose or else north to someplace where, if the government did have to feed them, it could at least do so more conveniently and without impinging the flow of supplies to its own armies. He offered the assistance of his troops and their supply wagons to transport the evacuees and their possessions. The mayor and city council protested the order, and Hood, on being informed by flag of truce to be ready to receive the refugees, wrote a letter condemning the action. Sherman was unmoved. To the mayor he wrote,

> We must have *peace*, not only at Atlanta, but in all America. To secure this, we must stop the war that now desolates our once happy and favored country. To stop war, we must defeat the rebel armies which are arrayed against the laws and Constitution that all must respect and obey. To defeat those armies, we must prepare the way to reach them in their recesses, provided with the arms and instruments which enable us to accomplish our purpose.[1]

That would mean that Atlanta would have to serve as a supply depot rather than a home for families, and the families might as well leave now, when they had a good opportunity of doing so. "You cannot qualify war in harsher terms than I will," Sherman continued:

> War is cruelty, and you cannot refine it; and those who brought war into our country deserve all the curses and maledictions a people can pour out. I know I had no hand in making this war, and I know I will make more sacrifices to-day than any of you to secure peace. But you cannot have peace and a division of our country. . . . You might as well appeal against the thunder-storm as against these terrible hardships of war. They are inevitable, and the only way the people of Atlanta can hope once more to live in peace and quiet at home, is to stop the war, which can only be done by admitting that it began in error and is perpetuated in pride. . . . I want peace, and believe it can only be reached through union and war, and I will ever conduct war with a view to perfect and early success. But, my dear sirs, when peace does come, you may call on me for any thing. Then will I share with you the last cracker, and watch with you to shield your homes and families against danger from every quarter.

The order stood, and Union troops helped the remaining citizens of Atlanta in moving their belongings out of town, either to the railroad for the trip north or to Confederate lines, whence they could continue their journey south.

In the weeks that followed, Hood chose not to attempt to defend the two-thirds of the state of Georgia Sherman had not yet taken but instead moved his army into northeastern Alabama. From there he advanced into North Georgia and attempted to cut Sherman's railroad supply line somewhere north of Atlanta. Sherman left enough troops to hold the city and with the rest of his force marched north to counter Hood and protect the railroad.

For the next several weeks, Union and Confederate forces maneuvered around northwestern Georgia without coming to grips while both commanders grew increasingly frustrated. Hood's men could tear up railroad tracks, but Sherman's repair teams had them running again within hours. What Hood could not do was destroy a facility, such as a tunnel, that would not be easily repairable. Nor could he seize and hold a position astride the railroad. Always the approach of Sherman's larger army compelled him to relinquish his grip on the railroad and beat a hasty retreat. Sherman, for his part, was confident that he could crush Hood's army in battle, but Hood would not hold still long enough, and Sherman could not catch him. Meanwhile the armies were marching up and down the same swath of country over which they had campaigned earlier that year.

Despite his success in keeping Sherman occupied in North Georgia and preventing any further Union offensive movements deeper into the Confederacy, Hood was the first to lose patience and tire of the game. He decided to march his army back into Alabama, then turn north and cross the Tennessee River. From there he planned to invade Middle Tennessee and possibly go all the way to the Ohio River or beyond. He began the movement in late October.

THE MARCH TO THE SEA

While Hood's army marched west, Sherman was contemplating movement in a different direction. He had for several weeks been corresponding with Grant about what his own next step should be. Sherman's proposal was to detach Thomas with two corps, plus the various Union garrisons in Tennessee, to deal with Hood while he, Sherman, took the remainder of his force, about sixty thousand men, on a march southeastward across nearly three hundred miles of Georgia to reach the sea at Savannah. Along the way, Sherman's troops would destroy factories, railroads, and public buildings and requisition food and livestock. The effect would be not only to destroy the South's logistical infrastructure but also to demoralize the white southerners in its path—as well as those who heard of it, including soldiers in the Confederate army far away in Virginia. "I can make this march," Sherman wrote to Grant, "and make Georgia howl."

In later generations, popular legend would have it that Sherman invented destructive warfare specially for use on this operation, and the claim would be taken up by some historians who ought to have known better. In fact, the practice of attacking an enemy's economy and infrastructure and thereby also his morale was as old as warfare, nor had it gone into disuse

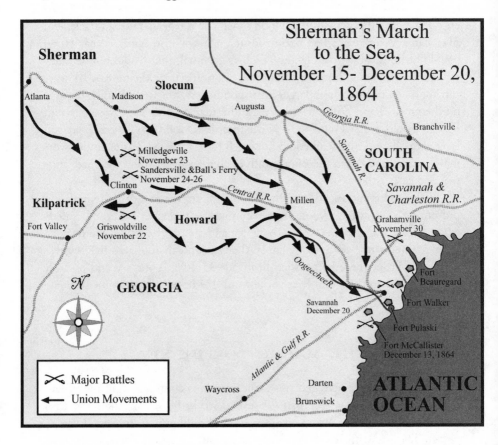

Sherman's March to the Sea, November 15- December 20, 1864

during the supposedly limited wars of the eighteenth century, much less those of the Napoleonic era. Such wars were certainly not limited in that way. All that Sherman proposed to do in Georgia was well within the existing laws and customs of war and not all that different, at least qualitatively, from what Lee and his army had practiced in Pennsylvania the preceding summer.

What was new and bold about Sherman's proposed operation was that it involved leaving an intact enemy army to his rear while marching his own army deep into the enemy's territory without any lines of supply or communication at all and on a scale of distance that would have been equivalent to Lee taking his army not merely to Gettysburg but all the way to New York City. True, Sherman had the advantage in numbers over Hood, but in an operation of this type, the more men he had, the sooner he would run out of supplies if enemy action should force him to halt. His army could continue living off the land only as long as it kept moving. To the trained military minds of the day, the plan seemed like asking to have his army trapped and captured. Grant was hesitant, but eventually his confidence in his old friend and faithful lieutenant prevailed, and he gave Sherman permission to go ahead.

On November 9 Sherman gave his army orders for the march, stating famously, "The army will forage liberally on the country during the march." He went on to state, however, that such gathering of foodstuffs was to be carried out by regularly organized foraging parties under the command of officers and that they were not to enter private dwellings or abuse civilians. The decision to burn a house, mill, or cotton gin was not to be made below the level of corps commander, and generally such destruction was to be reserved for neighborhoods in which overt acts of hostility—such as the burning of bridges—took place. Sherman told his men they could seize livestock as needed but admonished them, as in all their takings, to target the wealthy, slaveholding class and spare the poor and middling farmers.

The march began on November 15. Sherman had his men cut the telegraph wires and burn the railroads behind them as well as any installations of military usefulness left in Atlanta. Sherman's troops marched in two separate columns. As Sherman rode at the head of one of them that first day, he paused at the top of a rise and looked back at the smoke rising from Atlanta. He noticed that the troops marching past him were singing with one of the regimental bands the song "John Brown's Body." "John Brown's body lies amouldering in the grave," the lyrics repeated three times and then added, "His soul goes marching on." The tune was the same as that of "The Battle Hymn of the Republic," and the chorus had the same words. Sherman later reflected that he had never heard the words sung "with more spirit, or in better harmony of time and place."

For the most part, the troops obeyed Sherman's orders. They foraged so efficiently that the army never had to halt to gather supplies but continued its march at an average of about ten miles per day. Food was abundant, and the men ate well, afterward fondly remembering the hams and sweet potatoes of Georgia. Railroads, depots, factories, and the like went up in flames, as did the plantation house and outbuildings of Confederate cabinet member Howell Cobb but relatively few other private homes. A few soldiers fell out of ranks and foraged individually without orders. The troops referred to such men as bummers but later appropriated that name for all who had marched with Sherman. As in Sheridan's just concluded "Burning" in the Shenandoah Valley and all other Union operations in the South, peaceful civilians were safe from personal abuse or injury.

Sherman's troops tearing up railroad tracks in preparation for leaving Atlanta on their March to the Sea.

The march met little armed opposition. Hood had left his cavalry, under the command of Major General Joseph Wheeler, to harass Sherman, but Sherman's own cavalry was more than sufficient to keep Wheeler's horsemen well off the marching columns. Since the Confederate cavalrymen were also living off the land, the inhabitants of Georgia soon came to regard them as at least as bad a scourge as the passing Union army. Near Griswoldville, a division of Georgia militia composed mostly of middle-aged men and teen-aged boys attacked a brigade of Sherman's troops. Despite the militia's almost four-to-one advantage in numbers, experience proved to be the decisive factor, as the battle-hardened Union veterans easily repulsed the attack.

Near the town of Millen, one of Sherman's columns came upon one of

Ruins of the Atlanta railroad depot after Sherman's army left the city on its March to the Sea.

the infamous Confederate prison pens where thousands of Union prisoners of war had been cooped up inside a stockade, open to the weather, with neither tents nor adequate food. The Confederates had evacuated the place, but the mass graves as well as the emaciated corpses the Rebels had not had time to bury told the story all too plainly. Angry Union soldiers burned the town of Millen in retaliation.

Slaves welcomed the advancing Federals with demonstrations of joy that even the crusty Sherman found touching. Sherman was a racist in the abstract and sometimes said or wrote ugly things on the subject, but when he encountered blacks face-to-face, their humanity touched his, and always he treated them kindly. In conversations all along the march, he urged blacks to remain at their homes and await the imminent end of the war to give them freedom. In this daring raid deep into enemy territory, his army did not have the wherewithal to feed, shelter, or transport them. They would be safer, he urged, if they stayed put for now. But it was no use. Former slaves flocked after the army in long columns that trailed behind each of Sherman's corps, oblivious to prospects of food or shelter in their longing for freedom at the earliest possible moment.

Their presence led on at least one occasion to the sort of bad result that might be expected when masses of civilians followed an army deep in enemy territory. The march was nearing the coast when the Fourteenth Corps had to deploy its portable pontoon bridge to cross a broad stream known as Ebenezer Creek. Rumor had it that Confederate cavalry was shadowing the corps. If the corps commander left his pontoon bridge in place after the last of his soldiers got over, he ran the risk that the Confederates would capture or destroy it. That would trap his corps, which would then be unable to cross any of the remaining creeks and rivers that lay between it and the coast. No one could say how far the straggling column of fleeing slaves stretched out behind his last soldier. So he gave the order to take up the bridge. Blacks who had by then reached the bank panicked at the prospect of being returned to their contented way of life on the plantations and threw themselves into the creek, where a number of them drowned.

On December 10 Sherman's army reached the outskirts of Savannah, where Confederate Major General William J. Hardee held the fortifications with ten thousand men. On the thirteenth Sherman had one of his divisions storm outlying Fort McAllister. The assault lasted fifteen minutes, and when it was over the fort was in Union hands and the Ogeechee River open to the supply vessels and warships of the U.S. Navy, which had been cruising offshore awaiting Sherman's arrival. With a regular supply line and his men once more eating regular army rations of hardtack, salt pork, and beans, Sherman could take his time and besiege Hardee. Not relishing the prospect, the Confederate commander on December 20 withdrew into South Carolina before Sherman could close off that escape route. Sherman sent a telegram to Lincoln: "I beg to present you as a Christmas gift the City of Savannah, with one hundred and fifty guns and plenty of ammunition, also about twenty-five thousand bales of cotton."

HOOD'S TENNESSEE CAMPAIGN

While Sherman had marched through Georgia from Atlanta to the sea, Hood had proceeded with his preparations for a campaign into Tennessee. Logistical problems and poor planning delayed Hood's crossing of the Tennessee River until the third week of November, by which time Sherman had already left Atlanta behind and was deep in Georgia. Hood's army marched north from Florence, Alabama, on November 21. By that time Thomas, with his headquarters in Nashville, was well apprised of Hood's whereabouts and apparent intentions and had dispatched Schofield, whom Sherman had also detached for the defense of Tennessee, with two corps and orders to delay Hood's march. Schofield awaited Hood on the north bank of the Duck River near Columbia, Tennessee, squarely athwart the road to Nashville and about fifty miles south of the city.

Hood arrived on the south bank of the Duck at Columbia, and his troops skirmished with Schofield's. Well screened by Confederate cavalry commanded by Nathan Bedford Forrest, Hood on November 29 moved two of his three corps around Schofield's left and across the Duck east of Columbia. Before the Federal commander realized what was happening, most of Hood's army was bearing down on his line of communication and retreat near the village of Spring Hill, eleven miles north of Columbia. Around 3:00 that afternoon Schofield started his army marching north, out of Hood's trap, but the last of his units was not able to file out of the entrenchments along the Duck River until 10:00 that night.

Meanwhile, Hood's lead elements reached Spring Hill late that afternoon and skirmished with light Union forces guarding Schofield's line of communication. With their overwhelming advantage in numbers, the Confederates could easily have driven the Federals out of Spring Hill, capturing the town and thus cutting off Schofield's retreat. They could even more easily have moved directly against the Columbia Pike just south of Spring Hill, seizing the road and accomplishing the same purpose. Instead they did neither. The officer corps of the Confederacy's Army of Tennessee had never been characterized by mutual trust and cooperation but rather by backbiting, blame shifting, and a concern for protecting one's own record regardless of the consequences for the army or its mission. The result outside Spring Hill during the late afternoon and evening of November 29, 1864, was confusion and cross-purposes. Some officers thought their objective was the Columbia Pike. Others thought it was the town of Spring Hill itself and insisted that the movement against the pike be diverted in that direction. In the end, after indecisive skirmishing, they halted as darkness fell, just short of both objectives.

Hood arrived in person shortly thereafter, having ridden strapped to the saddle (because of his missing leg) since shortly after 3:00 that morning. Exhausted, he ordered a staff officer to find the two corps commanders and tell them to cooperate. Then, at about 9:00, he went to bed. About 2:00 in the morning Hood was awakened with a report that Union troops could just be seen somewhere out in front moving northward through the darkness, but Hood ignored the report and went back to sleep. North of Spring Hill Confederate cavalry patrols encountered Union supply wagons moving north along the road, but escorting Union infantry drove the Rebel horsemen back.

The next morning, November 30, Hood awoke to learn that during the night Schofield's entire army had marched up the Columbia Pike and through Spring Hill, passing along the front of the Confederate army within as little as a hundred yards of its outposts. Hood was, in the words of one of his officers, "as wrathy as a rattlesnake," and in a meeting with his generals that morning denounced them and their men as cowards. He ordered an immediate pursuit, and his army marched north, its generals enraged and humiliated.

They found Schofield at bay with his back to the Harpeth River at the town of Franklin, thirteen miles north of Spring Hill and about twenty miles south of Nashville. The Union commander had found the Harpeth River bridges badly damaged and needed time to repair them before he could continue his retreat. During previous operations in the area, Union troops had already built a substantial line of breastworks around the south side of Franklin, so Schofield put his troops into them, and into additional entrenchments they hastily dug, with orders to hold until the engineers could repair the bridges and the supply wagons were rolling toward Nashville again. Throughout the day the engineers made steady progress, and some of the wagons crossed via a nearby ford. With the bridges finished more wagons rolled north. Schofield was optimistic that by 6:00 p.m. he could pull all his troops back out of the entrenchments and evacuate the town, continuing his withdrawal to Nashville.

Hood and his unhappy army began arriving in front of the Union breastworks around 1:00 that afternoon and took up a position on Winstead Hill, about two miles south of town. Despite the absence of nearly a third of his infantry and most of his artillery, which had not caught up after diverting Schofield's attention on the south bank of the Duck during Hood's turning maneuver the previous day, Hood ordered an immediate all-out assault on the entrenched Federals.

Several of his generals protested the obvious folly of this course of action, and Forrest in particular claimed that with his cavalry plus a single division of infantry he could easily turn this position as they had turned Scho-field's position at Columbia. Hood, still seething from the affair at Spring Hill, would hear none of it and grimly insisted on the massed frontal assault. The sun would set around 4:30 that afternoon, and its rays were already steeply slanting as the twenty thousand Confederates advanced across the open plain two miles wide with colors flying while their bands played "Dixie" and "The Bonnie Blue Flag."

The assault should have had no chance of success at all. However, that afternoon the last Union division commander to bring his troops into the position, Brigadier General George D. Wagner, had mistaken his orders, possibly because, as some who were present later asserted, he was drunk, and had ordered his three brigades to take up a position straddling the Columbia Pike in the open field about half a mile in advance of the breastworks. Veteran brigade commander Colonel Emerson Opdyke had chosen simply to ignore his obviously addled division commander and had taken his brigade inside the breastworks, assuming a reserve position behind the point where the Columbia Pike entered the fortifications. Wagner's other two brigade commanders had obeyed orders and deployed in the hopeless position he had assigned.

Hood's troops deployed from column to line and swept forward, engulfing Wagner's two ill-fated brigades. Hundreds of Wagner's men surrendered, and the rest fled toward the main Union position, half a mile to the rear. The Confederates raced after them amid shouts of "Go into the works with them!" As the running mass of humanity neared the Union breastworks, the defenders held their fire rather than loose their volleys into the faces of their fleeing comrades. Yet the Confederates were only a few steps behind—in some cases almost among—Wagner's panting fugitives, and they surged over the works and swept the defenders back in a sector immediately on either side of the point where the Columbia Pike entered the lines. Opdyke led his brigade forward to fill the breach and drive back the Rebel penetration. Other Union troops rallied to join him. Hand-to-hand fighting raged around the buildings of the Carter plantation just inside Union lines. The Federals drove the Confederates back to the line of the breastworks, and then the two sides slugged it out across the parapet much as Lee and Grant's troops had done at the Bloody Angle of Spotsylvania though for a much shorter duration.

The fighting ceased after nightfall, and the Confederates who had been pinned down in front of the Union breastworks withdrew to a safer distance. In other sectors of the line the attack had made no headway at all, with the attackers being mowed down by the intense fire coming from the breastworks, where some of the defenders had repeating rifles. During the night, Schofield completed his withdrawal to the north bank of the Harpeth and continued his march to Nashville, leaving the town and battlefield to the Confederates, who took possession the next morning.

Hood's soldiers and Franklin civilians alike then busied themselves tending the 3,800 wounded and burying the more than 1,700 dead Rebels lying on the battlefield. Members of the Carter family found Captain Theodric "Tod" Carter of the Twentieth Tennessee Regiment lying badly wounded in front of the breastworks and brought him to the house that had been his boyhood home and the center of the previous evening's fiercest fighting. He died the next day, across the hall from the room in which he had been born, twenty-four years before.

In all, including missing and captured, Hood had lost more than 6,200 men. Among them were six generals killed or mortally wounded, seven more generals who would survive their wounds, and an additional general who was now on his way to Nashville as a prisoner of war—a loss of fourteen generals. Among the dead generals was Patrick R. Cleburne, widely believed, then and since, to be the best division commander in the Confederacy. In addition, Hood's army lost fifty-five regimental commanders. The Army of Tennessee was a wreck. Schofield's casualties, which had come mostly in Wagner's division and around the Carter house and outbuildings, numbered little more than one-third that many.

Since Schofield had left the battlefield in his hands, Hood claimed Franklin as a victory, though if Hood could have restrained his aggressiveness and perhaps his rage, Schofield would have been more than happy to have left Franklin and its environs to him without any battle at all. With little else to do in the wake of his Pyrrhic victory, Hood pursued Schofield to Nashville and encamped his army south of the town as if he could hope to besiege it with the thirty thousand or so men he still had left in the Army of Tennessee. Inside the extensive defenses of what was by then the most heavily fortified city on the continent other than Washington, D.C., Thomas by this time had some fifty-five thousand men. While Hood waited like Dickens's Mr.

Micawber for something to turn up, Thomas spent the next two weeks getting his army ready to take the offensive.

As day stretched into day of the odd standoff at Nashville, back in Virginia Grant grew concerned. He could see clearly that Hood's best move was not sitting in front of Nashville, where he could accomplish nothing but rather slipping past Thomas and setting off on a raid that might penetrate all the way to the Ohio River. Such a raid would be a desperate endeavor, but in the Confederacy's current state, as Grant's clear military insight perceived, no lesser effort made any sense for the Rebels. Though extremely unlikely to change the outcome of the war, such a raid could make a world of trouble for Grant, who feared that Hood might see as much and that any day Thomas might find his large army facing empty Confederate breastworks while Hood's army marched north bent on mischief. Grant sent Thomas one prodding message after another, each more pointed than the last, but nothing could budge the general whose army nickname was "Old Slow Trot."

On December 8 a heavy ice storm swept through Middle Tennessee, virtually paralyzing movement on roads or cross-country and ruling out an attack. Back in Virginia, Grant's impatience continued to mount. For him, the ice storm was just one more item in Thomas's long litany of reasons why he could not act promptly, and Grant had heard that song from Thomas before. On December 13 Grant decided he had waited long enough. John Logan, commander of the Fifteenth Corps in the Army of the Tennessee, happened to be on leave in Washington at the time, and Grant dispatched him to Nashville with orders to relieve Thomas and take command in Nashville unless Thomas had launched an attack by the time he arrived. Logan had no sooner started on his journey than Grant decided that nothing but his own presence would suffice and prepared to set out for Nashville himself.

In the end, neither man made the trip. Grant had not started and Logan had not gone far when word arrived that Thomas had finally launched his long-awaited attack against Hood. On Thomas's orders, two divisions of the U.S. Colored Troops, whose enlisted ranks were composed entirely of former slaves, advanced before dawn on December 15 and opened the battle with a diversionary attack on the Confederate right. Thomas's main attack struck the Confederate left and drove it back throughout the afternoon. The early end of a mid-December day gave Hood respite to regroup his army on higher ground about two miles to the rear of the position he had tried to hold that day. He anchored his new line on Shy's Hill on the left and Overton Hill on the right. It was a more compact position than the previous one, which was a necessity for his by now badly depleted army.

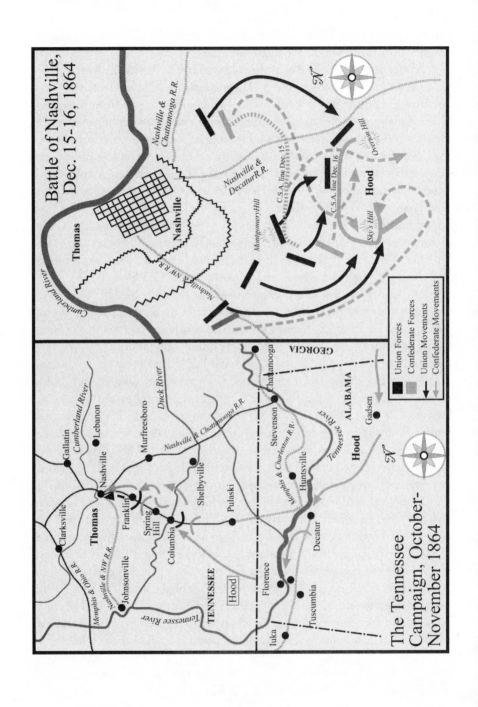

Battle of Nashville, Dec. 15-16, 1864

Cumberland River
Nashville & Chattanooga R.R.
Nashville
Thomas
Nashville & Decatur R.R.
Nashville & NW R.R.
C.S.A. line Dec. 15
C.S.A. line Dec. 16
Montgomery Hill
Overton Hill
Shy's Hill
Hood

Union Forces
Confederate Forces
Union Movements
Confederate Movements

The Tennessee Campaign, October-November 1864

Gallatin
Cumberland River
Lebanon
Clarksville
Nashville
Thomas
Franklin
Spring Hill
Columbia
Johnsonville
Memphis & Ohio R.R.
Nashville & NW R.R.
TENNESSEE
Tennessee River
Iuka
Florence
Tuscumbia
Decatur
Huntsville
Memphis & Charleston R.R.
Stevenson
Tennessee River
Gadsen
ALABAMA
Hood
GEORGIA
Chattanooga
Nashville & Chattanooga R.R.
Duck River
Murfreesboro
Shelbyville
Pulaski
Hood

Thomas renewed the assault the next day. His troops spent the morning hours moving up to confront Hood's new position. Then the attack once again opened against the Confederate left, followed by an even stronger Union assault against the right on Shy's Hill. After several hours of fighting, the Confederate lines crumbled on Shy's Hill, and then Hood's entire army collapsed. What had been a battle became a footrace, as individual Confederate soldiers sought to escape the pursuing Federals.

Once again early nightfall came to Hood's rescue, along with the onset of a steady rain. The Army of Tennessee regrouped again, this time to begin its long, weary trek out of its namesake state. In the days that followed, Union forces did their best to harass the retreat, which was ably screened by Forrest's cavalry and the ongoing spell of cold, rainy weather. The Battle of Nashville cost Thomas a total of about three thousand casualties and Hood twice that many. Three-quarters of the soldiers Hood lost at Nashville were missing or captured. Continuing his retreat through northern Alabama, Hood on Christmas Day crossed back to the south bank of the Tennessee River with roughly half of the thirty-six thousand men he had taken with him bound north little more than a month before. Three weeks later Hood formally asked to be relieved of command, and Davis promptly complied.

THE FALL OF FORT FISHER AND
THE LAST BID FOR A
NEGOTIATED PEACE

In the wake of Hood's crushing defeat in Tennessee and Sherman's capture of Savannah as the culmination of his March to the Sea, heavy blows rained down on the nearly prostrate Confederacy, and it hardly seemed to matter if one of them failed to land squarely. In that same month of December 1864, Union forces attempted to take Fort Fisher, a powerful Confederate bastion guarding the approaches to Wilmington, North Carolina, the last major southern port open to blockade-runners. Because the operation lay technically within Ben Butler's department, Grant had to allow that dismal political general to direct it, and the predictable result was failure. On December 27, Butler's troops reembarked on the powerful fleet of transports and warships that had brought them and returned to their bases.

Disgusted with Butler's performance and convinced that the political situation had now progressed to the point that this particular ambitious politician in uniform was no longer needed, Grant sacked Butler and ordered a new expedition against Fort Fisher, to depart immediately, this time under the command of Major General Alfred H. Terry. Like Butler, the thirty-eight-year-old Terry had been a lawyer without military background before the war. Unlike Butler, he had not been a politician and had started the war not as a general but rather as colonel of a regiment he had recruited. Several battles and two promotions later, Terry was a competent commander. Once again Rear Admiral David Dixon Porter and the strength of the Navy's North Atlantic Blockading Squadron would be on hand to support the assault with four monitors, the ironclad steam frigate USS *New Ironsides*, three of the fifty-gun steam frigates that had been the pride of the fleet when the war began, and more than fifty other warships.

Terry landed his troops on January 13. Two days later, under cover of the heaviest naval bombardment ever fired in American waters, the assault went in. A naval landing party composed of two thousand sailors and marines staged a direct assault across the beach against the fort's eastern, or sea, face, distracting the defenders' attention, while the nine thousand army troops launched the main attack against the fort's northern face. They fought their way into the fort and then fought their way through its multiple three-walled bays as the Confederates bitterly defended every inch of the fort. The battle lasted eight hours, and the two top-ranking Confederate officers were incapacitated by wounds before the fort was finally securely in Union hands.

With Fort Fisher lost, so too was the port of Wilmington as a haven for blockade-runners. That meant a final end to foreign manufactured war supplies for the Confederacy, including British Enfield rifles and Whitworth cannon. It even exacerbated the already dismal food supply situation for Lee's army, a strange development in view of the fact that the Confederacy was still full of food, as Sherman had just demonstrated and was about to demonstrate again. So wrecked was the Confederacy's transportation system that it was sometimes easier to feed Lee's troops by importing foreign food through Wilmington rather than moving abundant domestic produce up from points farther south. With Wilmington closed, Lee's scarecrow soldiers would have to take in their belts another notch.

Despite the steady drumbeat of military disasters, Davis would not even consider any negotiated peace agreement that did not begin with a clear acceptance of Confederate independence. Given Davis's known stubbornness, that fact was not really as surprising as the very fact that the opportunity for a negotiated peace still existed with the Confederacy nearing complete collapse. Indeed, Lincoln had not initially thought the prospect was worth the effort. As early as his December 1863 address to Congress on Reconstruction, in which he had spelled out his Ten Percent Plan, Lincoln had opined that nothing was to be gained by talks with Davis since "the insurgent leader," as Lincoln carefully styled him, had made clear on many occasions that he believed it his duty to accept nothing less than independence. Talks with Davis or with his emissaries would therefore be pointless, and the only hope lay in persuading the southern people to make peace without Davis and his administration.

Near the end of 1864 the intervention of two unusual men changed that. *New York Tribune* editor Horace Greeley had noticed that a peace movement of sorts existed within the Confederacy. Weak, scattered, disorganized, and diverse in its motivations and proposals, the Confederate peace movement included such men as North Carolina newspaper editor William Holden and Confederate Vice President Alexander H. Stephens. Like the peace movement in the North, these men generally claimed, perhaps disingenuously, that the chief national war aim, in this case, independence, could be achieved through an immediate cease-fire followed by negotiations. As war weariness grew and the Confederacy visibly tottered toward its ruin, the presence of such a peace movement became an increasing threat to Jefferson Davis and his determination to fight to the bitter end and beyond.

Greeley saw in this an opportunity and on December 15 suggested to Francis Preston Blair Sr., former adviser to the late President Andrew Jackson, that he should go to Davis with a half-baked proposal for the Union and the Confederacy to stop fighting each other and jointly turn on the French in Mexico. After they had whipped the forces of Napoleon III, concluding a formal peace agreement between North and South would presumably follow easily. Blair took the matter to Davis on January 12. The concept was the brightest glimmer for independence that the Confederate president had seen in some time, so he readily gave Blair a letter to Lincoln offering to appoint commissioners to a conference for the purpose of "securing peace to the two countries."

Blair brought the letter to Lincoln. The president dismissed the absurd notion of the Mexican gambit but, eager to try any realistic possibility of ending the bloodshed sooner, thought the idea of a peace conference sounded interesting. He gave Blair a letter, dated January 18, expressing his willingness to meet with whatever commissioners Davis might appoint "with the view of securing peace to the people of our one common country." Three days later Blair was in Richmond meeting with Davis. The Confederate president did not like Lincoln's reference to "one common country" and seized on an off-

hand suggestion of Blair's about settling the war through a military conference between Grant and Lee. Maybe Grant could be persuaded in the name
of soldierly camaraderie to give up essential Union war aims. Lincoln quickly
extinguished even that forlorn hope by immediately nixing the idea of any
such military conference.

That left Davis nothing but to appoint peace commissioners. He
shrewdly chose Stephens to lead the mission since it would almost inevitably
demonstrate the hollowness of the claims of the Confederate peace movement that peace could be had without reunion. Having the most visible leader
of the peace movement heading the delegation would discredit the peace
movement that much more. To accompany Stephens, Davis chose Confederate secretary of war (and former associate justice of the U.S. Supreme Court)
John A. Campbell and president pro tem of the Confederate senate, Robert
M. T. Hunter. Davis, on January 28, 1865, gave them a written commission
to meet with Lincoln "for the purpose of securing peace to the two countries."

That wording nearly got them turned back when they tried to pass
through Union lines under a flag of truce, but Grant intervened to let them
through anyway. They met with Lincoln and Secretary of State William H.
Seward on February 3 on board the steamboat *River Queen* on the body of
water called Hampton Roads at the mouth of the James River. The meeting
opened with pleasantries about Lincoln's and Stephens's former associations
in the old Whig Party, but when it turned to business the predictable impasse
arose immediately as Lincoln explained that peace was possible only with
reunion. Stephens brought up the Mexican business, but Lincoln dismissed
it. Campbell asked what terms the southern states could expect in case of
reunion at that time, and Lincoln replied that he would be as lenient as possible and would urge Congress to provide compensation to the former slaveholders for their lost human chattels.

Asked about such things as the continued existence of West Virginia or
the ongoing validity of the Emancipation Proclamation, Lincoln replied that
the courts would decide such things. This he could do since he had recently
replaced the late Chief Justice Roger B. Taney with the old-line abolitionist
Salmon P. Chase. He advised Stephens to go home and take Georgia out of
the Union and then have it ratify the recently introduced Thirteenth Amendment, which would end slavery throughout the United States. The Confederate vice president would do nothing of the sort. Carp as Stephens might
against the Davis administration, he lacked nerve for so bold a step. After
four hours the conference ended, and the members took their leave of one
another.

When the Confederate commissioners returned to Richmond, Davis skillfully exploited the outcome of the Hampton Roads Conference as proof that Lincoln would grant them no peace without their "submission," a term unspeakably odious to a ruling class comprised of slaveholders. Davis invoked the verbal imagery of slavery in an opposite sense in a fiery and impassioned speech at a mass meeting attended by an estimated ten thousand citizens in Richmond a few days later. The Confederacy would, Davis promised, "teach the insolent enemy who had treated our proposition with contumely in that conference in which he had so plumed himself with arrogance, [that] he [Lincoln] was, indeed talking to his masters." Even Davis's political enemies within the Confederacy had to confess that it had been "the most remarkable speech of his life," and Stephens, attending the meeting despite his despair, called the speech "brilliant," though he thought Davis "demented." Nothing more was heard from the Confederate peace movement. Confederate morale rose as reports of the conference and of Davis's remarks were read throughout the South. Even recently ravaged Georgia experienced a revival of fighting spirit, as southern whites rallied behind their president to follow the dream of a slaveholders' republic to its conclusion in blood and fire.[2]

13

"LET US STRIVE ON TO FINISH THE WORK"

SHERMAN'S CAROLINAS CAMPAIGN

Meanwhile, 450 miles to the south of Richmond in Savannah, Georgia, Sherman had been contemplating his next move and corresponding with Grant about the possibilities. Grant initially wanted Sherman to leave an adequate garrison in Savannah and ship the rest of his force by sea to join Grant in Virginia, but Sherman pointed out that it would take months to assemble the necessary shipping to transport his sixty thousand men to Virginia. As an alternative, he proposed to march his force north more than four hundred miles through the Carolinas and southern Virginia to join Grant outside Petersburg. Along the way his troops would wreak the sort of infrastructure damage they had done in Georgia and demoralize the civilian population. Grant gave his approval.

Sherman's troops were more than ready for such an operation. Their letters and diaries were virtually unanimous in expressing their longing to visit South Carolina. There secession had been born, and because of secession these men had spent the past three or four years living the hard life of soldiers and seeing many of their comrades killed or maimed. Many wrote during the weeks in Savannah of the debt they owed the Palmetto State and were eager to repay. The soldiers had been on their best behavior in Savannah, but Sherman knew it would be different once they crossed into South Carolina. "I almost tremble for [South Carolina]," he wrote, "but feel she deserves all that seems in store for her."

On February 1, two days before Lincoln and Seward met with the Confederate commissioners at Hampton Roads, Sherman's troops began their advance. As in Georgia they marched in two separate wings. The right was the Army of the Tennessee under Howard, comprised of the Fifteenth and Seventeenth corps. The left, newly named the Army of Georgia, was commanded by Henry W. Slocum and composed of the Fourteenth and Twentieth corps. This was to be a much different campaign than the previous one however. The March to the Sea had occurred in a season when good weather was to be expected and had enjoyed mostly good weather. The Carolinas Campaign would be carried out in the rainiest season of the year and would lead right through the low-country swamps. Whereas the campaign in Georgia had generally paralleled the major streams, that in the Carolinas would run perpendicular to all the rivers in those states. The troops would lay scores of miles of corduroy road to accommodate their wagons and would wade hip deep in cold water for miles at a time crossing the flooded swamps.

The Carolinas Campaign also differed from the March to the Sea in that regular Confederate troops attempted to oppose Sherman's march through the Carolinas. On February 3 a Confederate division of 1,200 men took advantage of overwhelming terrain advantages in trying to stop the Seventeenth Corps from crossing the Salkehatchie Swamp. Two brigades of Federals waded the swamp, sometimes under Confederate fire, and then outflanked the Rebels, forcing them to retreat. The same pattern was repeated again and again as Sherman's supremely confident veterans overcame natural barriers and steadily increasing numbers of Confederates with seeming ease. Joseph Johnston later wrote that when he heard of the progress of Sherman's men through the South Carolina swamps in winter, driving Confederate defenders before them, he became convinced that "there had been no such army since the days of Julius Caesar."

As anticipated, the soldiers destroyed much property in South Carolina. Besides feeding themselves and their draft animals on the produce of the land and also constantly renewing their stock of draft animals at the expense of the farms they passed, they burned many more houses than they had in Georgia. An occupied house was usually safe, but most South Carolinians had fled, leaving their houses empty and thus consigning them to the flames. Even in South Carolina the soldiers did not kill, rape, or otherwise abuse civilians. Day by day Union foraging parties ranged for miles on either side of the army, gathering food supplies and skirmishing with Confederate troops as

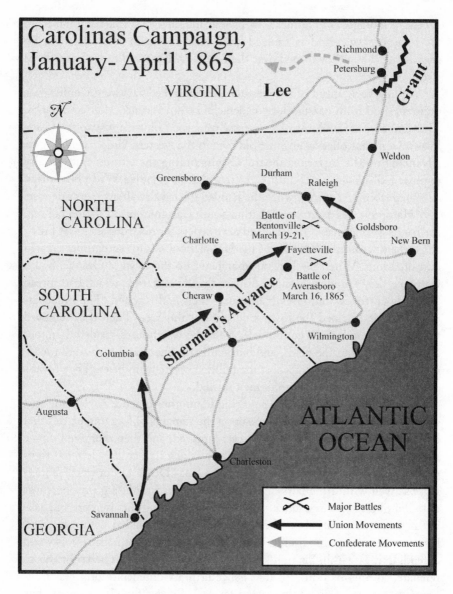

Carolinas Campaign, January- April 1865

necessary. Foragers sometimes took over abandoned grist mills and ran them for a day or two, grinding foraged grain until the main column caught up with them. Then they turned over their stock of flour and ranged out ahead again.

Falling back ahead of the steadily advancing Federals were Confederate units released from coastal duty or detached from various other commands. The remnants of the Army of Tennessee were soon on their way to the Carolinas to confront once again their old foes in the western Union armies, now advancing up the eastern seaboard. Commanding the Confederate cavalry opposing Sherman was South Carolina planter grandee Wade Hampton, detached from Lee's army, where he had led the cavalry after Stuart's demise.

Hampton was determined that no South Carolina cotton should fall into the hands of Sherman's Yankees and gave orders for his troopers to set fire to all stocks of cotton in advance of the Union troops. This sometimes created odd situations. When the Federals marched into the town of Orange, South Carolina, they found its business district already in flames, which had spread from the cotton warehouses Hampton's men had torched. The bluecoats pitched in and helped the townsmen put out the fires. Then they removed the remaining unburned cotton bales from the warehouses, hauled them out a safe distance into the fields, and burned them. Sherman's men were traveling light and could not transport the bulky, heavy cotton bales. They invariably burned any that Hampton's men missed.

But Hampton's men were engaging in another practice far less innocuous. Sherman's men began to come upon the remains of foraging parties that had been surrounded by superior forces, captured, and then murdered. Some had their throats cut. Others were hanged. Many had crudely lettered signs placed on or with them with statements such as "Death to Foragers." Foraging was well within the laws and customs of war. Murdering prisoners was not, and Sherman sent a letter to Hampton protesting the murders and asking if they were officially authorized. Hampton responded with a letter of his own, admitting that murdering prisoners was now his official policy and defending it as within his rights. The only way to stop such behavior was to retaliate, so Sherman ordered that henceforth a Confederate prisoner in his army's possession face a firing squad for each forager found murdered. The Federals carried out that grim step precisely once. The Rebel prisoner who drew the short straw was a middle-aged man, the father of several children, and had recently been conscripted. Thereafter no further retaliation took place, and Hampton's men went on murdering captured Federals literally up until the final days of the war.

On February 17 Sherman's troops marched into Columbia, the capital of South Carolina, past smoldering piles of half-burned cotton that Hampton's troopers had at least dragged into the streets before torching. That night high winds rose and fanned the heaps into flame, which spread to nearby buildings. Some of the Union soldiers had become drunk on liquor they found in the city and were determined to burn Columbia, as were some of their entirely sober comrades. Nor were they the only ones bent on conflagration that night. By many accounts, recently freed slaves as well as escaped prisoners from another of the infamous Confederate prison pens that had, until a few days before, been just outside of town, also engaged in setting fires, which sprang up at dozens of locations around the city.

Thousands of Union soldiers participated in the battle to fight the fires that night, both in units assigned to the task and as volunteers who hurried in from their camps outside of town. Meanwhile, some of their comrades with opposite intentions cut fire hoses and otherwise hindered the efforts to fight the fires. When the wind finally shifted and the fires went out, about one-third of Columbia, chiefly the business district, was in ashes or smoldering ruins. Among the relatively small number of residences to burn was Wade Hampton's palatial mansion, one of several he owned. First Baptist Church, scene of the convention that had declared South Carolina's secession almost four years before, escaped the flames. According to legend, the church's groundskeeper misdirected vengeance-minded Union soldiers to a nearby Methodist church instead.

Over the days that followed, the Federals methodically destroyed everything of military value in Charleston and then, on February 20, having left adequate food supplies for the population, marched north. As Sherman's soldiers marched away from the still-smoldering ruins of downtown Columbia, many soldiers speculated as to who or what had started the fire, but few if any would lose sleep over it. Whether they had fought the flames or lit them, Sherman's soldiers were unanimous in their belief that the fire had been a just retribution for South Carolina's sins.

On February 17, the same day Sherman's troops marched into Columbia, Confederate forces, threatened by Sherman's advance with the prospect of being cut off along the coast, evacuated Fort Sumter. The Union forces on the coast, which had been besieging and bombarding the fort for more than a year and a half, took possession of both the fort and the city of Charleston without opposition. With that, the place where Confederates had, almost four years before, fired the first shots of the war was back in Union hands.

On March 7 Sherman's troops crossed into North Carolina. They continued to forage, as they had to in order to eat, but the extraneous house burning ceased the moment they crossed the state line. On March 23 Sherman's columns reached Goldsboro, North Carolina, where they linked up with Schofield and his thirty thousand men. Transported by the navy to the Union-held coastal enclave on the North Carolina coast, Schofield's army advanced to Goldsboro to reinforce and resupply Sherman, whose force now totaled more than ninety thousand men. From Goldsboro it was less than 150 miles to Grant's and Lee's positions around Petersburg and Richmond.

Sherman's two great campaigns through the interior of the South, first through Georgia and then through the Carolinas, were enormously important in weakening both the ability and the will of the southern people to carry on a hopeless fight. The very fact that Sherman was able to march his troops hundreds of miles through the interior of what purported to be the Confederacy, seemingly unhindered by any efforts of the Confederate army, was evidence of the helplessness of the slaveholders' republic. The marches did enormous damage to the Confederacy's continued ability to support armies in the field, destroying warehouses, depots, stockpiles, factories, and hundreds of miles of railroad track.

More important, the mere presence of Sherman's troops, even though they did not abuse civilians—perhaps all the more because they did not abuse civilians—demoralized Confederates all across the South and especially in the Confederacy's armies. For southern boys who had given little thought to the issues of the war and enlisted simply to keep the Yankees out of their home counties, the presence of Union troops back home, methodically destroying factories and railroads and confiscating much of the food and livestock, was proof that the war was already lost. A steady trickle of desertion in Lee's army rose steadily throughout the fall and winter months. One study of a Georgia regiment in Lee's army revealed that the desertion rate in each company of the regiment was directly proportional to the amount of time Sherman's troops spent in that company's home county. More than the fall of Fort Fisher or even the operations around Petersburg, Sherman's marches tore the heart out of the Confederacy and hastened the end of the war.

Sherman's campaigns were also evidence that Union forces had by this time so dominated the Confederacy's western armies as to overrun all of the South east of the Mississippi, except for the part of Virginia between Richmond and the Blue Ridge. Now the main striking power of the Union's western armies was advancing northward, along the eastern seaboard, and was about to invade Virginia from the south. In a grand strategic sense the movement of the Union's western armies had been a right-wing left wheel on a continental scale. On the right end of the Union line and thus the outside edge of that enormous left wheel, Grant's own Army of the Tennessee had started out from Cairo, Illinois, at the beginning of the war; had advanced down the Mississippi Valley all the way to Vicksburg and beyond; had moved east to help secure Chattanooga and take Atlanta, then farther southeast to the Atlantic coast at Savannah; and finally moved north toward Virginia and the last enclave of the rebellion. Lee might continue to hold Richmond and its environs, but in the heartland of the Confederacy, where the really decisive action had taken place, the war was already over except for minor mopping-up operations.

CONFEDERATE DESPERATION
AND THE DECISION TO ENLIST
BLACK TROOPS

Desperation steadily increased inside the Confederate capital. In the press and elsewhere in Richmond, many complained bitterly of what they saw as the mismanagement of the war. In late January the dissatisfaction boiled up to the point that the Virginia state legislature passed a resolution calling for a wholesale cabinet shake-up. The real target of the criticism was Jefferson Davis, who had throughout the war maintained rigorous personal control of every decision. The censure was most galling for Secretary of War James A. Seddon, a Virginian and a capable administrator whose office nevertheless associated him most closely, second to Davis at any rate, with all that was going badly for the Confederacy. Humiliated by the censure of his home state's legislature, Seddon resigned on February 1. To replace him Davis chose former U.S. vice president, 1860 presidential candidate, and, more recently, Confederate general John C. Breckinridge.

The Confederate congress was also in a mood to clip the president's wings and in that frame of mind passed legislation creating the position of general in chief of the Confederate armies. The act was tailored to win Davis's acceptance, providing that the general in chief was to serve under the president's command, but the clear intent was to have someone else making the decisions that would guide the Confederate war effort. Even more clearly, the man the legislators had in mind was Lee. Davis signed the bill into law January 23 and on February 6 named Lee to fill it and to continue to serve as commander of the Army of Northern Virginia. The Confederate senate promptly approved the nomination. One of Lee's first actions as general in chief was to persuade Davis to return Joseph Johnston to command, this time in charge of the Confederate forces attempting to impede Sherman's northward march through the Carolinas. Davis reluctantly acquiesced, comforting himself with the reflection that perhaps with Lee to supervise him, Johnston would do better than he had in the past.

Desperate as might have been the step of reinstating Johnston, the Confederate president was prepared to go even farther. By early 1865 Davis was willing to consider sacrificing the institution of slavery if that was the price of survival. It was one of the strange ironies of war that white southerners who had set out to overthrow national authority in order to protect slavery were now willing to abandon slavery in order to resist national authority. Yet the Confederacy's shortage of manpower had become so acute as to suggest the hitherto unthinkable expedient of placing rifles in the hands of slaves and using them as soldiers.

Among the first to broach the idea, a year before Davis openly embraced it, was Army of Tennessee division commander Patrick R. Cleburne, who in January read a paper on the subject to his fellow generals of that army in its winter camp near Dalton, Georgia. The Irish-born-and-raised Cleburne may not have understood fully the visceral depth of the issue of slavery in the South. Some of his listeners that evening had gone away in stunned horror, most of the rest in a towering rage. Apprised of the event, Davis ordered it hushed up.

Now, more than a year later, with Cleburne in his grave not far from Franklin, Tennessee, the situation had become sufficiently desperate that the Confederate president had come around to the late general's point of view. "It is now becoming daily more evident to all reflecting persons," he wrote early in 1865, "that we are reduced to choosing whether the negroes shall fight for us or against us." Many others agreed with Davis. As early as October 6, 1864, the *Richmond Examiner* had come out in favor of enlisting slaves as Confederate soldiers. Others disagreed strongly despite the Confederacy's obviously desperate plight. Former Confederate cabinet member Howell Cobb of Georgia summed up their view when he astutely noted, "The day you make soldiers of them is the beginning of the end of the [Confederacy]. If slaves will make good soldiers our whole theory of slavery is wrong."[1]

Nevertheless, after intense debate the Confederate house of representatives on February 20, 1865, passed an act for the enlistment of slave soldiers. The Confederate senate approved the bill on March 13 by a one-vote margin, and Davis promptly signed it. A key factor in its passage was Lee's known advocacy of the use of black soldiers. The new law provided that slaves could be freed only with the consent both of their owners and of their home states. Davis, who at Lee's urging lost no time in implementing the act, therefore enlisted only those slaves whose masters volunteered them for service and subsequent emancipation. By the end of March, Confederate officers had enrolled two companies, or about two hundred black soldiers, though they had not yet issued them rifles. By that time, the U.S. government had fielded some two hundred thousand black troops.

LINCOLN'S SECOND INAUGURAL

The month of March also saw Abraham Lincoln's inauguration to a second term as president of the United States. As the Constitution provided in those days, the event took place on March 4 and, by custom, on a platform erected in front of the East Portico of the Capitol. The weather had been rainy of late, as was seasonable, and the day began under overcast skies. The sun broke through the clouds just as Lincoln stepped to the podium to give one of the most eloquent speeches of his remarkable career of public speaking. After briefly alluding to the path that had taken the nation into civil war and to the prayers of both sides to the same God, beseeching that the war might be avoided or that it might be quickly won, Lincoln concluded,

> The prayers of both could not be answered. That of neither has been answered fully. The Almighty has His own purposes. "Woe unto the world because of offenses; for it must needs be that offenses come, but woe to that man by whom the offense cometh." If we shall suppose that American slavery is one of those offenses which, in the providence of God, must needs come, but which, having continued through His appointed time, He now wills to remove, and that He gives to both North and South this terrible war as the woe due to those by whom the offense came, shall we discern therein any departure from those divine attributes which the believers in a living God always ascribe to Him? Fondly do we hope, fervently do we pray, that this mighty scourge of war may speedily pass away. Yet, if God wills that it continue until all the wealth piled by the bondsman's two hundred and fifty years of unrequited toil shall be sunk, and until every drop of blood drawn with the lash shall be paid by another drawn with the sword, as was said three thousand years ago, so still it must be said "the judgments of the Lord are true and righteous altogether."
>
> With malice toward none, with charity for all, with firmness in the right

as God gives us to see the right, let us strive on to finish the work we are in, to bind up the nation's wounds, to care for him who shall have borne the battle and for his widow and his orphan, to do all which may achieve and cherish a just and lasting peace among ourselves and with all nations.[2]

It was the shortest, most powerful, and most overtly religious inaugural address in the nation's history, and it came from a president who was so reticent about his own religion that the personal beliefs of this, the most intensively studied historical figure in America's past, remain a mystery. He had long since rejected the hard-shell Baptist faith of his parents and had been an atheist or an agnostic in his youth. In the 1850s he had come to believe in God's existence and seemed to be seeking, but what, if anything, he found, remains unknown. Through it all, the doctrinaire predestinationism of his Calvinist upbringing lingered in his thinking in the form of a vague fatalism, something he called "the doctrine of necessity." Man had no free will, he thought, but rather thought and did as some power, or Power, ordained he should think and do. Yet Lincoln did not act or speak consistently with that belief. In this, the most fatalistic of his public speeches, he nevertheless urged his listeners to have "firmness in the right as God gives us to see the right" and exhorted them to "strive on to finish the work we are in."

THE BATTLE OF FIVE FORKS AND THE FALL OF RICHMOND

Robert E. Lee was under no illusions as to the direction in which the war was trending. Grant's repeated probes and stabs as part of his quasi siege of Petersburg and Richmond were steadily stretching and sapping the Army of Northern Virginia. So too was the steady—and growing—trickle of desertions. Lee knew that his army was rapidly approaching the point at which it could not stretch any farther or hold its lines any longer. He believed the Confederacy's only remaining military option was for the Army of Northern Virginia to slip free of Grant's grasp, abandoning Richmond, and head south to link up with Johnston's small army in North Carolina. The combined Confederate armies would then defeat first Sherman and then Grant. In fact, this was the most forlorn of hopes. Even before Schofield reinforced Sherman, the latter's command would still have been roughly equal to the total number of troops remaining in the ranks of Lee's and Johnston's armies. Nevertheless, the plan was the only card left to play. Early in March Lee notified

Lincoln near the end of the war.

Davis, and the president accepted the fact that they would soon have to give up Richmond.

Down in North Carolina, Johnston on March 19 launched his first major offensive operation since the Battle of Fair Oaks, just outside Richmond almost three years before. With Sherman's forces advancing on a broad front that almost invited attack, Johnston took the bait and struck at Slocum's army near Bentonville, North Carolina. The Confederates scored some limited initial success, but then Sherman's veterans rallied and held their own. Howard's Army of the Tennessee moved in to support its comrades in Slocum's army, and had Johnston lingered a little longer before retreating or had Sherman possessed a bit more of the killer instinct, the Confederate army in North Carolina might have reached its demise there and then. As it was, in the three days of sporadic fighting, Johnston's army suffered more than 2,600 casualties to scarcely more than 1,500 Union losses.

Back up in Virginia Lee planned to attack a Union bastion named Fort Stedman, located along Grant's lines just east of Petersburg. If the attack was successful, Grant might have to pull back his left wing, which now extended ten miles to the southwest of Petersburg, in order to shore up his broken lines east of town. That would give Lee the opportunity to take his army and slip around the Union left to head for North Carolina and the hoped-for rendezvous with Johnston.

Lee entrusted the job to Major General John B. Gordon, now commanding the Second Corps of the Army of Northern Virginia. Gordon planned the operation meticulously, and the Confederates launched their assault in the predawn darkness at 4:15 a.m., March 25. Initially they had things all their own way, surprising the defenders and overrunning Fort Stedman and several smaller neighboring works. Then the attack bogged down in the disorganization that always followed the storming of defenses. Union artillery took the captured fort under heavy fire, and then a Union counterattack swept back over the captured positions, sending the surviving Confederate attackers fleeing back across no-man's-land under deadly fire of rifles and artillery.

It was over by 8:00 that morning. Union casualties totaled about one thousand, Confederate about four times that many. Union reserves in that sector had easily repulsed the brief penetration, and Grant had had no need to shift any troops from other sectors. Lincoln arrived at Grant's headquarters later that morning and mentioned the Battle of Fort Stedman in a cable he sent to Secretary of War Stanton informing him of his safe arrival: "There was a little rumpus up the line this morning, ending about where it began." Such was the impact the Army of Northern Virginia made in its last great offensive.

Grant had been planning an offensive of his own, to be led by Sheridan and aimed once again at the right flank of the Confederate position around Petersburg, aiming as always toward cutting the rail lines southwest of Petersburg. Along with his cavalry, Sherman would also have the Fifth Corps. His troops moved out on March 29, swinging well to the southwest, beyond the ends of both side's entrenchments. They clashed that first day with Confederate forces patrolling the roads and drove the Rebels back. The next day, however, saw heavy rain that turned the roads to quagmires, slowing the march. While Sheridan's men slogged through the mud, Lee recognized the threat and shifted George Pickett's division of infantry from the other end of the line out to a position to counter Sheridan. He also reinforced Pickett with the cavalry division of Major General W. H. F. Lee, the son of Robert E. Lee.

On the last day of March, Pickett's command met Sheridan's advance near Dinwiddie Court House. Though he suffered twice as many casualties as the Federals, Pickett managed to halt Sheridan's advance and even drive the blue-jacketed troopers back a short distance. Union mistakes and unfamiliarity with the lay of the land and the location of the Confederate positions were helpful to Pickett in that day's fighting. That night Pickett learned that a large formation of Union infantry (the Fifth Corps) was moving up from the east in support of Sheridan's cavalry. Fearing that he would be flanked, Pickett ordered his men to fall back from their position northwest of Dinwiddie Court House.

Learning of Pickett's withdrawal, Lee (the father) was displeased. Dinwiddie lay only about eight miles from the vital Southside Railroad, and Pickett's force was all Lee could spare for the vital task of keeping Sheridan away from the tracks. Though Pickett had planned to fall back to a position behind Hatcher's Run, scarcely a mile and a half from the railroad, Lee recognized that if Sheridan gained control of the key road junction known as Five Forks, three miles from the Southside, he would be in a position from which it would be almost impossible to prevent him from breaking the railroad. Lee therefore sent Pickett orders to entrench in front of the key intersection and "hold Five Forks at all hazards."

Pickett obeyed, and his men spent the morning of All Fools' Day digging in just south of the crossroads. By the middle of the day, Pickett felt confident enough in the strength of his position and doubtful enough as to whether Sherman would persevere in the operation after the check he had received the day before to accept an invitation from several of his fellow officers to attend a shad bake two miles to the rear. When he went, he neglected to inform subordinates of his absence, leaving his command effectively leaderless. While Pickett and his hosts enjoyed their meal of fish, Sheridan, having finally overcome the difficult terrain, struck hard at the position around Five Forks. As the Confederate lines crumbled, Pickett failed to hear the roar of battle, apparently because of unfavorable atmospheric conditions. By the time he returned to his command, it was reeling back in headlong retreat, and Sheridan held Five Forks.

Notified later that evening of the results of the fighting around Five Forks, Grant immediately recognized its significance. He ordered every cannon and mortar along the whole length of his lines to open fire on the Confederate positions and keep firing all through the night. At dawn Grant's infantry surged forward in a mass assault all along the front. The badly thinned Confederate lines broke in multiple places. Hurrying to a breach in his own sector, Confederate corps commander A. P. Hill encountered the advancing Union troops, who shot him dead. Elsewhere Confederate defenders clung tenaciously to several key forts, delaying the Union advance.

Desperately struggling to extricate his army from the collapsing position around Petersburg and Richmond, Lee hastily wrote to Davis notifying him that the two cities would fall that day and that if the Confederate government wanted to get out, the time had come. Davis was attending services at St.

Paul Episcopal Church in Richmond when the sexton quietly handed him the note from Lee. Davis silently read it, then rose and left, leaving the other congregants to guess its meaning. He supervised the hasty packing up of remaining government files, and then he and most of his cabinet boarded one of the last trains out of the city, hoping to reestablish the seat of government in Lynchburg, Virginia, a little more than one hundred miles to the west of Richmond. Back in the former Confederate capital, panic reigned and looting raged among the civilian populace as the Confederate rear guard set fire to military installations and depots to prevent their falling into Union hands. The flames spread and destroyed much of the city.

THE ROAD TO APPOMATTOX
COURT HOUSE

Lee succeeded in getting most of his troops out of the doomed enclave around Richmond and Petersburg and marched west, hoping to get clear of Grant's pursuit and turn southwest and then south to link up with Johnston's army. Lee's army, though much depleted, was in high spirits at being out of the entrenchments and back on open roads in unspoiled countryside, the sort of environment in which the army had won its great victories under Lee two years before. If anyone in the gray-clad ranks thought the army's demise was near, he generally kept quiet about it.

Grant was determined to make it happen. Thus far in the war no major army had been chased down after a defeat, trapped, and forced to surrender—unless one counted Pemberton's army, which had taken refuge in Vicksburg after its defeat at Champion Hill. Lee was no Pemberton and would not hole up in a fortress for Grant to besiege. Grant would have to catch him, and he set out to do so. He ordered his troops to follow Lee immediately. Only those that had been on the east side of Richmond actually got to pass through the newly captured city. The Army of the Potomac, which had striven to take Richmond since its days under McClellan three years before, bypassed the city, marching west in hot pursuit of its old nemesis the Army of Northern Virginia. While Meade and his army followed close at Lee's heels, Sheridan with his cavalry as well as Major General E. O. C. Ord, commanding the Army of the James in place of the finally discredited Butler, strove to pass Lee's flanks and block his escape.

While the armies marched rapidly west, Lincoln on April 4 arrived in Richmond by boat on the James River. The city had been in Union hands

Virginia (Confederate) capitol and ruins of burned outbuildings after the fall of Richmond.

less than twenty-four hours and was lightly occupied. Accompanied only by his son Tad, whose twelfth birthday this was, Lincoln went ashore at the landing and walked through the town. Alarmed at this appalling lapse of security, Porter hastily gathered a squad of armed sailors and set out after the president. While Richmond's whites glowered resentfully or peered at him through nearly shut window blinds, the black population flocked into the streets to greet and celebrate the man they considered their deliverer from bondage. Before leaving town, Lincoln visited the Confederate White House and sat pensively in a chair Jefferson Davis had occupied not two days earlier.

That same day, April 4, Lee's army reached Amelia Court House, on the Richmond & Danville Railroad about forty miles west-northwest of Petersburg and the same distance west-southwest of Richmond. There the elements of Lee's army that had been in the trenches around Petersburg joined those that had been holding the lines east of Richmond. More important, however, was what had not arrived at Amelia Court House. During the evacuation of the lines, Lee had given orders for the commissary department to load supplies from the Richmond depots onto several trains and ship them out the Richmond & Danville to Amelia Court House so that the army would find them waiting when it arrived. Somehow in the confusion of that last day in Richmond, the ammunition had moved out as ordered, but the much more desperately needed rations had gone astray. Now Lee found himself with nothing to feed his hungry army. Reluctantly he gave orders for the army to spend the next twenty-four hours at Amelia while foraging parties fanned out in the vicinity to seize food. They found little enough, and by the time the army marched on again, it had lost what little lead it had over Grant's pursuing columns.

The Confederates had gone little more than seven miles on their resumed march when they found Sheridan's cavalry blocking the southwest fork of the road at Jetersville. With Union infantry bearing down on the rear of his army, Lee could not afford to slow his pace in order to push the cavalry out of the way. That left no option but to continue to the west, not toward Danville now, as originally planned, but toward Lynchburg. The immediate goal was Farmville, where the commissary department gave Lee to understand he could expect to meet another shipment of rations. So the Army of Northern Virginia slogged wearily onward, no longer maneuvering toward Johnston and the forlorn hope of a combination against Sherman but simply fleeing like a deer half a step ahead of the pursuing wolf pack.

The next day, April 6, Lee's army marched by two roads, as armies always did when quick marching was necessary and parallel roads were available. Longstreet's large corps took the southerly road while the smaller corps of Ewell and of Richard H. Anderson took the northerly. Union infantry pressed close after the rear of the columns while Union cavalry, supported by more infantry, harassed both flanks. At Rice's Station, twelve miles beyond Jetersville, Longstreet again found Union troops, this time Ord's Army of the James, firmly blocking any possible turn to the south toward North Carolina and Johnston's army.

While Longstreet was busy skirmishing near Rice's Station, Union infantry pressed so close to the rear of Ewell's column that he had to turn at bay to hold them back. This caused the northerly of Lee's two columns to stretch thin, as Anderson's corps did not immediately halt. Sheridan, commanding the Union cavalry on that flank, saw the opportunity and sent two of his divisions in headlong attack. They ripped through Anderson's column, turned, and came crashing down on Ewell's flank and rear as his troops were fighting against Union infantry along the valley of Sayler's Creek. Trapped, Ewell's men surrendered in droves, and presently Ewell himself surrendered as well. In all, nearly three thousand Confederates were killed or wounded at Sayler's Creek, and another six thousand were captured. Union losses totaled a little more than one thousand. Lee personally rallied the fleeing remnants of Anderson's corps and borrowed troops from Longstreet to help stabilize the situation, but the debacle had cost his already badly depleted army almost a third of its strength.

"If the thing is pressed," Sheridan wrote Grant that day, "I think that Lee will surrender." A copy of the dispatch made its way back to Grant's supply base at City Point, east of Petersburg, where Lincoln was anxiously awaiting news of the campaign. On April 7 the president fired off a dispatch of his own to Grant, noting Sheridan's message and adding, "Let the *thing* be pressed." Grant had every intention of doing just that. He was already conducting the most aggressive pursuit by any major army in the war, and he was not about to let up. That same day he had sent Lee a message by a flag of truce: "The result of the last week must convince you of the hopelessness of further resistance on the part of the Army of Northern Virginia in this struggle. I feel that is so, and regard it as my duty to shift from myself the responsibility of any further effusion of blood, by asking of you the surrender of that portion of the C.S. Army known as the Army of Northern Virginia." While he waited for a reply, he kept his troops in rapid pursuit of Lee's dwindling force.

Lee's army continued its desperate retreat, crossing to the north bank of the Appomattox River and setting fire to the bridges behind it. Union troops were so close on their heels, however, that they were able to extinguish the fires and follow the Rebels across the river. With the Federals in hot pursuit, Lee had to keep his troops marching rapidly through Farmville, with little time to halt and eat the rations there. One more stockpile of rations lay ahead, twenty-five miles to the west at Appomattox Station, near the town of Appomattox Court House. Yet already the delays at Farmville and at the Appomattox crossing had cost Lee precious time and allowed Sheridan, already on Lee's left front with a combined force of cavalry and infantry, to gain ground in the race toward that destination.

On April 8, as the armies pushed west toward Appomattox Station, Grant received Lee's reply to his note. Lee did not agree that further resistance was hopeless but expressed agreement with Grant's desire "to avoid the useless effusion of blood." What terms, Lee wanted to know, would Grant offer if the Army of Northern Virginia were to surrender? Grant replied immediately: "Peace being my great desire, there is but one condition I would insist upon, namely that the men and officers surrendered shall be disqualified from taking up arms again against the Government of the United States until properly exchanged." Grant suggested they could meet later that day to conclude the surrender terms.

The terms were as generous as Lee could possibly have hoped, but a note came back from the Confederate general later that day stating that he "did not intend to propose the surrender of the Army of Northern Virginia, but to ask the terms of your proposition." Yet Lee still proposed to meet for a discussion with Grant. Grant was disappointed. This looked like another attempt to draw him into broader negotiations involving some kind of political agreement as Davis had attempted to set up in January and Lincoln had repeatedly warned Grant to avoid. He determined not to meet with Lee and resigned himself to continued military operations.

While the notes made their way back and forth the rival forces continued their rapid march to the west. By the evening of that Saturday, April 8, Sheridan's cavalry had won the race to Appomattox Station. George Armstrong Custer's division seized the supply trains there and burned them. The rest of Sheridan's command moved up, blocking Lee's route west toward Lynchburg and continued flight. The Confederate commander held a council of war with his generals that night to discuss what options remained open to the army. They agreed on a final breakout attempt. If nothing but Union cavalry blocked their path, they ought to be able to push it aside. With Longstreet's corps providing the rear guard, Gordon's infantry, supported by Fitzhugh Lee's cavalry, would attempt to break through at dawn the next day, Palm Sunday.

Before the Confederate attack stepped off that morning, Grant was up and writing his reply to Lee's message of the day before. He had, he said, "no authority to treat on the subject of peace," that is, a comprehensive agreement between the two governments. He would accept the surrender of Lee's army if it were offered. Otherwise the fighting must go on.

The fighting flared again early that morning as Gordon's men launched the Army of Northern Virginia's last advance. In front of Gordon's advancing line of battle, a skirmish line of dismounted Union cavalrymen fired and fell back, a process they repeated as the Confederate advance continued. Then Gordon's men topped a ridge and beyond it saw solid ranks of Union infantry, the Twenty-Fourth and Fifth corps, which had arrived after a hard march to support Sheridan's troopers. The last Rebel attack stopped almost as soon as it began, as the Confederate officers recognized at once that they, the

Army of Northern Virginia, were finally checkmated. "There is nothing left for me to do but to go and see General Grant," Lee said when informed of the situation Gordon had encountered, and then added, "and I would rather die a thousand deaths." He sent a flag of truce to arrange a meeting with Grant.

Considerable confusion followed. Headquarters were in motion, and at any given moment it was not easy to know the whereabouts of the commanding generals. The armies were already in contact, with Union forces even then beginning to move into position for attacks that would have overrun what was left of the Army of Northern Virginia. With some difficulty, Confederate staff officers got word to Grant as well as to other Union commanders on the opposite side of the Army of Northern Virginia, where Meade was eagerly preparing to launch a final assault that promised to be much different from all the doomed assaults the Army of the Potomac had staged over the past four years. With difficulty, the bloody finale was avoided. Staff officers arranged a meeting to take place in the home of Wilmer McLean in the village of Appomattox Court House. In a war full of ironies, the final one was that McLean had moved to this out-of-the-way settlement because two major battles had brought war to his front yard at his former residence near Manassas Junction. Now the final act of the war in Virginia was coming to his front parlor.

They met early that afternoon. Lee arrived early, accompanied by three staff officers. Grant had farther to go and arrived some time later, accompanied by Sheridan, Ord, and a number of staff officers. Having ridden hard in recent days, he was mud spattered, while Lee was resplendent in full-dress uniform. Grant and Lee had not met since the Mexican War, and Grant now tried to make a bit of small talk to ease the tension for Lee. He mentioned that he remembered Lee from Mexico, but Lee could not recall the slightly built young lieutenant of the Fourth Infantry.

Lee suggested that they proceed to business, and Grant gave Lee his written terms. They were even more generous than Grant had indicated in his note of the previous day. Not only would the members of the Army of Northern Virginia be paroled, but the terms of the agreement specifically protected them from future prosecution for what they had done the past four years. Military equipment was to be handed over, but officers were expressly permitted to retain their sidearms. Grant would not require Lee to acknowledge his defeat by formally yielding his sword to him at the surrender ceremony. Lee asked if the Confederate cavalrymen and artillerymen could keep their horses, which would soon be needed at home for the spring planting,

Robert E. Lee, April 1865

and Grant readily agreed. The Union general went on to offer to send enough rations to Lee's camps to feed his entire army, and Lee gratefully accepted.

With that, the meeting ended, and the two commanders returned to their armies. Grant allowed his men no cheering or noisy celebration. "The Confederates were now our countrymen," he later explained, "and we did not want to exult over their downfall." At the formal surrender ceremony three days later, Brigadier General Joshua L. Chamberlain, commanding the Union troops detailed to conduct the proceedings, gave his men the order "Present Arms" as the Confederates marched up, saluting the courage and fortitude of foes they had fought for four years. The former Rebels returned the salute, laid down their rifles as required, and marched away.

FINAL SURRENDERS AND THE
ASSASSINATION OF LINCOLN

When the war ended in Virginia, it was essentially over everywhere else because by the end of the war, Virginia was all that was left of the Confederacy. While Lee and his army had clung tenaciously to their enclave in the Old Dominion State, Union power had so thoroughly crushed Confederate strength throughout the rest of the South that by the time Lee surrendered, all that remained for Union forces in the rest of what had been the Confederacy was mopping up residual pockets of resistance. These dissolved quickly as other Confederate forces surrendered on learning of the outcome at Appomattox. Johnston and Sherman finalized the surrender of the former's army on April 26, and Confederate General Richard Taylor surrendered the remainder of Confederate forces east of the Mississippi on May 4. Confederate forces west of the Mississippi officially surrendered on May 26. Jefferson Davis remained on the lam until May 10, when Union cavalry apprehended him near Washington, Georgia. Throughout these weeks, men continued to shoot each other, in small numbers, as they would do throughout the twelve-year period of quasi peace that followed, but the clash of armies was over.

On the evening of April 11, Lincoln made a speech from a window of the White House to a jubilant crowd that gathered on the lawn and semicircular drive below. While his son Tad held a light nearby, the president read from a prepared script. This was a glad occasion, he observed, as the fall of Richmond and the surrender of Lee's army gave "hope of a righteous and speedy peace." In all of this, he admonished, "He from whom all blessings flow [i.e., God], must not be forgotten." As for himself, Lincoln disclaimed any credit for the recent events, giving it instead of Grant and his army.

Lincoln warned that the coming years would be "fraught with difficulty." Northerners who may have agreed on restoring the Union and even freeing the slaves disagreed strongly about what it would take to place the southern states back in what Lincoln called their "proper practical relation" to the rest of the Union and its people, and they even disagreed as to what that "proper practical relation" would look like. Lincoln defended the beginnings he had made in reconstructing southern state governments and said future plans should remain flexible. He hoped, however, that former black soldiers, at least, as well as other "very intelligent" blacks, would be granted the vote.

At least one of Lincoln's listeners was enraged by his endorsement of blacks voting. Prominent actor John Wilkes Booth was in the crowd that night. A bitter racist, Booth turned angrily to his companion David Herold. "That means nigger citizenship," Booth hissed. "Now, by God, I'll put him through." A few minutes later, as they left the White House grounds, Booth said to another associate, Lewis Powell, "That is the last speech he will ever give."

At twenty-six Booth was the youngest of the four actors in his renowned family. With black hair, striking black eyes, and athletic figure, Booth was celebrated by some as the most handsome man in the country and was said to be quite a favorite with the ladies. He was also known for his energetic acting, including occasional leaping stage entrances. Less well known was the fact that Booth was a Confederate sympathizer who hated blacks, abolitionists, and, most of all, Abraham Lincoln. During the war Booth had served as part of a network of Confederate agents in the Washington area. For the past few months, as the Confederacy tottered toward its end, Booth had headed a conspiracy of which both Herold and Powell were members to kidnap Lincoln and spirit him to Richmond. Whether this was an official Confederate operation remains disputed. After Appomattox, the plan changed, at least in Booth's mind, from kidnapping to assassination.

On the morning of Good Friday, April 14, Booth learned that the President and Mrs. Lincoln, as well as General and Mrs. U. S. Grant, would be sitting in the presidential box at Ford's Theater that night for the play *Our American Cousin.* Booth saw his chance. Throughout the day, while Lincoln held a cabinet meeting and then went for a pleasant, lighthearted carriage ride with his wife, the first such in years, Booth made preparations to assassinate the president that night while he watched the play. Two of Booth's accomplices were to assassinate the vice president and secretary of state, at their separate dwellings, thus decapitating the U.S. government. Other conspirators were ready to aid the three assassins' escape, and they could also rely on the Confederate espionage network in surrounding Maryland.

The Lincolns were late arriving at the theater that evening, and with them were not Ulysses and Julia Dent Grant but rather Mary Todd Lincoln's young friend Clara Harris and her fiancé, Major Henry Rathbone. The general had begged off at the urging of his wife, who had recently been offended by one of Mary Todd Lincoln's increasingly frequent jealous tirades toward any woman who came near her husband. Miss Harris and her fiancé were last-minute replacements. The actors paused as the president and his party entered and made their way up to the dress circle, or first balcony, and then around to the enclosed presidential box, overlooking the right-hand side of the stage as the audience viewed it. The orchestra played "Hail to the Chief," and, with the president and his companions in their seats, the play resumed.

Booth knew the piece well, a comedy about a gold-digging British mother and daughter and the American man they mistakenly believed to be heir to a great fortune. In act 3, scene 2, would come a point when the only

Ford's Theater after the assassination.

actor left on stage would bawl out a string of humorous insults directed at the recently exited actress portraying the mother. A roar of laughter was guaranteed to follow, and that would be Booth's moment. As the scene began, Booth silently crept into the presidential box, behind its occupants and shielded from the view of the audience except for perhaps a few seated in the dress circle on the far side of the stage, but their attention was directed to the action below, as was that of the Lincolns and their guests. It was about 10:11 p.m.

Holding his loaded and cocked, single-shot .44-caliber Deringer pistol, Booth edged closer to Lincoln's back, close enough to have reached out and touched the president, as actor Harry Hawk, in the role of Asa Trenchard, now held the stage alone and led up to his roundhouse denunciation of the avaricious Mrs. Mountchessington. "Don't know the manners of good society, eh?" bellowed Hawk. "Well, I guess I know enough to turn you inside out, old gal, you sockdologizing old mantrap."

As the house rang with laughter, few theatergoers noticed the muffled report of the pistol or the puff of white powder smoke in the presidential box.

The presidential box at Ford's Theater. President Lincoln was seated on the far right of the box. Mary Todd Lincoln was seated to his right, and Clara Harris and Henry Rathbone to her right, to the left of the portrait of George Washington.

In the seconds that followed, however, more of them became aware of what appeared to be a scuffle in the presidential box. Major Rathbone stepped toward Booth, who slashed the officer's arm with a large knife, then clambered over the rail and leaped to the stage. Catching one of his spurs on the bunting, he landed awkwardly and stumbled. Limping to center stage he waved his knife and shouted, "Sic semper tyrannis"—so always to tyrants. It was the state motto of Virginia and supposedly what Brutus had said when he killed Julius Caesar. Booth may also have added, "The South is avenged." Accounts vary. Then he turned and fled, slashing wildly and ineffectually at the terrified Hawk, who was only too eager to get out of his way. Offstage and out a back door of the theater went the assassin, then into the alley, where a horse was waiting for him. Hurriedly mounting despite the pain of what would turn out to be a broken bone in his lower leg, he was off for the Maryland countryside. The crowd, some of whom still thought that the whole bizarre spectacle was part of the evening's entertainment, had been too stunned to react.

Into the shocked moment of silence that followed came Major Rathbone's shout, "Stop that man!" and Clara Harris's cry, "He has shot the President!" Another moment of speechless silence, and then pandemonium broke loose. Among the bedlam, three off-duty army surgeons made their way to the box to tend Lincoln's wound. The bullet entered behind the president's left ear and lodged behind his right eye. A brief examination was all that was needed to show these men, who shared vast experience in gunshot wounds, that the president could not live more than a few hours. Believing the half-mile carriage ride on Washington's rutted streets might cause the president's immediate death, they carried him out of the crowded theater and across the street to the boardinghouse of William Peterson. There at 7:22 the next morning Lincoln died without having regained consciousness since the shooting.

At about the same time that Booth shot Lincoln, his accomplice Powell bluffed his way into the Seward house with the false story of being a deliveryman for a pharmacy. The secretary of war had recently suffered severe injury in a carriage accident and was confined to bed. Forcing his way through the house and into Seward's sickroom, Powell pistol-whipped the secretary's grown son, Frederick, and attacked the helpless man in his bed, stabbing him several times but failing to kill him. The brave resistance of Seward's male nurse, an army sergeant, as well as his other grown son, and the screams of Seward's daughter, which threatened to bring rescuers to the house, finally persuaded the hulking Powell to flee. George Atzerodt, whom Booth had assigned to assassinate Vice President Johnson at his room at the Kirkwood House, instead spent the night in a bar getting drunk.

Lincoln's death called forth a mighty wave of anger and grief throughout the North. Thousands filed past his casket as it lay in state under the rotunda of the Capitol. Hundreds of thousands more paid their respects at the many cities and towns where his funeral train paused in its twelve-day trip back to Springfield, retracing the roundabout route of Lincoln's journey from the Prairie State to Washington for his first inauguration little more than four years before. On the way, Lincoln lay in state in Philadelphia, New York City, Albany, Buffalo, Cleveland, Columbus, Indianapolis, and Chicago—

eleven cities in all. And between cities, among the small towns and farmlands not meriting formal stops, additional thousands of Americans stood with bowed heads along the railroad right-of-way as the brightly polished funeral train, draped in mourning and decorated with U.S. flags and a portrait of Lincoln just below the headlight, rolled by at a stately twenty miles per hour.

The anger was directed toward anyone whom people saw as being behind the assassination or in some way responsible for it or potentially profiting from it. The feeling was most dangerous among the hardhanded midwestern soldiers who filled the ranks of Sherman's armies, then encamped not far from Raleigh, North Carolina, while their commander negotiated for the surrender of Johnston's Confederate army. The Army of the Tennessee, the most consistently successful of the Union armies, had more regiments from Lincoln's home state of Illinois than from any other. On the night news arrived of the assassination, a large body of its troops set out in a blind rage with the purpose of laying the capital city of North Carolina in ashes. Even an appeal from John Logan, their favorite general, who had led them to victory at the Battle of Atlanta, went unheeded. Logan finally had to deploy a battery of artillery and threaten to blast his own men with canister before they would turn back. A number of soldiers wrote in diaries and letters that if the surrender negotiations should fall through and the war continue a few more weeks, the South would feel the hard hand of war to a degree not previously imagined. Fortunately, it never came to that. Many southerners also expressed sadness at Lincoln's murder if for no other reason than that it would obviously lead to much harsher treatment for the conquered South.

Booth and his accomplices were the subjects of an unprecedented manhunt, with massive rewards offered for information leading to their apprehension. After his escape from Washington immediately after the crime, Booth joined fellow conspirator David Herold and made his way southeastward through a part of Maryland in which support for the Confederacy had been strong, receiving help at several points along the way from members of the former Confederate espionage network. Dr. Samuel Mudd set Booth's broken leg early on the morning of April 15, while Lincoln still clung to life back at the Peterson House. Booth and Herold crossed the Potomac by boat on the night of April 23 and continued their journey south, still aided by members of the Confederate espionage ring of which Booth had been part. Tips from various sources led searching Union cavalry three nights later to the farm of Richard H. Garrett, south of the Rappahannock River in Caroline County, Virginia, where Booth and Herold were staying under aliases. Cornered in Garrett's tobacco barn, Herold came out and surrendered, but Booth, brandishing a revolver and visible through the slats in the building's semiopen sides, refused and was fatally shot by one of the cavalrymen.

In addition to Herold, seven more of Booth's accomplices were rounded up in the days following the assassination and subsequently tried and convicted. Herold, Powell, Atzerodt, and Mary Surratt, whose Washington boardinghouse had been the headquarters for the espionage ring and for the Lincoln murder conspiracy, were hanged in Washington that summer. The others received prison sentences, all of which concluded with their pardon in 1869 by Andrew Johnson.

The final surrender of Confederate troops east of the Mississippi took place at Citronelle, Alabama, on May 4, the same day Lincoln was buried up in Springfield. On May 10 Union cavalry captured Jefferson Davis, and President Johnson issued a proclamation stating that armed resistance was at an end, though the last skirmish between organized troops of the Union and Confederacy did not take place until May 12, at Brazos Santiago, Texas. On May 23 the Army of the Potomac paraded through the streets of Washington, between sidewalks packed with cheering citizens. The event was known as the Grand Review, and it continued the next day when Sherman's western armies paraded through Washington to a similar heroes' reception. The conventional war—the war of waving flags, marching armies, and thundering cannon—was over. But the conflict to shape the society that would emerge from the great struggle was only beginning.

14

RECONSTRUCTION

PRESIDENTIAL RECONSTRUCTION

E ver since 1865, people who have taken an interest in Reconstruction have asked themselves and each other how the process and the period might have been different if Lincoln had lived to preside over its first four years. Of course, we can never know what Lincoln would have done, but we can take an educated guess or two based on his previous actions.

As president-elect, Lincoln had been willing to accept even a constitutional amendment stipulating that the Constitution could never be amended so as to ban slavery, if such an amendment would satisfy white southerners and persuade them to step back from secession. Southern leaders were not satisfied, and so the proposal went nowhere. In his first inaugural address, Lincoln had gone out of his way to reassure southerners of his peaceful intent. "In your hands, my dissatisfied fellow-countrymen, and not in mine," Lincoln had said, "is the momentous issue of civil war. The Government will not assail you. You can have no conflict without being yourselves the aggressors. You have no oath registered in heaven to destroy the Government, while I shall have the most solemn one to 'preserve, protect, and defend it.'" But when the secessionists had become the aggressors, Lincoln had held firm to his oath and his purpose of preserving the Union and had accepted war. He had held to a conciliatory policy during the first year of the war, hoping the Rebels would not persevere in secession. When they proved intransigent, he took the further step of emancipation.

Throughout the deepening crisis, Lincoln had shown himself eager to conciliate but willing to be firm if pushed. At the heart of Lincoln's greatness as a statesman was the fact that he kept a firm grip on a few very clear moral goals and pursued them unflinchingly, no matter where that led him. He was committed to securing freedom for the slaves, and for Lincoln freedom included the opportunity of bettering one's lot in life. He was also on record that at least some of the slaves should vote. It is easy to imagine that had he lived, he would have shaped his course by those landmarks. Perhaps he would have met southern cooperation with generosity, but in the face of intransigence, he might well have shown as much firmness, determination, and willingness to take harsh measures as he had done during the war's conventional phase. We can never know. One thing is certain, though, and that is that the process of Reconstruction was going to be much more difficult without Lincoln.

His successor, Andrew Johnson, had been born to poverty in Raleigh, North Carolina, in 1808. Apprenticed as a tailor, young Johnson had run away to Greeneville, Tennessee, several years later, where he married a wife who bore him five children and taught him to read and cipher. Elected alderman at age twenty-one, Johnson went on, through the usual ups and downs of politics, to be mayor, state legislator, congressman, governor, and finally U.S. senator. That was the office he held at the outbreak of the Civil War. Johnson saw himself as the champion of the poor and middling whites of the South, hostile to slaveholders but at best indifferent to their slaves. He was a Buchanan Democrat in the 1850s, but when secession came, Johnson, alone among U.S. senators from seceding states, remained loyal to the Union. In 1862 Lincoln appointed him military governor over the Union-occupied portion of the state, and two years later the Republicans, in their National Union Party guise, tapped him as Lincoln's second-term vice president.

He got off to a bad start as vice president. Johnson, who did not have the reputation of a problem drinker, was sick with typhoid fever on inauguration day and had taken a drink or two of whiskey, which in those days was considered to have medicinal value. The Senate chamber, in which the vice-presidential inauguration took place, was stuffy, and the liquor seemed to affect Johnson more strongly than he anticipated. After taking the oath of office, he gave a rambling, incoherent speech that did nothing to enhance his standing in the capital city.

In the aftermath of the Lincoln assassination, however, it appeared that Johnson would get along very well with the most powerful political faction in town, the Radical Republicans. He talked tough about punishing traitors, and leading members of the Radical faction expressed the belief that now that

Johnson was in charge, there would be no difficulty about Reconstruction, none of the tension between president and Congress that had shown up in the dispute over the Wade-Davis Bill. They were in for a surprise.

During the seven months between his taking the oath of office as president in April and Congress's convening for its next session in December, Johnson took several key steps in the Reconstruction process. He issued a proclamation offering amnesty to former Confederates who would take the oath of allegiance. The offer was good for any Rebel except those in certain specified classes, including Confederate civil officials, high-ranking army and navy officers, and those owning more than twenty thousand dollars of taxable property. He also recognized the four state governments Lincoln had established in former Confederate states before the end of the war. Johnson went on and set up similar governments in the remaining seven states of the former Confederacy, stipulating that the new governments must accept emancipation, nullify secession, and repudiate the debts their states had incurred during the rebellion. He also encouraged the restored southern state governments to extend the vote to literate blacks. This was very close to Lincoln's final announced Reconstruction policy except that it left out the vote for former black soldiers.

As it turned out, the finer points of Johnson's position on black suffrage were irrelevant since every one of the new state governments ignored his recommendation to extend the vote to at least some blacks. Some southerners cited the *Dred Scott* decision as proof that blacks were not citizens. It was almost as if the preceding decade with its more than half a million war deaths had never happened. No former Confederate state enfranchised a single black man, and some states even declined to repudiate their wartime debts. Rather than reacting as Lincoln always had with increased firmness and severity in the face of defiant white southerners, Johnson tamely acquiesced.

As the summer wore on, Radicals criticized Johnson's actions, while white southerners flattered him. Gradually Johnson slid more and more into sympathy with the former Rebels. In August he allowed the provisional governor of Mississippi to set up a state militia composed of former Confederate soldiers, and he rebuked two U.S. Army generals stationed in Mississippi who objected to the governor's ominous move. Meanwhile former Confederates who were members of the special classes excluded from Johnson's previous pardon flocked to the White House in droves seeking from the president the special, individual pardons that would restore them to full political privileges. Johnson swelled with pride to see members of the southern aristocracy finally treating him with deference, and he granted pardon after pardon—an average of five hundred a day during the month of September. In all, Johnson granted 90 percent of the fifteen thousand or so pardon requests he received.

Meanwhile the amazing political recovery of the recent Rebels was having a direct effect on the former slaves, who were often called freedmen. Congress, on March 3, 1865, had passed a bill for the establishment of the Bureau of Refugees, Freedmen, and Abandoned Lands, usually known as the Freedmen's Bureau. Under the leadership of its commissioner, General Oliver O. Howard, the bureau strove to help the former slaves make the transition to freedom. During the tumultuous final days of the war and the early months of peace, the bureau provided emergency food, housing, and medical care to displaced freedmen as well as to white refugees.

Increasingly thereafter, its chief task was helping the freedmen find gainful employment. At first, there were high hopes that this might be accomplished by settling the former slaves as landowning farmers on small parcels carved from the abandoned (during the war) plantations of many of their former owners who had been active Rebels. Johnson quickly put a stop to that and saw to it that the pardoned Rebels got their land back. Next, the Freedmen's Bureau tried to help the former slaves get fair work contracts to farm on the lands of their former masters, with mixed success. Old attitudes died hard, and many of the former slaveholders tried as much as possible to treat the blacks as if they were still in bondage. The political resurgence of the former Rebels made the task of the Freedmen's Bureau more difficult.

Keeping the blacks in a subordinate role was the chief purpose of special "black codes" passed by the newly restored legislatures of the former Confederate states. Before the war, every slave state had had, as part of its laws, a slave code, containing the laws that enabled, supported, and protected slavery. Now that slavery was gone, a number of the former Confederate states replaced their slave codes with black codes that provided a separate—and lower—legal status for blacks, a sort of legal netherworld between slavery and freedom. The Freedmen's Bureau, together with the army occupation forces in the South, suspended the operation of the more onerous portions of the slave codes.

The southern states were by no means alone in an unwillingness to accord legal equality to blacks. That year three northern states—Connecticut, Wisconsin, and Minnesota—had rejected referenda that would have given the vote to blacks in those states. However, the passage of a specific black code went farther than a mere denial of the vote. It was more blatant, and it smacked of an attempt to continue many of the features of slavery. The southern black codes, combined with a rising tide of violence against blacks and Unionists in the South, helped convince many congressional Republicans that the former Confederate states were rejecting the outcome of the war.

CONGRESS ASSERTS ITS AUTHORITY

In December 1865 the Thirteenth Amendment, banning slavery throughout the United States, received the needed ratification by three-fourths of the states and went into effect. The amendment supported and broadened the impact of Lincoln's Emancipation Proclamation and removed any possibility that the proclamation might be challenged in the courts. Slavery, which had been at the heart of the sectional crisis and the rebellion, was at last dead. It remained to be seen, however, how effective the rebellious states would be in setting aside the result of the war by creating for the blacks a legal status that, if it was not quite slavery, was nevertheless well short of freedom.

When Congress convened in that same December 1865, the Republicans, who controlled both houses, refused to seat the representatives and senators from the former Confederate states. They believed these states were still, in effect, in rebellion though not openly in arms because they were continuing to reject the outcome of the war. To remedy the situation, Congress passed two bills. One broadened the powers of the Freedmen's Bureau to protect blacks in the South, and the other was aimed at extending civil rights to the blacks, canceling the legal legacy of the *Dred Scott* decision and according blacks citizenship and the "full benefit of all laws and proceedings for the security of person and property as is enjoyed by white citizens." The bill stopped short of requiring states to allow blacks to vote or to sit on juries or of forbidding segregation.

Johnson vetoed both bills. Some of the arguments he put forward in his veto messages would have been sound in ordinary times of peace but ignored the fact that the nation was still in the process of restoring peace and stability after a massive civil war or of working out the war's chief effect of ending slavery. Regarding the Freedmen's Bureau Johnson pointed out that the Constitution made no provision for a "system for the support of indigent persons." He objected to the civil rights bill for infringing on the rights of the states. Both bills, he maintained, were unacceptable because when they were passed, "there was no Senator or Representative in Congress from the eleven States which are to be mainly affected by [their] provisions." This last argument begged the question of whether the state governments he had set up without congressional authorization were actually legitimate. It also negated any possibility of enforcing the outcome of the war in the southern states.

The vetoes alone would have been enough to incur the wrath not only of the Radical Republicans but of the former moderates as well, virtually uniting the majority party in opposition to Johnson. But the president went farther. In shrill and intemperate speeches Johnson denounced the party that had elected him to the vice presidency as a band of traitors and likened himself to Christ and the Republicans to Judas, plotting his death. This sort of overheated rhetoric had always played well for him on the stump in backwoods Tennessee, but it shocked the nation when coming from the White House. Johnson fell far short of Lincoln's political skills either in dealing with potential political opponents or in explaining his views to the American people and persuading them to support him. Lincoln would no doubt have needed every bit of his skill to navigate the difficult political waters of Reconstruction. Johnson was lost at sea.

Congressional Republicans, now much closer to unity between Radicals and moderates, overrode both vetoes in the spring and summer of 1866. During that time the congressional Joint Committee on Reconstruction hammered out the provisions of another constitutional amendment, the Fourteenth. Meant to address most of the outstanding issues of Reconstruction, the Fourteenth Amendment became a grab bag of different provisions. Section 1, aimed at securing black civil rights on a solid constitutional basis, was at once the most sweeping and the most succinct:

> All persons born or naturalized in the United States, and subject to the jurisdiction thereof, are citizens of the United States and of the State wherein they reside. No State shall make or enforce any law which shall abridge the privileges or immunities of citizens of the United States; nor shall any State deprive any person of life, liberty, or property, without due process of law; nor deny to any person within its jurisdiction the equal protection of the laws.

Section 2 was intended to prevent white southerners from experiencing an increase in the congressional overrepresentation they had already enjoyed as a result of the Three-Fifths Compromise. Under that compromise, though no southern state allowed slaves to vote, three-fifths of slave numbers counted toward a state's representation in Congress. Now that the slaves were free, their whole number would count toward representation of the states in which they lived, but they still could not vote. Whites in slave states were thus overrepresented in Congress relative to people living in other parts of the country, and emancipation ironically threatened to make the problem worse. To remedy this, the Fourteenth Amendment reduced the congressional representation of any state in proportion to any segment of its adult male population to which it denied the vote.

Section 3 banned from civil or military office anyone who had previously taken an oath to uphold the Constitution of the United States but then had participated in a rebellion. This meant that men who had held civil or military office in the United States before the war but then had supported the Confederacy could not subsequently return to such office in the United States after the war. Its provisions disqualified most of the congressional delegations that Johnson's hastily reconstructed states had sent to Washington. The section further provided that Congress could make exceptions to the rule but only by a two-thirds vote of both houses.

Section 4 of the amendment guaranteed repayment of the U.S. national debt but forbade repayment of any state debt contracted in support of the rebellion or of any compensation for the loss of alleged property in slaves.

The first section of the amendment has been the subject of much litigation over the past century and a half, much of it unrelated to the purposes for which the amendment was passed. The earnest members of the Joint Committee on Reconstruction, as well as those who subsequently passed and ratified the amendment, would have been amazed if they could have seen the interpretations the Supreme Court would make of their words in the twentieth century, but then so would the original framers of the Constitution.

Both houses of Congress passed the amendment by the necessary two-thirds majorities, and it went to the states for ratification.

With the election of 1866 approaching, Johnson and the Republicans campaigned vigorously against each other. Johnson made a whistle-stop campaign speaking tour from Washington to Chicago to St. Louis and back. His behavior was unpresidential, as he traded insults with hecklers and suggested that abolitionists ought to be hanged. Most voters were unimpressed. Johnson's cause was further discredited by a race riot in New Orleans in July in which former Confederate soldiers attacked a convention that had met to advocate black suffrage. The rioters killed thirty-seven of the blacks and three white supporters of black civil rights. Disturbed by this indication of continued rebellion in the South as well as the president's repulsive statements, the voters gave Republicans a landslide victory and a three-to-one ascendancy in both houses of Congress.

With the election over, Congress passed a Military Reconstruction Act, providing for military occupation and administration of the still-rebellious states of the South. The act provided that any state could be readmitted to the Union and its representatives admitted to Congress as soon as it ratified the Fourteenth Amendment and adopted a state constitution banning slavery. Johnson vetoed the act, and both houses of Congress overrode his veto the same day.

That day, March 2, 1867, was a busy day in Congress. Both houses also passed, once again over a presidential veto, two additional acts. One was the Tenure of Office Act, stipulating that the president could not dismiss a cabinet member without the consent of the Senate. Congress wanted to make sure that Johnson did not fire Secretary of War Stanton, who supported its policies. The second act was an army appropriations bill containing a rider stipulating that all of Johnson's orders to the army had to go through the general of the army, Grant, and further requiring that Johnson could not fire Grant without the Senate's approval. Like many other Americans, Grant had been deeply disturbed by the previous summer's race riot in New Orleans and by Johnson's stubborn refusal to recognize the continued rebellion in the former Confederate states. He would see to it that Johnson did not issue orders to the army that would nullify the Military Reconstruction Act. Three weeks later Congress passed a second Military Reconstruction Act, directing the army to begin registering voters, including former slaves, in the occupied states, setting in motion the process of adopting the new constitutions that would restore those states to their proper function within the Union.

CONGRESS ASCENDANT

Johnson continued to fight Reconstruction tooth and nail, interpreting the laws in such a way as to negate most of their intended effect. Early in 1867 Republicans considered trying to impeach him but found that they were not unified on the question of whether to take such an extreme step. Yet as Johnson continued his obstinate resistance to everything the Republicans tried to do, support for impeachment steadily rose. In August Johnson took the opportunity of the Senate's adjournment to dismiss Stanton, at least pending the Senate's reconvening. As interim secretary of war Johnson appointed Grant, who accepted the job only in order to try to protect the army from more of Johnson's efforts to hamstring it and its mission of Reconstruction. Despite his best efforts, however, Grant was unable to stop Johnson from relieving Sheridan as military governor of Texas and Louisiana and assigning in his place a general more amenable to the maintenance of white supremacy in those states. Johnson's efforts encouraged white southerners to stand fast against the ratification of the new state constitutions or any move toward the acceptance of black suffrage or civil rights.

In December 1867 the Senate reconvened and the following month voted to disapprove Johnson's removal of Stanton as secretary of war. In obedience to the Tenure of Office Act, Grant vacated the office, and Stanton resumed his old duties. On February 21 Johnson openly defied the act by firing Stanton again and appointing the army's adjutant general, Lorenzo Thomas, as interim replacement. This was a blatant violation of law, and the House of Representatives reacted by impeaching Johnson three days later.

The Constitution provides that an official impeached by the House should then be tried by the Senate and, if found guilty, removed from office. Impeachment by the House is analogous to indictment by a grand jury in a criminal case, and the Senate stands in the place of the trial court. Johnson's trial in the Senate began on March 4, 1868, eight days after his impeachment by the House. Johnson's team of very skillful defense lawyers argued that since violation of the Tenure of Office Act was not a crime for which an ordinary citizen could be indicted, it was not impeachable either. They further argued that Johnson was merely trying to have the constitutionality of the act tested by the Supreme Court and that in any case the act did not apply to him in Stanton's case since Stanton had been appointed by Lincoln, not Johnson.

Of more practical aid to Johnson's case was the discomfort some moderate Republicans in the Senate felt about the process. Removal of a president seemed disturbingly radical. Worse, if Johnson were removed, the notorious longtime abolitionist and Radical Speaker of the House Benjamin Wade was in line to become president. Some of the moderate Republicans quietly reached out to Johnson through intermediaries to suggest that perhaps it might not be necessary to impeach him if he would show some restraint. For once, Johnson took a hint. He stopped making incendiary speeches and started enforcing the Reconstruction acts. When the roll call vote was taken on Johnson's removal from office, the tally was thirty-five yea and nineteen nay. The shift of a single senator's vote would have been enough remove Johnson from office. As it was, seven Republican senators had voted to acquit, joined by the Senate's twelve Democrats.

Over the course of the next several months, one southern state after another adopted the necessary state constitution abjuring slavery and embracing black suffrage and ratified the Fourteenth Amendment, fulfilling the terms of the Military Reconstruction Act so as once again to have senators and representatives accepted in Congress. By the end of 1868, seven former Confederate states had been readmitted to representation in Congress. Despite the setback they had suffered in failing to remove Johnson from office, the Congressional Republicans had scored a major success in their program of Reconstruction.

Many white southerners had fought the process with all their might and would continue to do so. Employers and landowners tried to intimidate their black employees or tenants into staying away from the polls. Some whites organized themselves into night-riding organizations to carry out murders, beatings, and other acts of terror against blacks and their white allies. Chief among these night-riding organizations was the Ku Klux Klan.

Founded in 1865 in Pulaski, Tennessee, by bored former Confederate soldiers, the Klan was initially a relatively innocuous fraternal organization. By 1868, however, it had become a terrorist organization, frequently murdering politically active blacks, as well as Scalawags and Carpetbaggers, as the opponents of civil rights referred to southern Unionists and northern settlers in the South, respectively. Additional Klan targets included freedmen's schools and their teachers along with any "uppity" blacks. Klansmen dressed in a variety of outlandish costumes, often featuring robes (frequently but not always white) and white, conical hats or hoods. Too cowardly to own up to their deeds, they generally covered their faces with masks. At the head of the Klan was its "Grand Wizard," former Confederate general Nathan Bedford Forrest. Local Klan chapters acted more or less independently, with the Grand Wizard serving mainly as an inspirational figure. As the election of 1868 approached, Forrest publicly announced that if the authorities attempted to use the militia to prevent the Klan from suppressing Republican voting in Memphis, his men would murder every Republican political leader in the city.

THE GRANT ADMINISTRATION

As the 1868 election campaign got under way, the Republicans nominated Grant for president. The Democrats passed over Andrew Johnson, who had hoped for their endorsement. Instead the party gave its nomination to Horatio Seymour. New York's wartime Copperhead governor, Seymour had referred to the New York rioters of 1863 as "my friends." The Democratic campaign appealed strongly to racism, demanding that the government should remain strictly a white man's concern. The night riders went all out, committing more than two hundred murders in the state of Arkansas alone, including the killing of a U.S. congressman. Georgia saw somewhat fewer murders but more beatings. Louisiana, on the other hand, saw not only numerous assassinations but at least three anti-Republican riots and had a total death toll well over one thousand. The intimidation worked, and tens of thousands of southern blacks stayed away from the polls, allowing the Democrats to carry several southern states despite majorities of black voters in those states. In the North, however, Grant ran as well as Lincoln had in 1864, carrying almost exactly the same states and localities for a total of 214 electoral votes to Seymour's 80. The Republicans retained dominant majorities in both houses of Congress.

One of the first goals of Congress after the election was the passage of yet another constitutional amendment, the third of three amendments known as the Reconstruction Amendments and the fifteenth overall. This one stipulated that the right to vote was not to be denied by any state on the account of race. It was much needed in the North as well as the South since eleven of the twenty-one northern states still did not permit black suffrage, and referenda allowing suffrage had gone down to defeat in a number of northern states since the war. Congress approved the amendment in February 1869. All across the North, Republican-controlled legislatures ratified it, and Democratic ones rejected it. Four southern states—Virginia, Georgia, Mississippi, and Texas—had still not been readmitted to representation in Congress, so Congress required them to ratify both the Fourteenth and the Fifteenth amendments in order to regain their seats in the national legislature. All four states did so and were restored to representation in 1870. That same year the Fifteenth Amendment became part of the Constitution.

Grant has gone down in history, unfairly, as one of the nation's worst presidents. In truth, he was not as good a president as he was a general. He had been a master of the political nuances of wartime generalship, but he was less skillful in coping with the far different set of political problems generated by life in the White House at the very center of the political cauldron that was Washington, D.C. He had been an exceptionally good judge of the character and ability of officers with whom he served closely in wartime, and he had prospered as a general in part by surrounding himself with a team of such trusty subordinates. Yet even during the war he was far less effective in judging the traits of generals with whom he merely held interviews, as his experience with Butler and Meade demonstrated.

As president, Grant was sometimes sadly lacking in the ability to judge which men would be trustworthy in the turbid waters of Washington politics or New York high finance. Scrupulously honest himself, Grant tended to trust those around him. When he misjudged men who were not worthy of his trust, the result could be costly, as when Secretary of the Interior (and former general) William W. Belknap betrayed Grant's trust by engaging in corruption or when financiers Jay Gould and Jim Fisk misused indirect connections to Grant in order to promote their attempt to corner the market on gold, leading to the Black Friday crash. Grant was free of wrongdoing in both affairs.

Some of the opprobrium heaped on Grant's administration for its supposed corruption actually involved the administration's exposure and cleanup of graft that had been carried out under the previous administration. Such was the case of the Crédit Mobilier scandal of 1872. The United States had completed its first transcontinental railroad in 1869, along the general route that Stephen A. Douglas had envisioned a decade and a half before. Douglas's efforts to pave the way politically for such a railroad had resulted in the Kansas-Nebraska Act back in 1854 and had moved the nation another large step closer to civil war. As Douglas and virtually everyone else at that time had assumed was necessary, the railroad had been built with hefty subsidies from the federal government. Unfortunately, government money attracts corruption the way a carcass draws flies, and the transcontinental railroad was no exception. The builders of the railroad set up a dummy company called Crédit Mobilier and used it to skim millions of dollars in excess construction costs from the government, generously bribing members of Congress to grease the wheels along the way. Grant's administration exposed and cleaned up the mess, but, partially thanks to hostile Democratic newspapers, the public associated the scandal with Grant.

Grant's administration pressed the issue of Britain's responsibility for the financial losses caused by raiding vessels such as the CSS *Alabama* and other instances of tacit—or at least negligent—support of the Confederacy. Some in Congress, notably Senator Charles Sumner, believed that Canada would be about the right compensation. After several years of tense negotiations, American diplomats persuaded Britain to accept a treaty submitting the disputed claims to international arbitration. The three arbitrating countries—Switzerland, Italy, and Brazil—ruled unanimously in favor of the United States, awarding $15.5 million in damages. Great Britain paid the claims, opening the way for a period of steadily improving Anglo-American relations that would have important consequences in the twentieth century.

The depredations of the Ku Klux Klan continued apace, and Republican state governments in the South proved unable to suppress the terrorist organization. Congress and the Grant administration set out to take the matter in hand in 1870, passing and enforcing an act making it a federal offense to interfere with voting rights. When this measure proved too weak to break the Klan, Congress in 1872 added a second enforcing act, known as the Ku Klux Klan Act, strengthening the provisions of the first act and authorizing the president to deploy the army and to suspend the writ of habeas corpus when and where necessary. Grant sent troops to the South, and over the next few months his administration made thousands of arrests and secured hundreds of convictions. Other Klansmen fled the country to escape arrest. The campaign broke the power of the Klan, which officially disbanded. However, other similar night-riding organizations, such as the Red Shirts, continued to terrorize blacks and other southern Republicans in their relentless quest to rid the South of any taint of black equality or civil rights.

In 1872 the Republicans nominated Grant for a second term. The main issue of the campaign was Grant's "bayonet rule" in the South and his supposedly cruel and tyrannical suppression of the Ku Klux Klan. A different twist was added when members of Grant's own Republican Party took up the accusation, splitting from the rest of the party and calling themselves the Liberal Republican Party. They were an odd conglomeration of men with personal grudges against Grant, idealistic nineteenth-century liberals (something like what would be called libertarians in the twenty-first century), and people who had simply become tired of the effort to suppress southern terrorism and just wanted to move on.

As their presidential candidate the Liberal Republicans nominated the always unstable but tremendously well-known newspaper editor Horace Greeley. Their platform called for the reduction or removal of protective tariffs, a blanket amnesty for all former Rebels, repentant or not, and an end to the army's protection of civil rights in the South. The Democrats knew a good thing when they saw it and added their endorsement to Greeley's Liberal Republican nomination. However formidable the alliance of Democrats with a splinter faction of the Republican Party may have seemed at the outset, it proved less so in the actual campaign. When election day came, Grant won reelection in one of the most impressive landslides since the days of Andrew Jackson.

THE ELECTION OF 1876 AND THE
END OF RECONSTRUCTION

Throughout the years of Reconstruction, the majority of white southerners never accepted the legitimacy of the changes the Civil War had brought, and many of them kept up a constant struggle to extinguish black political activity and black civil rights and to reestablish white supremacy in their states. Democratic Party politics made up one arm of this effort, and night-riding terrorism was the other. As long as the North retained the political will to enforce the Fourteenth and Fifteenth amendments and to protect blacks and white Republicans in the South, the efforts of the white supremacists proved mostly in vain.

But in the mid-1870s northern political will began to weaken. Americans are not very good at long, low-intensity wars. Eager to get on with their lives and their profitable enterprises, they readily tire of contending with the same, almost faceless enemy year after year. So it was in the 1870s. Besides that, racism was not limited to the South by any means, and those who favored civil rights for the former slaves had struggled to maintain power even in the North. After nearly a decade of guerrilla war against white-supremacist terrorism in the South, four years of the nation's bloodiest war before that, and decades of political strife against the slave power before that, Americans were growing very, very weary of the great struggle. Their generation had accomplished much, very much, in ending slavery, but it was nearing the end of its strength.

One by one, southern states fell under Democratic rule—Tennessee in 1869, Virginia and North Carolina the following year, Georgia in 1871, Texas in 1873, and Arkansas and Alabama the year after that. And as the Republican state governments went down, black voting and civil rights winked out, state by state. As the election of 1876 approached, only four states—Mississippi, South Carolina, Florida, and Louisiana—still had Republican governments, and Mississippi fell to Democratic rule and white supremacy that year.

The Republican convention that year passed up front-runner James G. Blaine and instead nominated Civil War veteran Rutherford B. Hayes of Ohio. The Democrats nominated New York governor Samuel J. Tilden. Since Tilden had suppressed the Democratic Party's Tammany Hall, his Democratic supporters touted him as the antidote to the corruption they had for years been claiming characterized the Grant administration. Republicans emphasized that the plight of the southern freedmen and their white allies was at stake as well as the fruits of the Civil War. When election day came, Tilden carried his home state of New York, plus the Democratic Party's most reliable northern stronghold, New Jersey. He also succeeded in snagging the northern states of Connecticut and Indiana. The rest of the North went for Hayes.

In the South, however, the Democrats carried every single former slave state with the exception of the three states where U.S. Army troops were still protecting black voting rights: South Carolina, Florida, and Louisiana. Elsewhere throughout the South, the night riders of the White League and the Red Shirts, considering themselves the armed wing of the Democratic Party, had carried out the same tactics that had brought Democratic victory in Mississippi only a few months before. Brutally and aggressively they broke up Republican rallies; threatened, beat, or murdered Republican leaders and party workers; and intimidated potential voters into staying home. The tactic worked.

The Democrats also claimed victory in South Carolina, Florida, and Louisiana, but Republican state authorities were able to identify more than enough blatant fraud and voter intimidation (despite the army's efforts to keep order) to yield revised returns showing Republican victory in all three states. Slates of electors for both parties from each state demanded recognition of their votes. Hayes needed the votes of all three states to win. Tilden would triumph if he gained any one of the three.

Faced with a constitutional crisis not quite like any it had encountered before, Congress passed a bill setting up a complicated system for deciding the dispute. The law called for a fifteen-member Electoral Commission to investigate the rival claims and decide who should get the votes of the three disputed states. The commission's members would include five senators— three from the majority Republicans and two from the minority Democrats. Five more members would come from the House—three from the Democrats, who then held the majority there, and two from the Republicans. The final five members would come from the Supreme Court—two Republicans, two Democrats, and one other chosen by those four. When the fifteen members were in place, the commission spent the month of February listening to arguments from lawyers for both sides. Then in a series of eight-to-seven votes it decided to award all twenty disputed electoral votes to Hayes, giving him the election.

The commission finished its work and adjourned on March 2. Inauguration day was two days away, and Congress still had to give its formal acceptance to the commission's findings. Congressional Republicans naturally backed acceptance, as did the leadership of the Democratic Party, but a coterie of disaffected Democratic senators threatened a filibuster to prevent approval. This would at least delay inauguration day and exacerbate the constitutional crisis. In the end, the recalcitrant southern senators refrained, possibly, as some have suggested, because of informal discussions with representatives of Hayes who had promised them that in exchange for their acquiescence in his inauguration, Hayes would withdraw federal troops from the three remaining southern states, throwing their Republican governments to the night-riding wolves. In fact, Hayes had been talking about a pullout even before the election, and Grant had withdrawn the troops from Florida before inauguration day. If such discussions did take place, they concluded not in a formal deal but, at the most, in an informal understanding that came to be known as the Compromise of 1877.

Thus Reconstruction came to an end. The North, politically weary after decades of sectional conflict, finally gave in to white southern intransigence on the issues of voting rights and civil rights for southern blacks. White Democratic regimes came to power in all of the southern states, and they used both legal means (such as literacy tests and poll taxes) and the well-tried illegal means of lynching and intimidation to maintain their control and deny blacks the right to vote. White supremacy was maintained, and blacks were relegated to a legal netherworld of second-class citizenship known as "Jim Crow."

By the 1890s, a renewed emphasis on national unity and sectional reconciliation led to northern acceptance of a substantial segment of the white South's mythology regarding the nature of the conflict. In the new reconciliationist version of history, embraced on both sides of the Mason-Dixon Line, the war had never had any fundamental relationship to issues of race or slavery. Each side had, so the story ran, fought nobly for a different aspect of the American ideal—the South for self-determination and the North for majority rule.

The claim of the Declaration of Independence that all men were "created equal and endowed by their Creator with certain unalienable rights" was best not remembered in connection with the Civil War, though it had been Lincoln's theme from start to finish. Also better forgotten in the reconciliationist synthesis of the 1890s and beyond were the blacks themselves, who became the innocent bystanders of the war. In exchange, white southerners allowed that the restoration of the Union had been a good thing after all. That was the story the country maintained, for the most part, for the next three generations, and so the history books were written. Only in the second half of the twentieth century, with the centennial of the Civil War rapidly approaching, did Americans (or some of them) begin to recognize a much different story in the diaries, letters, and speeches of the participants, a story well known during the war but forgotten or out of the nation's conscious memory for almost three-quarters of a century.

"THERE IS MORE INVOLVED
IN THIS CONTEST"

The Civil War remains one of the largest phenomena in U.S. history, and in the nineteenth century it dwarfs all other events. About 2.9 million men served as Union soldiers during the course of the conflict, about 1.5 million of them under regular three-year enlistments. Total enrolled Confederate soldiers came to roughly 1.2 million men, of whom perhaps eight hundred thousand were long-term enlistees. This means that about one in every four northern men served in the army during the course of the war and almost one in three southern white men. Additionally, a little more than one in nine African American men served as soldiers during the war.

In numbers of casualties the Civil War far exceeded any other American conflict. The roughly 620,000 soldiers who died between Fort Sumter and Appomattox was almost half again the total U.S. dead in World War II, the nation's second-costliest conflict. When the war dead are considered as a percentage of the country's population at the time, the cost of the Civil War appears in even starker terms. The dead of the Civil War made up 8 percent of the total male population of the United States between the ages of thirteen and forty-three. The 360,000 northern dead equaled 6 percent of northern males of that age-group, while the South's 260,000 deaths took an appalling 18 percent of that cohort of its population. In addition to the dead, 270,000 Union and at least 90,000 Confederate soldiers suffered wounds. To this day, about half of all the American men who have died in the nation's wars were casualties of the Civil War.

The war brought devastation to the South, where most of the fighting and marching to and fro of armies had taken place. Many public buildings, factories, and warehouses had been destroyed, as had private houses in some areas. Thousands of miles of railroad track had been torn up and destroyed, the ties burned, and the rails heated over the fires and then twisted or else bent around trees or telegraph poles into what had been nicknamed Sherman neckties. Crops had been trampled, consumed, or burned by the armies. Burning was also the fate of untold thousands of miles of rail fence, the only barriers protecting growing crops from grazing animals. Not that there were as many grazing animals as there had been four years before. Nineteenth-century wars had a voracious appetite for horses and mules, which died in their thousands—shot, starved, or worked to death. Hogs, cattle, and poultry had found their way into the stomachs of the passing armies in vast numbers.

Nearly one-third of the white men—and those the most active and vigorous—had been absent for most of the past four years, while their farms had languished and been overrun by weeds. Worst of all, the South had lost its chief capital investment and a large part of its labor force in the form of almost four million slaves, freed by the Emancipation Proclamation and the Thirteenth Amendment. The region would take decades to recover economically.

Although the conventional military phase of the conflict most commonly called the Civil War lasted from 1861 to 1865, Reconstruction represented an unconventional phase of conflict. Though unconventional, it was still very much a civil war, often with real bloodshed though not in the vast quantities the conventional phase had elicited. The U.S. government won a clear and overwhelming victory in the conventional phase of the conflict because of a combination of superior resources and manpower and superior civilian and military leadership, which overcame the Confederate advantages of the strategic defensive, the vast size of its territory, and the tangible nature of its war aims. Thanks especially to Lincoln's superb civilian leadership, northern will to fight endured long enough to allow northern superiority in numbers and generalship to crush the Confederacy's uniformed armies.

In Reconstruction, however, the phase of the conflict that followed 1865, the advantages went the other way. The American people have never been very good at coping with a situation that is not quite open war but not quite peace. They have also fared poorly at waging a disputed occupation far from home against a hostile local civilian population. Lincoln was gone, and even he would have had difficulty making the aim of continued struggle clear to northern voters and convincing those voters that the goal was worth the effort, especially since many even in the North partook of the racist assumptions of their day. In the end, a desperate white southern commitment to maintain white supremacy finally wore out the North's will to complete a revolutionary transformation of society that almost no one had envisioned when the guns first spoke at Fort Sumter almost sixteen years before. The result was a modification of the original peace terms. The Union was preserved and slavery abolished, but if the slaves were not slaves any more, neither were they fully free American citizens.

Yet in noting the failure of the Civil War generation to complete the overwhelming task it faced, we should not lose sight of the amazing things it did accomplish. These were twofold. First, the Civil War generation established that a free government truly could function and survive—that, as Lincoln said, it need not be either too strong to allow its people liberty or else too weak to secure its own survival. Second, the Americans of this generation removed the blot of slavery from the escutcheon of American freedom. In doing so they had answered the question Lincoln had put to the 164th Ohio in August 1864 as to "whether your children and my children shall enjoy the privileges we have enjoyed." If they had left the final working out of all the fruits of their accomplishments to future generations, the Americans of the 1860s had nevertheless, in what they had accomplished, risen "to the height of a generation of men worthy of a free Government."[1]

ACKNOWLEDGMENTS

I t is a pleasure to acknowledge with gratitude the kind assistance of several who have aided in the preparation of this book. Justin Solonick read and critiqued the chapters and offered many excellent suggestions for revisions. Similarly, Niels Aaboe of Rowman & Littlefield offered good ideas for the development of the work. Both have contributed to the significant improvement of the final product. Niels and the rest of the staff at Rowman & Littlefield were very supportive and patient throughout the process of writing and publishing the book. Charles D. Grear was a very helpful and competent mapmaker. His knowledge of the Civil War made the process of deciding what should go into the maps infinitely easier than would otherwise have been the case. Finally, my wife, Leah, proofread the manuscript for me and provided valuable moral support. To all I extend my sincere thanks.

SOURCES AND NOTES

PROLOGUE

1. Jim Leeke, ed., *A Hundred Days to Richmond: Ohio's "Hundred Days" Men in the Civil War* (Bloomington: Indiana University Press, 1999), 193.
2. Abraham Lincoln, Speech to the 164th Ohio Regiment, Washington, D.C., August 18, 1864, Lincoln, Abraham, 1809–1865, in Roy P. Basler, ed., *Collected Works of Abraham Lincoln*, 9 vols. (New Brunswick, NJ: Rutgers University Press, 1953–1955), 7:504–5.

CHAPTER 1: AMERICA'S LONG ROAD TO CIVIL WAR

On the development of slavery in colonial Virginia, see Edmund S. Morgan, *American Slavery, American Freedom: The Ordeal of Colonial Virginia* (New York: Norton, 2003). For a history of the somewhat different course of slavery in colonial South Carolina, see Peter Wood, *Black Majority: Negroes in Colonial South Carolina from 1670 through the Stono Rebellion* (New York: Knopf, 1974). For a brief discussion of the crises leading to the Missouri Compromise and the Compromise of 1850 as well as that stemming from the Kansas-Nebraska Act, with their relevance to the coming of the Civil War, see Don E. Fehrenbacher, *The South and Three Sectional Crises* (Baton Rouge: Louisiana State University Press, 1980). On Nat Turner's Rebellion, see Stephen B. Oates, *The Fires of Jubilee: Nat Turner's Fierce Rebellion* (New York: Harper & Row, 1975). On the abolitionist movement, see Frederick J. Blue, *No Taint of Compromise: Crusaders in Antislavery Politics* (Baton Rouge: Louisiana State University Press, 2005). On the Nullification Crisis, see William W. Freehling, *Prelude to Civil War: The Nullification Controversy in South Carolina, 1816–1836* (New York: Oxford University Press, 1992). On the Gag Rule and the long and determined fight against it by former president John Quincy Adams, see William Lee Miller, *Arguing about Slavery: The Great Battle in the United States Congress* (New York: Knopf, 1996). On how the sectional expansion of the 1840s gave new urgency to the slavery controversy, see Steven E. Woodworth, *Manifest Destinies: America's Westward Expansion and the Road to the Civil War* (New York: Knopf, 2010). On the Compromise of 1850, see John C. Waugh, *On the Brink of Civil War: The Compromise of 1850 and How It Changed the Course of American History* (Wilmington, DE: Scholarly Resources, 2003). The classic biography of Stephen A. Douglas is by Robert W. Johannsen (New York: Oxford University Press, 1973). Several works deal with Lincoln's political career during the 1850s. For a classic account, see Don E. Fehrenbacher, *Prelude of Greatness: Lincoln in the 1850's* (Stanford, CA: Stanford University Press, 1962). Two excellent recent books are John C. Waugh, *One Man Great Enough: Abraham Lincoln's Road to Civil War* (Orlando: Harcourt, 2007), and Gary Ecelbarger, *The Great Comeback: How Abraham Lincoln Beat the Odds to Win the 1860 Republican Nomination* (New York: Thomas Dunne Books, 2008). A dated but still somewhat useable overview of the 1850s is David E. Potter's *The Impending Crisis, 1848–1861* (New York: Harper & Row, 1976). For a more modern treatment of the decade, see Eric H. Walther, *The Shattering of the Union: America in the 1850s* (Wilmington, DE: Scholarly Resources, 2004). On the Fire-Eaters, see Walther's book of that title (Baton Rouge: Louisiana State University Press, 1992). For a classic and still-profound treatment of the Lincoln-Douglas Debates, see Harry Jaffa, *Crisis of the House Divided: An Interpretation of the Issues in the Lincoln-Douglas Debates* (Garden City, NY: Doubleday, 1959). For an excellent and thought-provoking modern treatment of the debates, see Allen Guelzo, *Lincoln and Douglas: The Debates that Defined America* (New York: Simon & Schuster, 2008).

1. Paul Leicester Ford, ed., *The Works of Thomas Jefferson, Volume 12* (New York: G. P. Putnam's Sons, 1905), 159.

2. Thomas Jefferson to John Holmes, April 22, 1820, Library of Congress.

3. Abraham Lincoln, *Collected Works of Abraham Lincoln*, 9 vols. (New Brunswick, NJ: Rutgers University Press, 1953), 2:461–62.

CHAPTER 2: AND THE WAR CAME

On John Brown and his raid on Harpers Ferry, see David S. Reynolds, *John Brown, Abolitionist: The Man Who Killed Slavery, Sparked the Civil War, and Seeded Civil Rights* (New York: Vintage, 2006), and Evan S. Carton, *Patriotic Treason: John Brown and the Soul of America* (Lincoln, NE: Bison Books, 2009). On the entire secession crisis, see James L. Abrahamson, *The Men of Secession and Civil War* (Wilmington, DE: SR Books, 2000). On Lincoln's rise to the presidency, see John C. Waugh, *One Man Great Enough: Abraham Lincoln's Road to Civil War* (New York: Harcourt, 2007); Gary Ecelbarger, *The Great Comeback: How Abraham Lincoln Beat the Odds to Win the 1860 Republican Nomination* (New York: Thomas Dunne, 2008); and Harold Holzer, *Lincoln at Cooper Union: The Speech That Made Abraham Lincoln President* (New York: Simon & Schuster, 2004). On the First Battle of Bull Run, see Ethan S. Rafuse, *A Single Grand Victory: The First Campaign and Battle of Manassas* (Wilmington, DE: SR Books, 2002), and William C. Davis, *Battle at Bull Run: A History of the First Major Campaign of the Civil War* (Baton Rouge: Louisiana State University Press, 1981).

1. Abraham Lincoln, *Collected Works of Abraham Lincoln*, 9 vols. (New Brunswick, NJ: Rutgers University Press, 1953), 4:271.

2. Lincoln, *Collected Works*, 8:332 (emphasis in the original).

3. Some have claimed that Taney did not assert that this was true but rather only claimed that it was the opinion at the time of the writing of the Constitution. In fact,

Taney quoted it approvingly and implied that since it was, in his opinion, the belief at the time of the founding, it should still prevail in his day.
4. Lincoln, *Collected Works*, 4:532.

CHAPTER 3: ALL QUIET ALONG
THE POTOMAC

On the dispute within the Confederate high command regarding the responsibility for the failure to reap major dividends from the victory at Bull Run, see Steven E. Woodworth, *Davis and Lee at War* (Lawrence: University Press of Kansas, 1995). On George B. McClellan, see Stephen W. Sears, *George B. McClellan: The Young Napoleon* (New York: Ticknor & Fields, 1988), the definitive biography of this troubled general. For a contrarian (favorable) interpretation of McClellan, see Ethan S. Rafuse, *McClellan's War: The Failure of Moderation in the Struggle for the Union* (Bloomington: Indiana University Press, 2005).

For an outstanding treatment of all aspects of the events surrounding the Battle of Wilson's Creek, see William Garrett Piston and Richard W. Hatcher III, *Wilson's Creek: The Second Battle of the Civil War and the Men Who Fought It* (Chapel Hill: University of North Carolina Press, 2000). On the end of Kentucky neutrality, see Steven E. Woodworth, *Jefferson Davis and His Generals: The Failure of Confederate Command in the West* (Lawrence: University Press of Kansas, 1990).

On Ulysses S. Grant, see Brooks D. Simpson, *Ulysses S. Grant: Triumph over Adversity, 1822–1865* (Boston: Houghton Mifflin, 2000), the first volume of an anticipated two-volume biography and much of the best work on Grant. On Grant's operations around Cairo and in command of what was to become the Army of the Tennessee, see Steven E. Woodworth, *Nothing but Victory: The Army of the Tennessee, 1861–1865* (New York: Knopf, 2006).

On the Joint Committee for the Conduct of the War, see Bruce Tap, *Over Lincoln's Shoulder: The Committee on the Conduct of the War* (Lawrence: University Press of Kansas, 1998).

On naval operations in the Civil War, see Spencer C. Tucker, *A Short History of the Civil War at Sea* (Wilmington, DE: Scholarly Resources, 2002). For a specialized account of blockade-running, see Stephen R. Wise, *Lifeline of the Confederacy: Blockade Running during the Civil War* (Columbia: University of South Carolina Press, 1988).

For a discussion of Union policy toward the black residents of the Port Royal enclave, see Willie Lee Rose, *Rehearsal for Reconstruction: The Port Royal Experiment* (Indianapolis: Bobbs-Merrill, 1964).

On Confederate efforts to use cotton as a source of diplomatic leverage, see Frank L. Owsley, *King Cotton Diplomacy: Foreign Relations of the Confederate States of America* (Chicago: University of Chicago Press, 1931). On U.S. foreign relations during the war, see Howard Jones, *Union in Peril: The Crisis over British Intervention in the Civil War* (Chapel Hill: University of North Carolina Press, 1992); Howard Jones, *Abraham Lincoln and a New Birth of Freedom: The Union and Slavery in the Diplomacy of the Civil War* (Lincoln: University of Nebraska Press, 1999); R. J. M. Blackett, *Divided Hearts: Britain and the American Civil War* (Baton Rouge: Louisiana State University Press, 2001); Norman Ferris, *Desperate Diplomacy: William H. Seward's Foreign Policy* (Knoxville: University of Tennessee Press, 1976); and Dean B. Mahin, *One War at a Time: The International Dimensions of the American Civil War* (Washington, DC: Brassey's, 1999). On the work of the outstanding U.S. minister to Britain during the war, see Martin B. Duberman, *Charles Francis Adams, 1807–1886* (Boston: Houghton Mifflin, 1961). On the Trent Affair itself, see Norman Ferris, *The Trent Affair: A Diplomatic Crisis* (Knoxville: University of Tennessee Press, 1977).

1. Alexander H. Stephens, "Cornerstone Address, March 21, 1861," in *The Rebellion Record: A Diary of American Events with Documents, Narratives, Illustrative Incidents, Poetry, etc.*, vol. 1, ed. Frank Moore (New York: O. P. Putnam, 1862), 44–46.

2. James D. Richardson, *A Compilation of the Messages and Papers of the Presidents*, vol. 6 (Washington, DC: Government Printing Office, 1907), 430.

3. Hammond's complete speech can be found in *Selections from the Letters and Speeches of the Hon. James H. Hammond, of South Carolina* (New York: John F. Trow & Co., 1866), 311–22.

4. Jasper Ridley, *Lord Palmerston* (New York: Dutton, 1971), 554.

5. David Herbert Donald, *Lincoln* (New York: Simon & Schuster, 1995), 330.

CHAPTER 4: THE EMERGENCE OF GRANT

On Lincoln's relations with his generals and his efforts to get action out of McClellan, see T. Harry Williams, *Lincoln and His Generals* (Baton Rouge: Louisiana State University Press, 19). On Davis's struggles with Beauregard and Joseph E. Johnston, see Steven E. Woodworth, *Davis and Lee at War* (Lawrence: University Press of Kansas, 1995). On Davis's relations with Albert Sidney Johnston, see Woodworth, *Jefferson Davis and His Generals: The Failure of Confederate Command in the West* (Lawrence: University Press of Kansas, 1990).

On the battles of Fort Henry and Fort Donelson, see B. Franklin Cooling, *Forts Henry and Donelson—The Key to the Confederate Heartland* (Knoxville: University of Tennessee Press, 1987); Spencer C. Tucker, *Andrew Foote: Civil War Admiral on Western Waters* (Annapolis, MD: Naval Institute Press, 2000); and Kendall D. Gott, *Where the South Lost the War: An Analysis of the Fort Henry-Fort Donelson Campaign, February 1862* (Mechanicsburg, PA: Stackpole Books, 2003). On the role of what would become the Confederate Army of Tennessee in this and subsequent campaigns, see Thomas Lawrence Connelly, *Army of the Heartland: The Army of Tennessee, 1861–1862* (Baton Rouge: Louisiana State University Press, 1967). For the role of the opposing Union army that was to become the Army of the Tennessee in this and subsequent campaigns, see Steven E. Woodworth, *Nothing but Victory: The Army of the Tennessee, 1861–1865* (New York: Knopf, 2006).

On the Pea Ridge Campaign, see William L. Shea and Earl J. Hess, *Pea Ridge: Civil War Campaign in the West* (Chapel Hill: University of North Carolina Press, 1992). On the New Mexico Campaign and the Battle of Glorieta Pass, see Thomas S. Edrington and John Taylor, *The Battle of Glorieta Pass: A Gettysburg in the West, March 26–28, 1862* (Albuquerque: University of New Mexico Press, 1998), and Donald S. Frazier, *Blood and Treasure: Confederate Empire in the Southwest* (College Station: Texas A&M University Press, 1995).

Several good books cover the Shiloh Campaign. They include Edward Cunningham, Gary D. Joiner, and Timothy B. Smith, *Shiloh and the Western Campaign* (El Dorado Hills, CA: Savas Beatie, 2009); Steven E. Woodworth, ed., *The Shiloh Campaign* (Carbondale: Southern Illinois University Press, 2009); Larry J. Daniel, *Shiloh: The Battle That Changed the Civil War* (New York: Simon & Schuster, 1997); Wiley Sword, *Shiloh: Bloody*

April (New York: Morrow, 1974); and James Lee McDonough, *Shiloh: In Hell before Night* (Knoxville: University of Tennessee Press, 1977).

1. William E. Dodd, *Jefferson Davis* (Philadelphia: George W. Jacobs, 1907), 265.
2. Ulysses S. Grant, *Personal Memoirs of Ulysses S. Grant*, 2 vols. (New York: Charles L. Webster, 1885), 1:368.

CHAPTER 5: MCCLELLAN'S
GREAT CAMPAIGN

On Lincoln's interaction with McClellan, see T. Harry Williams, *Lincoln and His Generals* (New York: Knopf, 1952). On the naval battle of Hampton Roads, see William C. Davis, *Duel between the First Ironclads* (Mechanicsburg, PA: Stackpole Books, 1994); Gene A. Smith, *Iron and Heavy Guns: Duel between the Monitor and Merrimac* (Fort Worth, TX: Ryan Place Publishers, 1996); and Spencer C. Tucker, *A Short History of the Civil War at Sea* (Wilmington, DE: Scholarly Resources, 2002).

On the Peninsula Campaign, see Stephen W. Sears, *To the Gates of Richmond: The Peninsula Campaign* (New York: Ticknor & Fields, 1992). On Jackson's Shenandoah Valley Campaign, see Robert G. Tanner, *Stonewall in the Valley: Thomas J. "Stonewall" Jackson's Shenandoah Valley Campaign, Spring 1862* (Mechanicsville, PA: Stackpole Books, 1996). On Davis's interaction with Johnston and Lee during these operations, see Steven E. Woodworth, *Davis and Lee at War* (Lawrence: University Press of Kansas, 1995). On Robert E. Lee, see Emory M. Thomas, *Robert E. Lee: A Biography* (New York: Norton, 1995). For a more critical view of Lee, see Alan T. Nolan, *Lee Considered: General Robert E. Lee and Civil War History* (Chapel Hill: University of North Carolina Press, 1991). For the definitive biography of Jackson, see James I. Robertson Jr., *Stonewall Jackson: The Man, The Soldier, The Legend* (New York: Macmillan, 1997).

1. William W. Averell, "With the Cavalry on the Peninsula," in Robert U. Johnson and Clarence C. Buel, eds., *Battles and Leaders of the Civil War*, 4 vols. (New York: Thomas Yoseloff, 1956), 2:432.

CHAPTER 6: CONFEDERATE
HIGH TIDE

On the career of George B. McClellan, see Stephen W. Sears, *George B. McClellan: The Young Napoleon* (New York: Ticknor & Fields, 1988). On the Maryland Campaign and the Battle of Antietam, see Sears's *Landscape Turned Red: The Battle of Antietam* (New Haven, CT: Ticknor & Fields, 1983).

On the handful of women who disguised themselves as men to enlist in the Civil War armies, see DeAnne Blanton and Lauren M. Cook, *They Fought Like Demons: Women Soldiers in the American Civil War* (Baton Rouge: Louisiana State University Press, 2002).

For an excellent discussion of Lincoln's progress toward emancipation as well as the significance of the Emancipation Proclamation, see Allen C. Guelzo, *Lincoln's Emancipation Proclamation: The End of Slavery in America* (New York: Simon & Schuster, 2004).

On the second Bull Run Campaign, see John J. Hennessy, *Return to Bull Run: The Campaign and Battle of Second Manassas* (New York: Simon & Schuster, 1993). On Lee's conduct of the summer campaigns of 1862 and his relations with Jefferson Davis, see Steven E. Woodworth, *Davis and Lee at War* (Lawrence: University Press of Kansas, 1995). On the significance of Lee's victories on Confederate morale and nationalism, see Gary W. Gallagher, *The Confederate War* (Cambridge, MA: Harvard University Press, 1997).

1. Roy Edgar Appleman, ed., *Abraham Lincoln: From His Own Words and Contemporary Accounts* (Washington, DC: U.S. Department of the Interior, National Park Service, 1942), 31.

2. Appleman, *Abraham Lincoln*, 31.

3. U.S. War Department, *The War of the Rebellion: Official Records of the Union and Confederate Armies*, 128 vols. (Washington, DC: Government Printing Office, 1881–1901), series 1, vol. 12, pt. 3, p. 474 (Hereinafter cited as OR; except as otherwise noted, all references are to series 1).

4. John J. Hennessy, *Return to Bull Run: The Campaign and Battle of Second Manassas* (Norman: University of Oklahoma Press, 1993), 241–42; A. Wilson Greene, *The Second Battle of Manassas* (Fort Washington, PA: Eastern National, 2006), 38.

CHAPTER 7: LINCOLN TAKES
NEW MEASURES

On Lincoln and the Emancipation Proclamation, see Allen C. Guelzo, *Lincoln's Emancipation Proclamation: The End of Slavery in America* (New York: Simon & Schuster, 2004). On British reaction to the Emancipation Proclamation, see Howard Jones, *Abraham Lincoln and a New Birth of Freedom: The Union and Slavery in the Diplomacy of the Civil War* (Lincoln: University of Nebraska Press, 1999).

On the Confederate invasion of Kentucky, see Kenneth W. Noe, *Perryville: This Grand Havoc of Battle* (Lexington: University Press of Kentucky, 2001), and Steven E. Woodworth, *Jefferson Davis and His Generals: The Failure of Confederate Command in the West* (Lawrence: University Press of Kansas, 1990), which also covers the activities of Van Dorn and Price in Mississippi. Similarly, Earl J. Hess, *Banners to the Breeze: The Kentucky Campaign, Corinth, and Stones River* (Lincoln: University of Nebraska Press, 2000), covers both campaigns as well as the later Battle of Stones River. For a brief account of the Kentucky Campaign, see James McDonough, *War in Kentucky: From Shiloh to Perryville* (Knoxville: University of Tennessee Press, 1994).

On the Battle of Fredericksburg, see George C. Rable, *Fredericksburg! Fredericksburg!* (Chapel Hill: University of North Carolina Press, 2002). On the battles of Corinth, Iuka, and the Hatchie River, see, in addition to Woodworth's and Hess's works mentioned above, Steven E. Woodworth, *Nothing but Victory: The Army of the Tennessee, 1861–1865* (New York: Knopf, 2006), and, for a brief account, Steven Nathaniel Dossman, *Campaign for Corinth: Blood in Mississippi* (Abilene, TX: McWhiney Foundation Press, 2006). On Ulysses S. Grant, see Brooks D. Simpson, *Ulysses S. Grant: Triumph over Adversity, 1822–1865* (Boston: Houghton Mifflin, 2000). On the Battle of Stones River, in addition to Hess's work mentioned above, see James McDonough, *Stones River—Bloody Winter in Tennessee* (Knoxville: University of Tennessee Press, 1994).

1. OR vol. 30, p. 442.

CHAPTER 8: "PEACE DOES NOT APPEAR SO DISTANT AS IT DID"

On discouragement within Grant's Army of the Tennessee during the winter encampment in front of Vicksburg, see Steven E. Woodworth, *Nothing but Victory: The Army of the Tennessee, 1861–1865* (New York: Knopf, 2006). On the focus of Confederate morale and nationality on Lee's army, see Gary W. Gallagher, *The Confederate War* (Cambridge, MA: Harvard University Press, 1997). On dissension within the high command of Bragg's Army of Tennessee, see Steven E. Woodworth, *Jefferson Davis and His Generals: The Failure of Confederate Command in the West* (Lawrence: University Press of Kansas, 1990), and Thomas L. Connelly, *Autumn of Glory: The Army of Tennessee, 1862–1865* (Baton Rouge: Louisiana State University Press, 1971).

There are a number of excellent works on Grant's Vicksburg Campaign. They include Michael B. Ballard, *Vicksburg: The Campaign That Opened the Mississippi* (Chapel Hill: University of North Carolina Press, 2004); William L. Shea and Terrence J. Winschell, *Vicksburg Is the Key: The Struggle for the Mississippi River* (Lincoln: University of Nebraska Press, 2003); Warren E. Grabau, *Ninety-Eight Days: A Geographer's View of the Vicksburg Campaign* (Knoxville: University of Tennessee Press, 2000); and Edwin C. Bearss's encyclopedic three-volume *The Campaign for Vicksburg* (Dayton, OH: Morningside, 1985–1986). Additional insights on the opposing commanders can be found in Brooks D. Simpson, *Ulysses S. Grant: Triumph over Adversity* (Boston: Houghton Mifflin, 2000), and Michael B. Ballard, *Pemberton* (Jackson: University Press of Mississippi, 1991).

On the Battle of Chancellorsville, see Ernest B. Furgurson, *Chancellorsville 1863: The Souls of the Brave* (New York: Knopf, 1992). For an alternative interpretation of the battle, strongly favorable to Hooker, see Stephen W. Sears, *Chancellorsville* (Boston: Houghton Mifflin, 1996).

Thanks in part to the myth that it was somehow the turning point or decisive battle of the Civil War, Gettysburg has attracted a voluminous literature, of which the following is a minute selection. For a short overview of the campaign and battle, see Steven E. Woodworth, *Beneath a Northern Sky: A Short History of the Gettysburg Campaign* (Lanham, MD: Rowman & Littlefield, 2008). The classic work on the campaign is Edwin B. Coddington, *The Gettysburg Campaign: A Study in Command* (New York: Scribner's, 1968). A more recent comprehensive study of the campaign is Stephen W. Sears, *Gettysburg* (Boston: Houghton Mifflin, 2003). On the decision by the Confederate cabinet to allow Lee to keep Longstreet's corps and invade Pennsylvania, see Steven E. Woodworth, *Davis and Lee at War* (Lawrence: University Press of Kansas, 1995). On the first day's fighting at Gettysburg, see Warren W. Hassler, *Crisis at the Crossroads: The First Day at Gettysburg* (Tuscaloosa: University of Alabama Press, 1970), and Harry W. Pfanz, *Gettysburg: The First Day* (Chapel Hill: University of North Carolina Press, 2001). On the second day, see Harry W. Pfanz, *Gettysburg: The Second Day* (Chapel Hill: University of North Carolina Press, 1987). On the fighting on Culp's and Cemetery hills, spanning the second and third days, see Harry W. Pfanz, *Gettysburg: Culp's Hill and Cemetery Hill* (Chapel Hill: University of North Carolina Press, 1993). On the third day's fighting, see Jeffry D. Wert, *Gettysburg: Day Three* (New York: Simon & Schuster, 2001). On the assault known as Pickett's Charge, see George Ripley Stewart, *Pickett's Charge: A Microhistory of the Final Attack at Gettysburg, July 3, 1863* (Boston: Houghton Mifflin, 1959); John Michael Priest, *Into the Fight: Pickett's Charge at Gettysburg* (Shippensburg, PA: White Mane, 1998); and Earl J. Hess, *Pickett's Charge: The Last Attack at Gettysburg* (Chapel Hill: University of North

Carolina Press, 2001). On Lee's retreat from Gettysburg and the impressive haul of supplies that his army took with it to Virginia, see Kent Masterson Brown, *Retreat from Gettysburg: Lee, Logistics, and the Pennsylvania Campaign* (Chapel Hill: University of North Carolina Press, 2005).

On the Tullahoma Campaign, see Steven E. Woodworth, *Six Armies in Tennessee: The Chickamauga and Chattanooga Campaigns* (Lincoln: University of Nebraska Press, 1998), and Michael R. Bradley, *Tullahoma: The 1863 Campaign for the Control of Middle Tennessee* (Shippensburg, PA: Burd Street Press, 2000).

    1. OR vol. 25, pt. 2, p. 4.

    2. OR ser. 3, vol. 3, p. 734.

CHAPTER 9: "THE
UNFINISHED WORK"

On Confederate finance, see Mark Thornton and Robert B. Ekeland Jr., *Tariffs, Blockades, and Inflation: The Economics of the Civil War* (Wilmington, DE: Scholarly Resources, 2004), and Douglas B. Ball, *Financial Failure and Confederate Defeat* (Urbana: University of Illinois Press, 1991). On the Richmond Bread Riot, see Emory M. Thomas, *The Confederate State of Richmond: A Biography of the Capital* (Baton Rouge: Louisiana State University Press, 1971). On Union conscription and how it was administered, see Eugene C. Murdock, *One Million Men: The Civil War Draft in the North* (Madison: State Historical Society of Wisconsin, 1971). On the New York City draft riot, see Edward K. Spann, *Gotham at War: New York City, 1860–1865* (Wilmington, DE: SR Books, 2002). On civil liberties in the Union during the war, see Mark E. Neely, *The Fate of Liberty: Abraham Lincoln and Civil Liberties* (New York: Oxford University Press, 1991). For a contrasting study of civil liberties in the Confederacy, see Neely's *Confederate Bastille: Jefferson Davis and Civil Liberties* (Milwaukee, WI: Marquette University Press, 1993). On Clement Vallandigham, see Frank L. Klement, *Limits of Dissent: Clement L. Vallandigham and the Civil War* (New York: Fordham University Press, 1998).

    On the Chickamauga and Chattanooga campaigns, see Steven E. Woodworth, *Six Armies in Tennessee: The Chickamauga and Chattanooga Campaigns* (Lincoln: University of Nebraska Press, 1998). On the Battle of Chattanooga, see also Wiley Sword, *Mountains Touched with Fire: Chattanooga Besieges* (New York: St. Martin's Press, 1995). On the Gettysburg Address and Lincoln's oratorical skill in general, see Ronald C. White Jr., *The Eloquent President: A Portrait of Lincoln through His Words* (New York: Random House, 2005).

    1. Archer Anderson, "The Campaign and Battle of Chickamauga," *Southern Historical Society Papers*, 52 vols. (Richmond: Virginia Historical Society, 1876–1959), 9:396.

    2. Roy P. Basler, ed., *Collected Works of Abraham Lincoln*, 9 vols. (New Brunswick, NJ: Rutgers University Press, 1953–1955), 7:23.

CHAPTER 10: FROM THE RAPIDAN
TO THE JAMES TO THE POTOMAC

On Grant's plans for the 1864 campaign, see Brooks D. Simpson, *Ulysses S. Grant: Triumph over Adversity, 1822–1865* (Boston: Houghton Mifflin, 2000). On the campaign from the Wilderness to Spotsylvania to North Anna and Cold Harbor, see Mark Grimsley's excellent short summary *And Keep Moving On: The Virginia Campaign, May–June 1864* (Lincoln: University of Nebraska Press, 2002). Gordon Rhea has provided a more detailed treatment of the campaign in his excellent series of books, *The Battle of the Wilderness, May 5–6, 1864* (Baton Rouge: Louisiana State University Press, 1994), *The Battles for Spotsylvania Court House and the Road to Yellow Tavern, May 7–12, 1864* (Baton Rouge: Louisiana State University Press, 1997), *To the North Anna River: Grant and Lee, May 13–25, 1864* (Baton Rouge: Louisiana State University Press, 2000), and *Cold Harbor: Grant and Lee, May 26–June 3, 1864* (Baton Rouge: Louisiana State University Press, 2002).

On Butler's Bermuda Hundred Campaign, see William Glenn Robertson's *Back Door to Richmond: The Bermuda Hundred Campaign, April–June 1864* (Newark: University of Delaware Press, 1987). On Sigel's unsuccessful campaign in the Shenandoah Valley, see William C. Davis, *The Battle of New Market* (Harrisburg, PA: Stackpole Books, 1993). For two excellent accounts of Early's raid on Washington, see Benjamin Franklin Cooling's books, *Jubal Early's Raid on Washington* (Tuscaloosa: University of Alabama Press, 2007), and *Monocacy: The Battle That Saved Washington* (Shippensburg, PA: White Mane, 1997).

1. Joseph T. Glatthaar, *Partners in Command: The Relationships between Leaders in the Civil War* (New York: Free Press, 1994), 153.

2. Brooks D. Simpson, *Ulysses S. Grant: Triumph over Adversity, 1822–1865* (Boston: Houghton Mifflin, 2000), 298–99.

3. Jean Edward Smith, *Grant* (New York: Simon & Schuster, 2001), 345.

4. Mark Grimsley, *And Keep Moving On: The Virginia Campaign, May–June 1864.* (Lincoln: University of Nebraska Press, 2002), 148.

CHAPTER 11: THE
ATLANTA CAMPAIGN

On the Atlanta Campaign, see Stephen Davis, *Atlanta Will Fall: Sherman, Joe Johnston, and the Yankee Heavy Battalions* (Wilmington, DE: Scholarly Resources, 2001), and Richard M. McMurry, *Atlanta 1864: Last Chance for the Confederacy* (Lincoln: University of Nebraska Press, 2000). On the climactic Battle of Atlanta, see Gary L. Ecelbarger, *The Day Dixie Died: The Battle of Atlanta* (New York: St. Martin's Press, 2010). Recent decades have seen the publication of several biographies of Sherman. These include John F. Marszalek, *Sherman: A Soldier's Passion for Order* (New York: Free Press, 1993); Lee B. Kennett, *Sherman: A Soldier's Life* (New York: HarperCollins, 2001); Stanley P. Hirshson, *The White Tecumseh: A Biography of General William T. Sherman* (New York: Wiley, 1997); and Steven E. Woodworth, *Sherman* (New York: Palgrave Macmillan, 2009). Craig L. Symonds makes the best case he can for Johnston in his ably researched and written *Joseph E. Johnston: A Civil War Biography* (New York: Norton, 1992). On Hood, see Richard M. McMurry, *John Bell Hood and the War for Southern Independence* (Lincoln: University of Nebraska Press, 1992), and David Coffey, *John Bell Hood and the Struggle for Atlanta* (Abilene, TX: McWhiney Foundation Press, 1998).

On the election campaign of 1864, see John C. Waugh, *Reelecting Lincoln: The Battle for the 1864 Presidency* (New York: Crown, 1997).

1. Dunbar Rowland, ed., *Jefferson Davis, Constitutionalist: His Letters, Papers, and Speeches*, 10 vols. (Jackson: Mississippi Department of Archives and History, 1923), 6:295.

2. Wiley Sword, *The Confederacy's Last Hurrah: Spring Hill, Franklin, and Nashville* (Lawrence: University Press of Kansas, 1993), 32.

3. Arthur Brooks Lapsley, ed., *The Writings of Abraham Lincoln*, 7 vols. (New York: G. P. Putnam's Sons, 1906), 7:152.

CHAPTER 12: LAST CHANCES FOR
THE CONFEDERACY

On the Battle of Jonesboro and the final operations around Atlanta, see Stephen Davis, *Atlanta Will Fall: Sherman, Joe Johnston, and the Yankee Heavy Battalions* (Wilmington, DE: SR Books, 2001), and Richard M. Mcmurry, *Atlanta 1864: Last Chance for the Confederacy* (Lincoln: University of Nebraska Press, 2000). On the chase and sinking of the CSS *Alabama* and the Battle of Mobile Bay, see Craig L. Symonds, *The Civil War at Sea* (Santa Barbara, CA: Praeger, 2009), and Spencer C. Tucker, *Blue and Gray Navies: The Civil War Afloat* (Annapolis, MD: Naval Institute Press, 2006) and *A Short History of the Civil War at Sea* (Wilmington, DE: SR Books, 2002). On Sheridan's Campaign in the Shenandoah Valley and the Battle of Cedar Creek, see Roy Morris Jr., *Sheridan: The Life and Wars of General Phil Sheridan* (New York: Crown, 1992); Thomas A. Lewis, *The Guns of Cedar Creek* (New York: Harper & Row, 1988); and David Coffey, *Sheridan's Lieutenants: Phil Sheridan, His Generals, and the Final Year of the Civil War* (Lanham, MD: Rowman & Littlefield, 2005).

On the election of 1864, see John C. Waugh, *Reelecting Lincoln: The Battle for the 1864 Presidency* (New York: Crown, 1997).

On Sherman's March to the Sea, see Edward Caudill and Paul Ashdown, *Sherman's March in Myth and Memory* (Lanham, MD: Rowman & Littlefield, 2008); Mark Grimsley, *The Hard Hand of War: Union Military Policy toward Southern Civilians, 1861–1865* (New York: Cambridge University Press, 1995); Lee Kennett, *Marching through Georgia: The Story of Soldiers and Civilians during Sherman's Campaign* (New York: HarperCollins, 1995); and Anne J. Bailey, *War and Ruin: William T. Sherman and the Savannah Campaign* (Wilmington, DE: SR Books, 2003) and *The Chessboard of War: Sherman and Hood in the Autumn Campaigns of 1864* (Lincoln: University of Nebraska Press, 2000). The last of these also covers Hood's 1864 Tennessee Campaign. On that campaign, see also Wiley Sword, *Embrace an Angry Wind: The Confederacy's Last Hurrah: Spring Hill, Franklin, and Nashville* (New York: HarperCollins, 1992).

On the Hampton Roads Conference and attempts to open peace negotiations, see Mark Grimsley and Brooks D. Simpson, eds., *The Collapse of the Confederacy* (Lincoln: University of Nebraska Press, 2001).

1. OR vol. 39, pt. 2, pp. 418–19.

2. William J. Cooper Jr., *Jefferson Davis, American* (Baton Rouge: Louisiana State University Press, 2000), 513.

CHAPTER 13: "LET US STRIVE ON
TO FINISH THE WORK"

On Sherman's Carolinas Campaign and the burning of Columbia, see John G. Barrett, *Sherman's March through the Carolinas* (Chapel Hill: University of North Carolina Press,

1956); Marion B. Lucas, *Sherman and the Burning of Columbia* (Columbia: University of South Carolina Press, 1976); Nathaniel Cheairs Hughes Jr., *Bentonville: The Final Battle of Sherman and Johnston* (Chapel Hill: University of North Carolina Press, 1996); and Mark L. Bradley, *The Battle of Bentonville: Last Stand in the Carolinas* (Mason City, IA: Savas Publishing, 1996).

On the Confederate decision to enlist black troops, see Robert F. Durden, *The Gray and the Black: The Confederate Debate on Emancipation* (Baton Rouge: Louisiana State University Press, 1972).

On Lincoln's thought, see Allen C. Guelzo, *Abraham Lincoln: Redeemer President* (Grand Rapids, MI: Eerdmans, 1999), and on Lincoln's speeches, see Ronald C. White Jr., *The Eloquent President: A Portrait of Lincoln through His Words* (New York: Random House, 2005).

On the Appomattox Campaign and other events of April 1865, see Jay Winik, *April 1865: The Month That Saved America* (New York: HarperCollins, 2001). On Lincoln's assassination and the search for his killer, see also James L. Swanson, *Manhunt: The Twelve-Day Chase for Lincoln's Killer* (New York: William Morrow, 2006).

1. Both quotations from William J. Cooper Jr., *Jefferson Davis, American* (Baton Rouge: Louisiana State University Press, 2000), 517–18.

2. Roy P. Basler, ed., *Collected Works of Abraham Lincoln*, 9 vols. (New Brunswick, NJ: Rutgers University Press, 1953–1955), 8:333.

CHAPTER 14: RECONSTRUCTION

1. Abraham Lincoln, Speech to the 164th Ohio Regiment, Washington, D.C., August 18, 1864, Lincoln, Abraham, 1809–1865, in Roy P. Basler, ed., *Collected Works of Abraham Lincoln*, 9 vols. (New Brunswick, NJ: Rutgers University Press, 1953–1955), 7:504–5.

INDEX

Note: Page numbers in italics refer to illustrations.

ABOUT THE AUTHOR

Steven E. Woodworth is professor of history at Texas Christian University and author, coauthor, or editor of twenty-seven books. He is a two-time winner of the Fletcher Pratt Award of the New York Civil War Round Table, a two-time finalist for the Peter Seaborg Award of the George Tyler Moore Center for the Study of the Civil War, and a winner of the Grady McWhiney Award of the Dallas Civil War Round Table for lifetime contribution to the study of Civil War history. He is the author, most recently, of *Manifest Destinies: America's Westward Expansion and the Road to the Civil War* (2010).